MW01630249

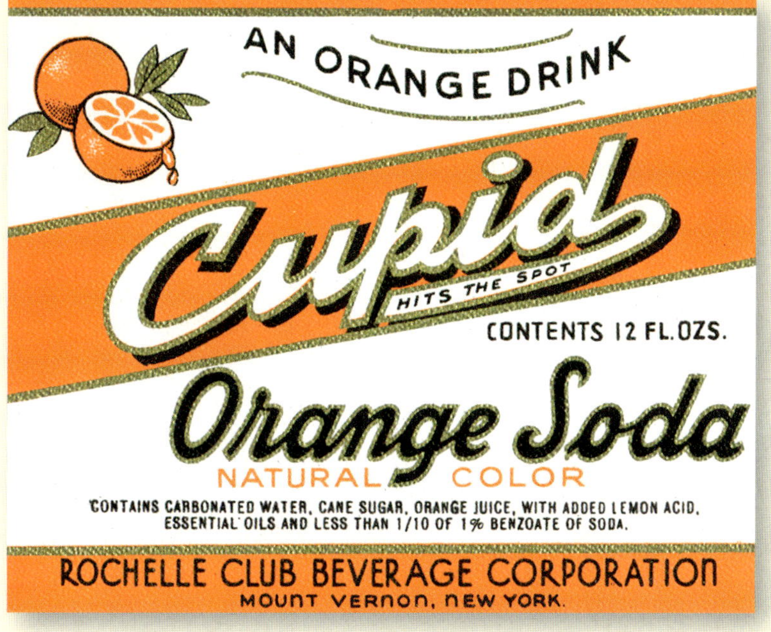

AN ORANGE DRINK
Cupid
HITS THE SPOT
CONTENTS 12 FL. OZS.
Orange Soda
NATURAL COLOR
CONTAINS CARBONATED WATER, CANE SUGAR, ORANGE JUICE, WITH ADDED LEMON ACID,
ESSENTIAL OILS AND LESS THAN 1/10 OF 1% BENZOATE OF SODA.
ROCHELLE CLUB BEVERAGE CORPORATION
MOUNT VERNON, NEW YORK.

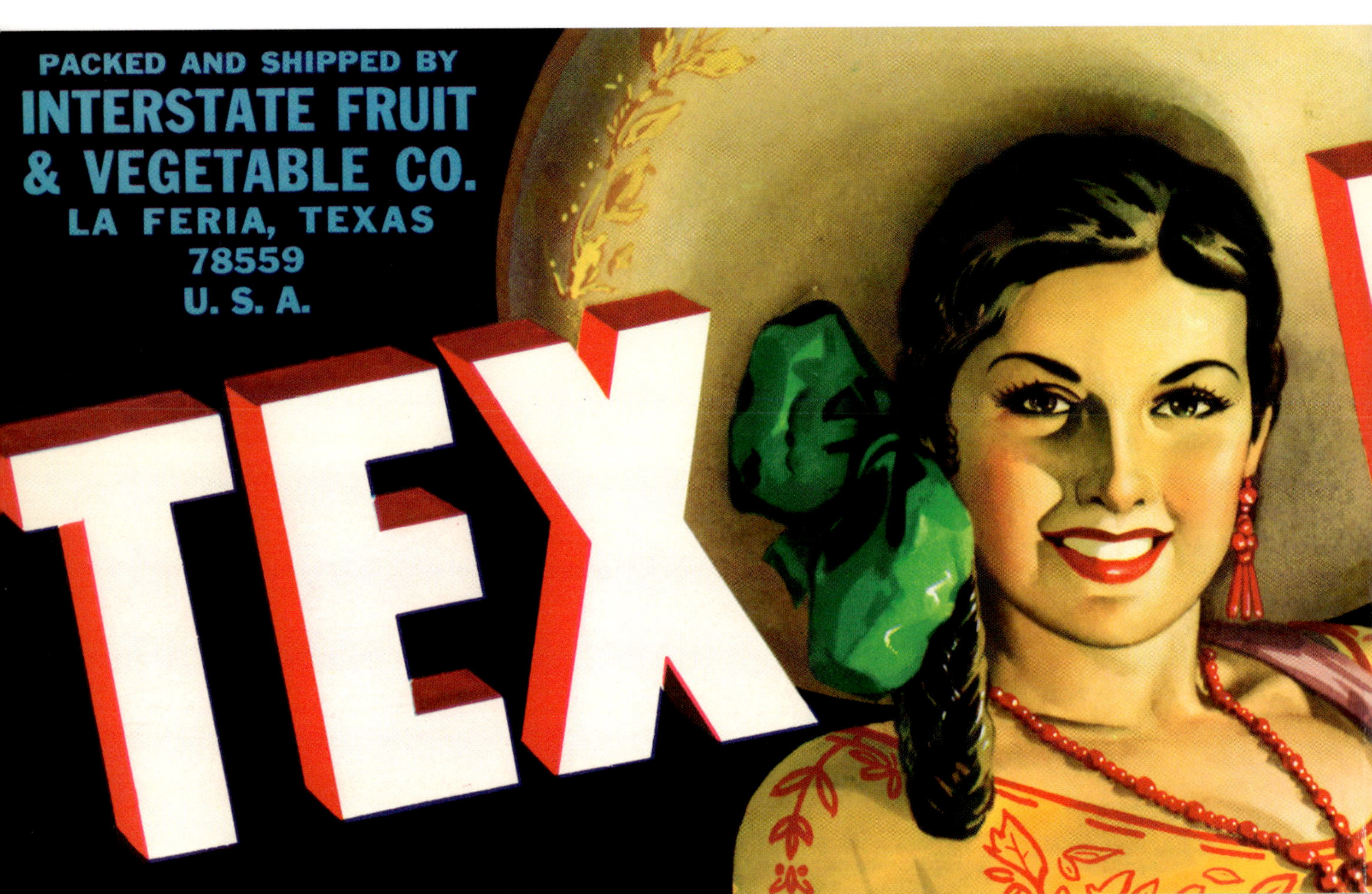

PACKED AND SHIPPED BY
INTERSTATE FRUIT
& VEGETABLE CO.
LA FERIA, TEXAS
78559
U. S. A.
TEX

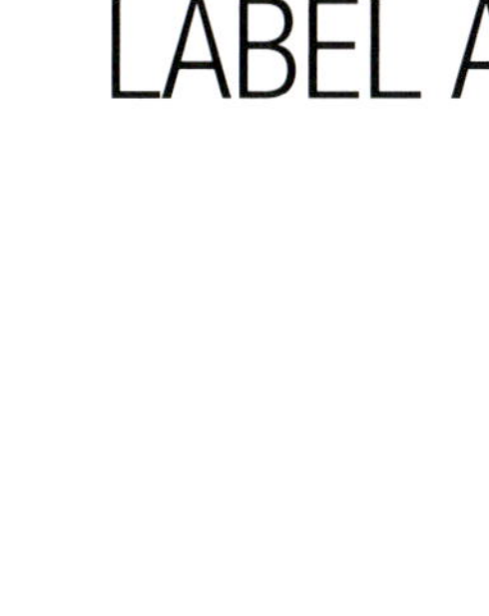

LABEL ART

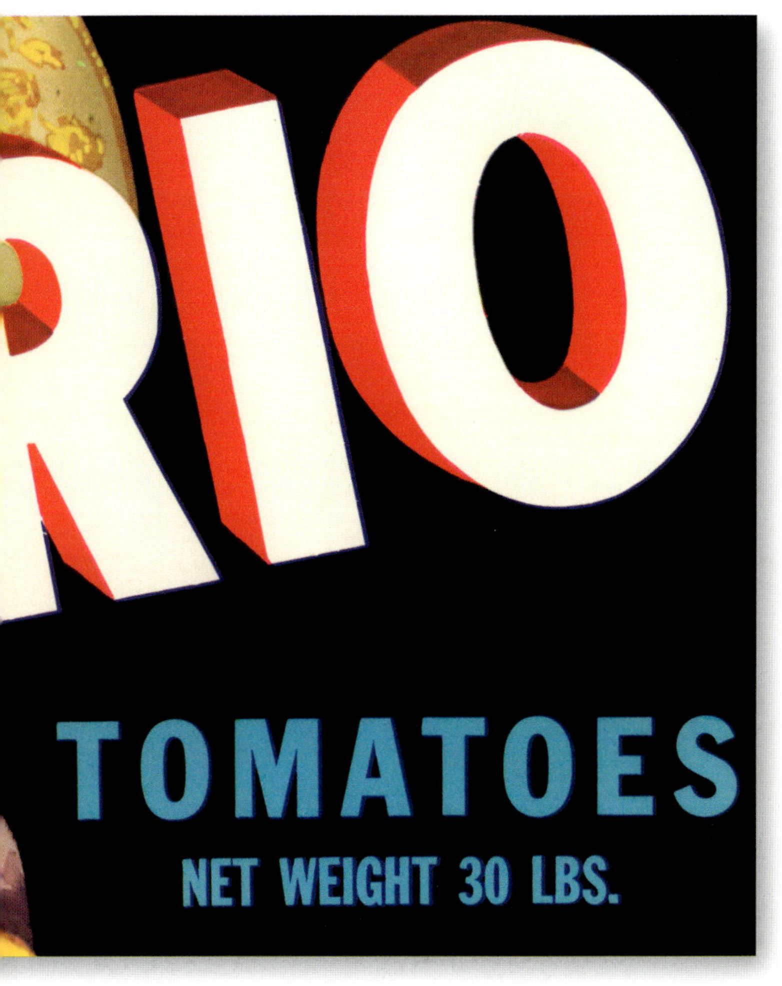

RIO
TOMATOES
NET WEIGHT 30 LBS.

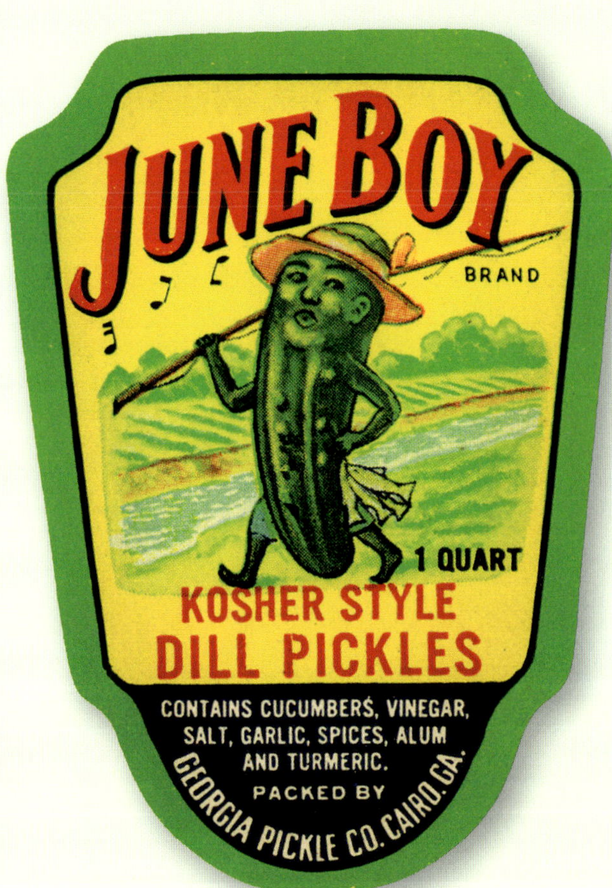
JUNE BOY
BRAND
1 QUART
KOSHER STYLE
DILL PICKLES
CONTAINS CUCUMBERS, VINEGAR,
SALT, GARLIC, SPICES, ALUM
AND TURMERIC.
PACKED BY
GEORGIA PICKLE CO. CAIRO, GA.

LABEL ART

DOVERPICTURA

DOVER PUBLICATIONS, INC. | Mineola, New York

By Alan Weller.
Designed by Joel Waldrep.

Label Art is a new work, first published by Dover Publications, Inc.,
in 2008.

The CD-ROM file names correspond to the images in the book. All of the artwork
stored on the CD-ROM can be imported directly into a wide range of design and
word-processing programs on either Windows or Macintosh platforms. No further
installation is necessary.

ISBN 10: 0-486-99753-7
ISBN 13: 978-0-486-99753-7
Manufactured in the United States of America
Dover Publications, Inc., 31 East 2nd Street, Mineola, NY 11501
www.doverpublications.com

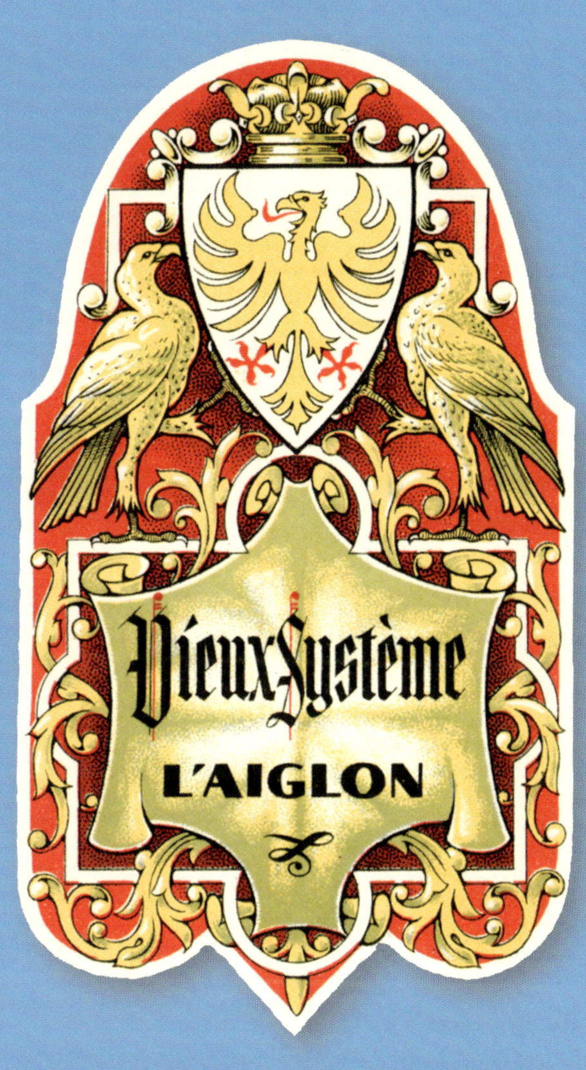

Vieux Système
L'AIGLON

VALENCIAS
GOLDEN EAGLE
BRAND
AN EXCLUSIVE
CHAPMAN PACK
GROWN IN
U.S.A.
GROWN & SHIPPED BY
PLACENTIA ORCHARD COMPANY
OPERATED UNDER PERSONAL DIRECTION OF CHARLES C. CHAPMAN FOR MORE THAN FIFTY YEARS
FULLERTON, CALIFORNIA
ORANGE COUNTY

005

DUCKWALL
D-B
BRAND
TRADEMARK REG.
U.S. PAT. OFF.
DISTRIBUTED BY
DUCKWALL BROS. Inc.
HOOD RIVER, OREGON
U.S.A.
HOOD RIVER
PEARS
CONTENTS
4/5 BUSHEL

006

QUAIL
BRAND
CONTRA COSTA
BARTLETTS
NET
WEIGHT
46 LBS.
CALIFORNIA FRUIT EXCHANGE
SACRAMENTO, CALIFORNIA
BLUE
ANCHOR
CALIFORNIA FRUIT EXCHANGE
UNITED STATES
OF AMERICA

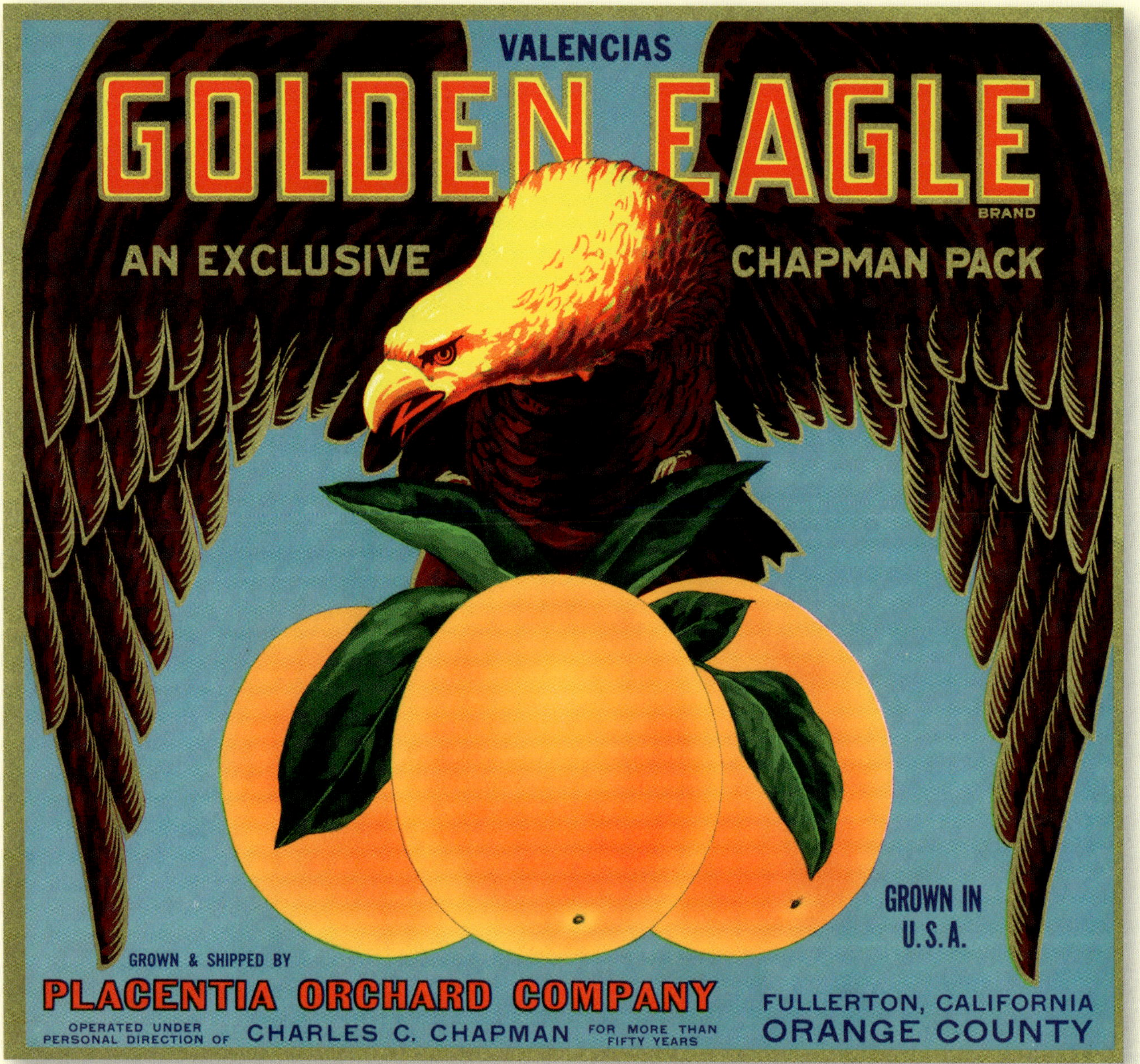

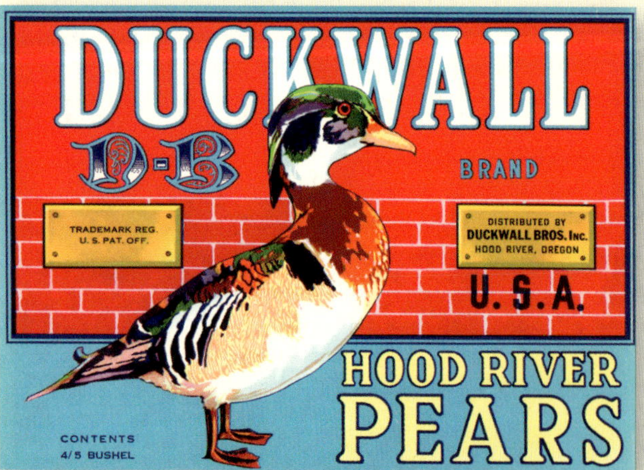

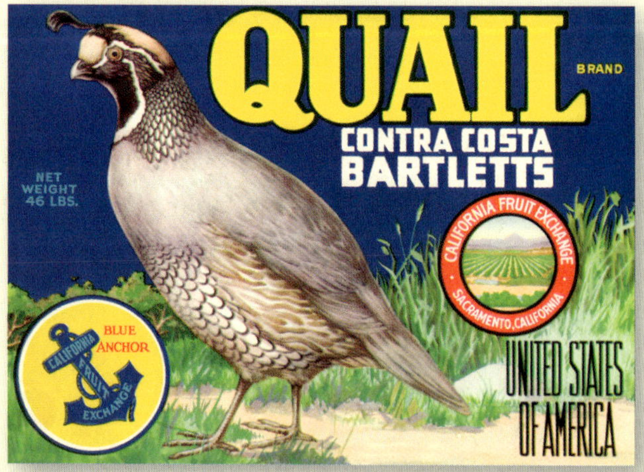

007

'mornin Judge'
RIO GRANDE VALLEY
Texsun
CITRUS EXCHANGE
GRAPEFRUIT & ORANGES
PACKED AND SHIPPED BY
DONNA CITRUS ASSOCIATION
DONNA, TEXAS
PRODUCE OF U.S.A.
CONTENTS 1 3/5 BU.

008

SWAN
BRAND
Perham Fruit Company Yakima, Washington. U.S.A. DISTRIBUTOR
APPLES
UNITED STATES OF AMERICA
CONTENTS ONE U.S. BUSHEL

009

SNOW OWL
BRAND
APPLES
PERHAM FRUIT CORPORATION YAKIMA, WASHINGTON. U.S.A. DISTRIBUTOR
CONTENTS ONE U.S. BUSHEL
UNITED STATES OF AMERICA

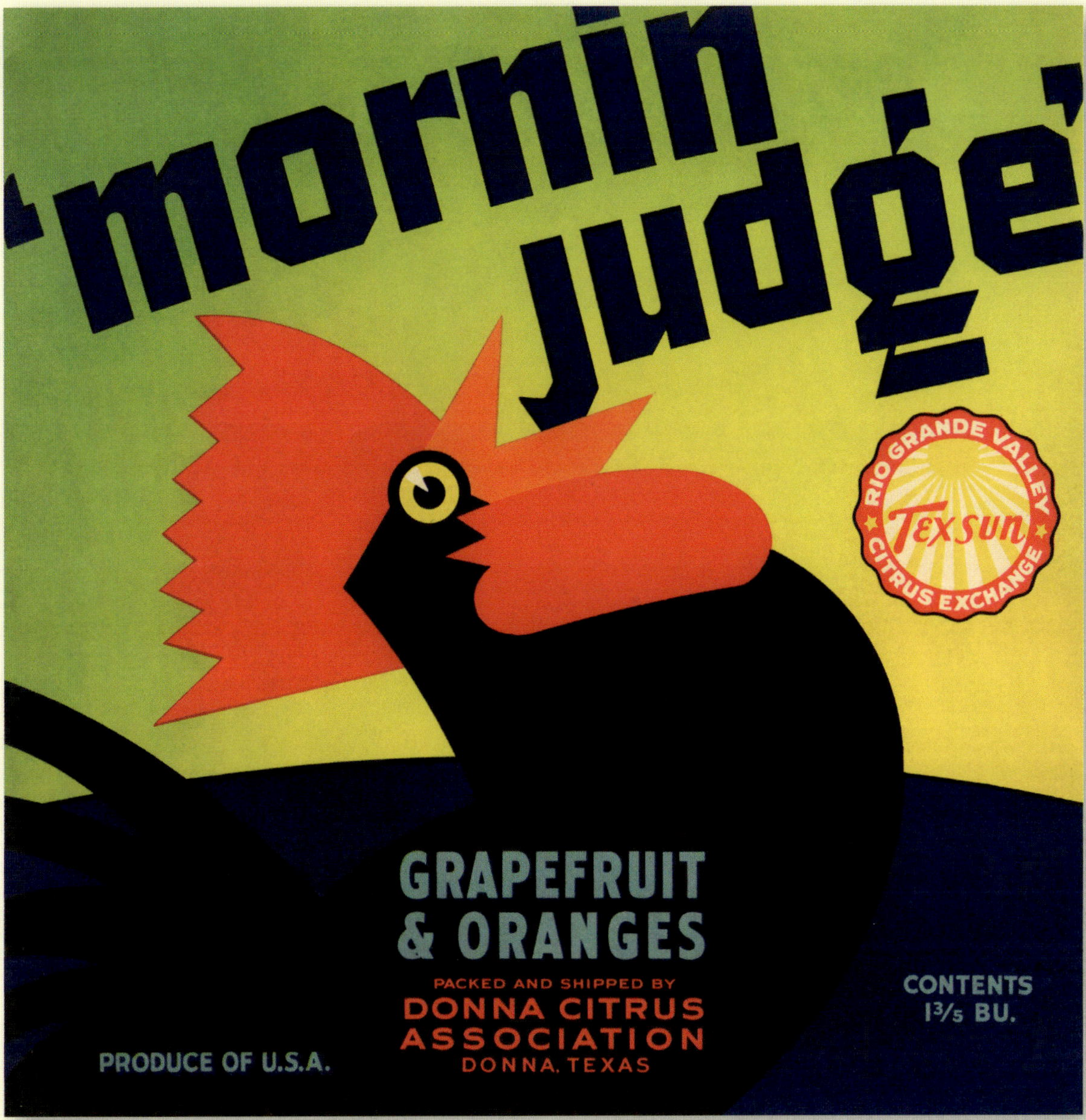

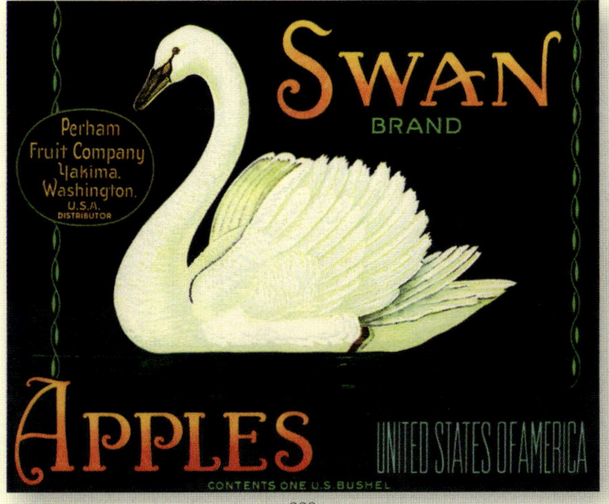

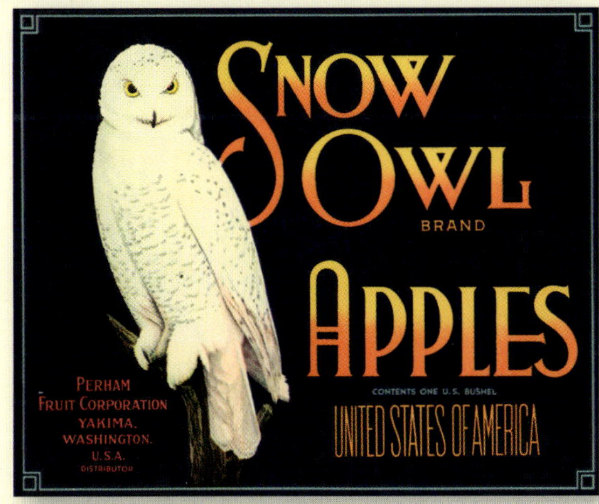

010

PRODUCE OF U.S.A.
POLAR BIRD
BRAND
ROYAL VALLEY FRUIT GROWERS ASS'N.
REEDLEY, CALIFORNIA
A. CARLISLE & CO.

011

PRODUCE OF U.S.A.
J.
John J. Kovacevich
GROWER SHIPPER
P.O. BIN 488,
ARVIN, CALIF. 93203
PRIME QUALITY
REG. U.S. PAT. OFF.
J.
BRAND

012

BLUE
BEAK
Seald Sweet
1/5 more 4 Juice
BRAND
UMATILLA CITRUS GROWERS ASS'N
UMATILLA, FLORIDA

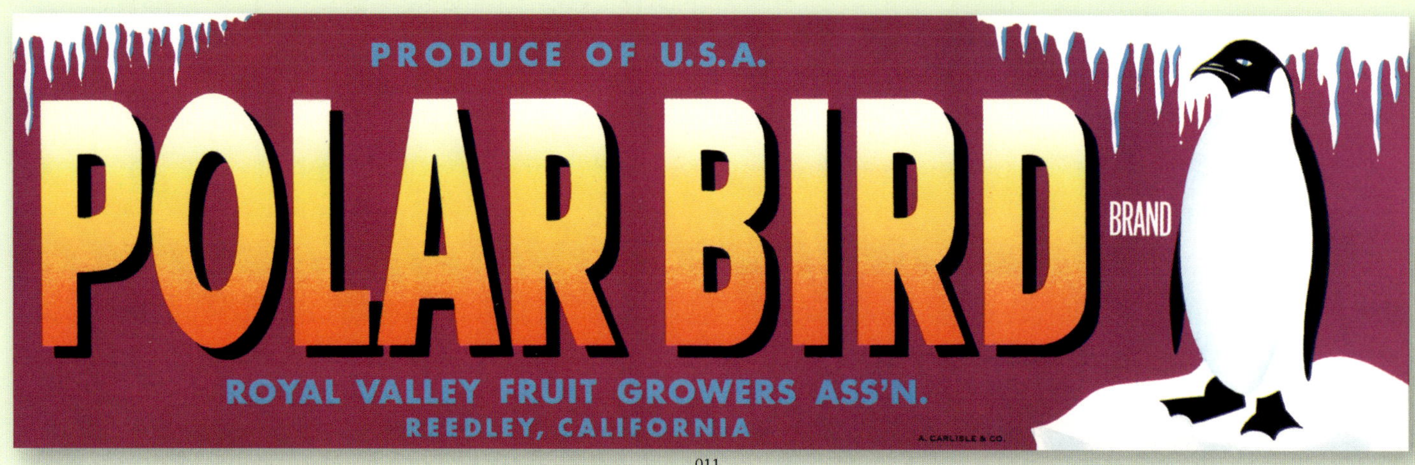

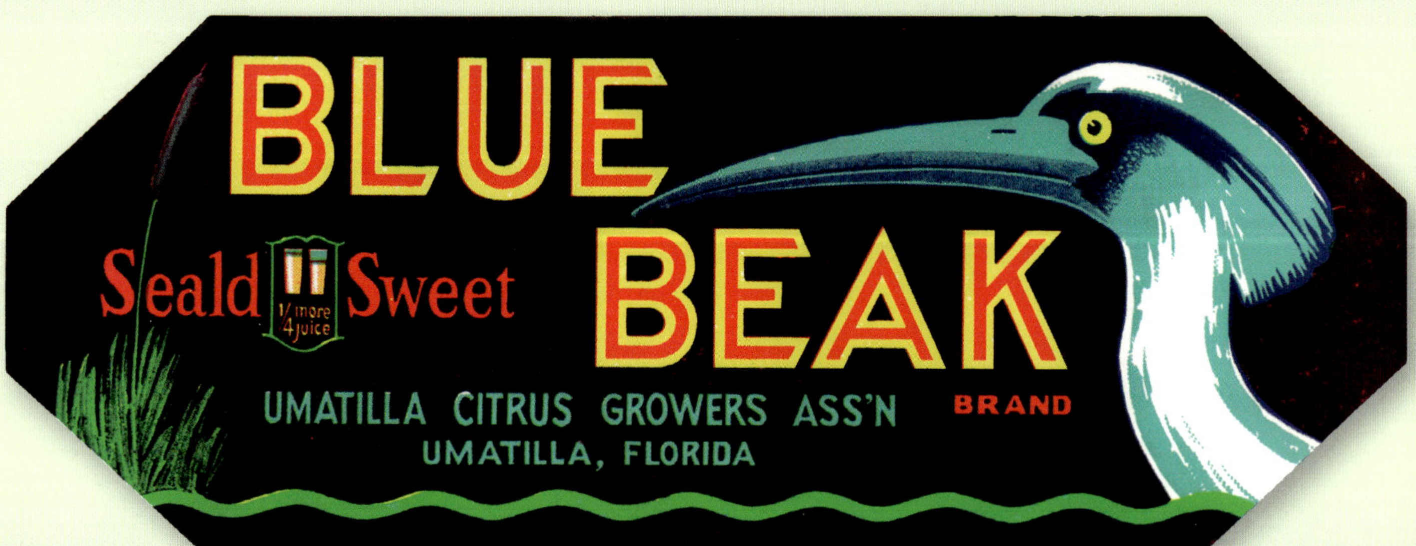

013

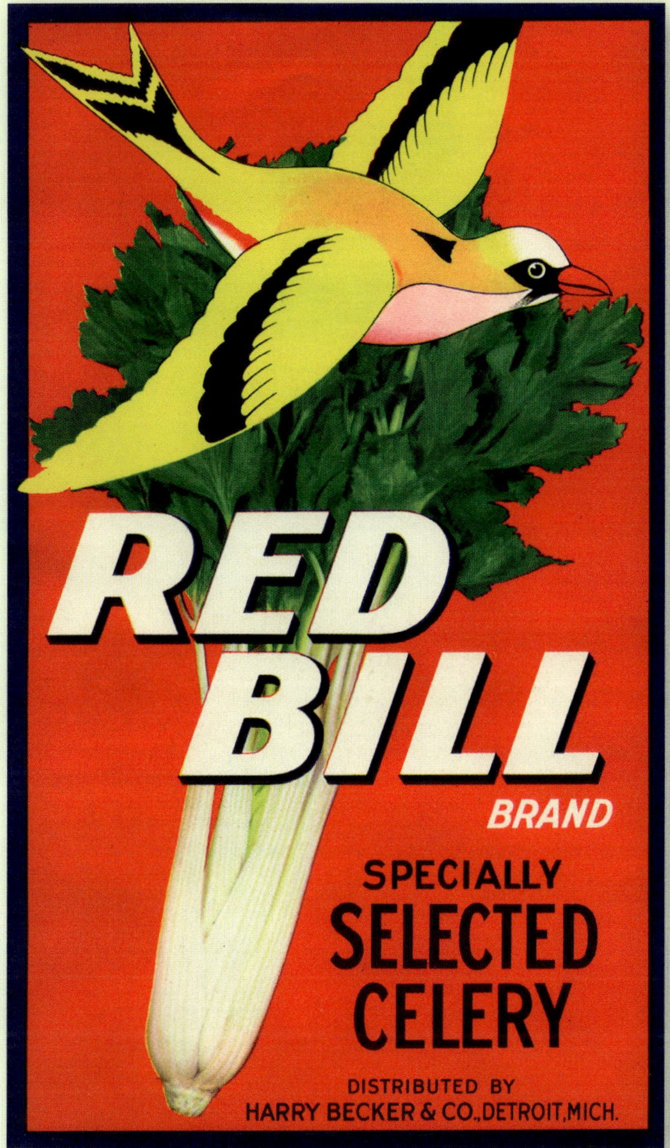

014

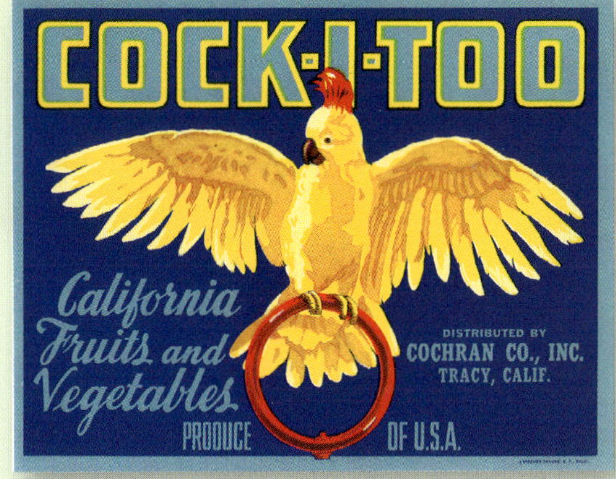

015

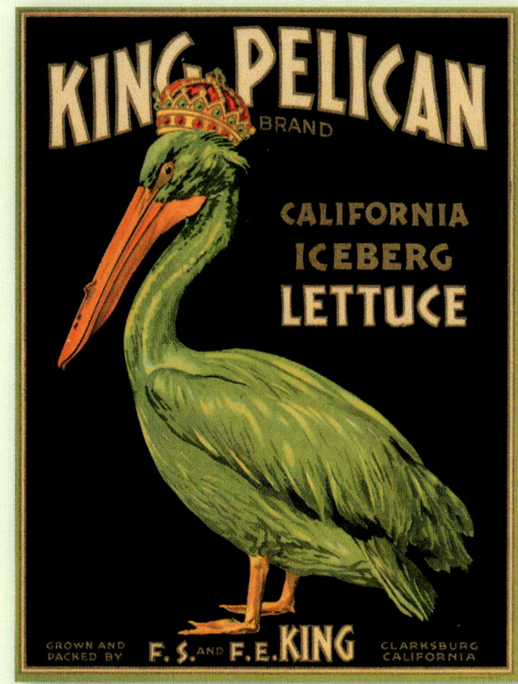

016

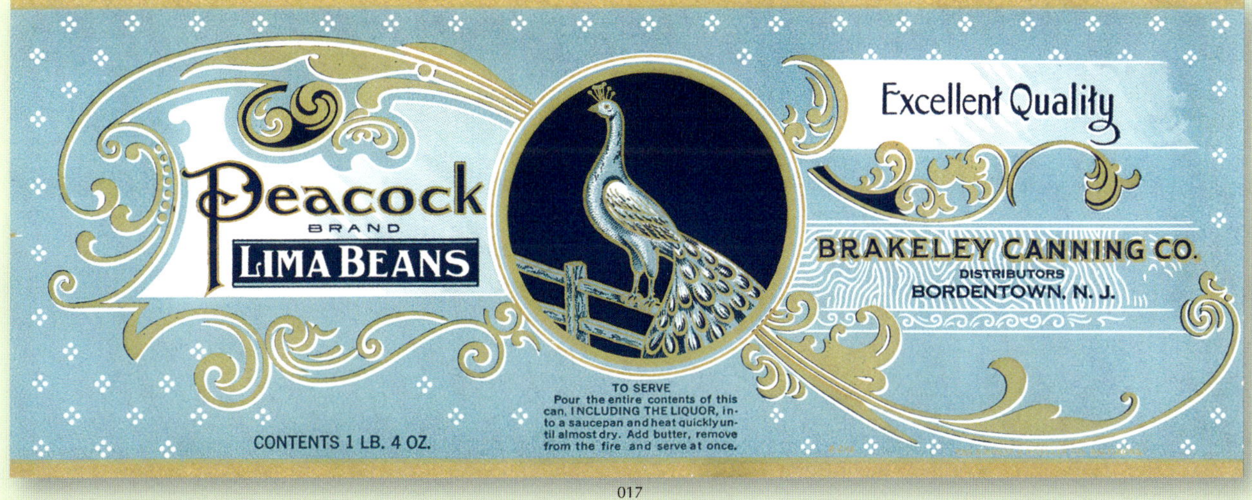

017

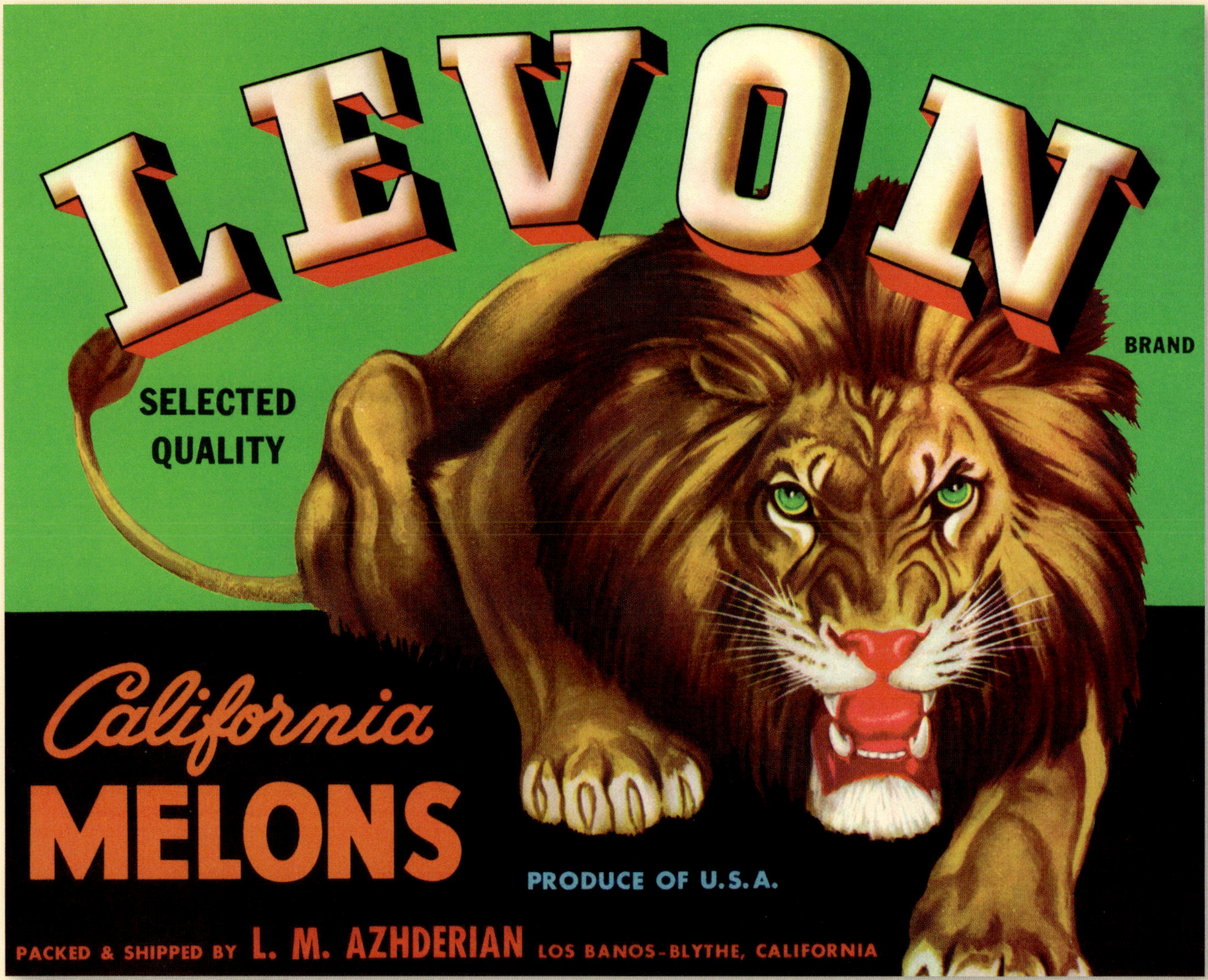

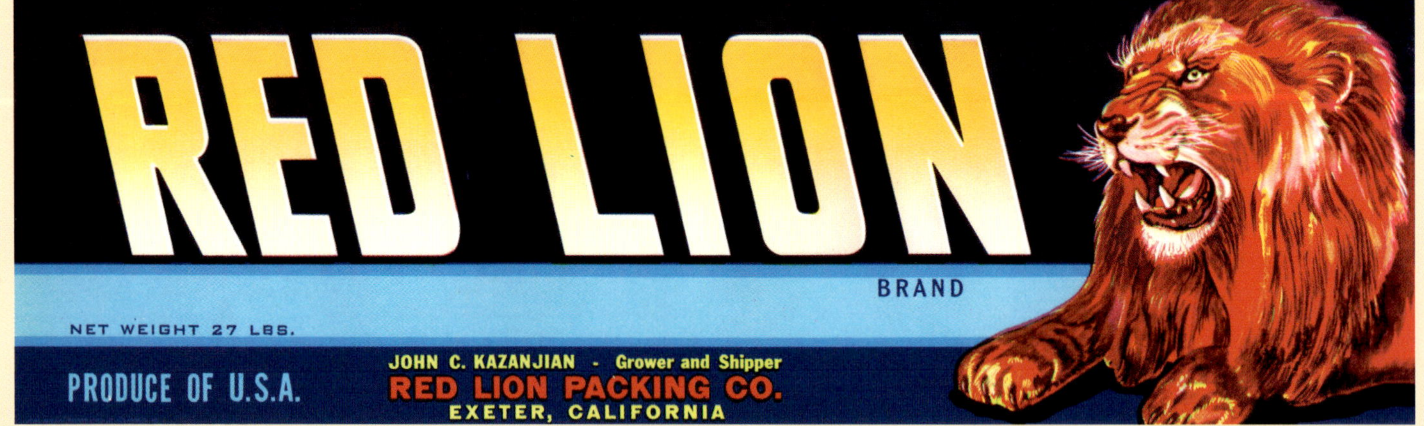
LEVON
BRAND
SELECTED QUALITY
California
MELONS
PRODUCE OF U.S.A.
PACKED & SHIPPED BY L. M. AZHDERIAN LOS BANOS-BLYTHE, CALIFORNIA
018
RED LION
BRAND
NET WEIGHT 27 LBS.
PRODUCE OF U.S.A.
JOHN C. KAZANJIAN - Grower and Shipper
RED LION PACKING CO.
EXETER, CALIFORNIA
019

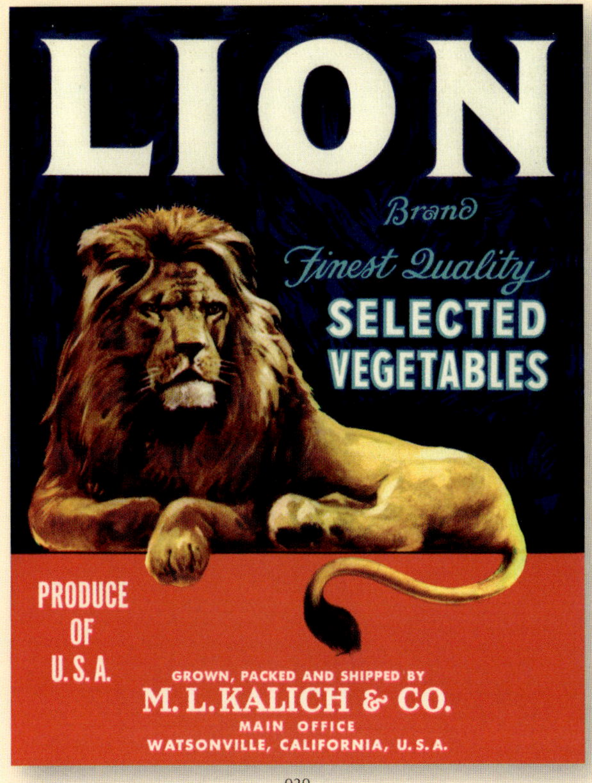

020

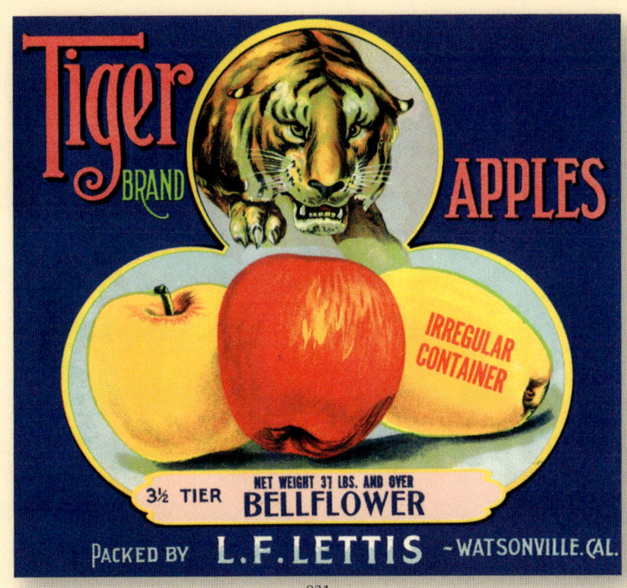

021

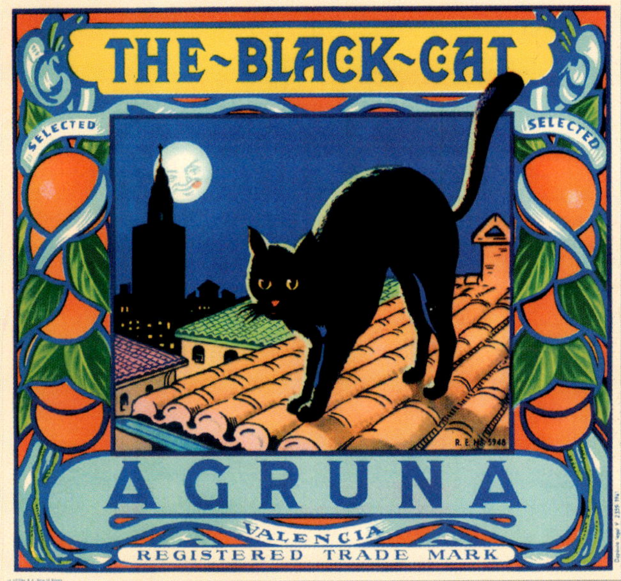

023

022

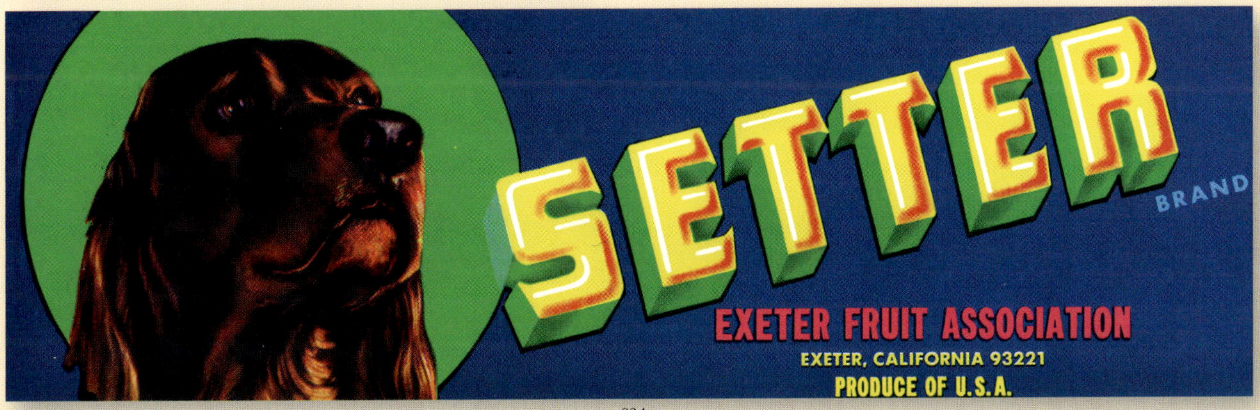

024

46 LBS. NET
BUCKINGHAM
BRAND
CALIFORNIA BARTLETTS
W.H. BUCKINGHAM
VACAVILLE,
CALIFORNIA.

025

Piggy Pears
BRAND
MEDFORD
OREGON
CONTENTS 4/5 BUSHEL
HIGHCROFT
ORCHARDS
PRODUCE OF U.S.A.

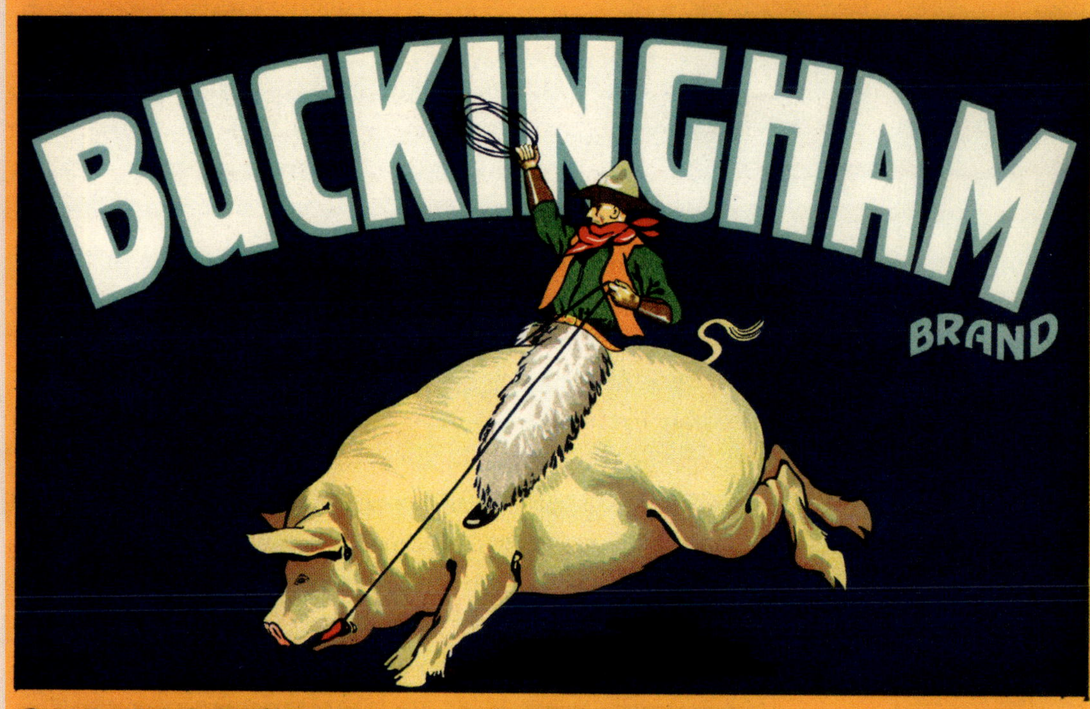

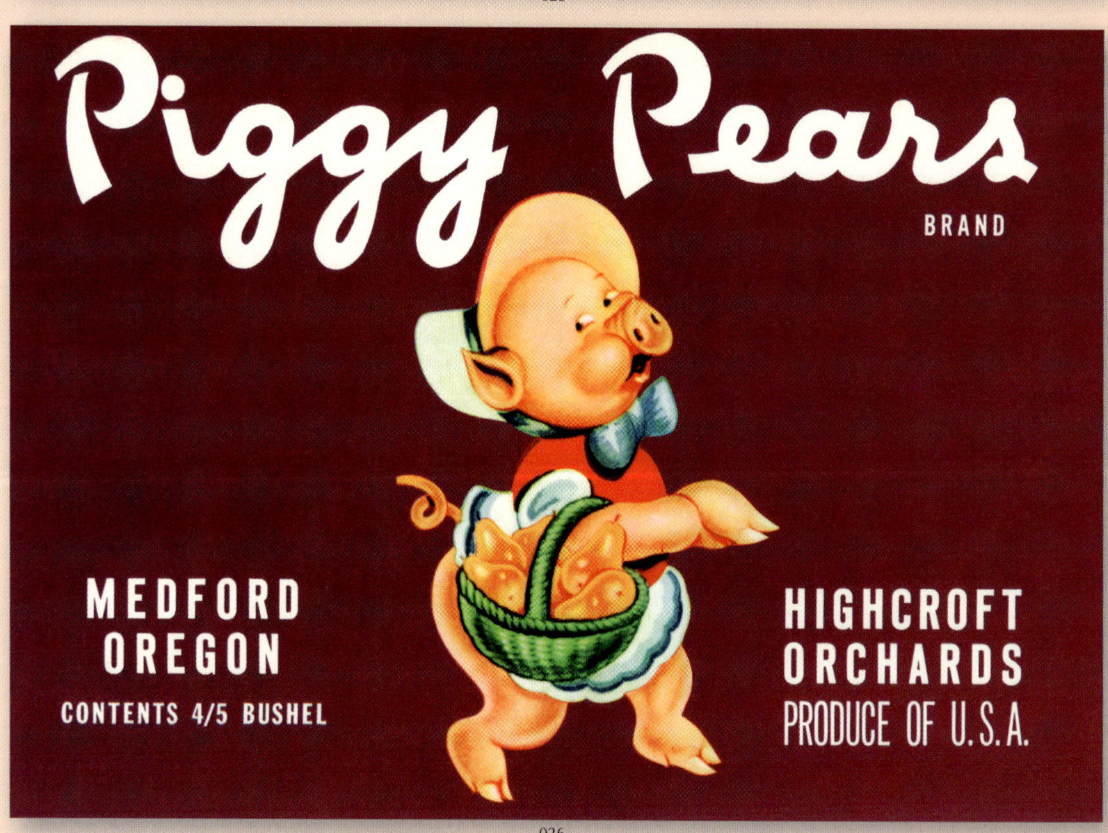

026

CONTENTS ONE VOLUME BUSHEL
TROUT
BRAND
"Quality Boxed Apples
Grown in Nature's Selected
Lake Chelan Apple District"
WENOKA
APPLES
TRADE MARK
PRE-COOLED
AND
COLD STORED
AT
SHIPPING POINT
PACKED BY
PRODUCE OF U.S.A.
LAKE CHELAN FRUIT GROWERS
CHELAN, WASHINGTON, U.S.A.

027

DUCK
BRAND
PICKED AND PACKED BY
SAN DIMAS LEMON ASSOCIATION
SAN DIMAS, LOS ANGELES CO. CAL.

028

Gagnant
ANTONIO ESCANDELL
CARCAGENTE
(ESPAÑA)

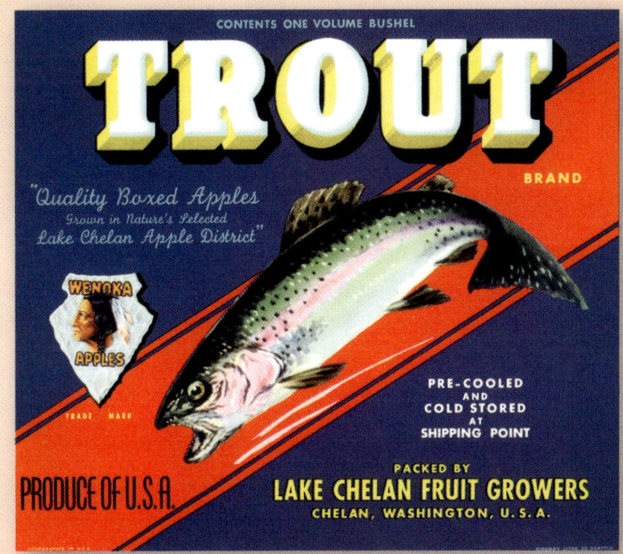

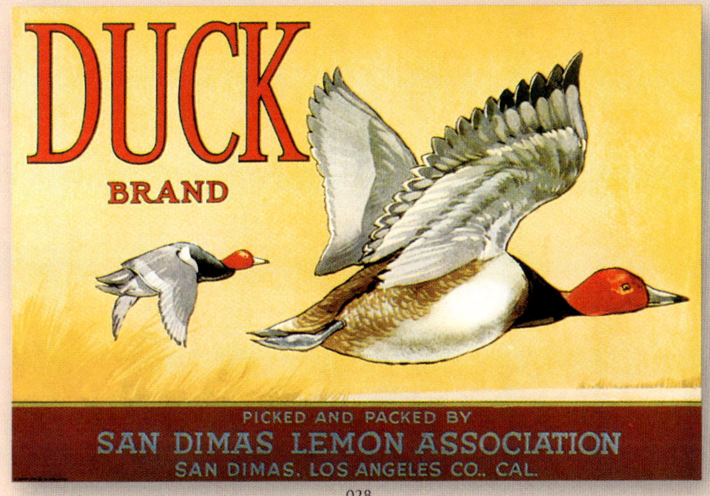

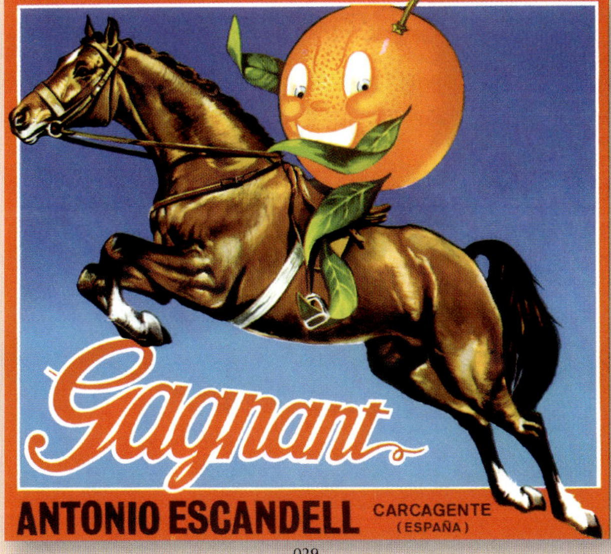

029

BLACK BEAR
ZINFANDEL
NORTHERN CALIFORNIA FRUIT CO.
VICTOR, CALIFORNIA
PRODUCE OF U.S.A.
NET WEIGHT 36 LBS.
BLACK JUICE GRAPES

030

SILVER TIP
PRODUCE OF U.S.A.
CALIFORNIA GRAPES
BRAND
PACKED AND SHIPPED BY: CALRIPE INC., STRATHMORE, CALIFORNIA 93267

031

Giant Tree
BRAND
CALIFORNIA FRUIT EXCHANGE
BLUE ANCHOR
SEQUOIA FOOTHILL FRUIT GROWERS
WOODLAKE, CALIF.
PRODUCE OF U.S.A.

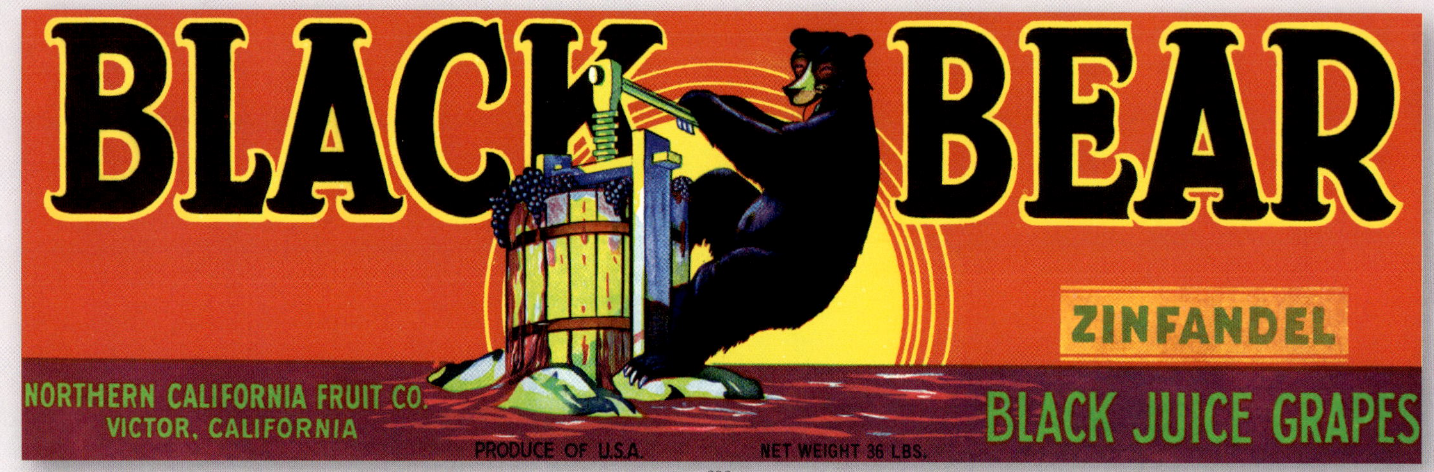

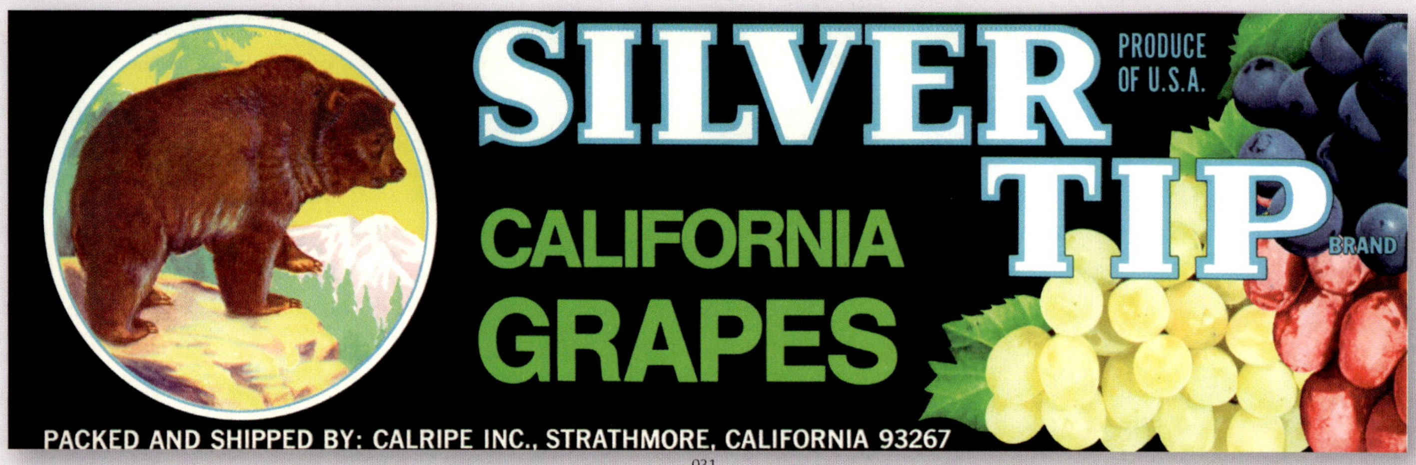

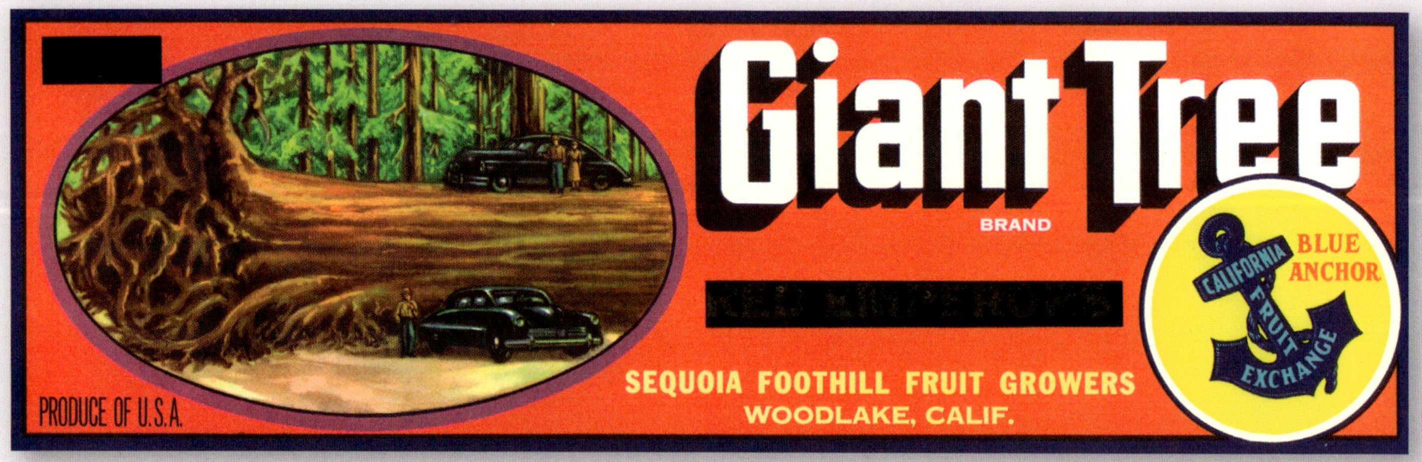

032

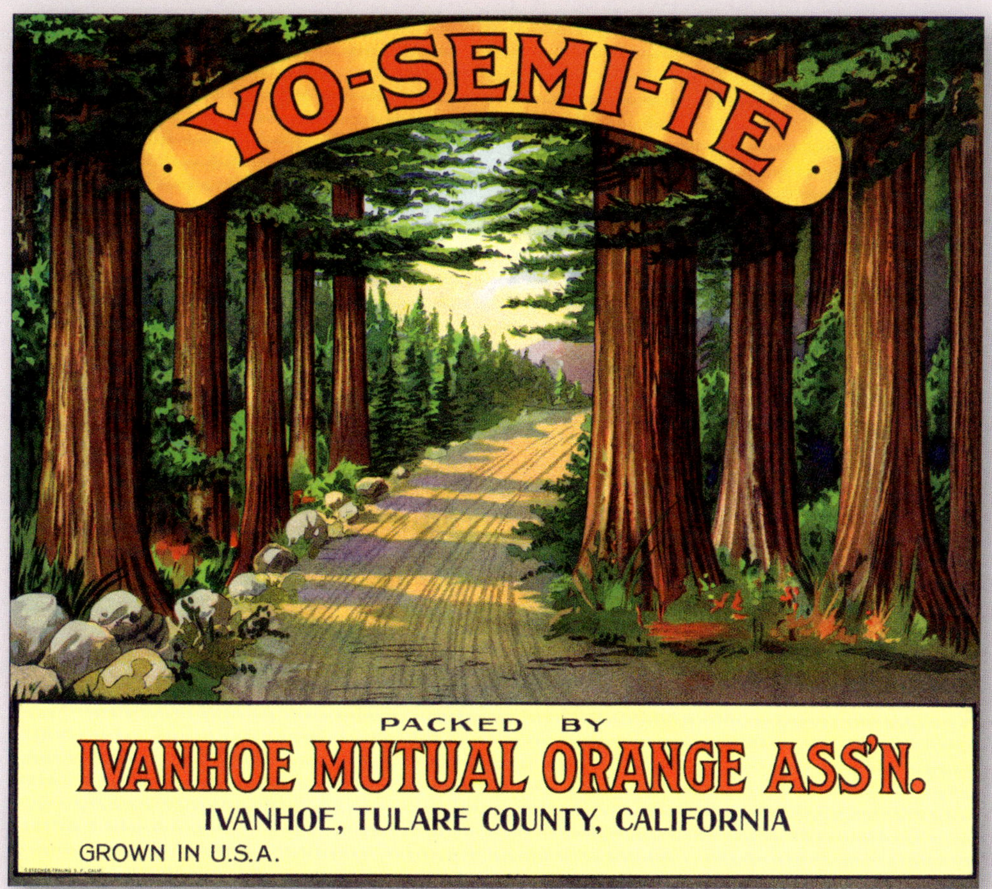
YO-SEMI-TE
PACKED BY
IVANHOE MUTUAL ORANGE ASS'N.
IVANHOE, TULARE COUNTY, CALIFORNIA
GROWN IN U.S.A.

NET WT. 46 LBS.
MT. SHASTA
BRAND
CALIFORNIA
PEARS
PRODUCE OF U.S.A.
PACKED BY
JAMES MILLS GROWERS SERVICE CO.
HAMILTON CITY, CALIF.

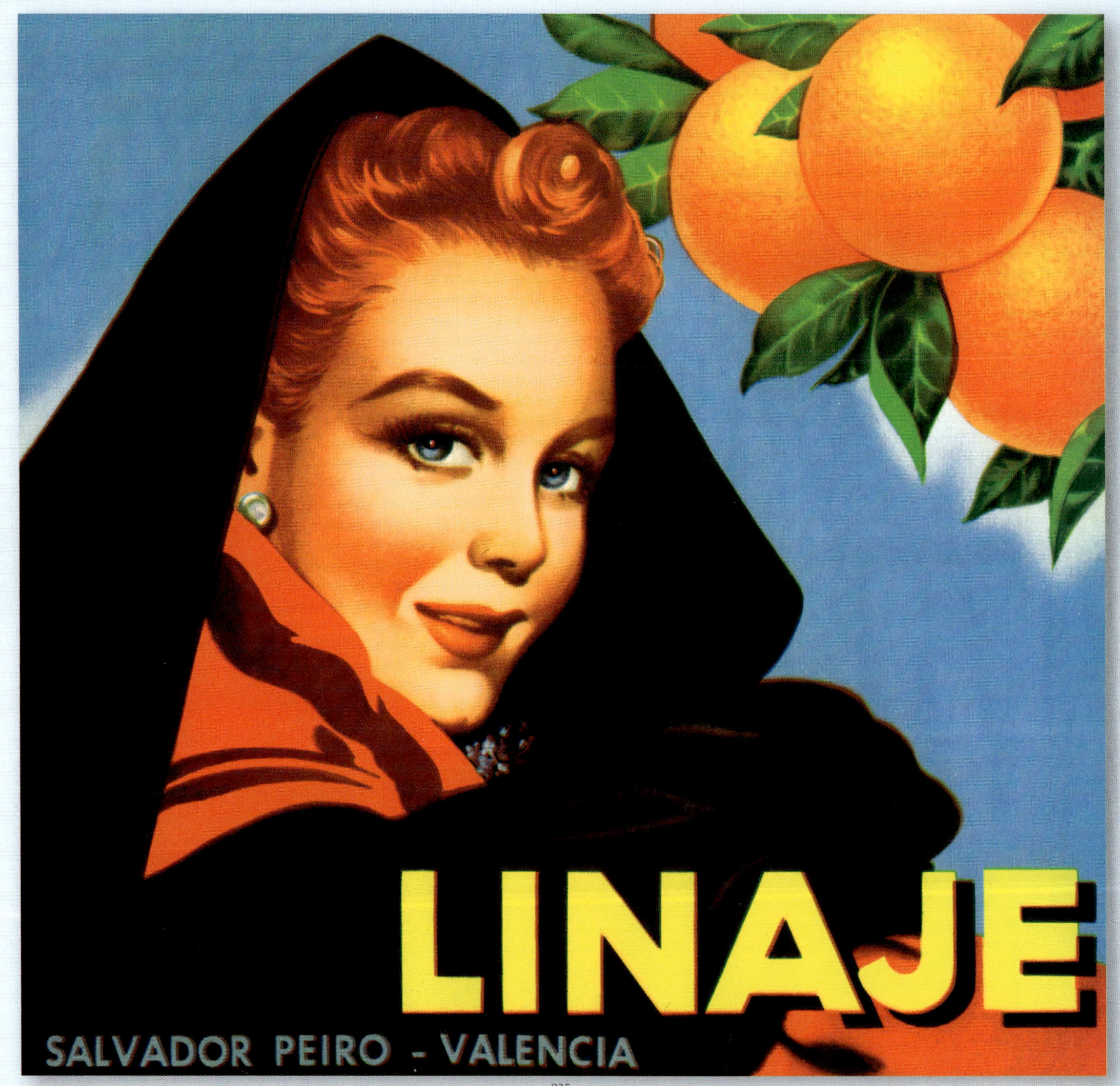
LINAJE
SALVADOR PEIRO - VALENCIA
035

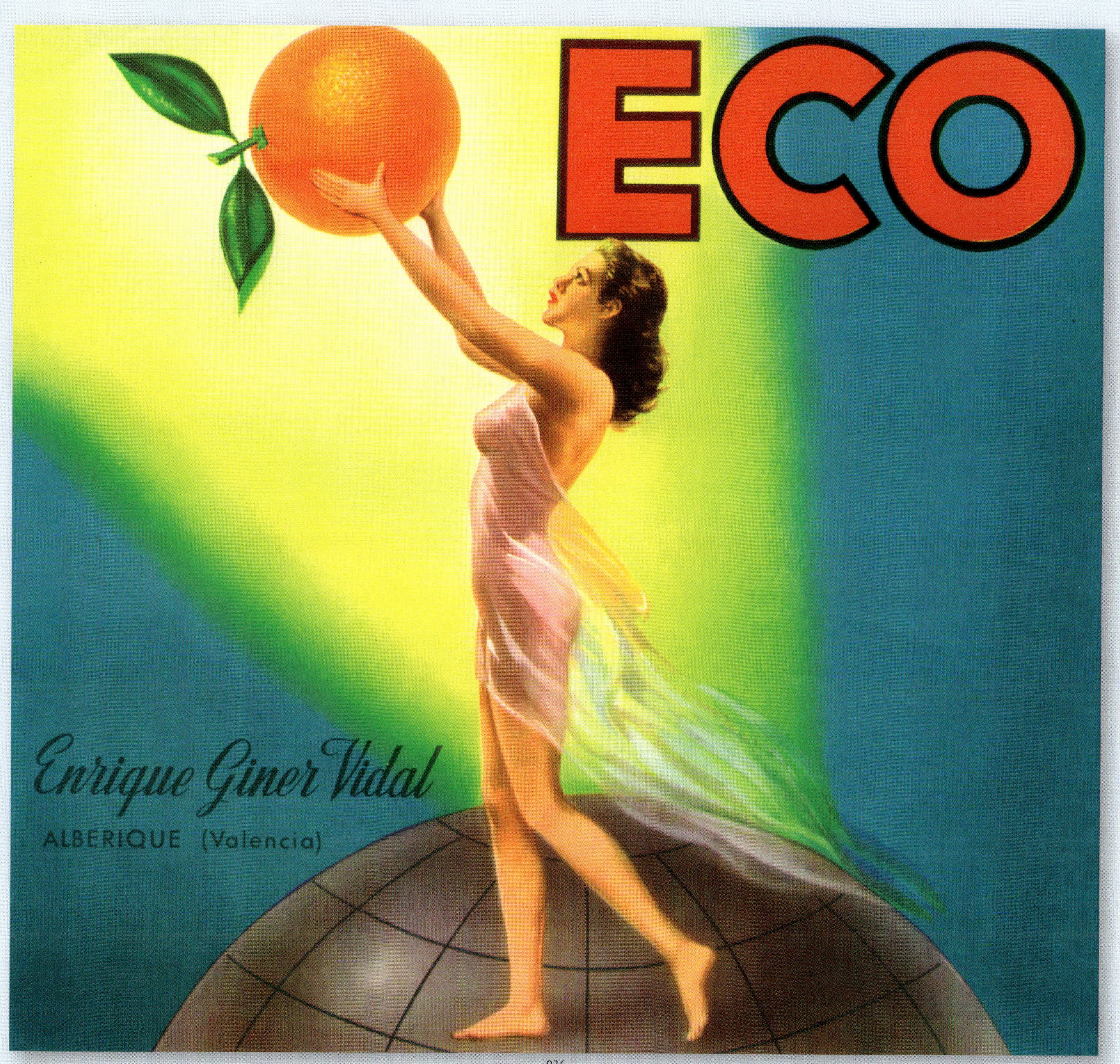

ECO
Enrique Giner Vidal
ALBERIQUE (Valencia)
036

Pride of Mexico!
Sweetmex
ORANGES
SHIPPED BY CHAS. A. ROGERS & SONS WESLACO, TEXAS
PRODUCE OF MEXICO

037

La Reina
GROWN IN U.S.A.
RIALTO ORANGE CO.
RIALTO
SAN BERNARDINO CO.
CALIFORNIA

038

RAMONA MEMORIES
SAN FERNANDO HEIGHTS
LEMON ASSOCIATION
SAN FERNANDO LOS ANGELES CO. CALIFORNIA

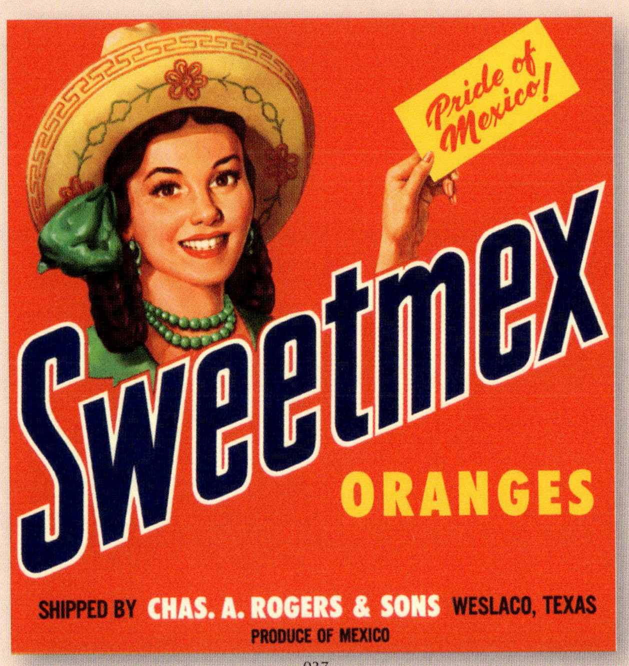

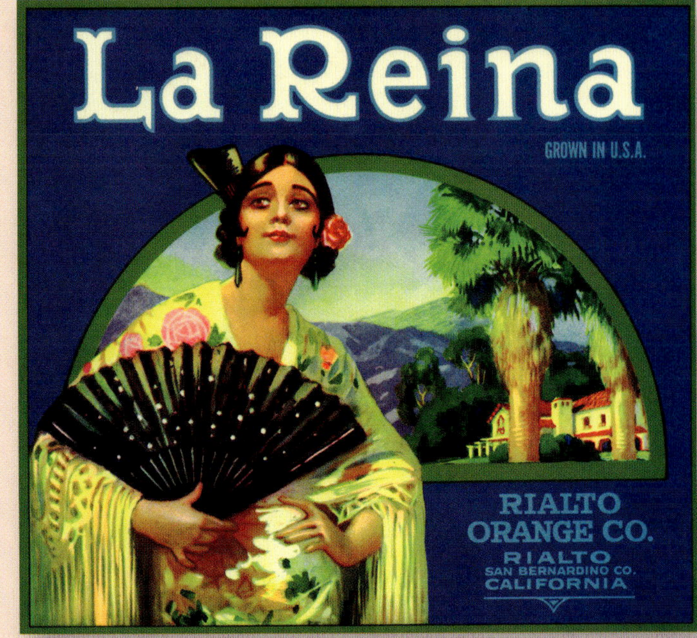

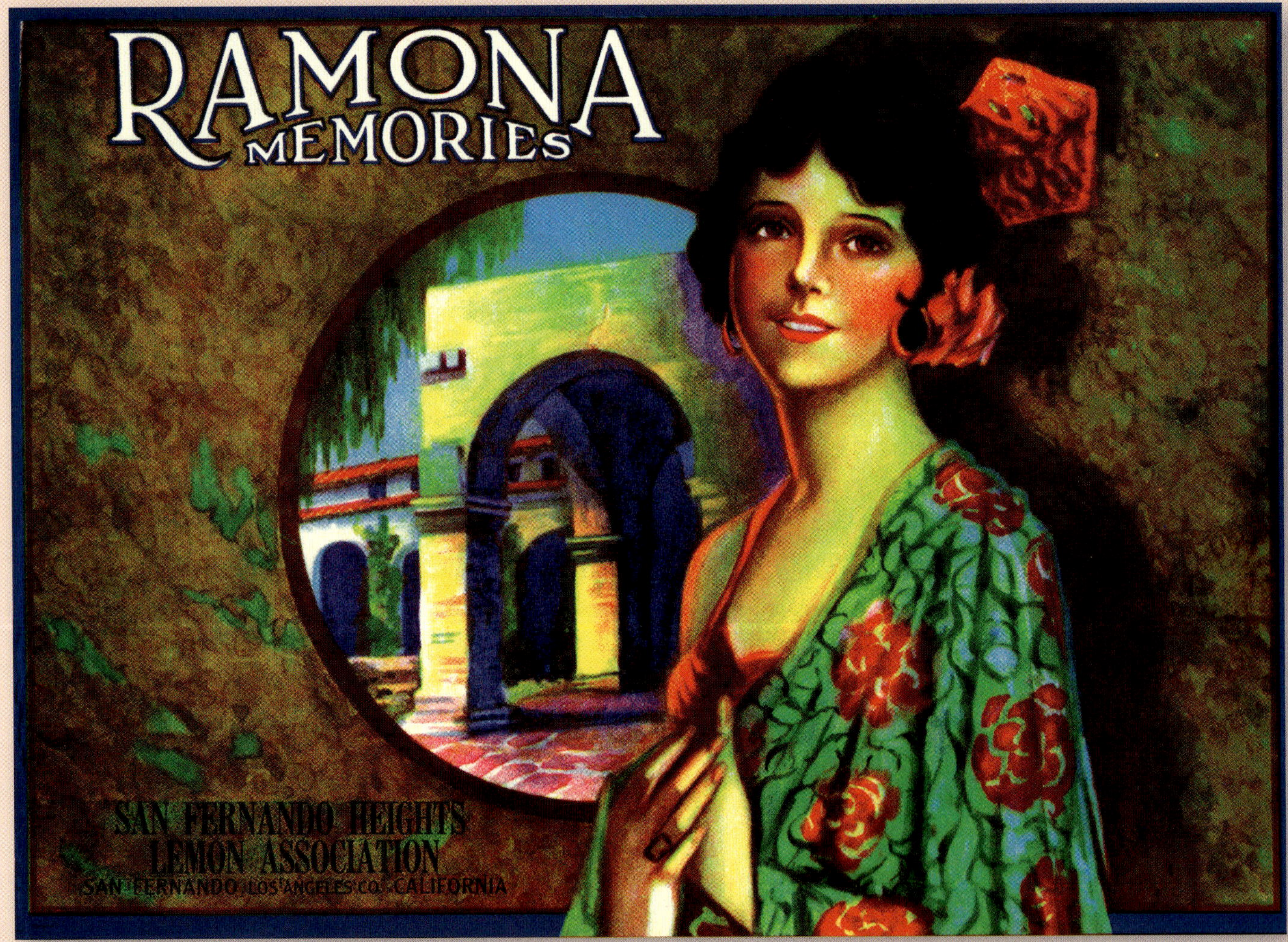

039

BROGDEX
REDUCES DECAY
RETARDS SHRINKAGE
CO-ED
BRAND
GROWN AND PACKED BY
COLLEGE HEIGHTS
ORANGE & LEMON ASS'N.
CLAREMONT
LOS ANGELES CO.
CALIFORNIA
SELLING AGENTS
San Antonio Fruit Exchange
CLAREMONT, CALIF.

040

GOLDEN GIRL
BRAND
APPLES
PRODUCE OF U.S.A. • CONTENTS ONE BUSHEL
GHISELLI BROS. SAN FRANCISCO, CALIF.
DISTRIBUTORS

041

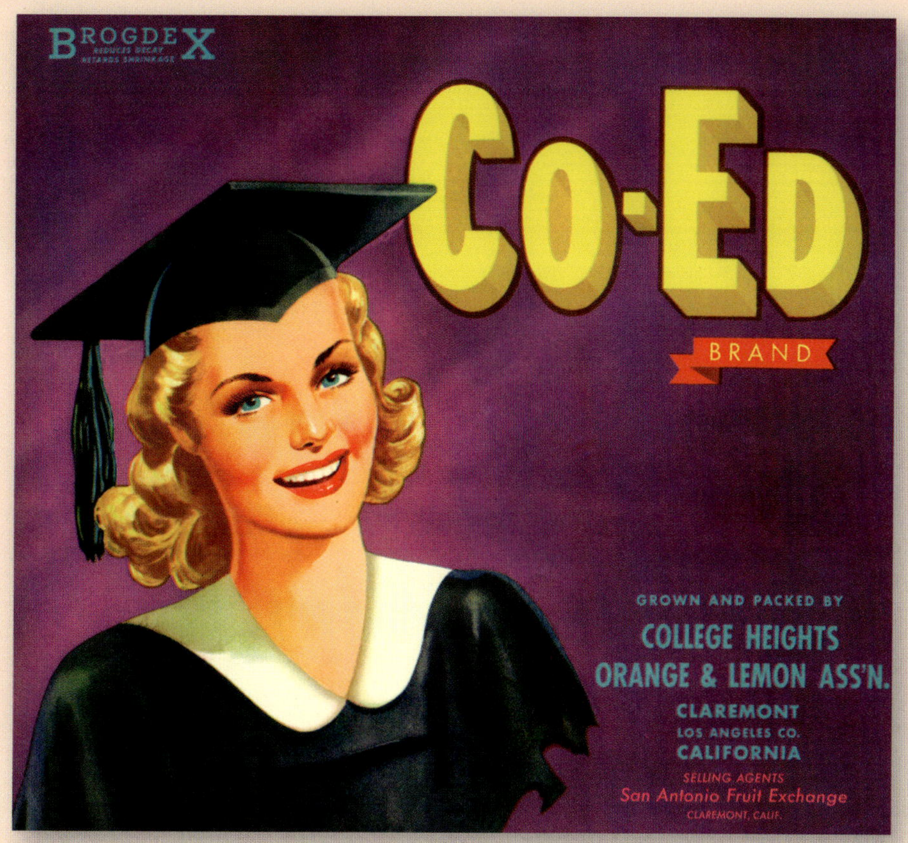

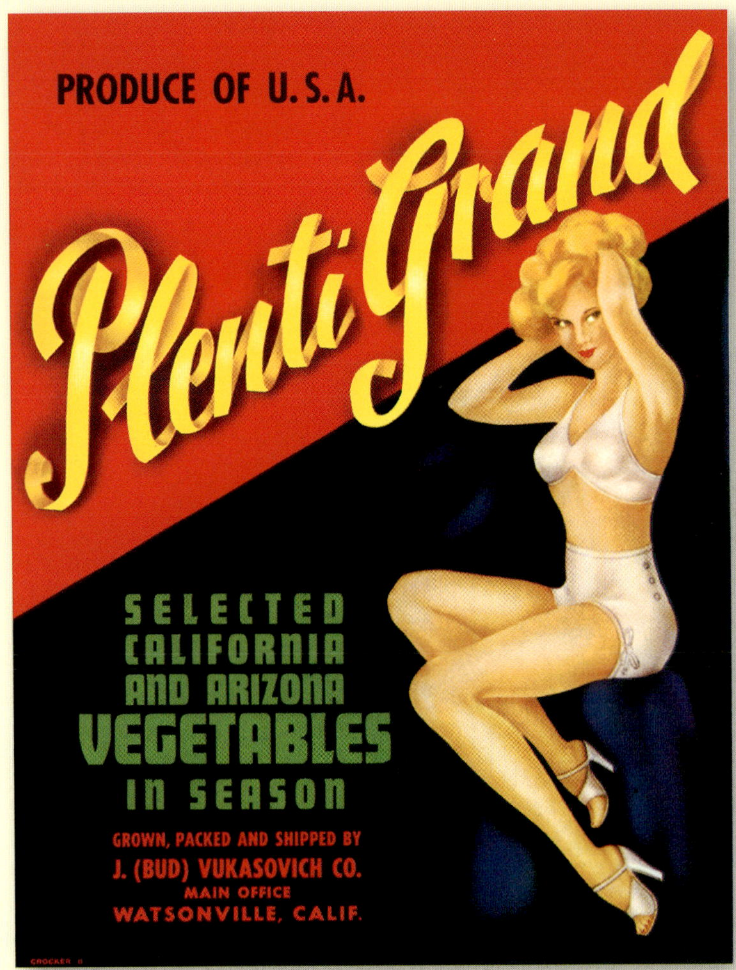

042

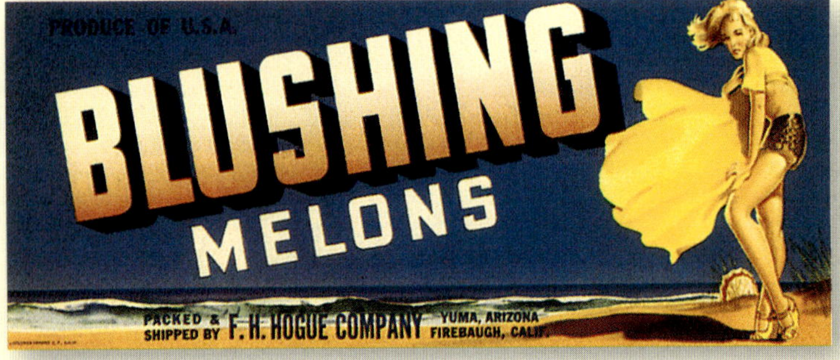

043

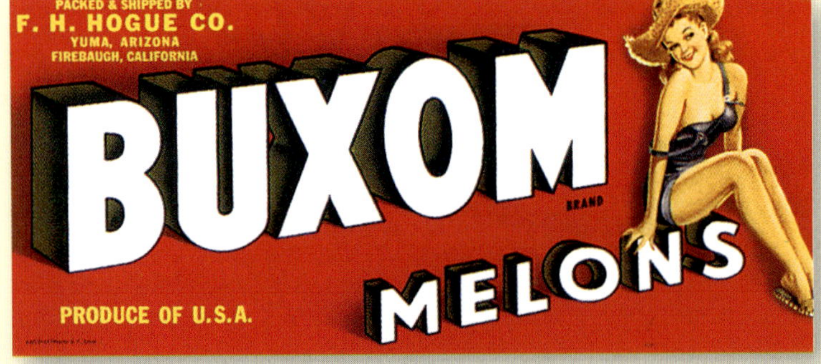

044

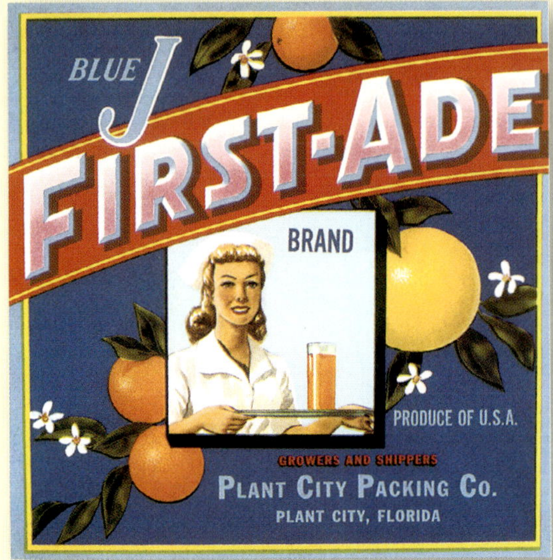

045

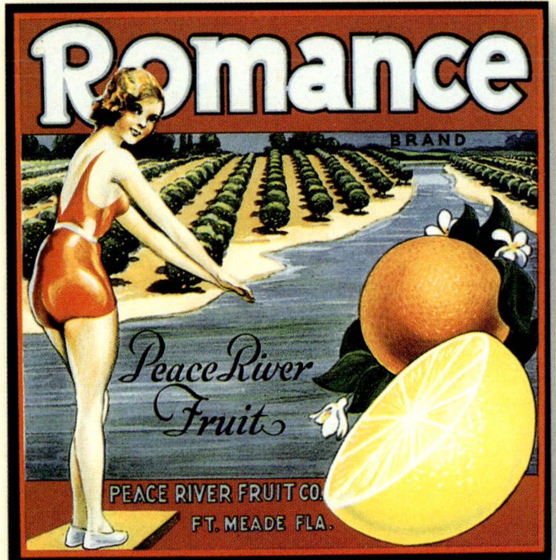

046

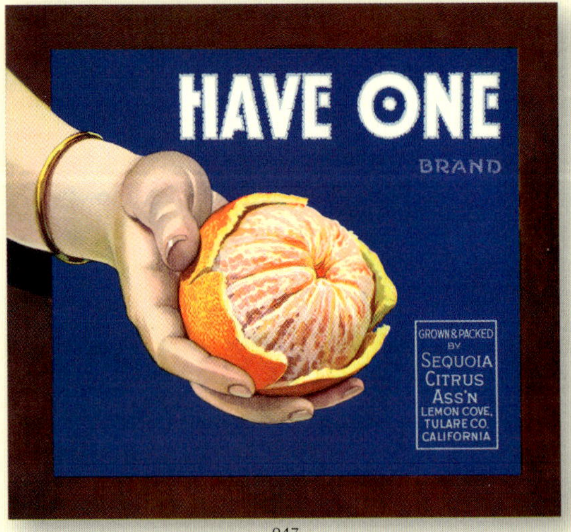

047

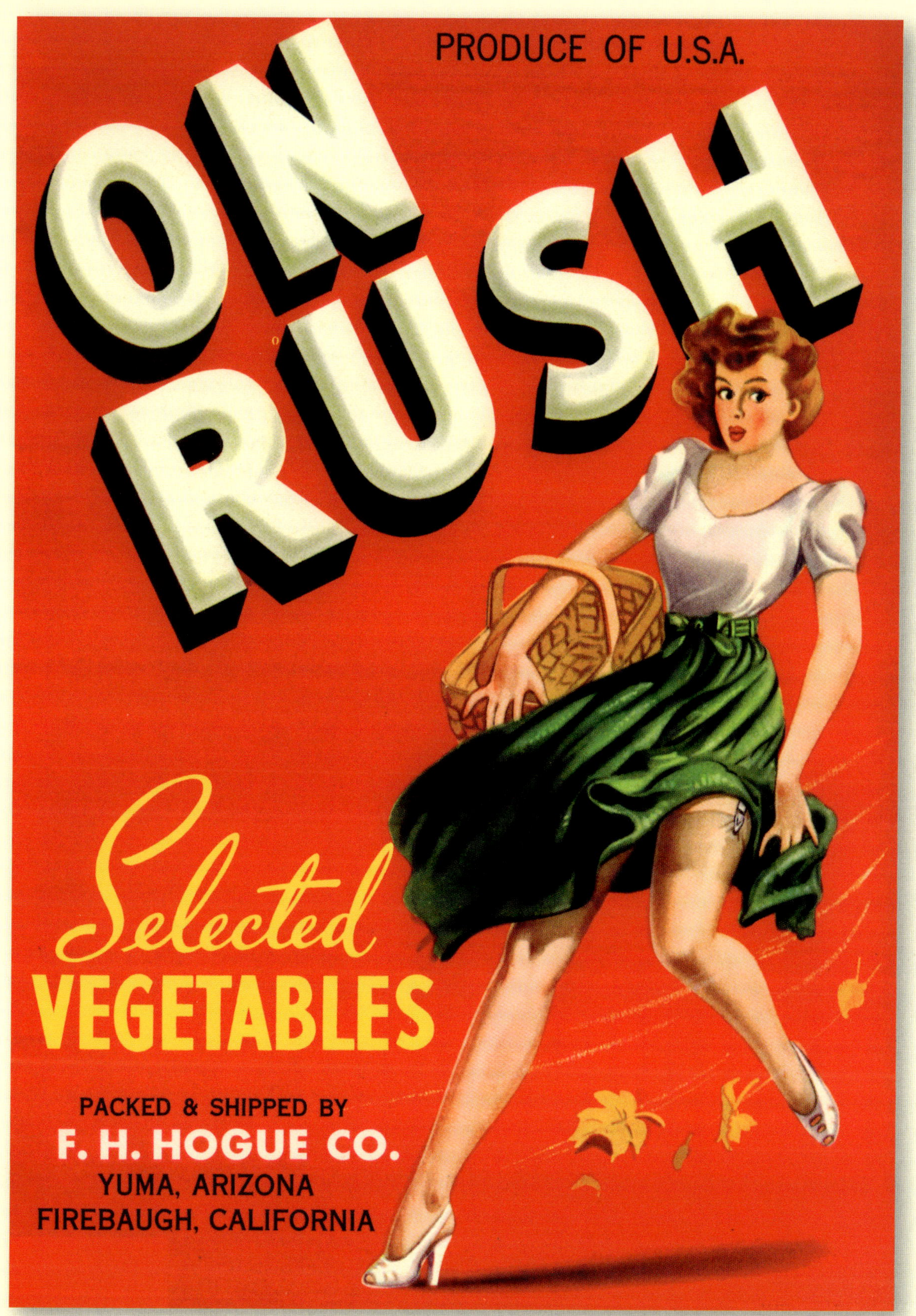

PRODUCE OF U.S.A.
ON RUSH
Selected
VEGETABLES
PACKED & SHIPPED BY
F. H. HOGUE CO.
YUMA, ARIZONA
FIREBAUGH, CALIFORNIA

Glamour Girl
BRAND
PRODUCE OF U.S.A.
"TOP QUALITY"
CALIFORNIA VEGETABLES
GROWERS AND SHIPPERS HALF-MOON BAY GROWERS ASSN., SAN FRANCISCO, CALIF.
ROESCH CO. LITHO. S.F.
ACROBAT
BRAND
Florida CITRUS FRUIT
WINTER HAVEN
CITRUS GROWERS ASSN.
WINTER HAVEN, FLORIDA

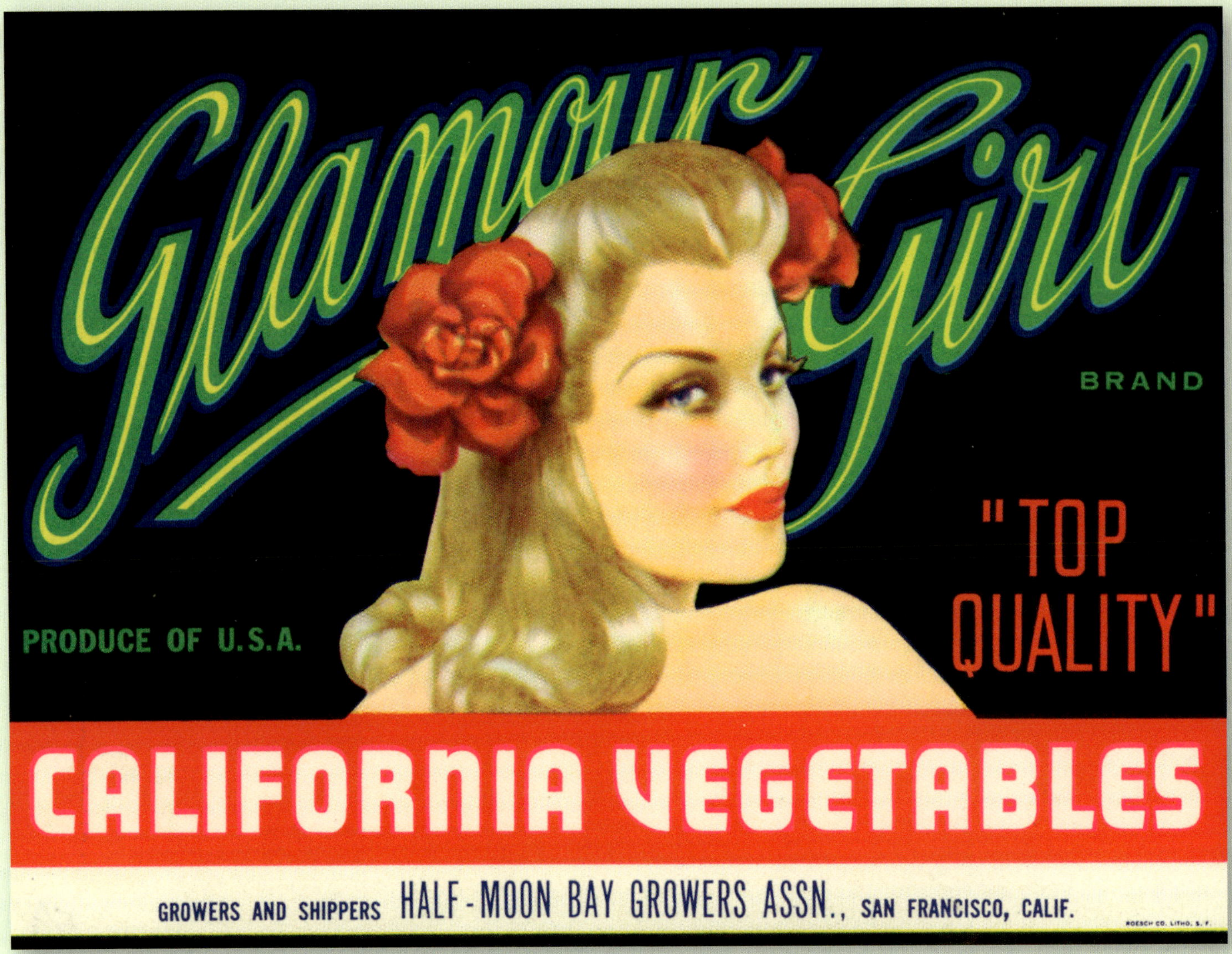

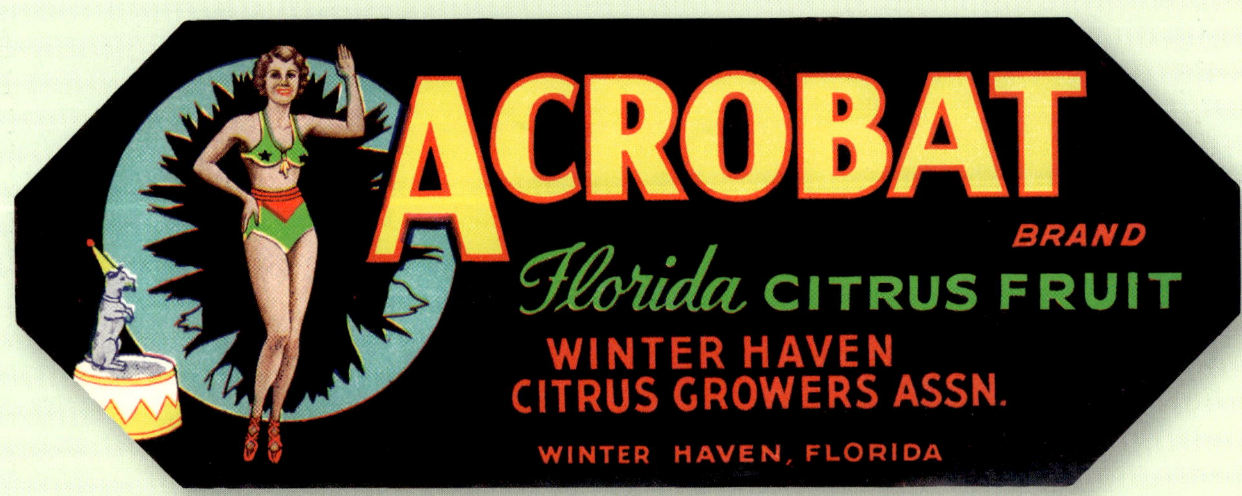

049

050

COAST QUEEN
California
BROCCOLI
PACKED AND SHIPPED BY
SANTA CRUZ ARTICHOKE
& SPROUT GROWERS ASSN.
SANTA CRUZ, CALIF.

051

PRODUCE OF U.S.A.
Lady Rowena
BRAND
CALIFORNIA FRUITS
BLUE ANCHOR
CALIFORNIA FRUIT EXCHANGE
NET WEIGHT 28 LBS.
PACKED AND SHIPPED BY
IVANHOE FRUIT ASSOCIATION
IVANHOE, CALIFORNIA

052

NET WEIGHT 28 LBS.
PRODUCE OF U.S.A.
Lady Rowena
BRAND
CALIFORNIA FRUITS
EMPERORS
BLUE ANCHOR
CALIFORNIA FRUIT EXCHANGE
PACKED AND SHIPPED BY
IVANHOE FRUIT ASSOCIATION
IVANHOE, CALIFORNIA

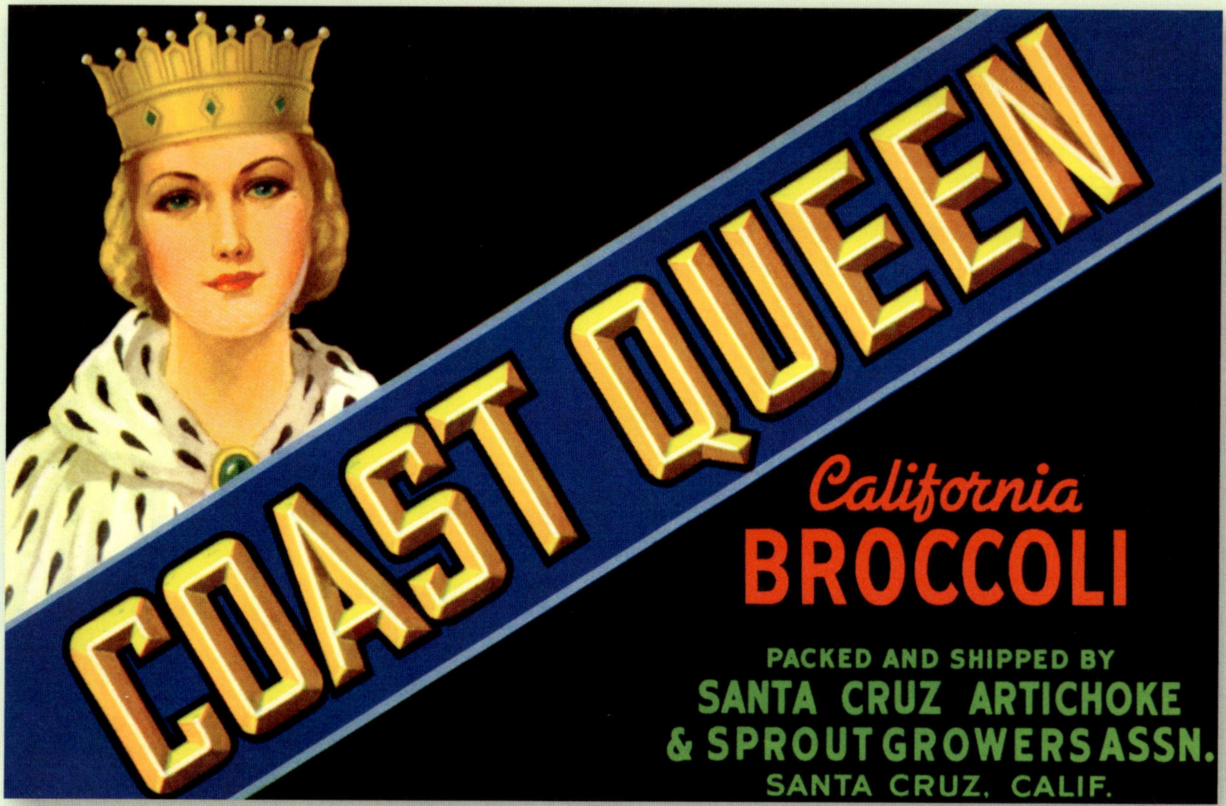

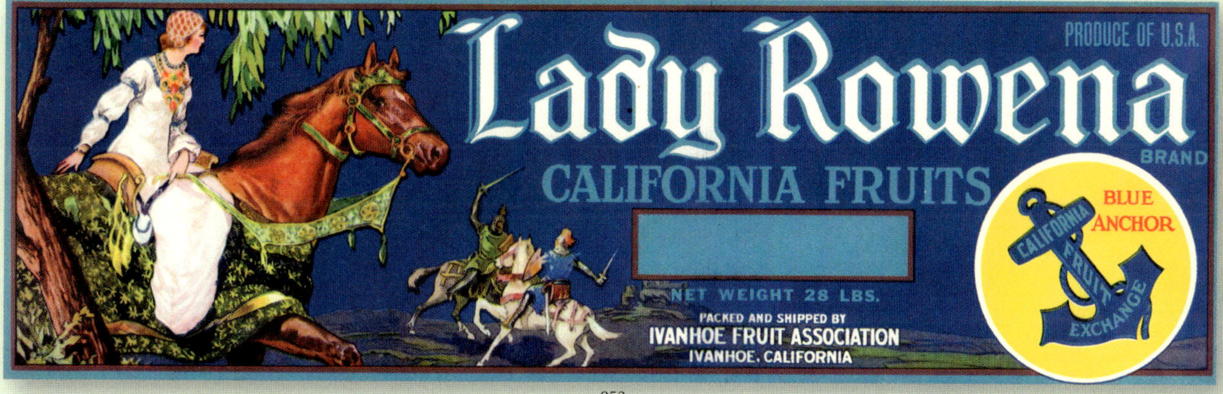

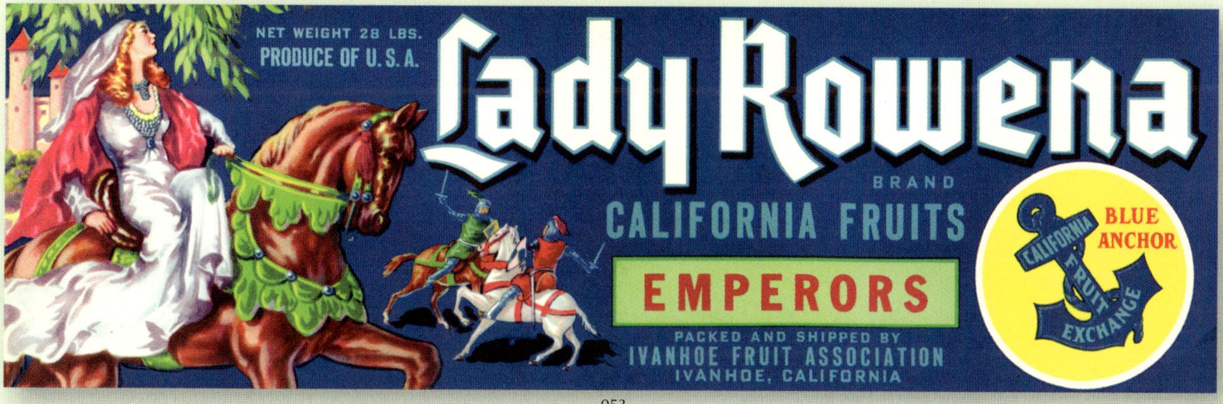

053

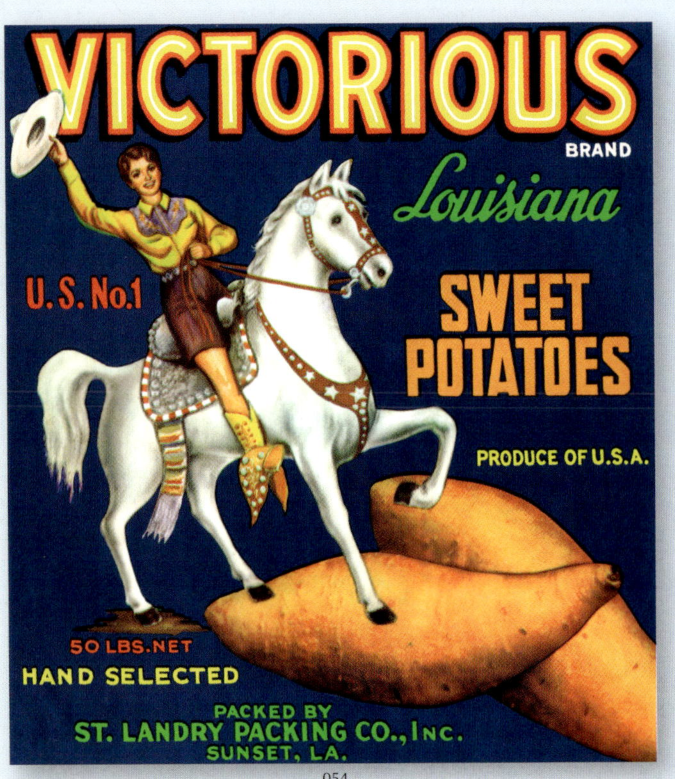

054

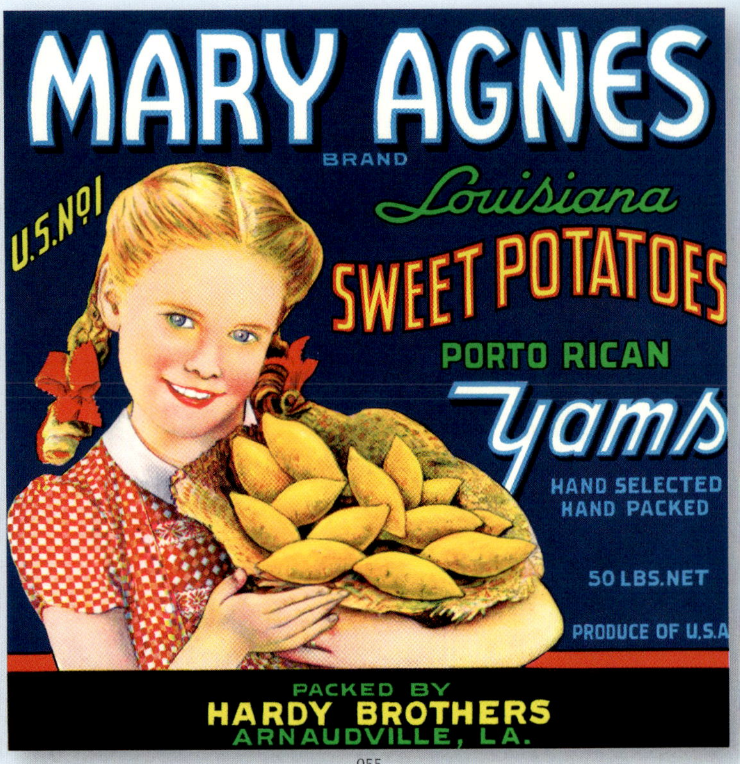

055

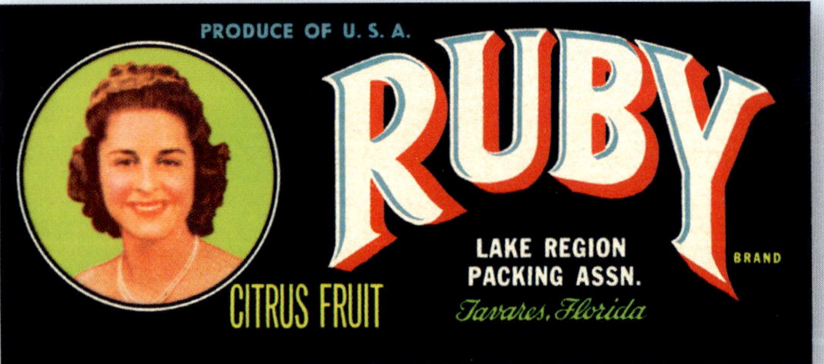

056

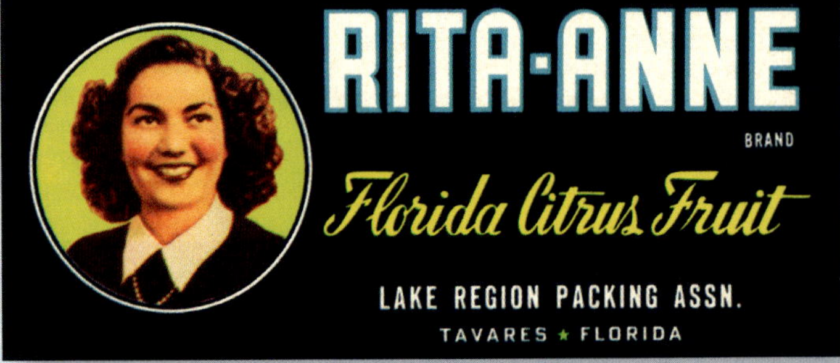

057

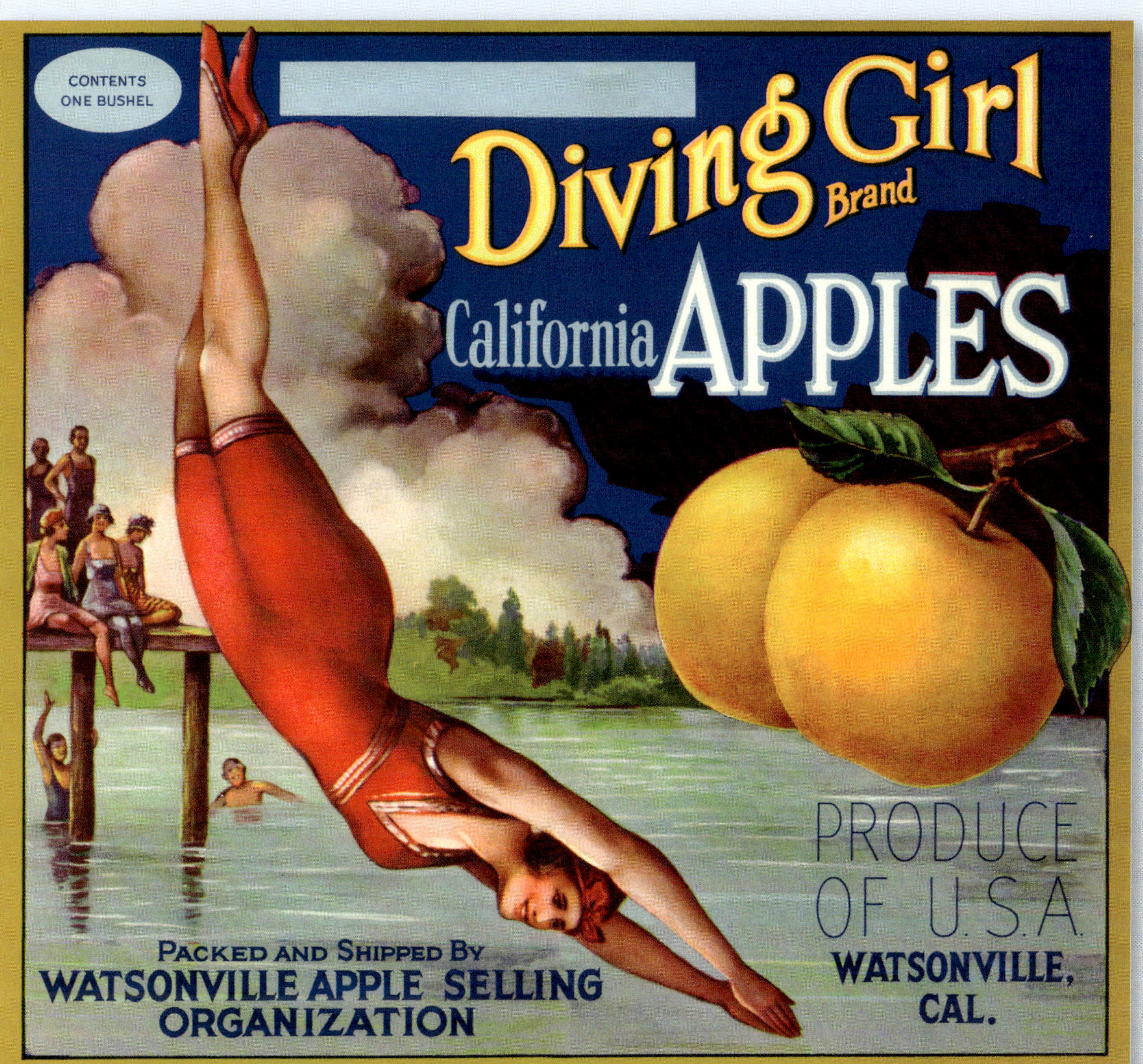

CONTENTS ONE BUSHEL
Diving Girl Brand
California APPLES
PRODUCE OF U.S.A.
WATSONVILLE, CAL.
PACKED AND SHIPPED BY
WATSONVILLE APPLE SELLING ORGANIZATION

EDUARDO ROSELLÓ
SUNBEAM
VALENCIA
SPAIN

059

COLOR GUARD
BRAND
WASHINGTON STATE
APPLES
PRODUCE OF U.S.A.
DISTRIBUTED BY
PAUL BRIANT FRUIT CO.
WENATCHEE-YAKIMA, WASHINGTON
CONTENTS
ONE VOLUME BUSHEL

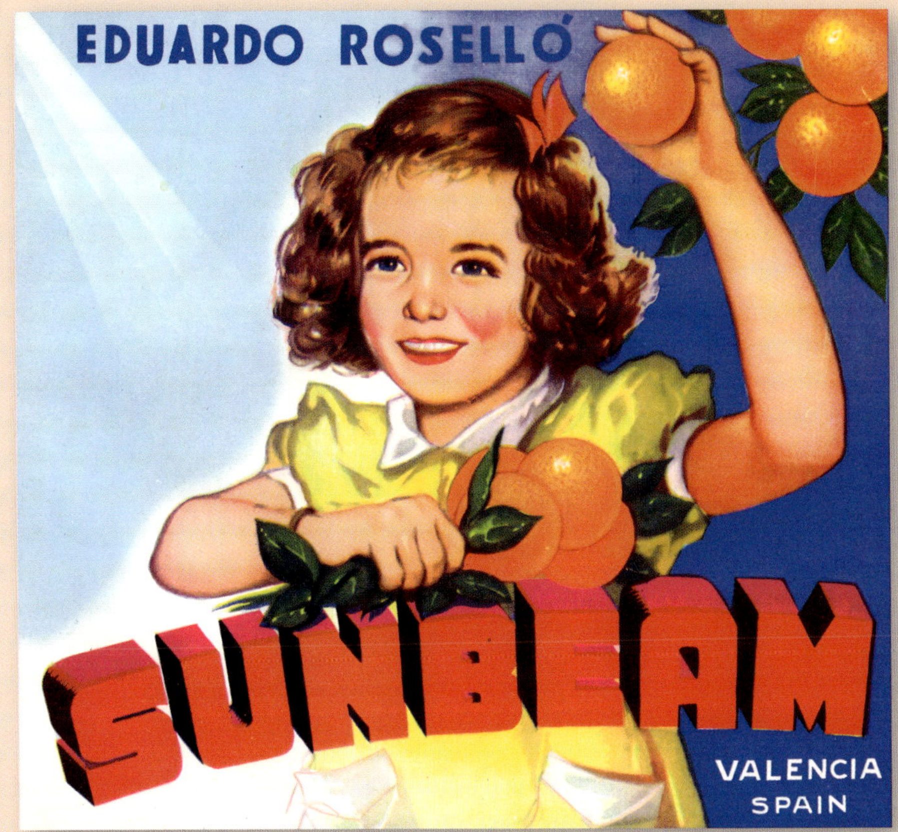

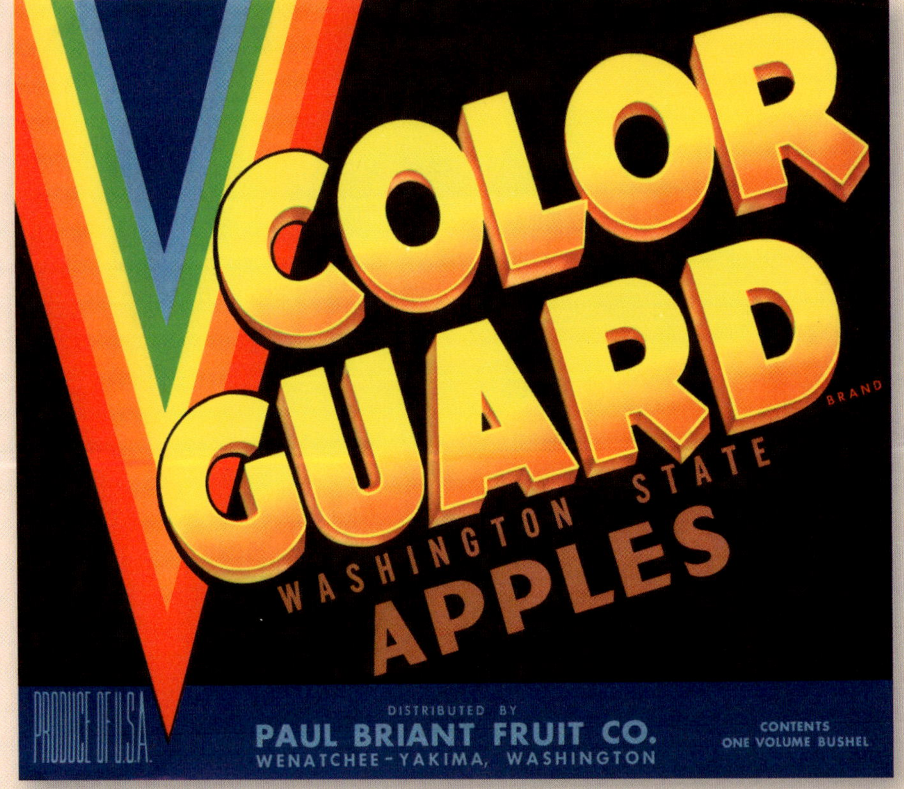

060

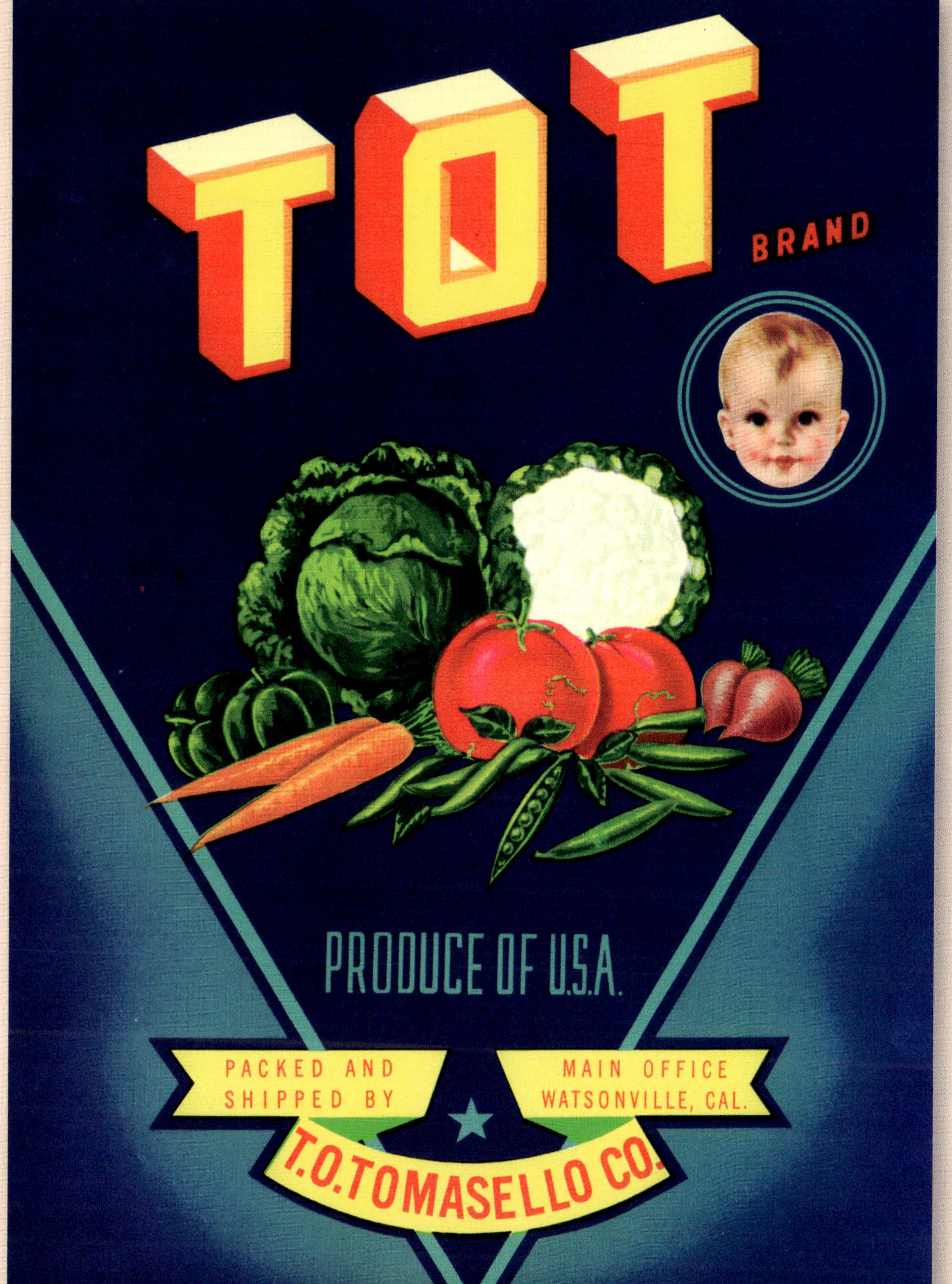

TOT
BRAND
PRODUCE OF U.S.A.
PACKED AND
SHIPPED BY
MAIN OFFICE
WATSONVILLE, CAL.
T.O.TOMASELLO CO.

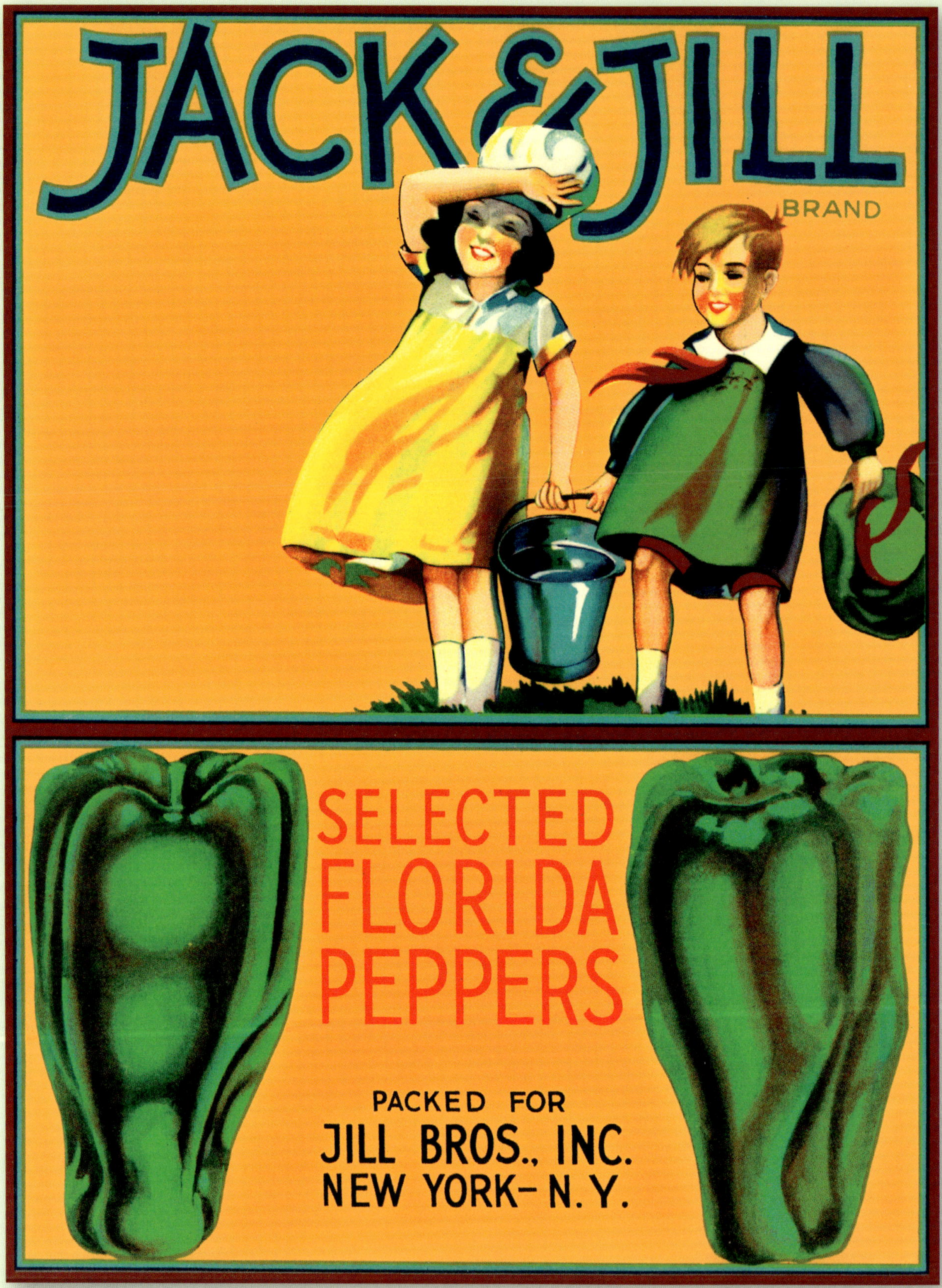

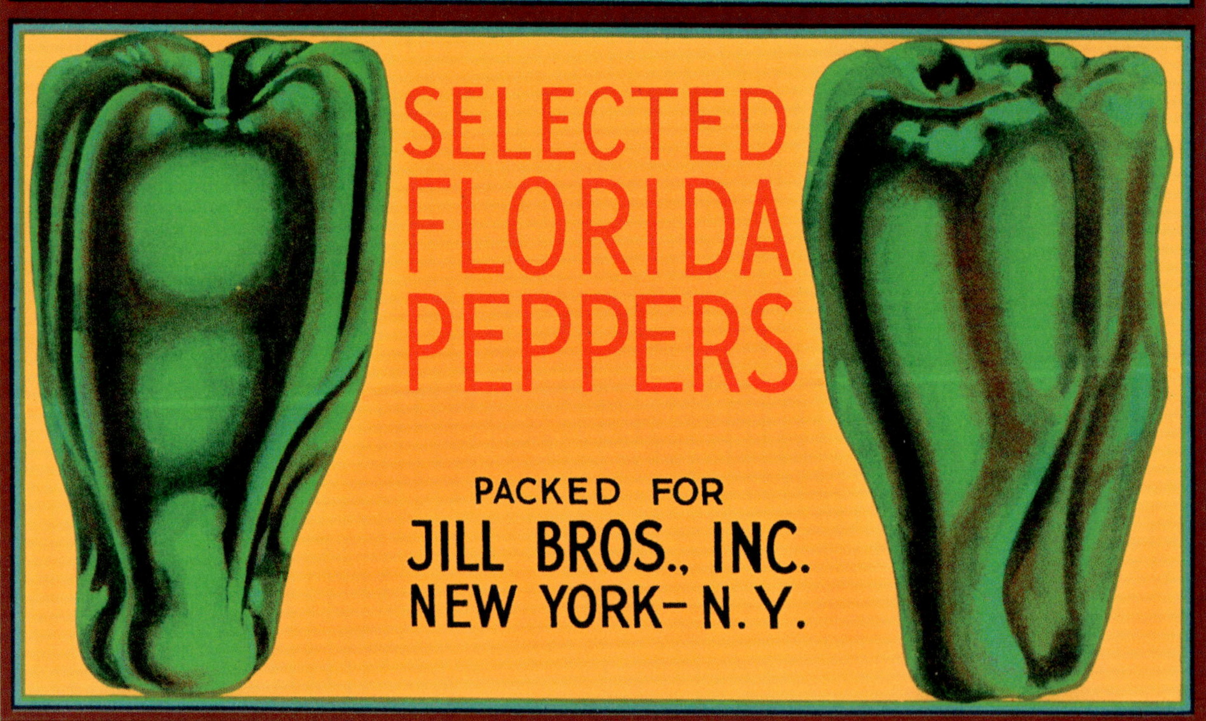

JACK & JILL
BRAND
SELECTED
FLORIDA
PEPPERS
PACKED FOR
JILL BROS., INC.
NEW YORK— N.Y.

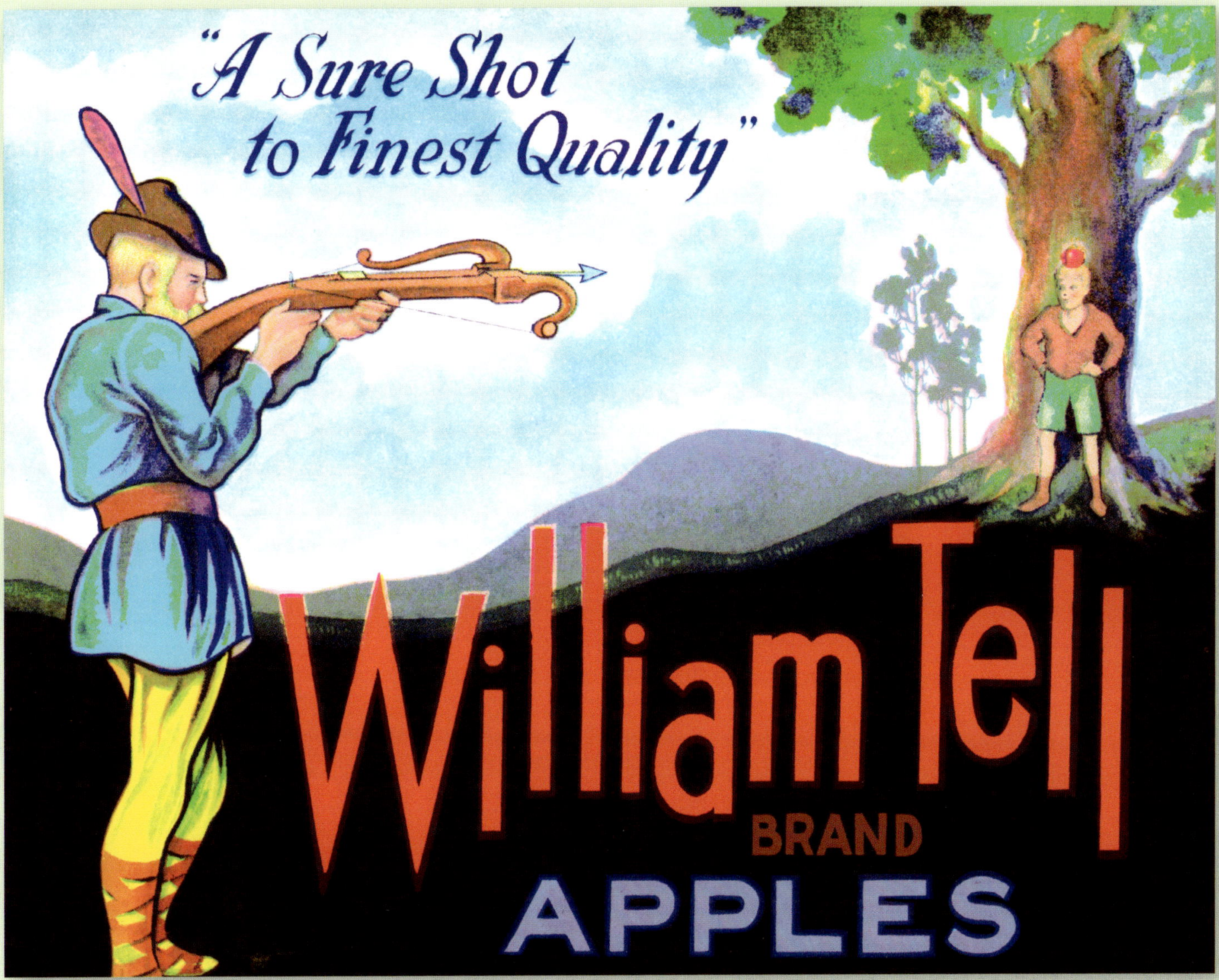

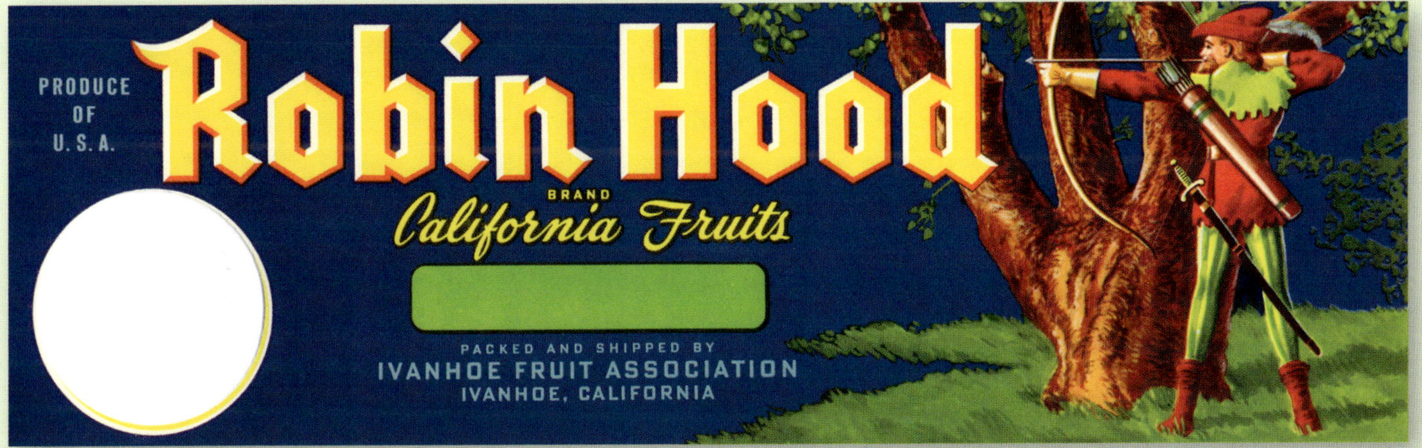
"A Sure Shot
to Finest Quality"
William Tell
BRAND
APPLES
063

PRODUCE
OF
U.S.A.
Robin Hood
BRAND
California Fruits
PACKED AND SHIPPED BY
IVANHOE FRUIT ASSOCIATION
IVANHOE, CALIFORNIA
064

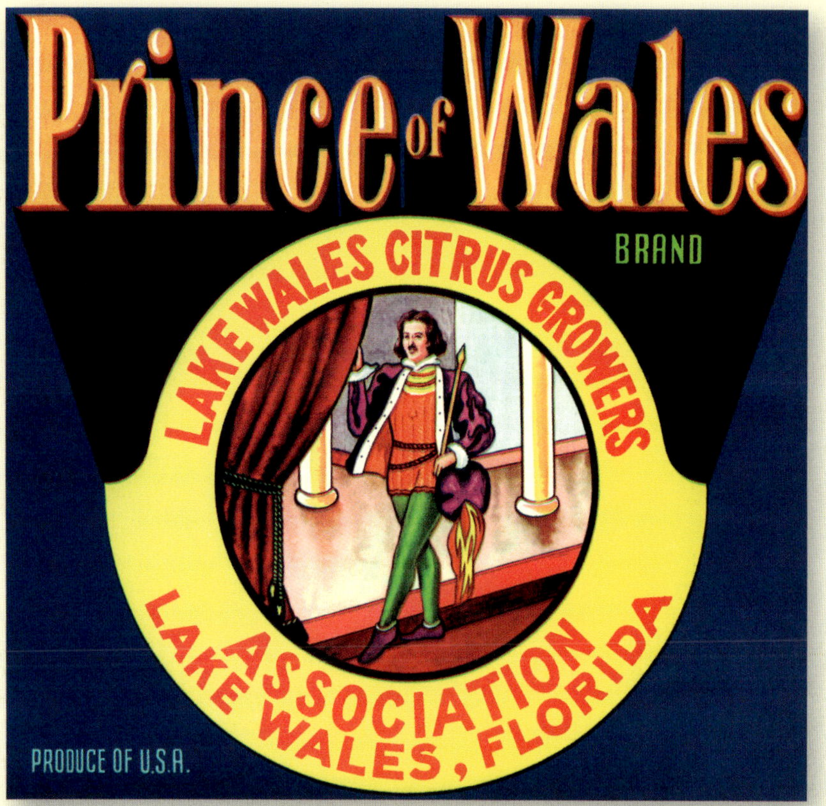

065

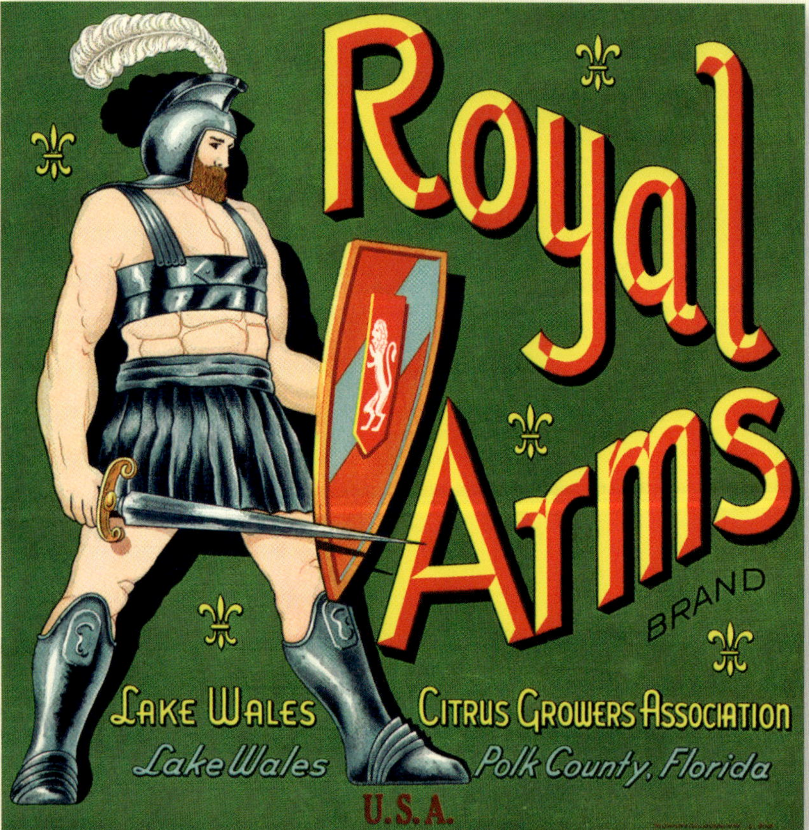

066

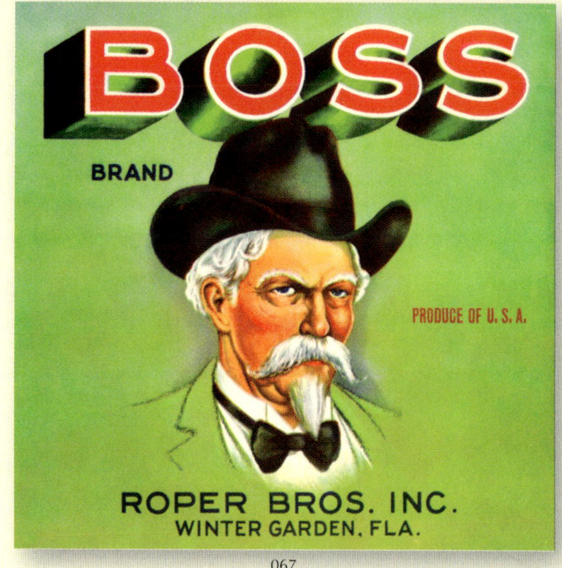

067

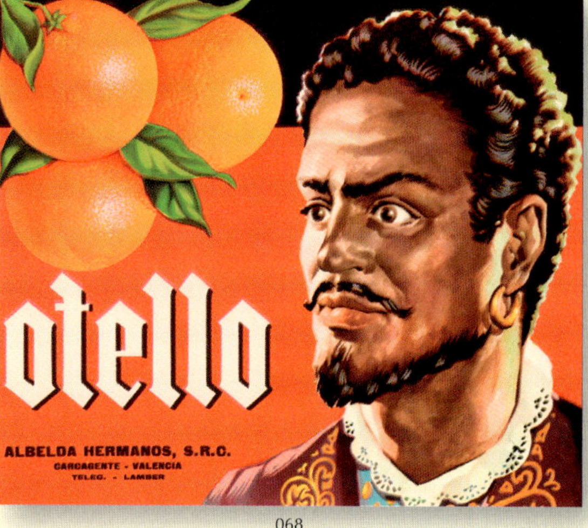

068

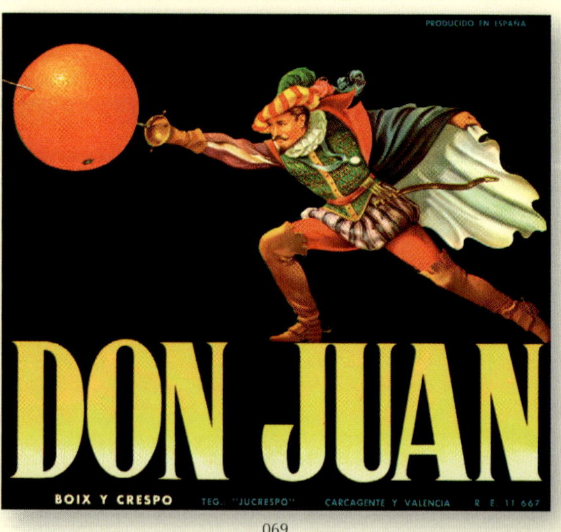

069

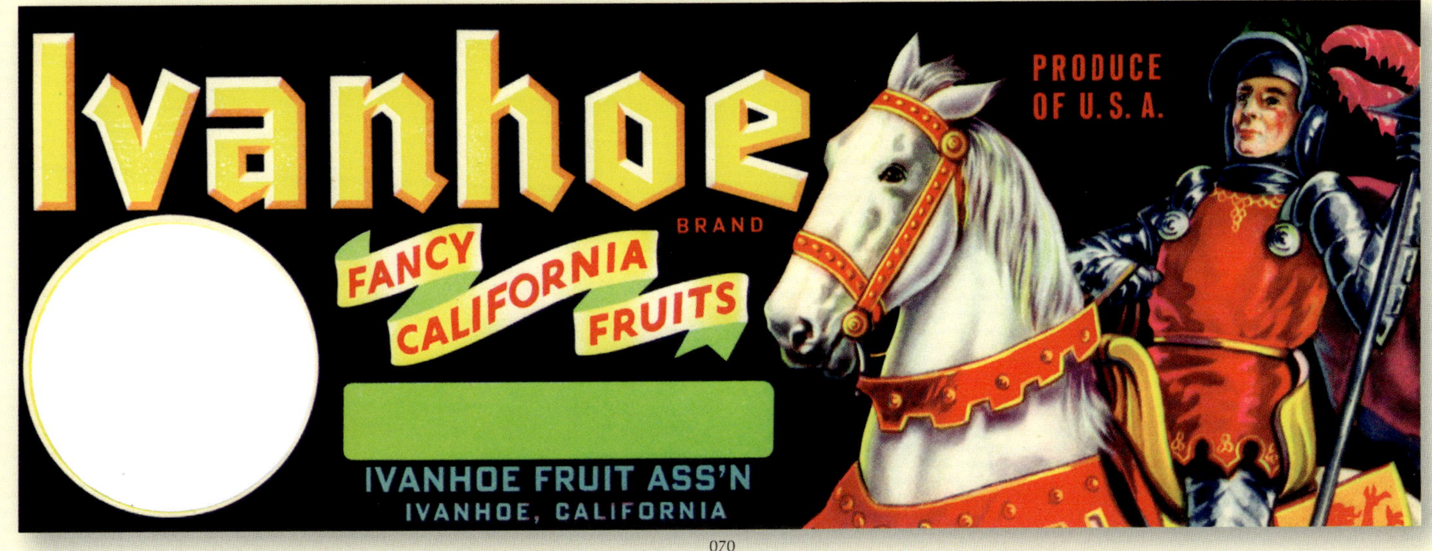

070

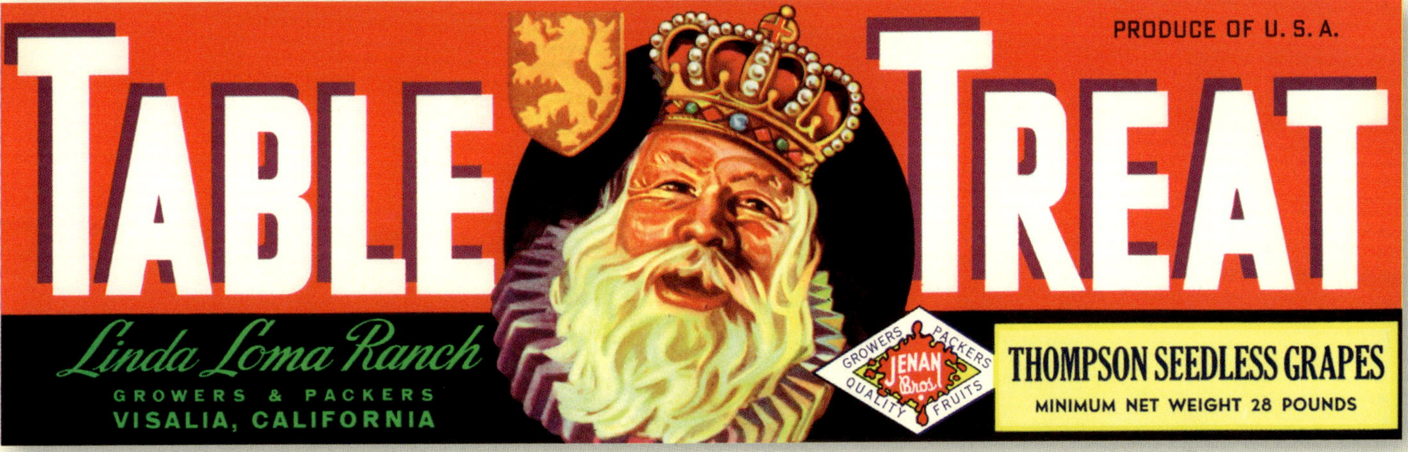

071

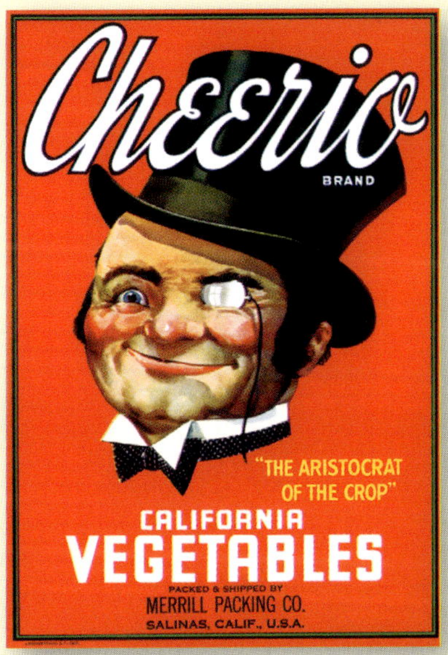

072

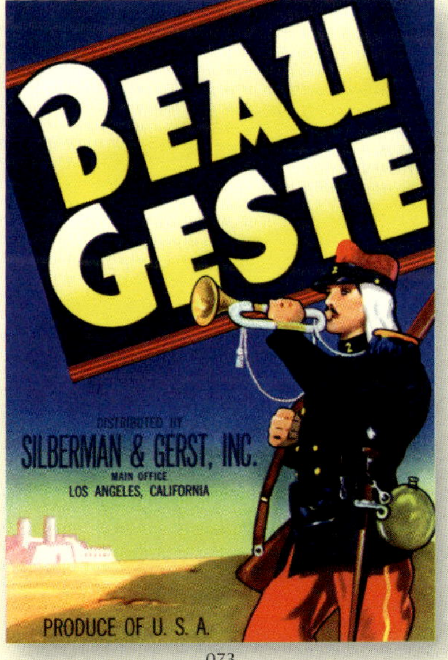

073

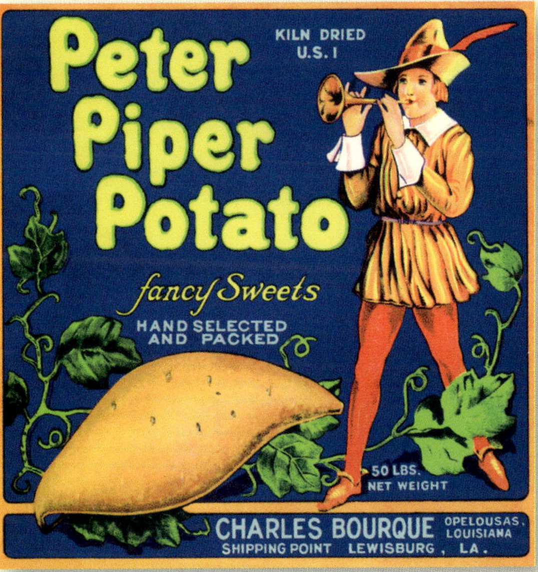

074

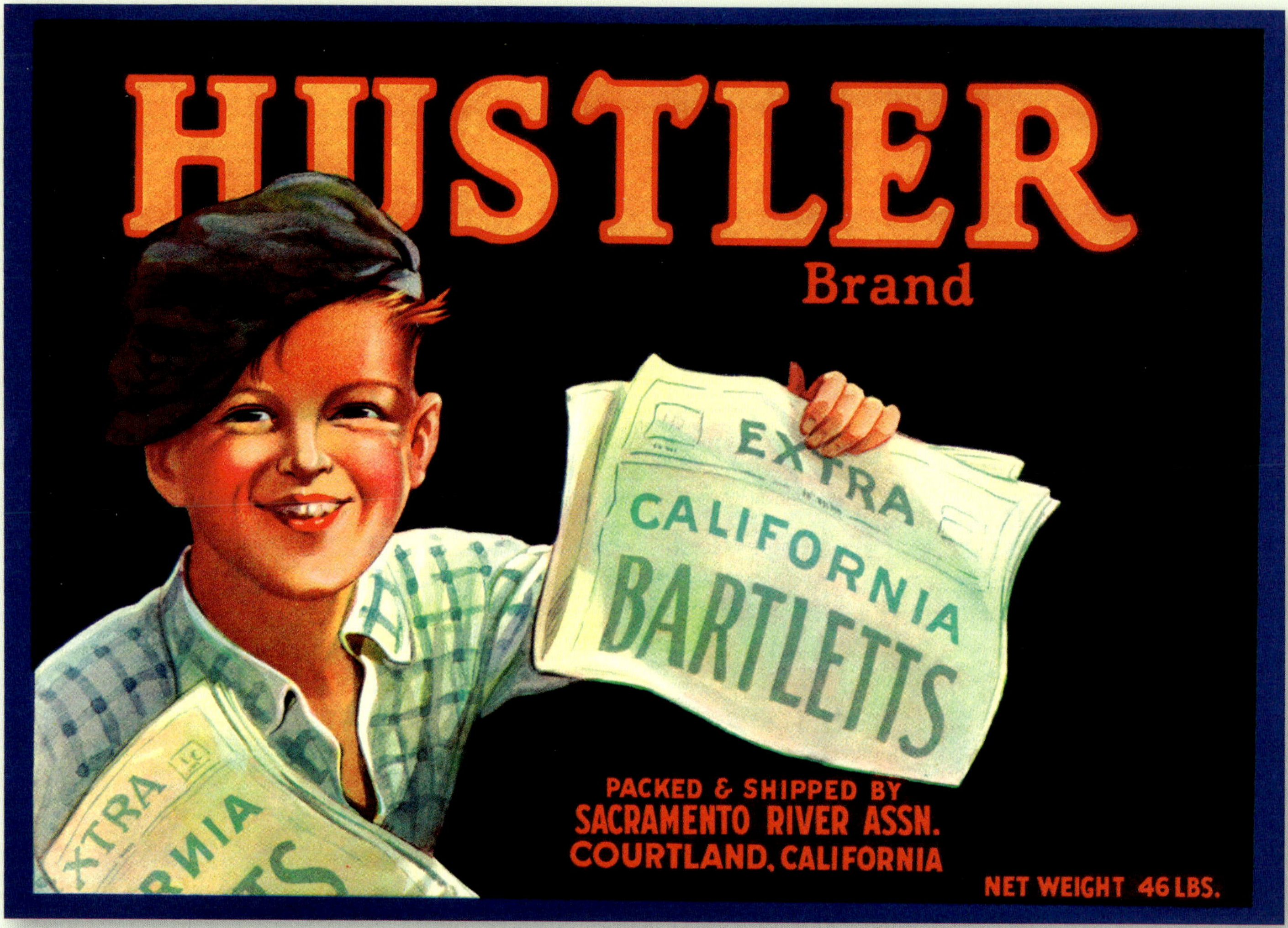

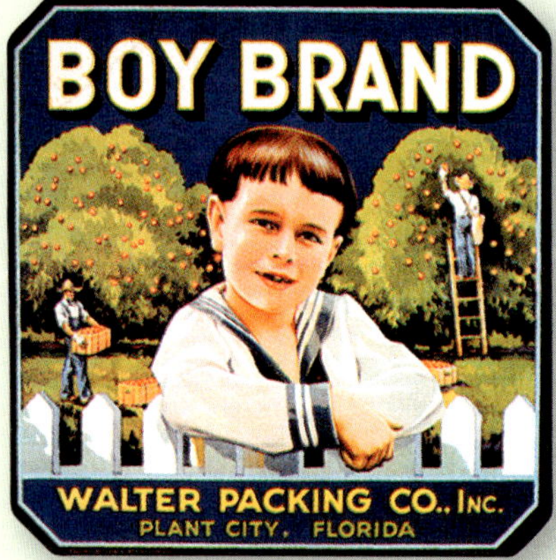

076

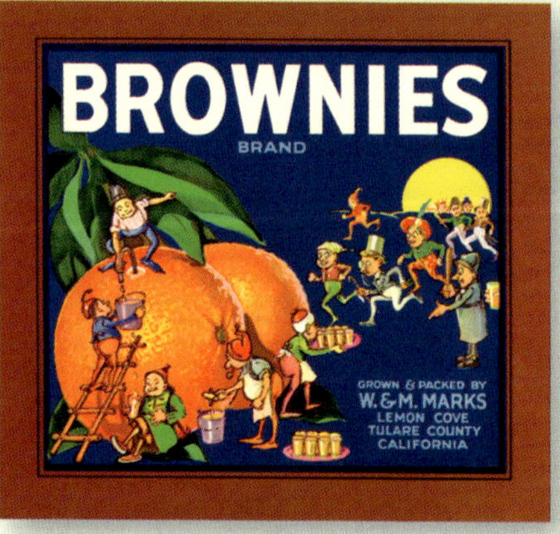

077

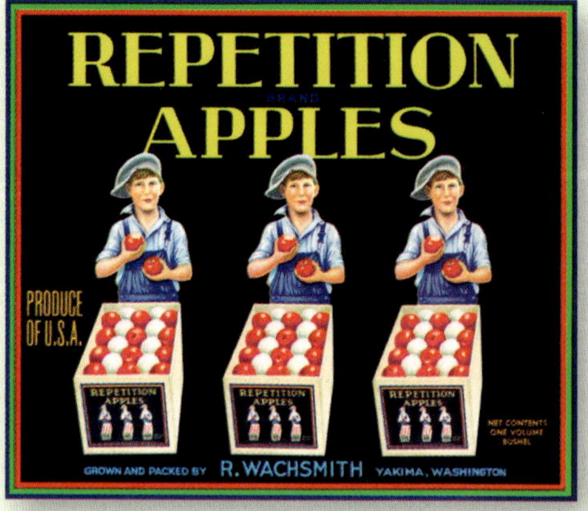

078

075

UNITED STATES OF AMERICA
RED WAGON
BRAND
ROYAL VALLEY FRUIT GROWERS ASS'N.
REEDLEY, CALIFORNIA

079

BUDDY BRAND
The Northwest's Finest Apples
ANDREWS BROTHERS
AB
DETROIT, MICH.

080

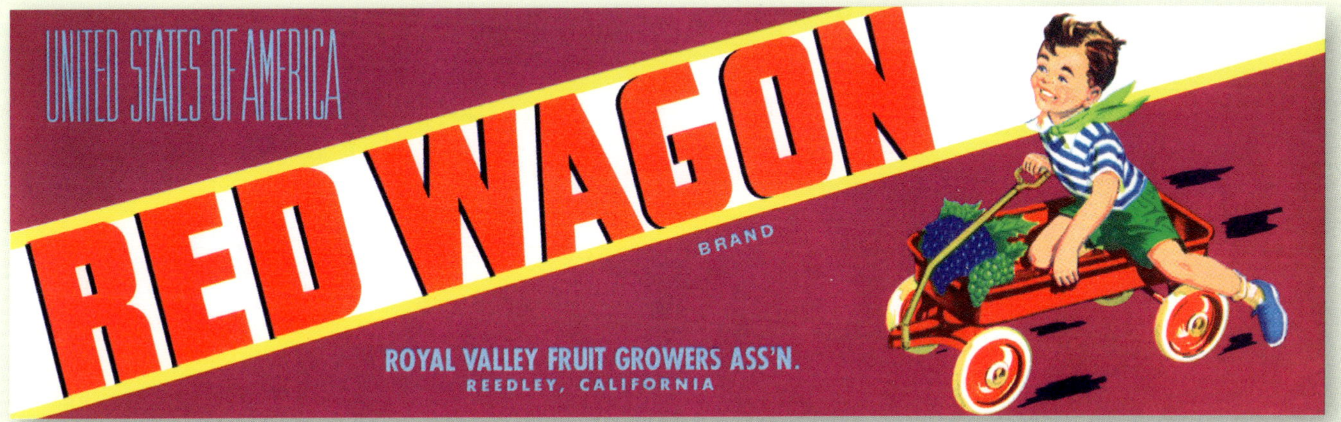

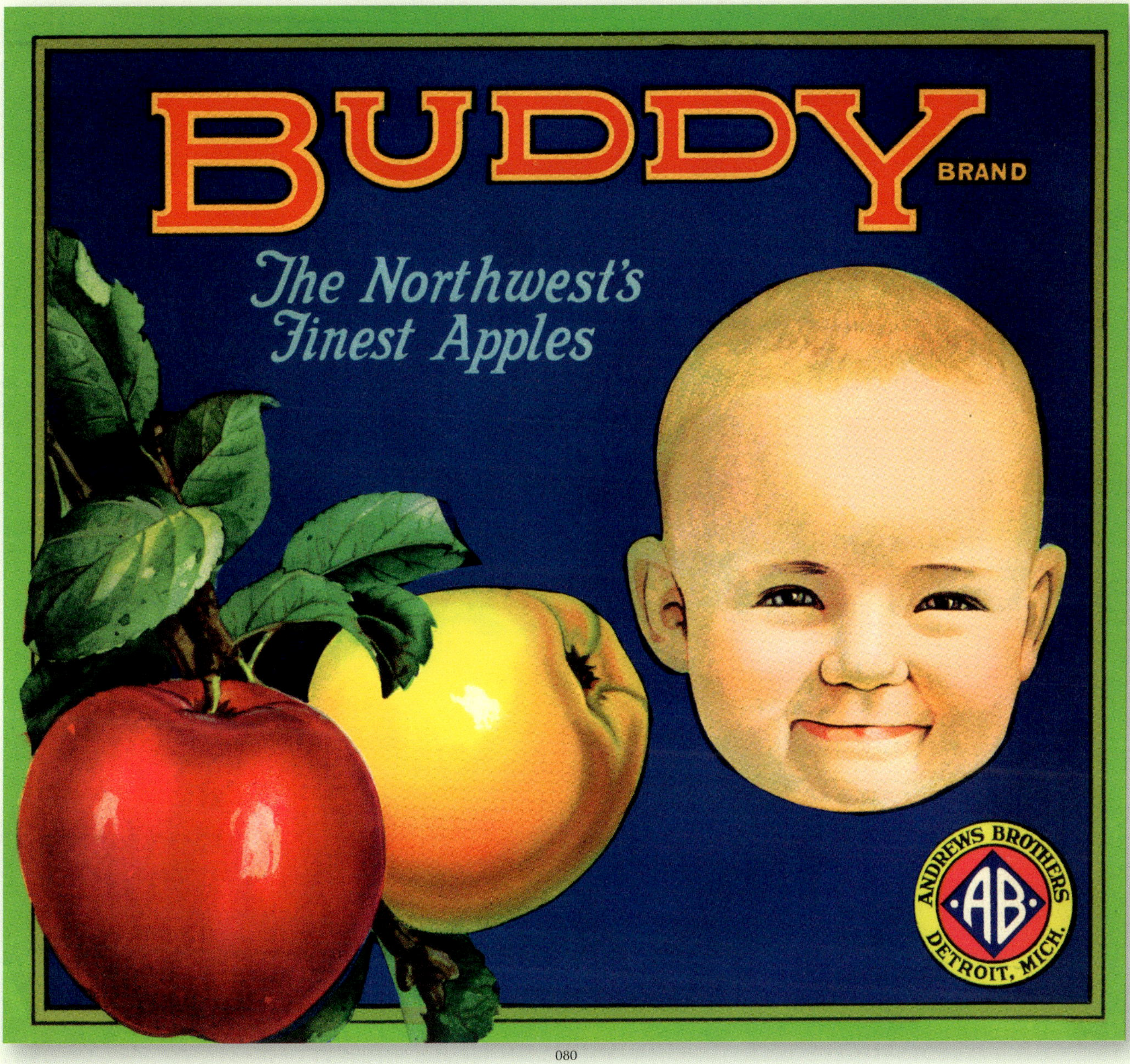

50 LBS. NET
CHAMP
BRAND
LOUISIANA
SWEET POTATOES
YAMS
LOUISIANA
YAM SWEET POTATOES
PRODUCE OF U.S.A.
HAND SELECTED
HAND PACKED
PACKED BY
DUPUIS PRODUCE
COMPANY
BREAUX BRIDGE, LA.
081
TOUCHDOWN
CALIFORNIA DECIDUOUS FRUITS
PACIFIC FRUIT EXCHANGE
EMPEROR GRAPES
DISTRIBUTORS
MAIN OFFICE
SAN FRANCISCO, CALIFORNIA
GROWN IN U.S.A.
NET WEIGHT 28 LBS.
LEHMANN, S.F.
082

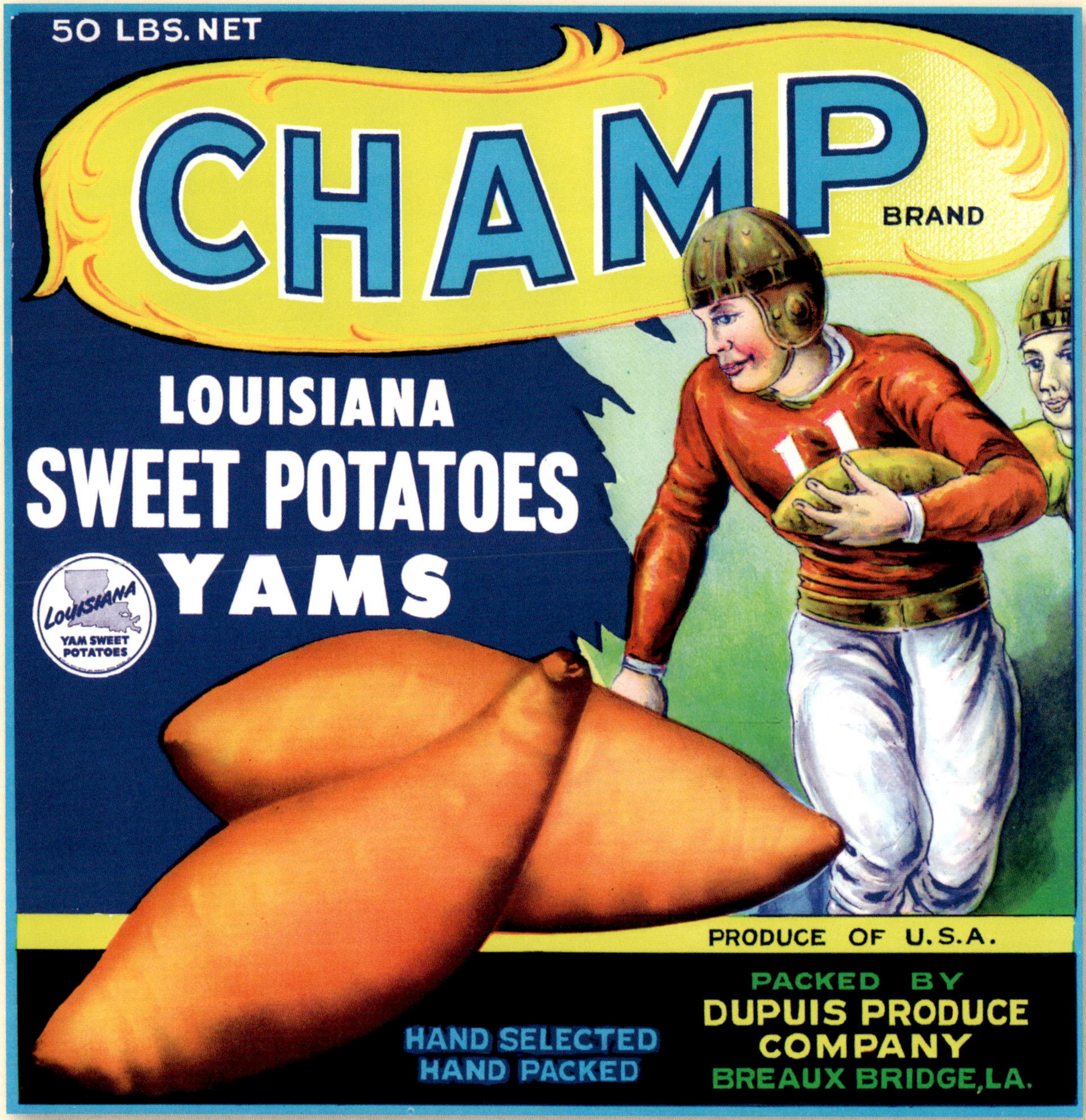

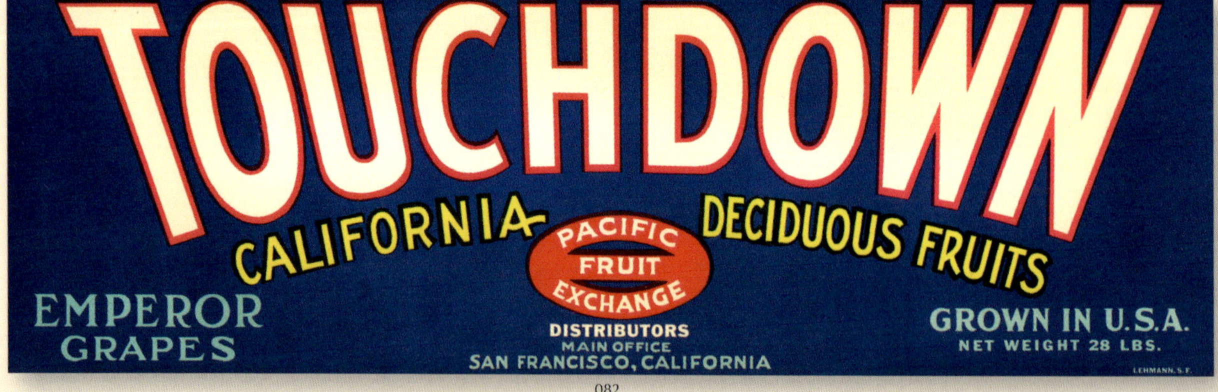

36

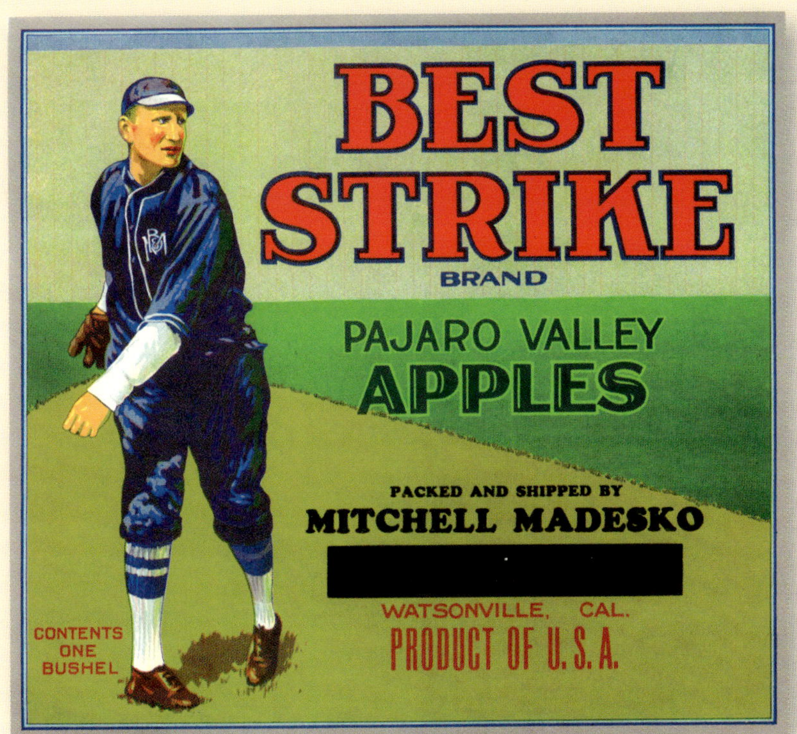

083

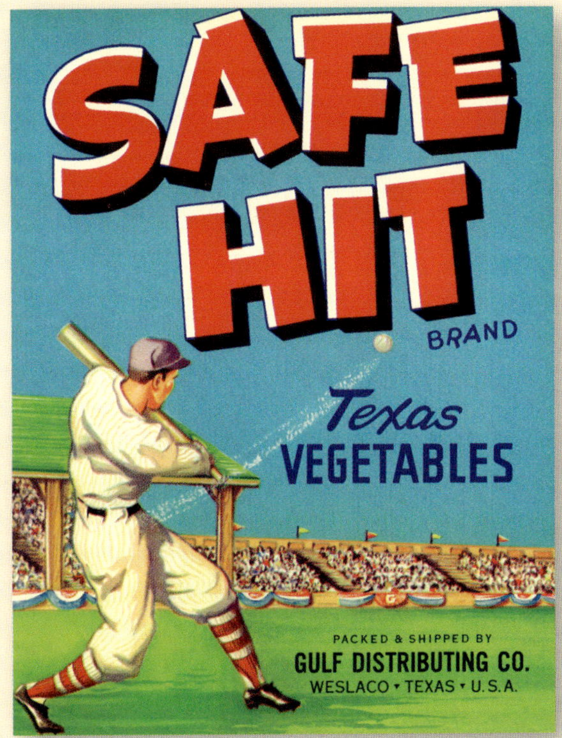

084

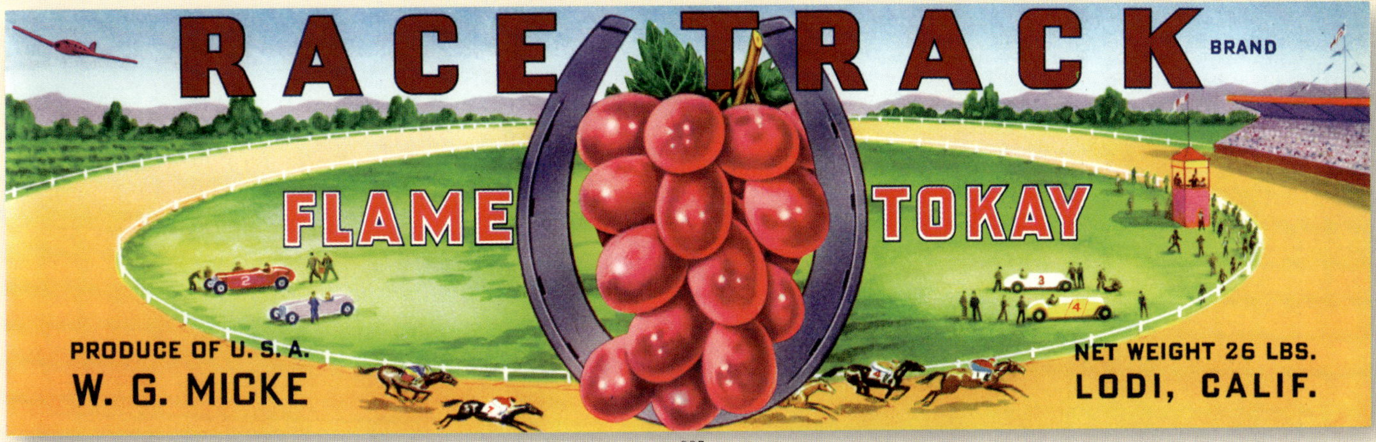

085

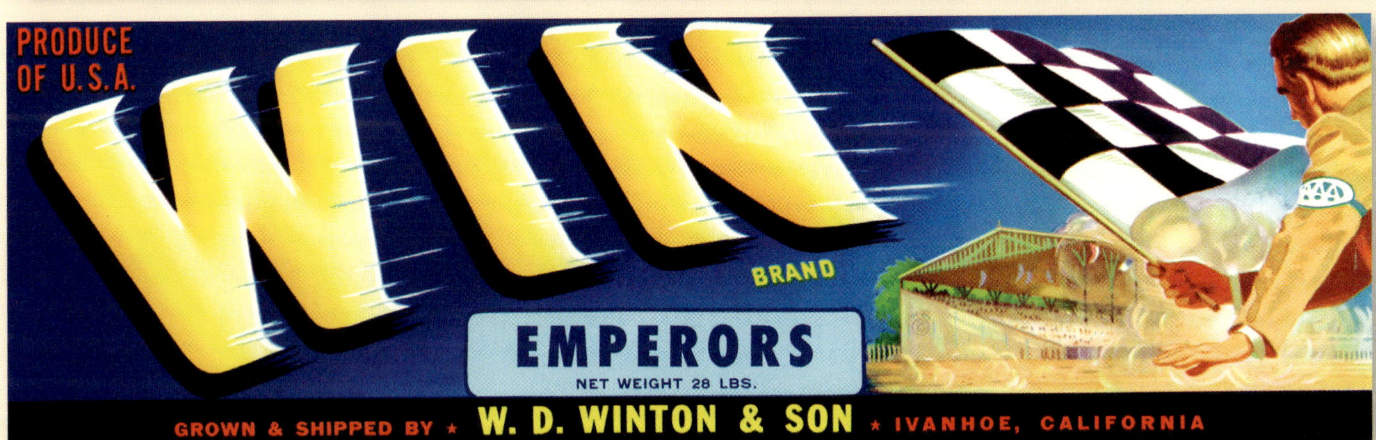

086

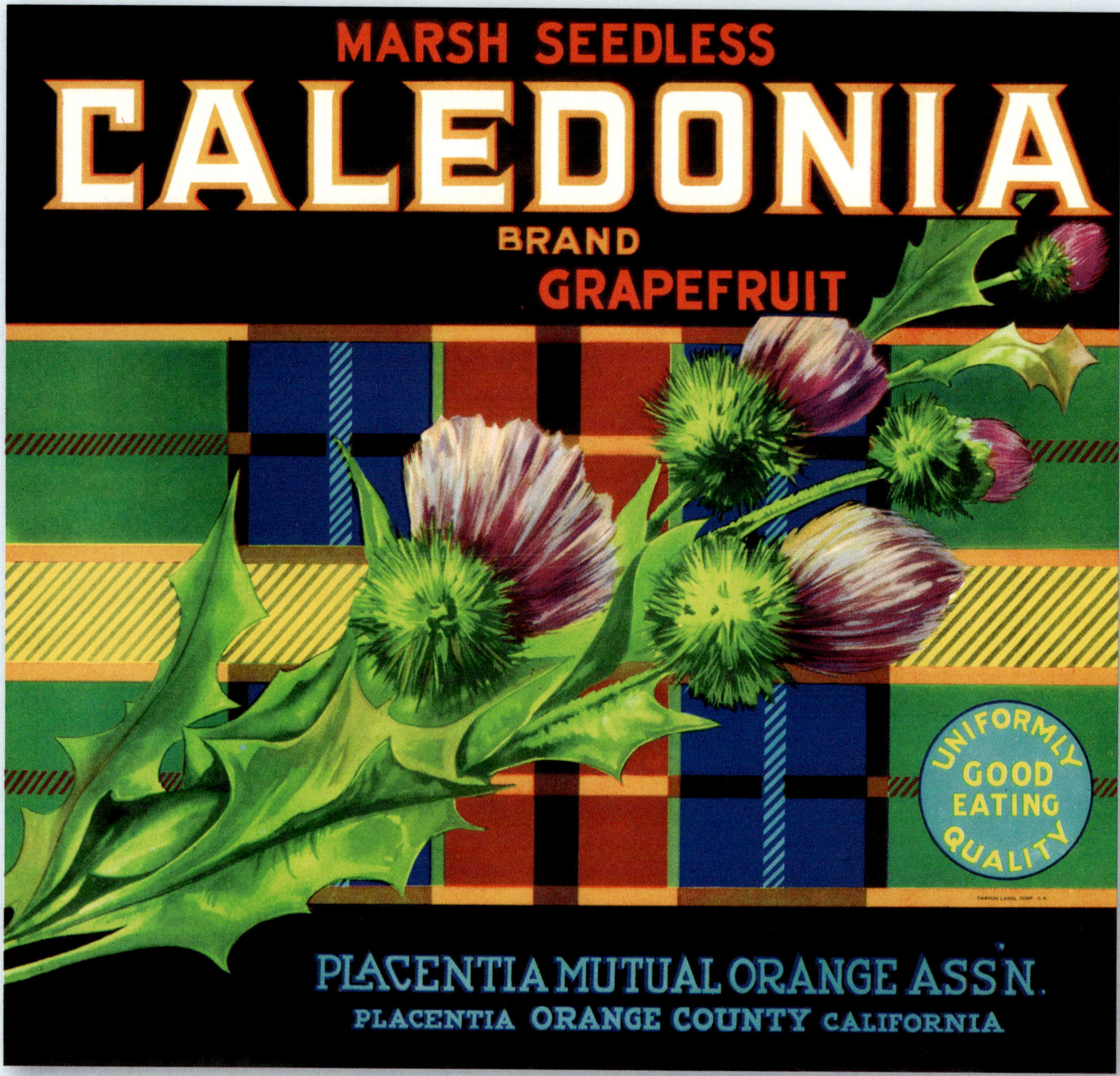

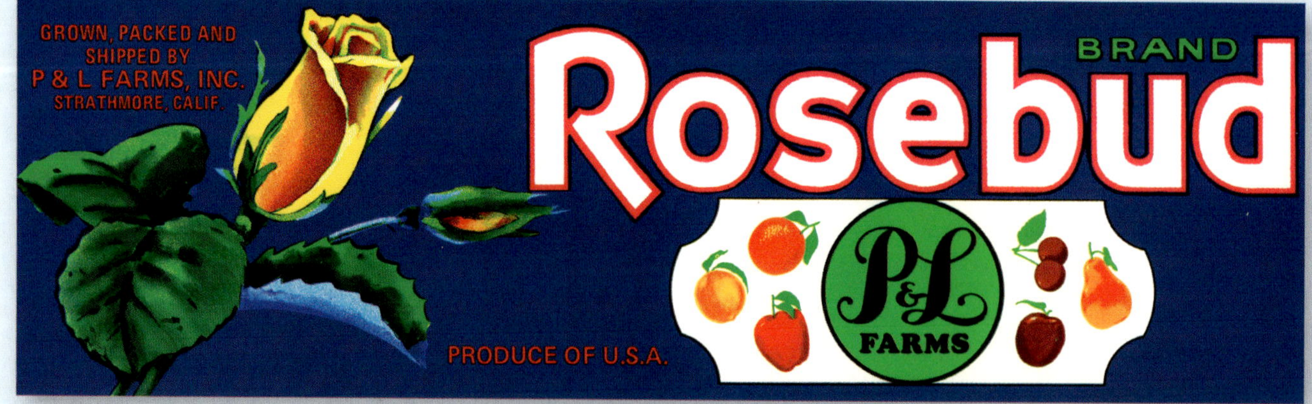
MARSH SEEDLESS
CALEDONIA
BRAND
GRAPEFRUIT
UNIFORMLY GOOD EATING QUALITY
PLACENTIA MUTUAL ORANGE ASS'N.
PLACENTIA ORANGE COUNTY CALIFORNIA
GROWN, PACKED AND SHIPPED BY
P & L FARMS, INC.
STRATHMORE, CALIF.
BRAND
Rosebud
P&L FARMS
PRODUCE OF U.S.A.

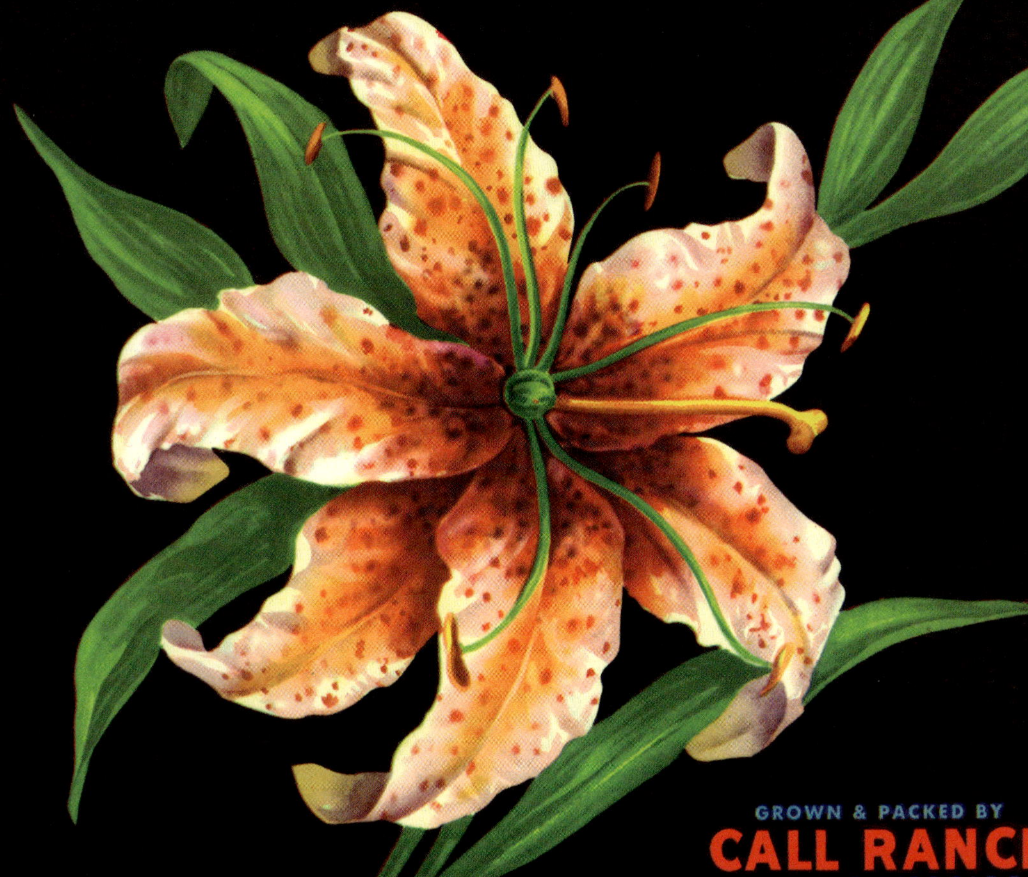

CORONA LILY
BRAND
GROWN & PACKED BY
CALL RANCH
CORONA - RIVERSIDE CO.
CALIFORNIA

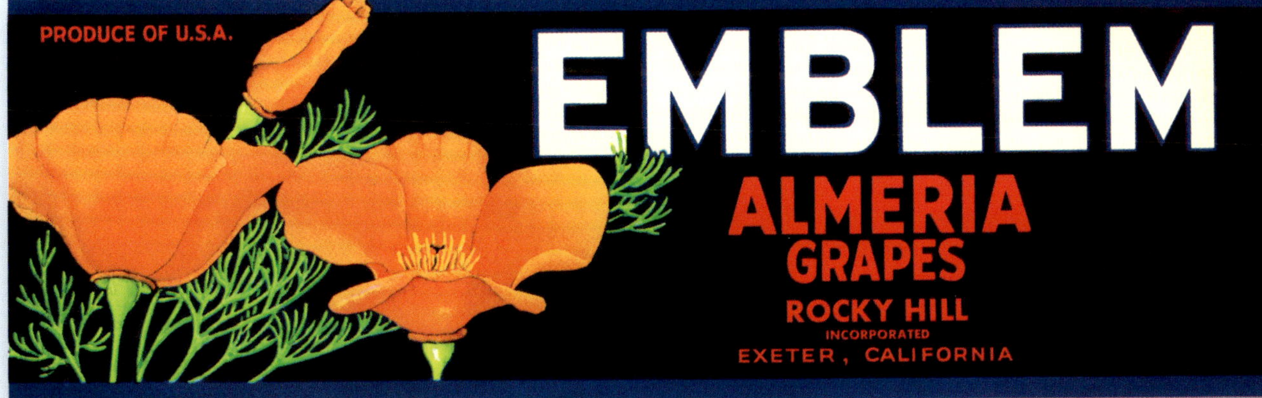

PRODUCE OF U.S.A.
EMBLEM
ALMERIA
GRAPES
ROCKY HILL
INCORPORATED
EXETER, CALIFORNIA

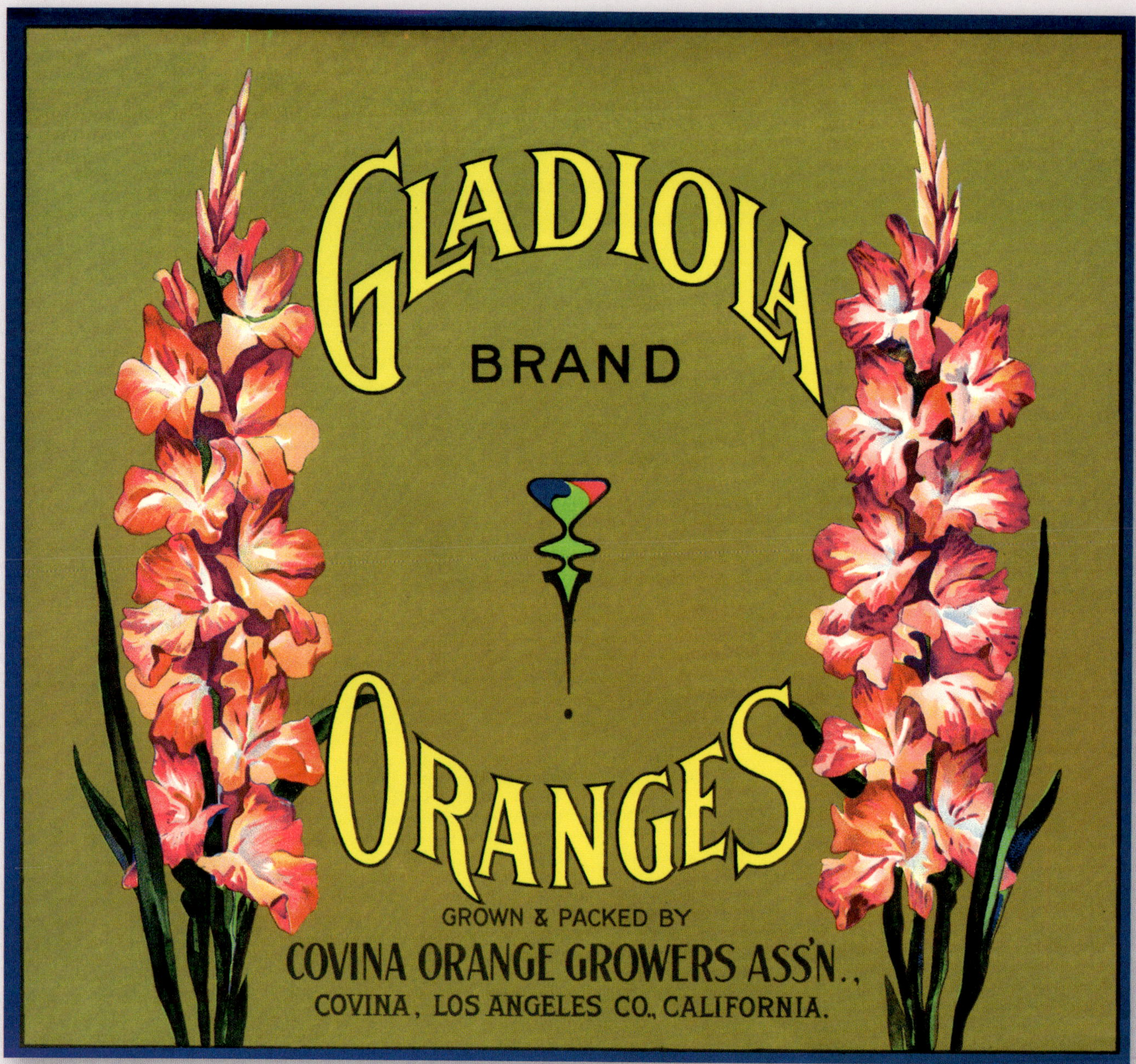

GLADIOLA
BRAND

ORANGES
GROWN & PACKED BY
COVINA ORANGE GROWERS ASS'N.,
COVINA, LOS ANGELES CO., CALIFORNIA.

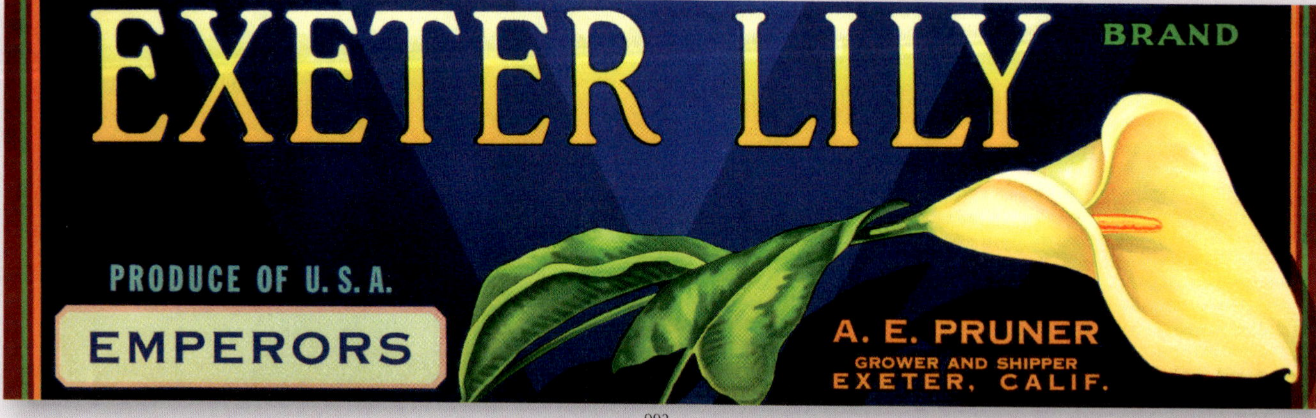

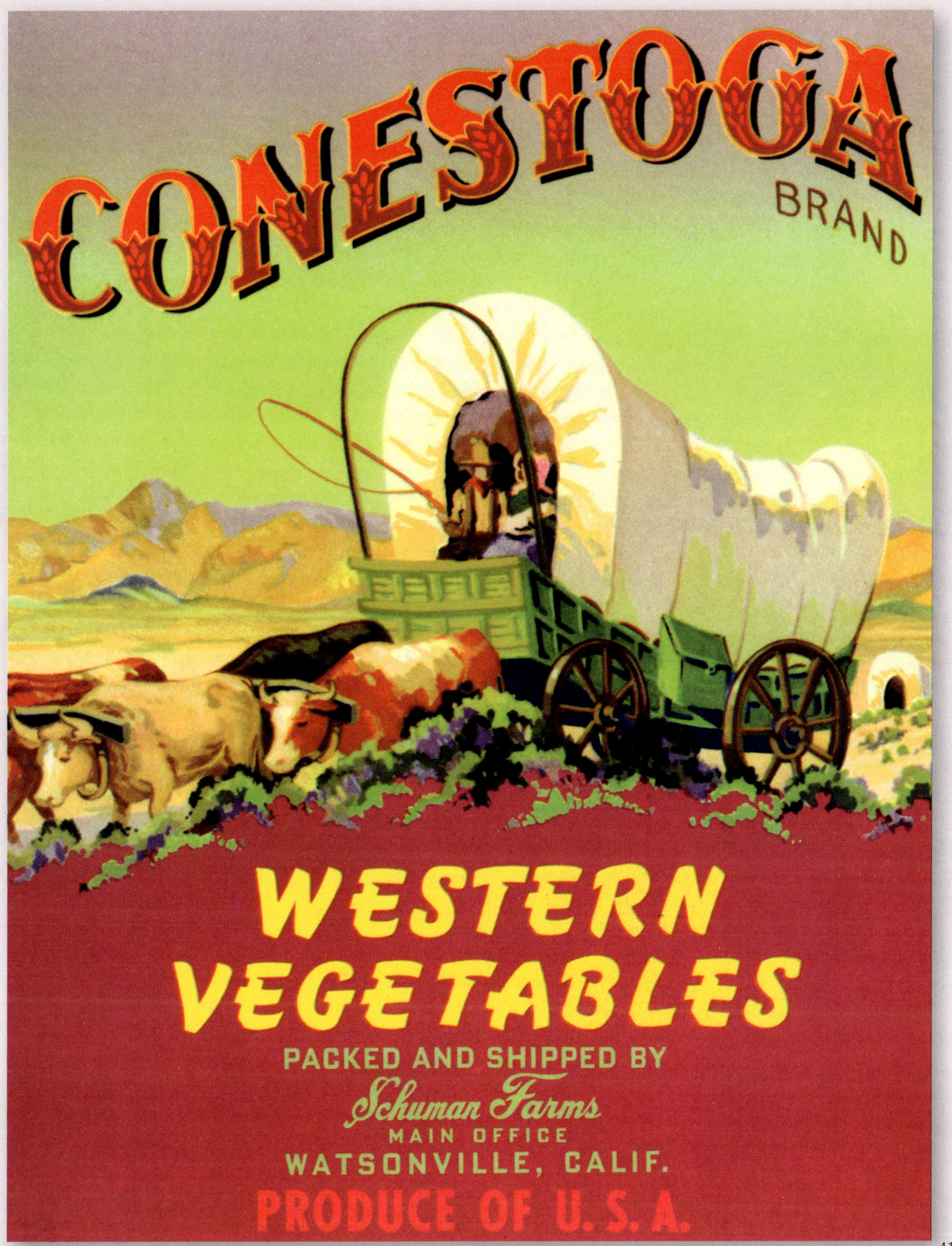

CONESTOGA
BRAND
WESTERN
VEGETABLES
PACKED AND SHIPPED BY
Schuman Farms
MAIN OFFICE
WATSONVILLE, CALIF.
PRODUCE OF U. S. A.

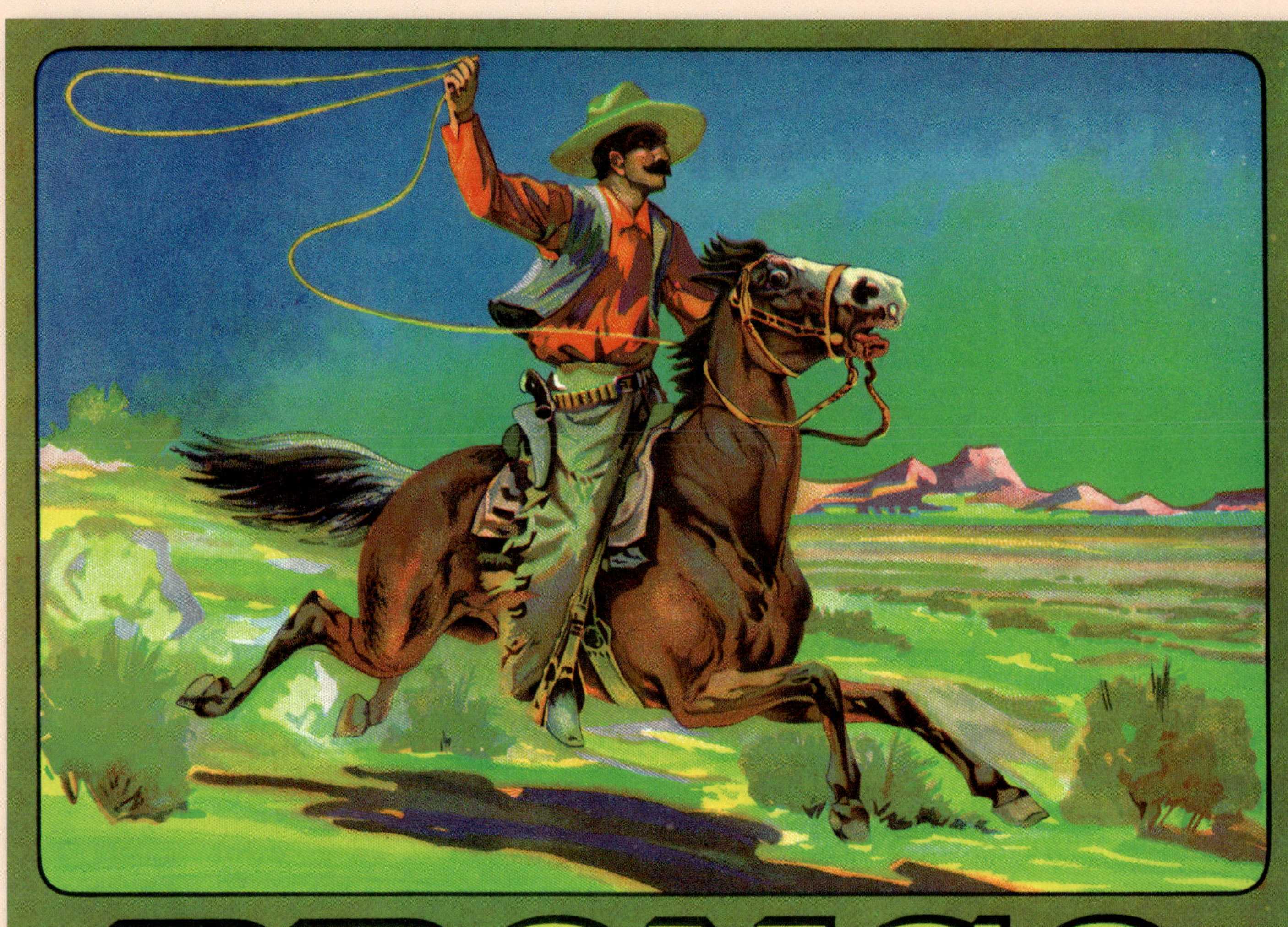

BRONCO
PACKED BY
REDLANDS FOOTHILL GROVES
REDLANDS, CALIFORNIA
BRAND
094

PRODUCE OF U.S.A.
MUSTANG
DISTRIBUTED BY
AMERICAN FRUIT GROWERS INC.
LOS ANGELES, CALIFORNIA

095

BLANKET
BRAND
COLORADO PEACHES
GROWN & PACKED BY
OSCAR HUFFINGTON
ESCALANTE FORKS
COLORADO
MINIMUM NET WEIGHT 16 LBS.

096

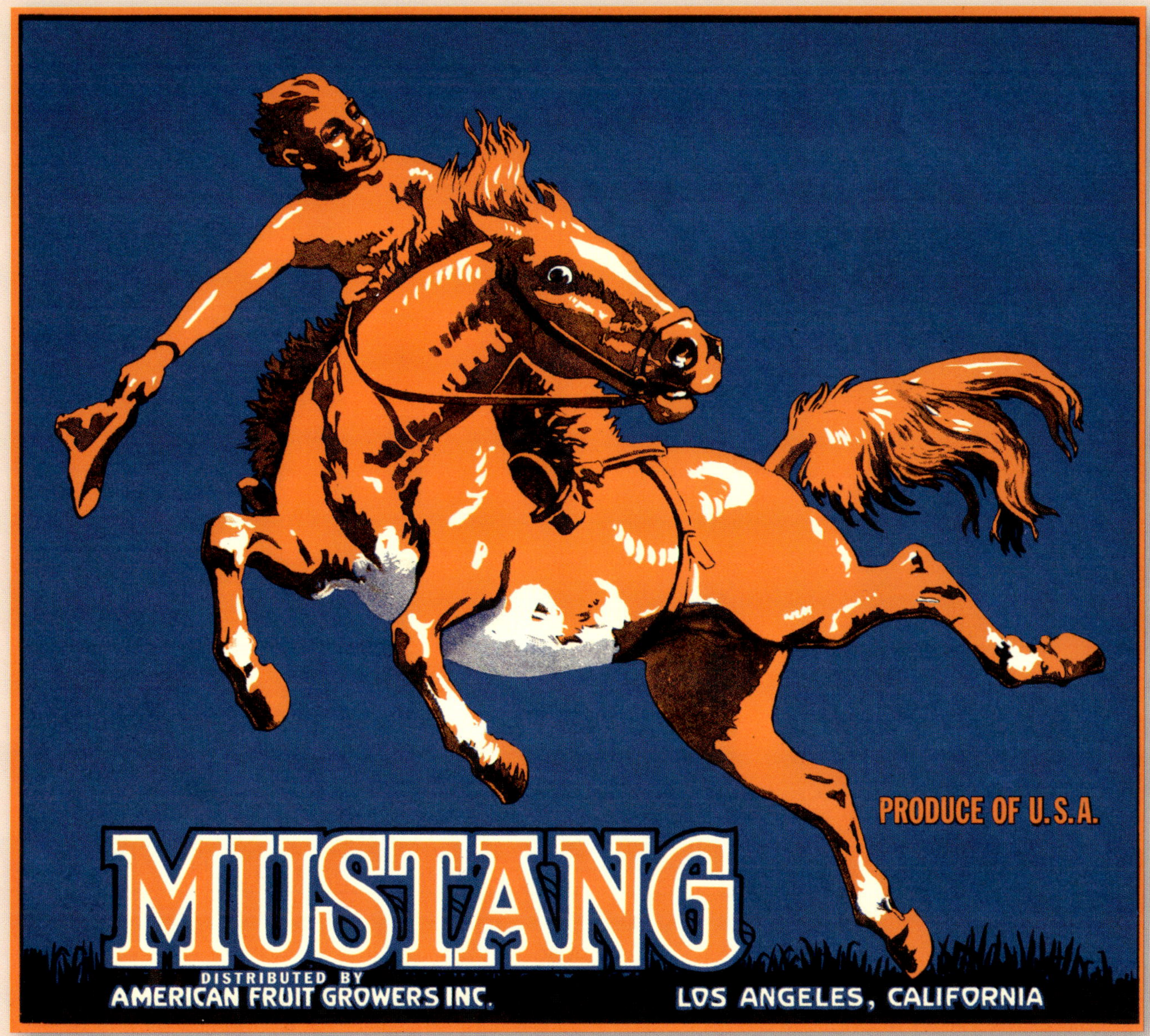

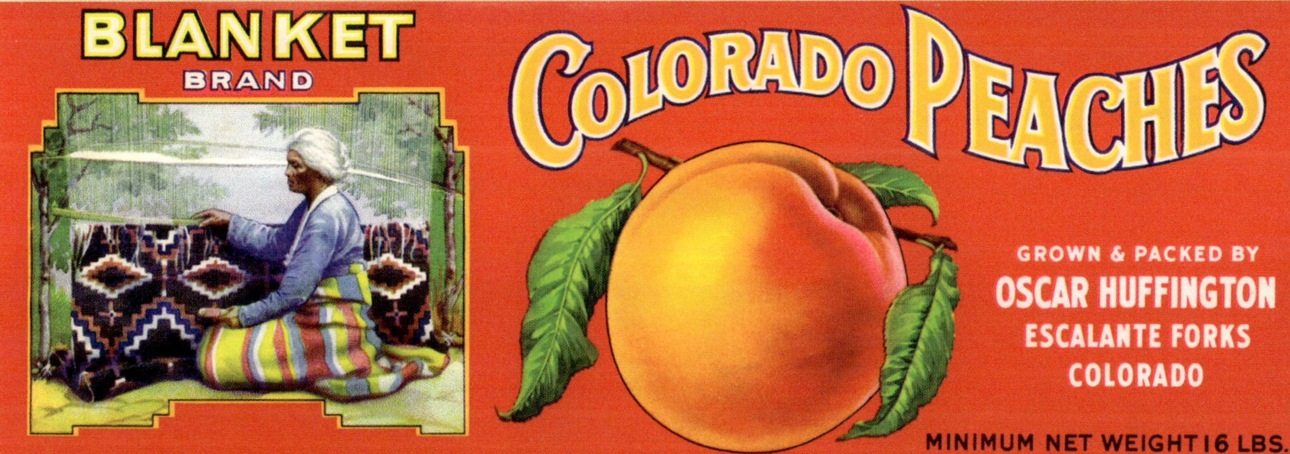

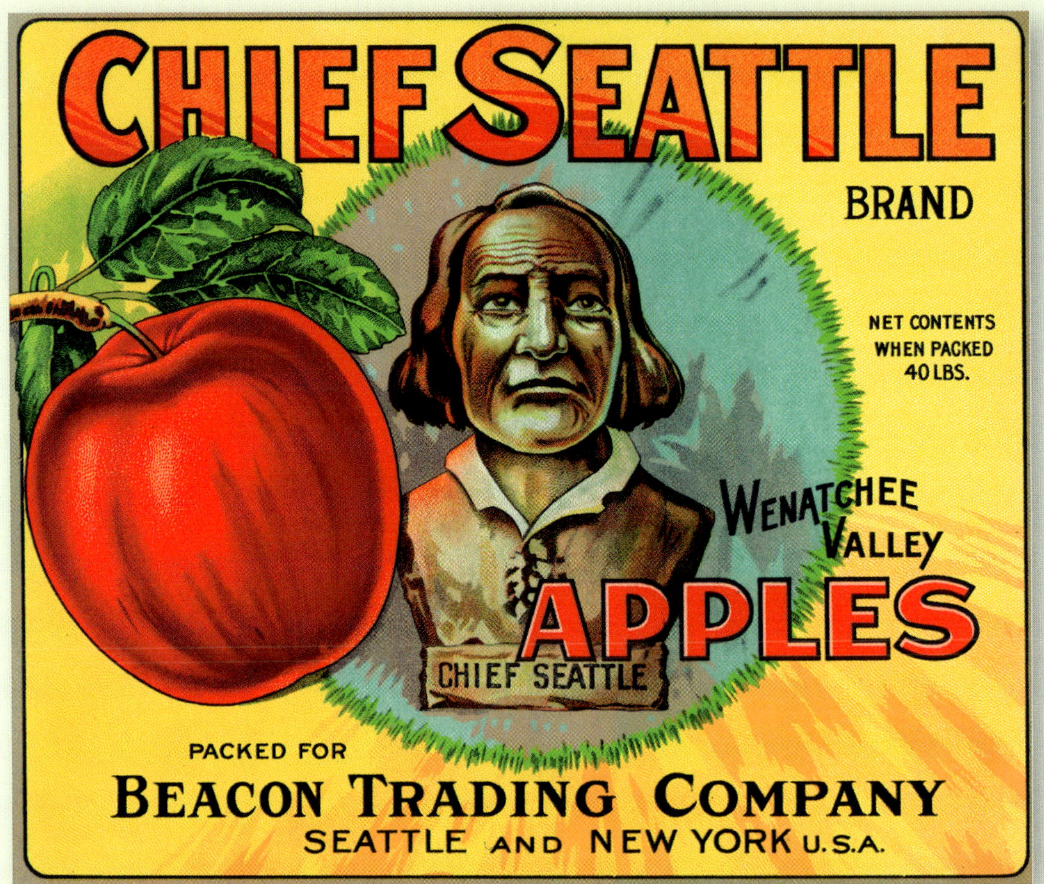
CHIEF SEATTLE
BRAND
NET CONTENTS
WHEN PACKED
40 LBS.
WENATCHEE VALLEY
APPLES
CHIEF SEATTLE
PACKED FOR
BEACON TRADING COMPANY
SEATTLE AND NEW YORK U.S.A.

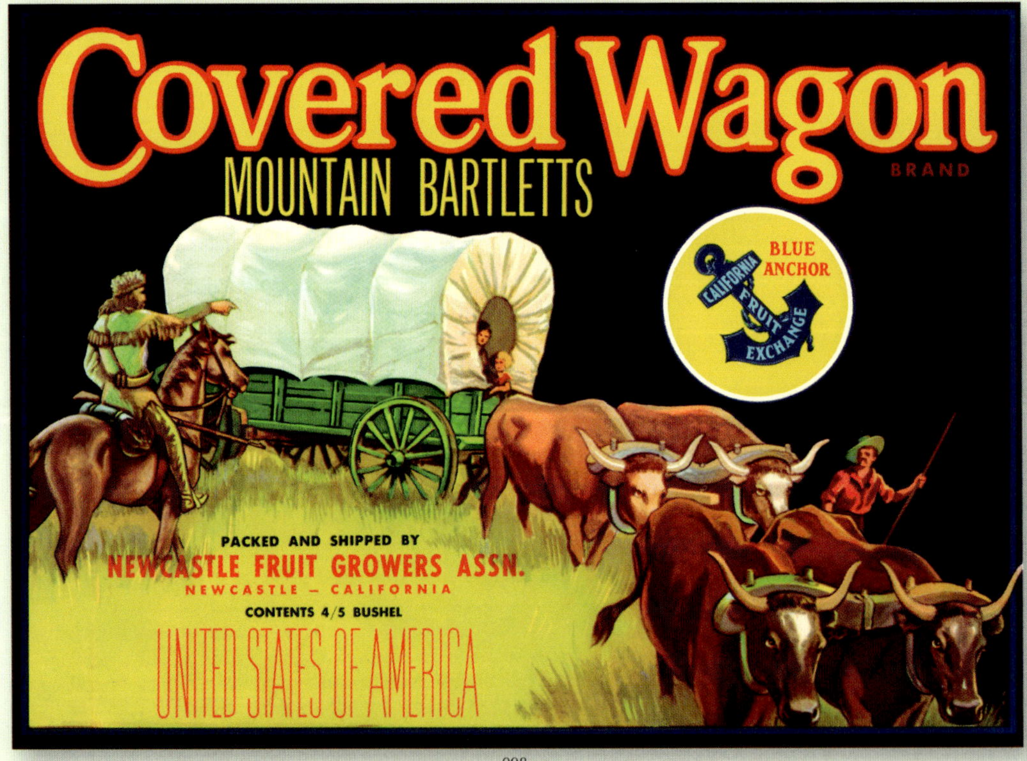
Covered Wagon
BRAND
MOUNTAIN BARTLETTS
BLUE ANCHOR
CALIFORNIA FRUIT EXCHANGE
PACKED AND SHIPPED BY
NEWCASTLE FRUIT GROWERS ASSN.
NEWCASTLE — CALIFORNIA
CONTENTS 4/5 BUSHEL
UNITED STATES OF AMERICA

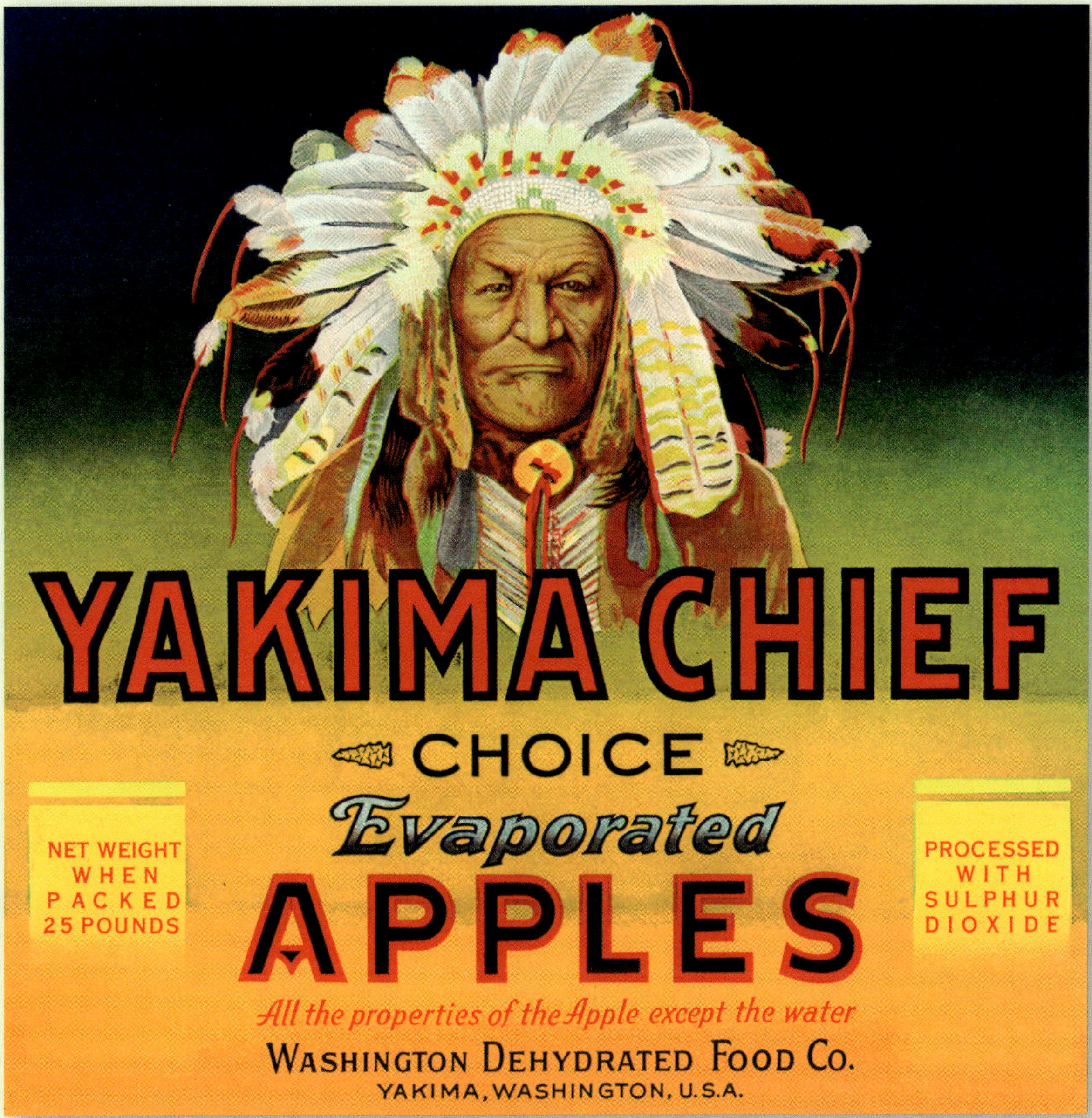

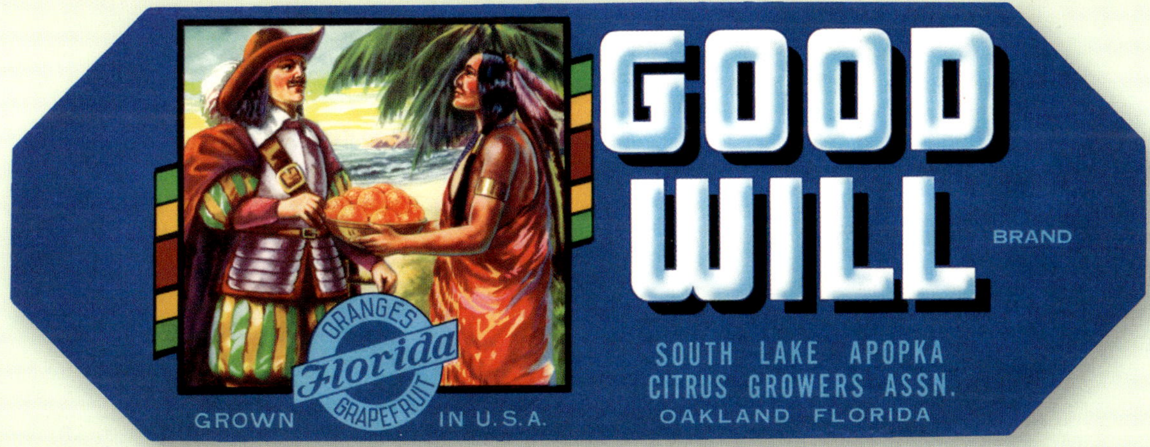
YAKIMA CHIEF
CHOICE
Evaporated
APPLES
NET WEIGHT
WHEN
PACKED
25 POUNDS
PROCESSED
WITH
SULPHUR
DIOXIDE
All the properties of the Apple except the water
Washington Dehydrated Food Co.
YAKIMA, WASHINGTON, U.S.A.
099
GOOD WILL
BRAND
ORANGES
Florida
GRAPEFRUIT
GROWN IN U.S.A.
SOUTH LAKE APOPKA
CITRUS GROWERS ASSN.
OAKLAND FLORIDA
100

ONE BUSHEL
EXTRA FANCY
Skookum
Apples
LAKE CHELAN
BRAND
LAKE CHELAN GROWERS UNION
CHELAN, WASHINGTON, U.S.A.
INSPECTED AND CERTIFIED
BY THE SKOOKUM PACKERS ASSOCIATION
Skookum Packers Association
Wenatchee, Washington, U.S.A.
UNITED STATES OF AMERICA

101

UP
NORTH
BRAND
Apples
DWINNELL BROS. ORCHARDS
OROVILLE, WASH.
PRODUCE OF U.S.A.
1 U.S. BUSHEL BY VOLUME

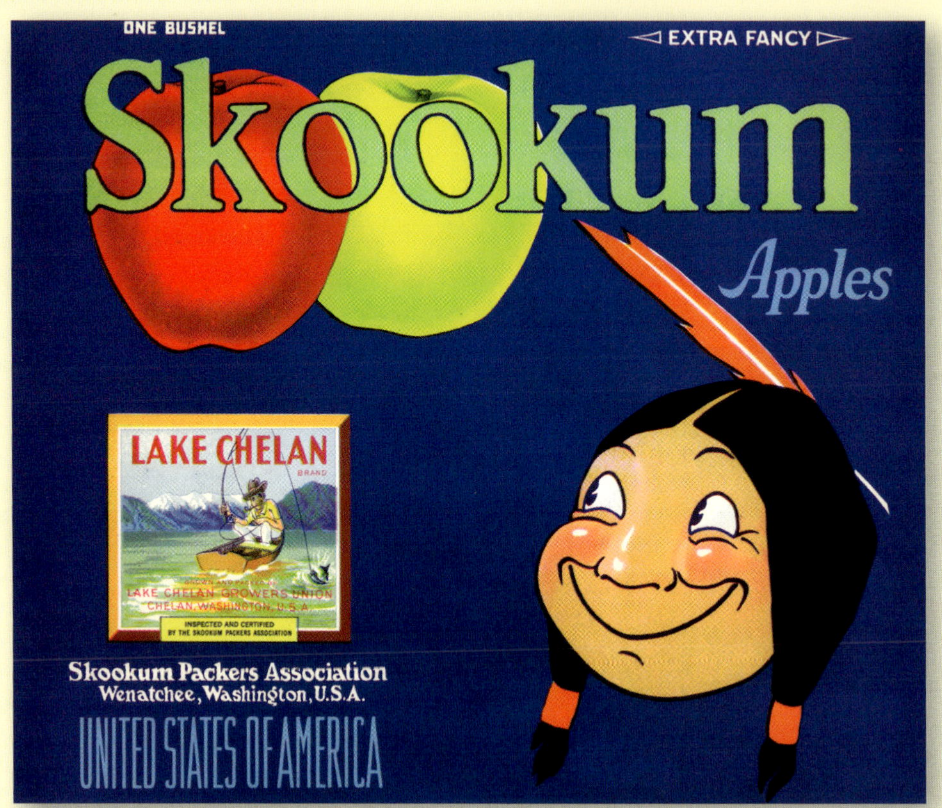

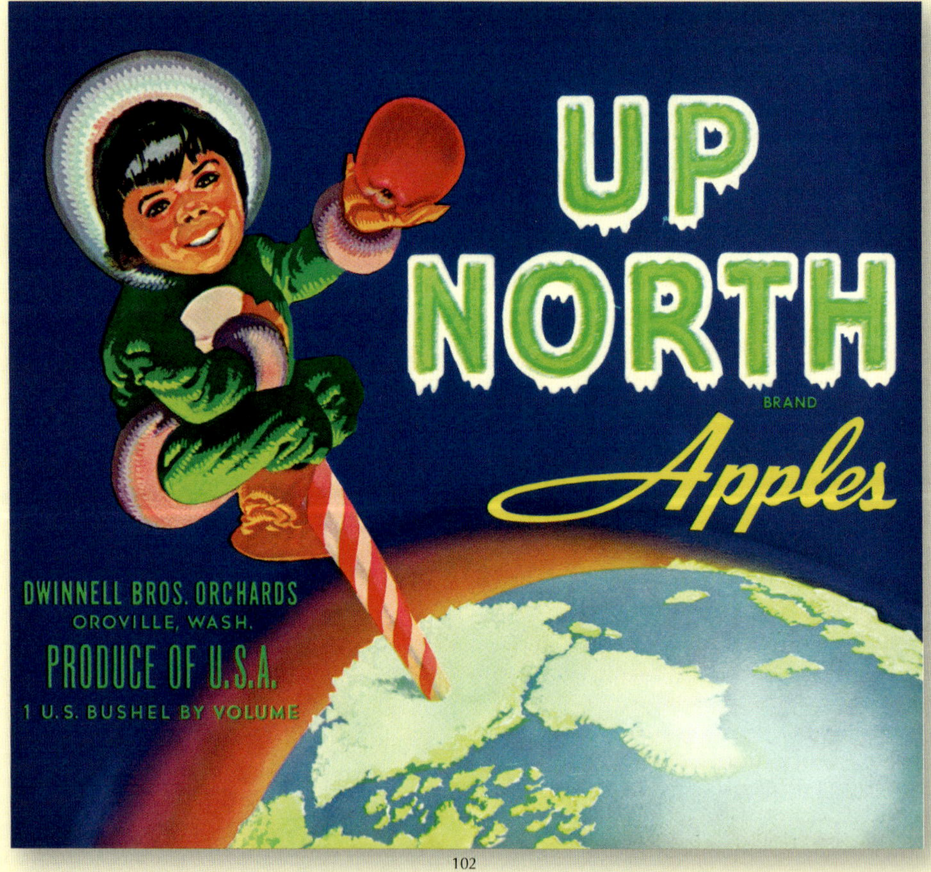

102

BUFFALO
BRAND
Pajaro Valley
APPLES
PRODUCE OF U.S.A.
NEWTOWN PIPPINS
CONTENTS 1 BUSHEL NET
Packed by
J. P. BRAYCOVICH CO.
WATSONVILLE · CALIFORNIA · U·S·A

103

SQUAW
BRAND
SQUAW
BRAND
CONTENTS
1 LB. 4 OZ.
PACKED BY
CENTERVILLE CANNING CO.
CENTERVILLE, MD.
EXTRA SIFTED PEAS

104

MARYLAND CHIEF
BRAND
MARYLAND CHIEF BRAND
PACKED
BY
J. LANGRALL & BRO. INC.
BALTIMORE
MD.
CONTENTS
1 LB. 3 OZ.
TRADE MARK REGISTERED 1878.
STRINGLESS BEANS
PACKED IN U.S.A.
STRINGLESS BEANS
CONTENTS 1 LB. 3 OZ.

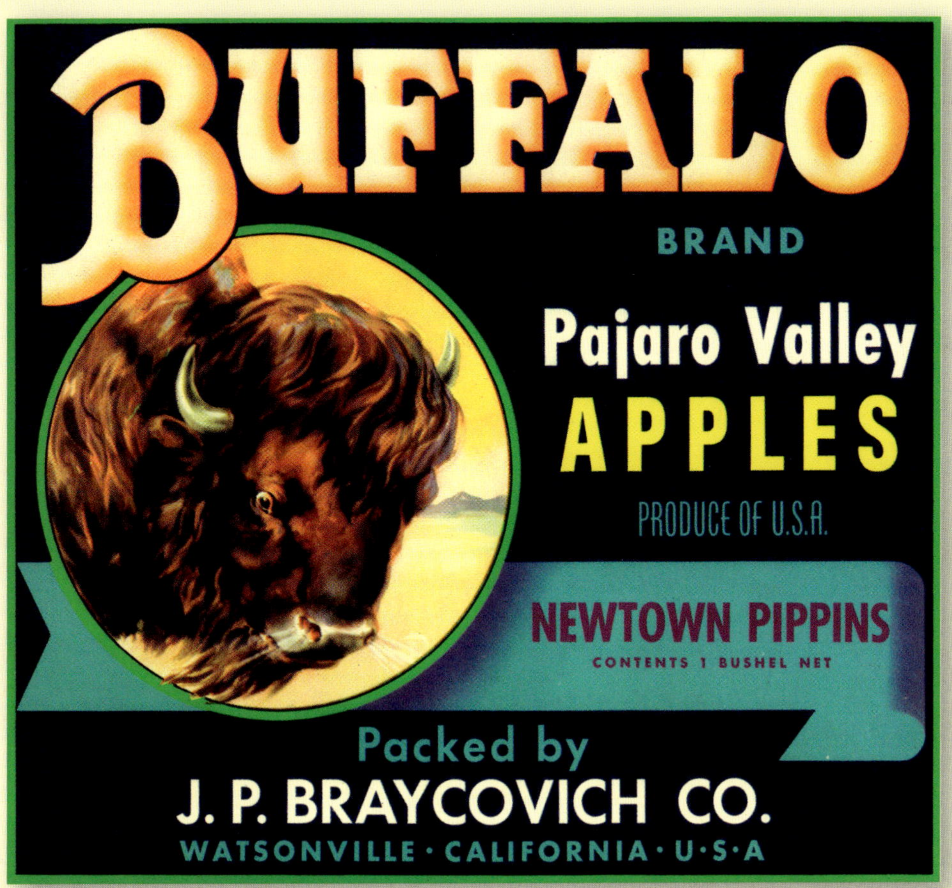

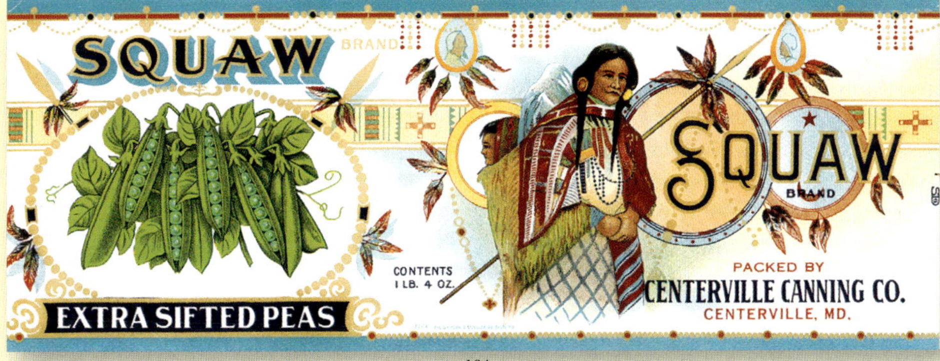

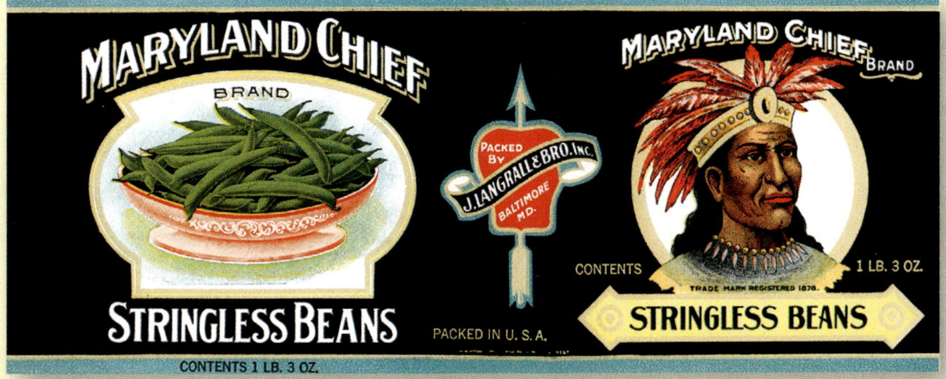

105

MUSTANG
BRAND
California
VEGETABLES
PRODUCE OF U.S.A.
WESTERN PACKING CO.
PACKERS - SHIPPERS   GUADALUPE, CALIF.

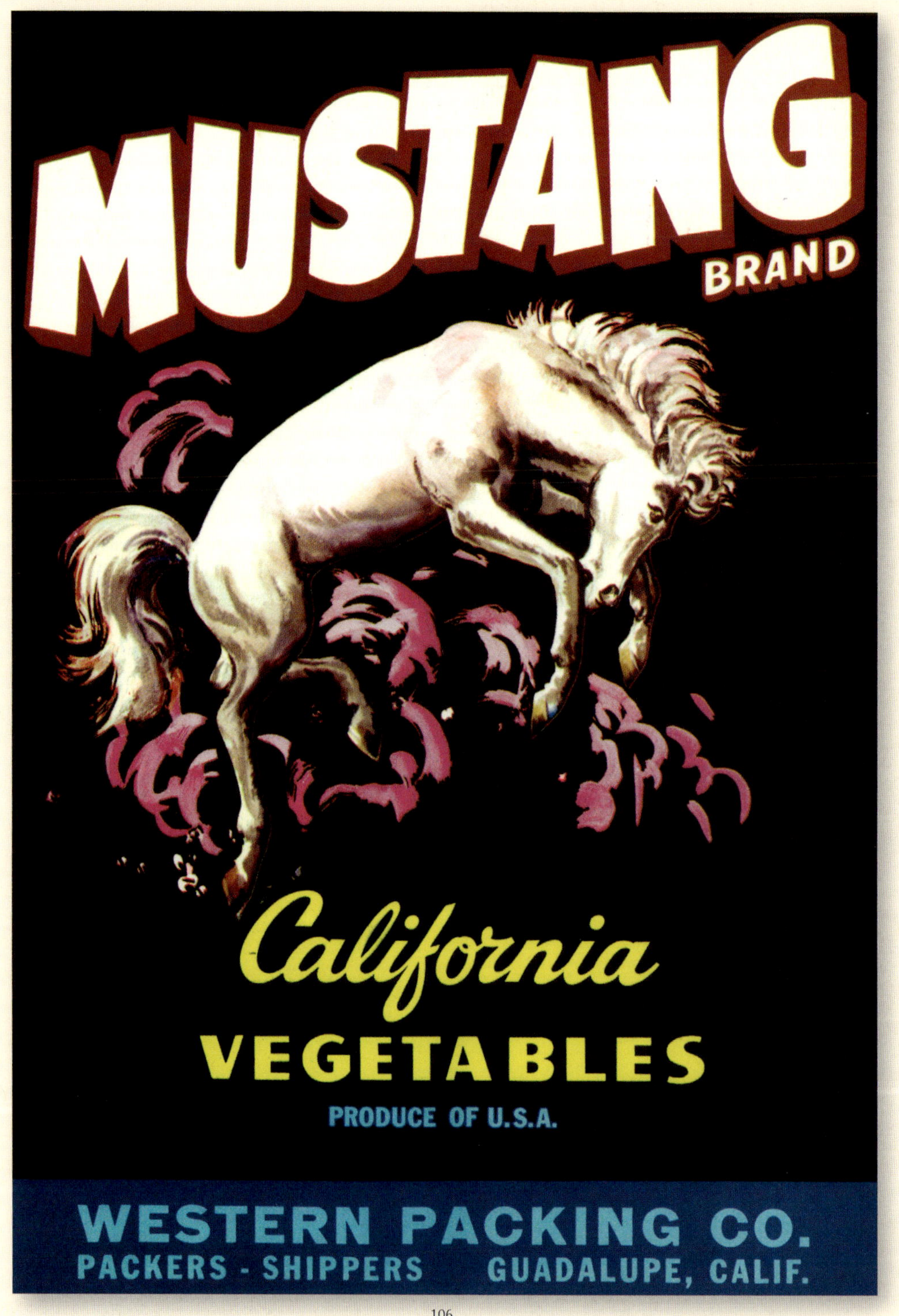

106

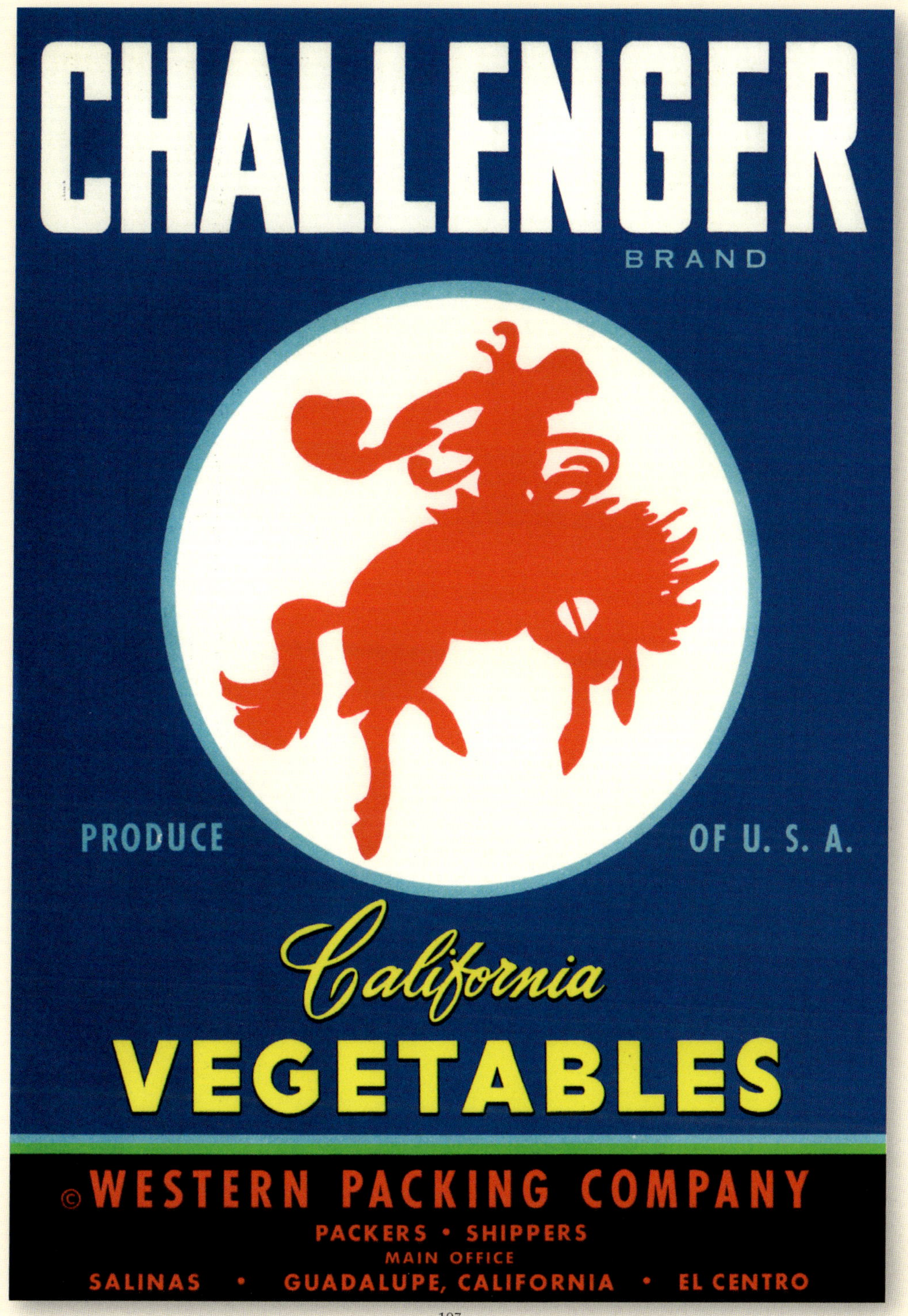

CHALLENGER
BRAND
PRODUCE
OF U. S. A.
California
VEGETABLES
© WESTERN PACKING COMPANY
PACKERS • SHIPPERS
MAIN OFFICE
SALINAS • GUADALUPE, CALIFORNIA • EL CENTRO
107

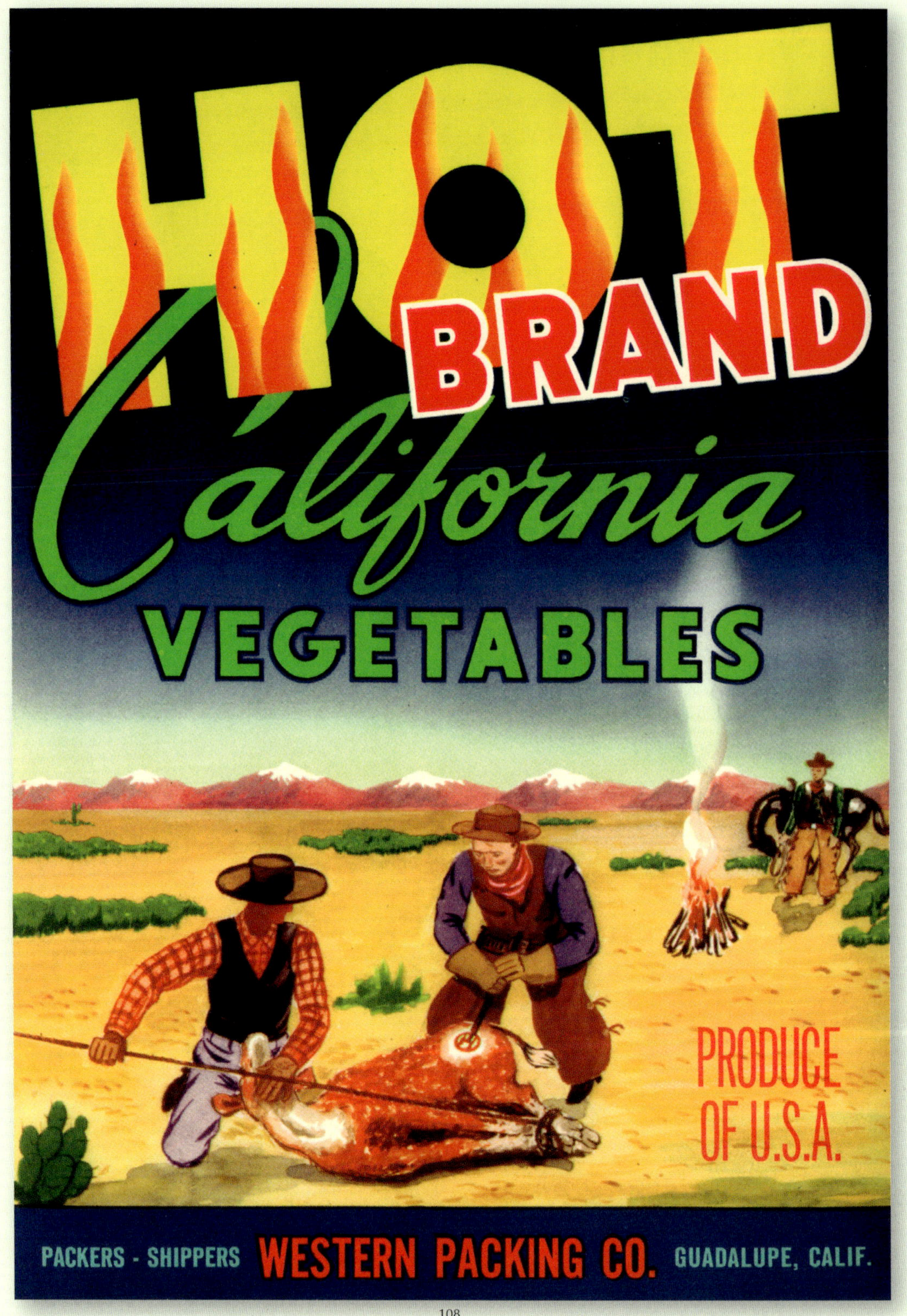

HOT
BRAND
California
VEGETABLES
PRODUCE OF U.S.A.
PACKERS - SHIPPERS WESTERN PACKING CO. GUADALUPE, CALIF.
108

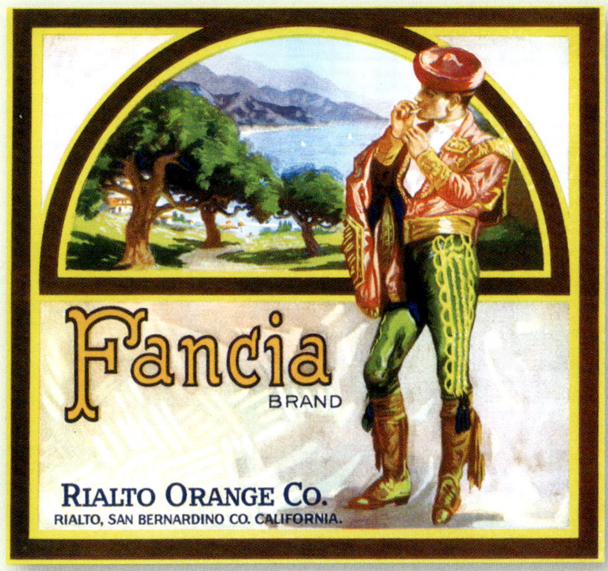

109

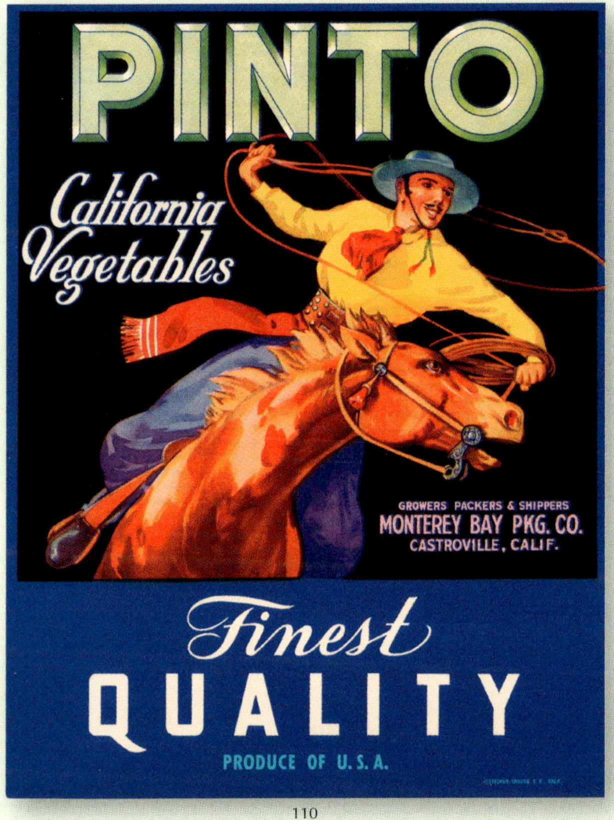

110

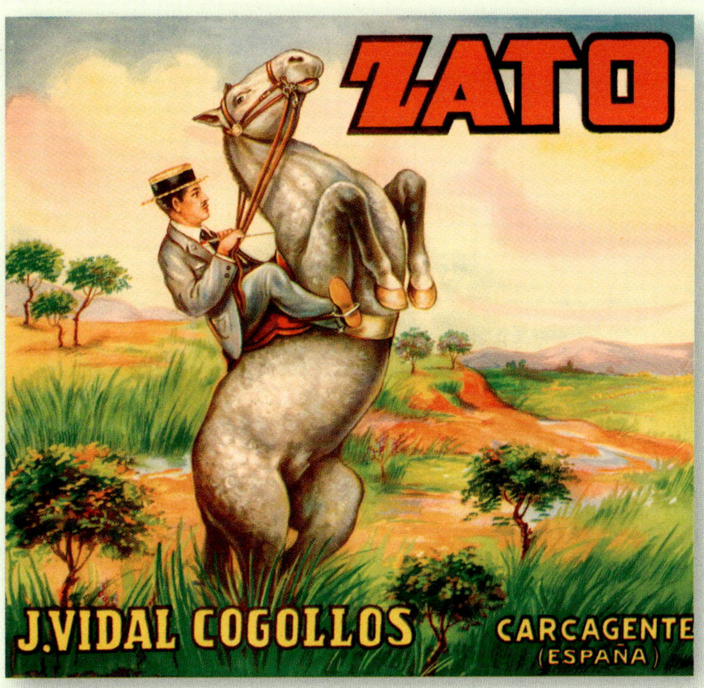

111

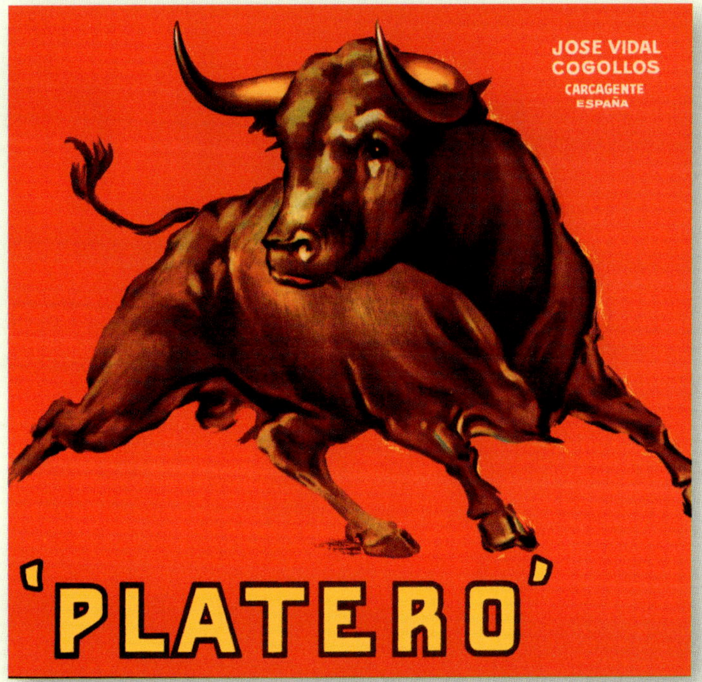

112

TOP CARD
PRODUCE OF U.S.A.
SUISUN
BARTLETTS
A
LEAPS AHEAD
NET WEIGHT 46 LBS.
LAMBERT MARKETING CO.
MAIN OFFICE
SACRAMENTO, CALIF.

113

HIGH-HAND
HAND GRADED
MOUNTAIN FRUIT
LOOMIS
FRUIT GROWERS ASSOCIATION
GROWERS, PACKERS & SHIPPERS
LOOMIS, CALIFORNIA 95650

114

TALK O' THE TOWN
NET WEIGHT 28 LBS.
EMPERORS
W. D. WINTON & SON

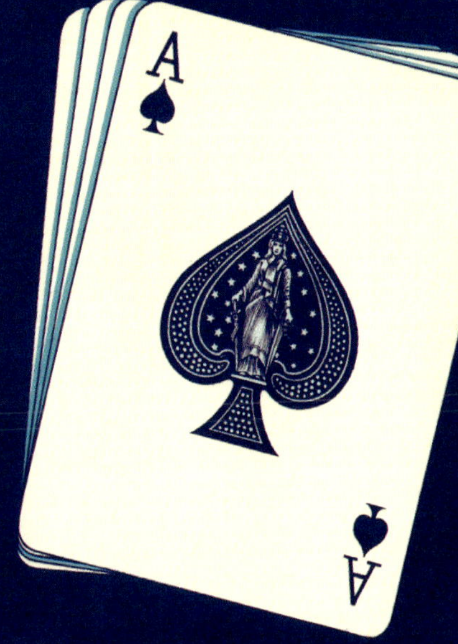

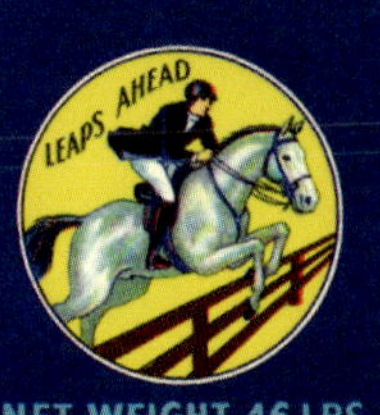

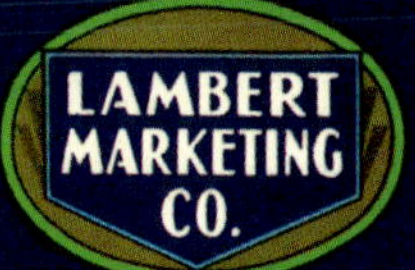

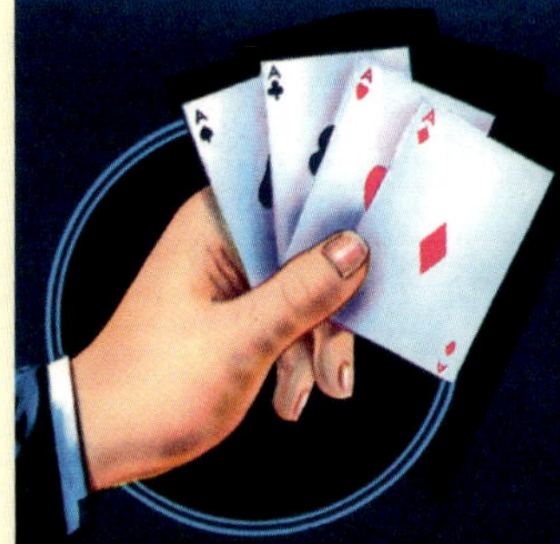

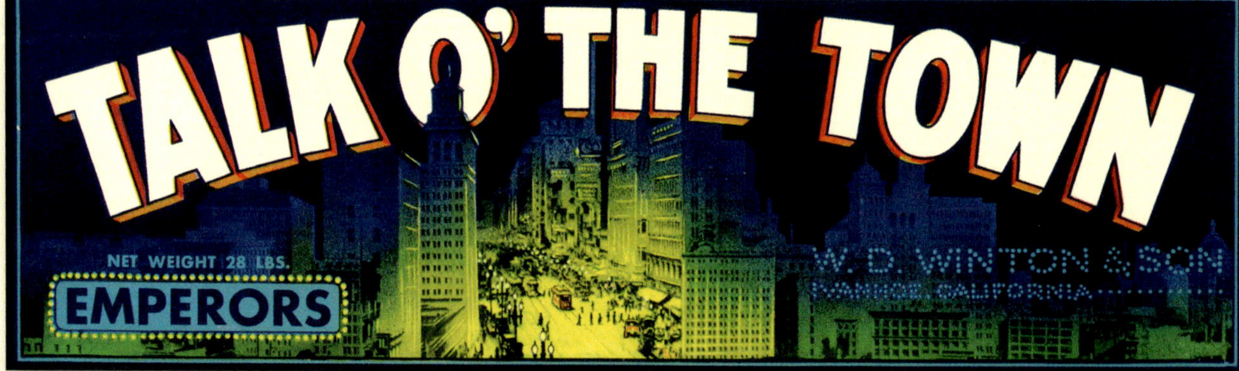

115

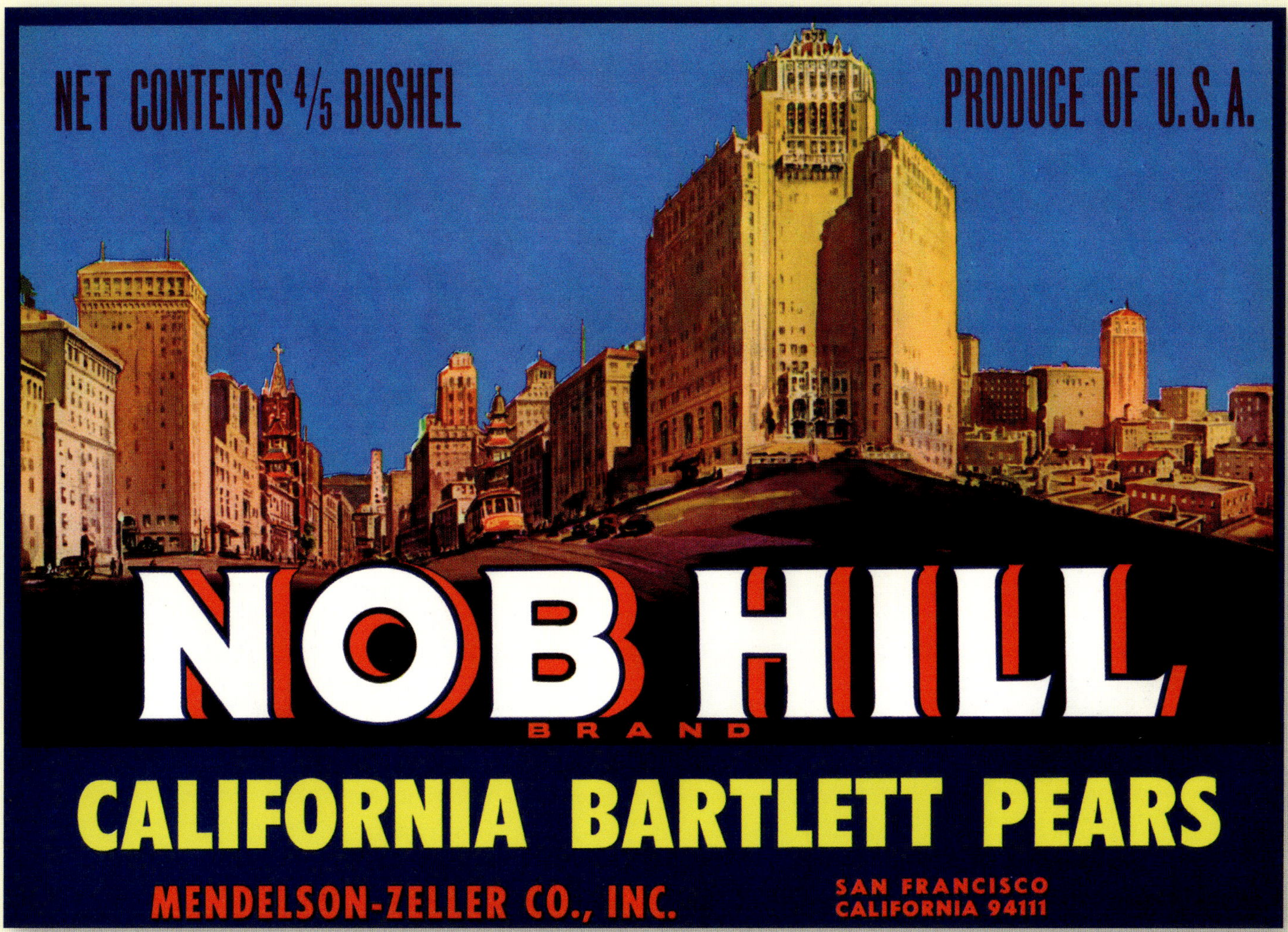

NET CONTENTS 4/5 BUSHEL
PRODUCE OF U.S.A.
NOB HILL
BRAND
CALIFORNIA BARTLETT PEARS
MENDELSON-ZELLER CO., INC.
SAN FRANCISCO
CALIFORNIA 94111

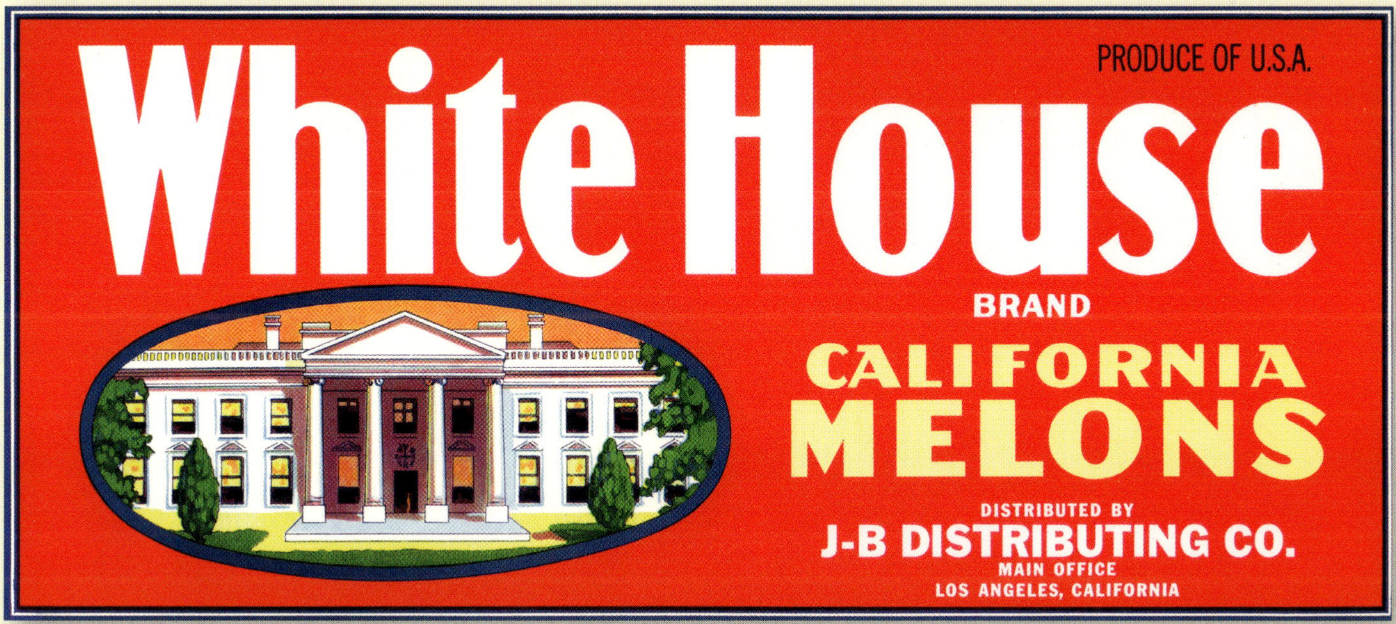

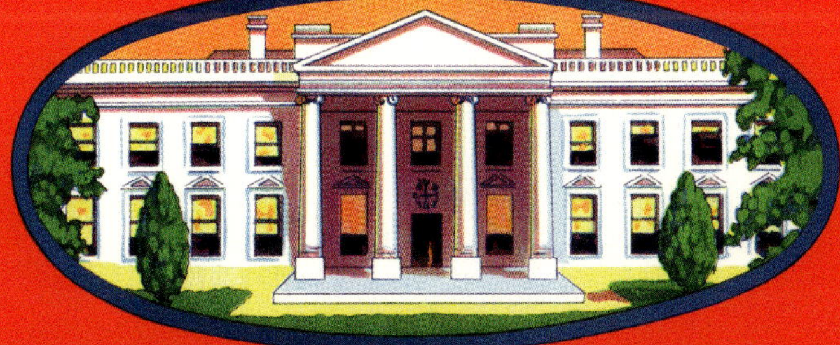

PRODUCE OF U.S.A.
White House
BRAND
CALIFORNIA
MELONS
DISTRIBUTED BY
J-B DISTRIBUTING CO.
MAIN OFFICE
LOS ANGELES, CALIFORNIA

WALDORF
BRAND
APPLES
NET CONTENTS
ONE BUSHEL
S. ALBERTSON CO. INC. YAKIMA WASH. BOSTON MASS.
SHIPPERS DISTRIBUTORS
PRODUCE OF U.S.A.

118

BIG CITY
PRODUCE OF U·S·A·
LAMBERT MARKETING CO.
MAIN OFFICE
WEST SACRAMENTO
CALIF. 95691
CALIFORNIA
BARTLETT PEARS
CONTENTS 4/5 BUSHEL

119

GOLDEN
LIMITED BRAND
PEARS
PACKED & SHIPPED BY
MYRON ROOT & CO. INC.
MEDFORD, OREGON
CONTENTS ½ BUSHEL

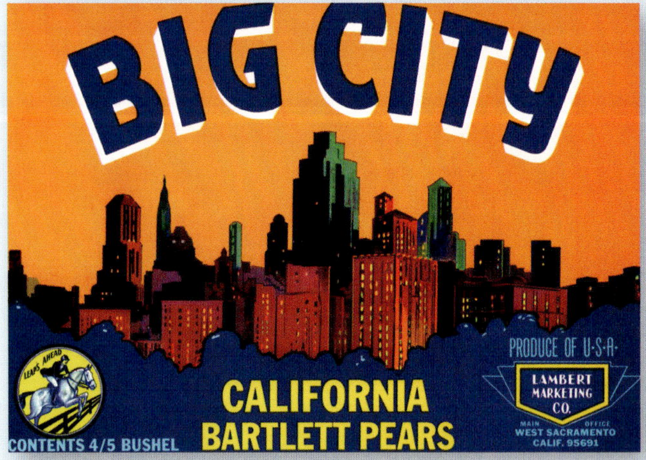

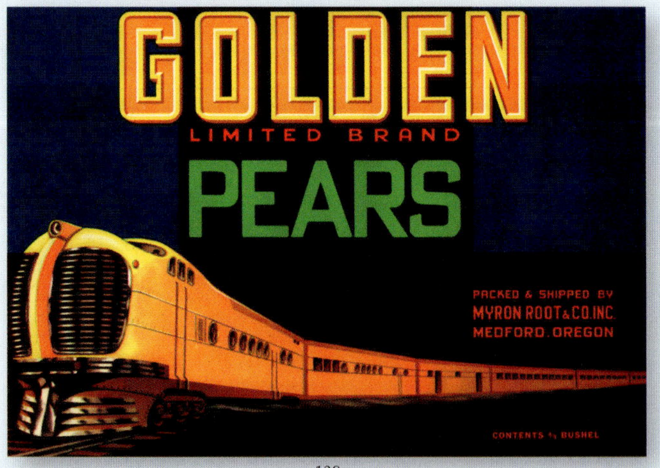

120

RUBAIYAT
BRAND
Packed by
REDLANDS
ORANGEDALE
ASSOCIATION
REDLANDS, CALIFORNIA
GROWN IN
U.S.A.

121

RICORDO
PRODUCE OF U.S.A.
BRAND
CHINCHIOLO BROS.
MAIN OFFICE
STOCKTON, CAL.
ZINFANDELS

122

NILE
BRAND
CALIFORNIA
ALICANTE BOUSCHET GRAPES
VINEYARDS
MINKLER & WAHTOKE
CALIFORNIA
GROWN & PACKED BY
ERICKSON BROTHERS
MINKLER (SANGER P.O.) CALIFORNIA.

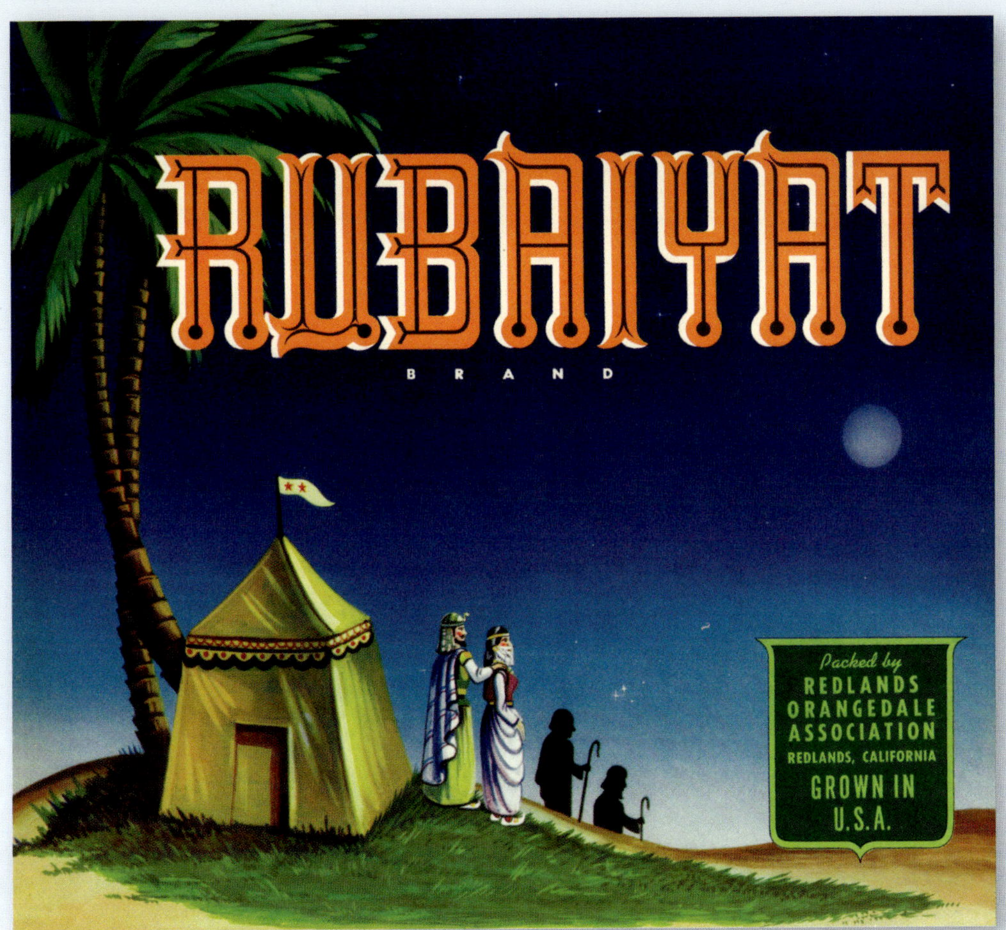

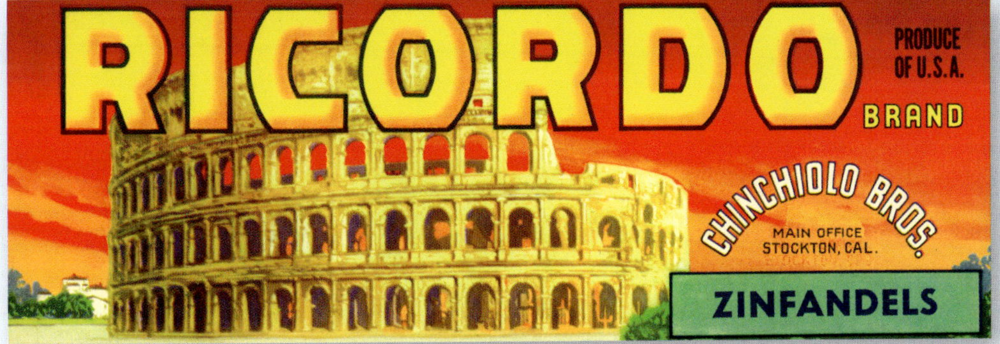

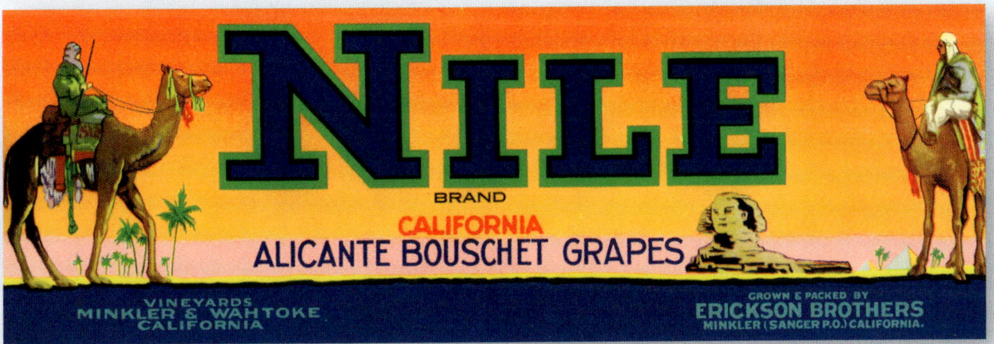

123

GROWN AND PACKED BY
EXETER FRUIT ASSOCIATION
EXETER, CALIFORNIA
93221
PRODUCE OF U.S.A.
PURSUIT
CALIFORNIA FRUIT EXCHANGE
BLUE ANCHOR

124

PACKED & SHIPPED BY
T. O. TOMASELLO CO.
MAIN OFFICE
WATSONVILLE
CALIFORNIA
PRODUCE OF U.S.A.
DOMINATOR
BRAND
TOMATOES
MINIMUM NET WT.
30 LBS.

125

EAST WEST
EMPERORS
GROWN & PACKED BY
PAUL DOBSON
EXETER, CALIFORNIA
NET WEIGHT 25 LBS.

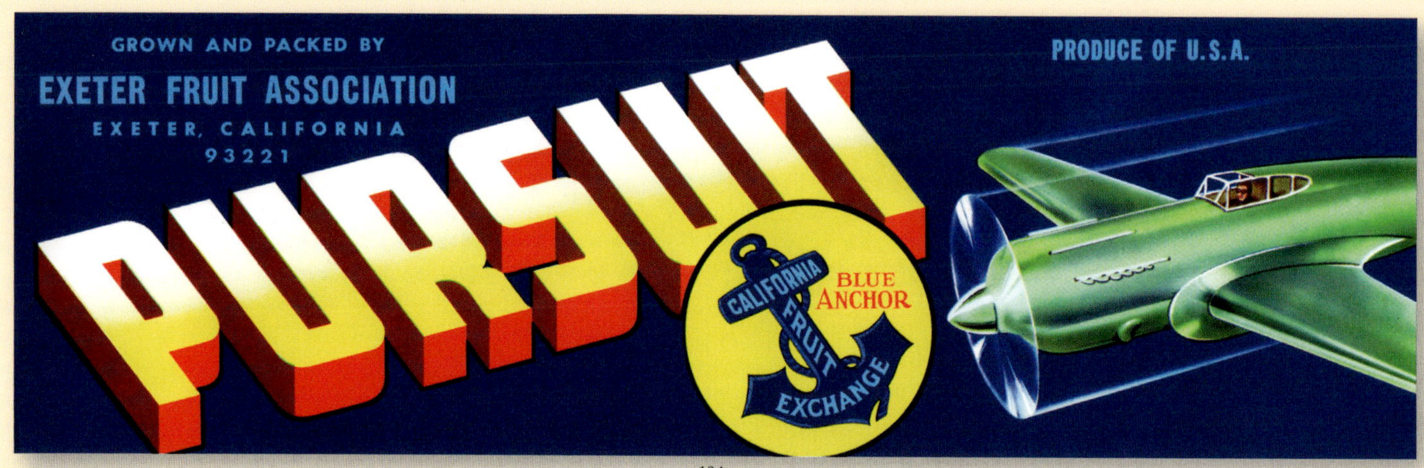

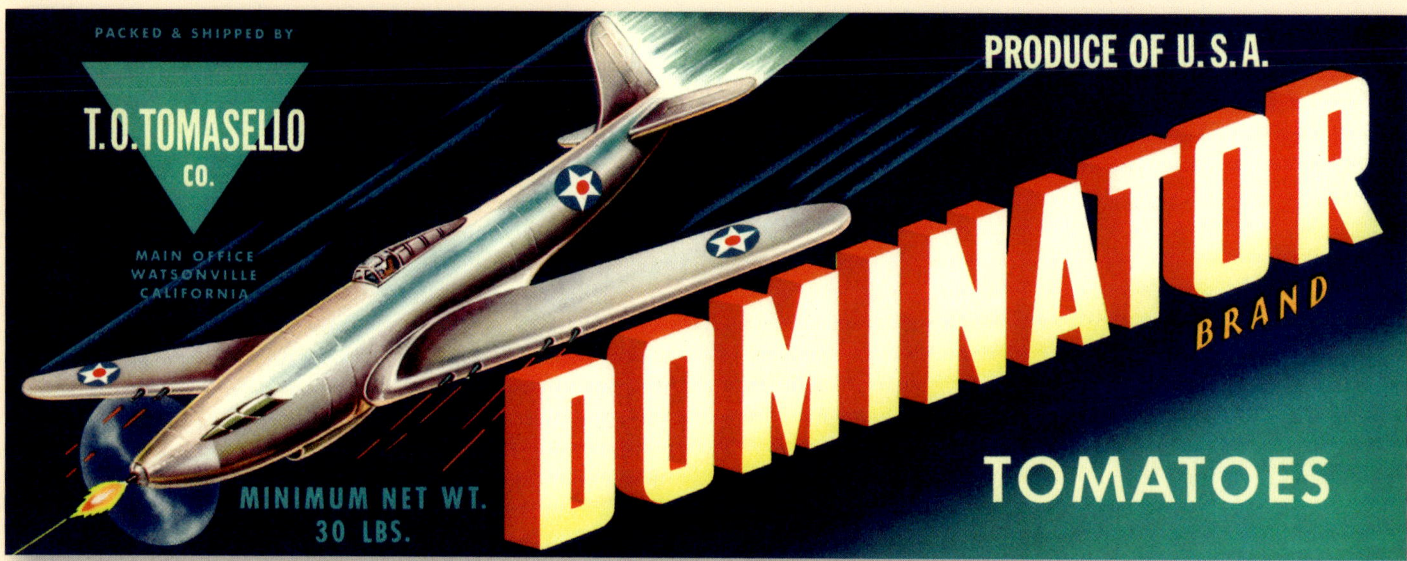

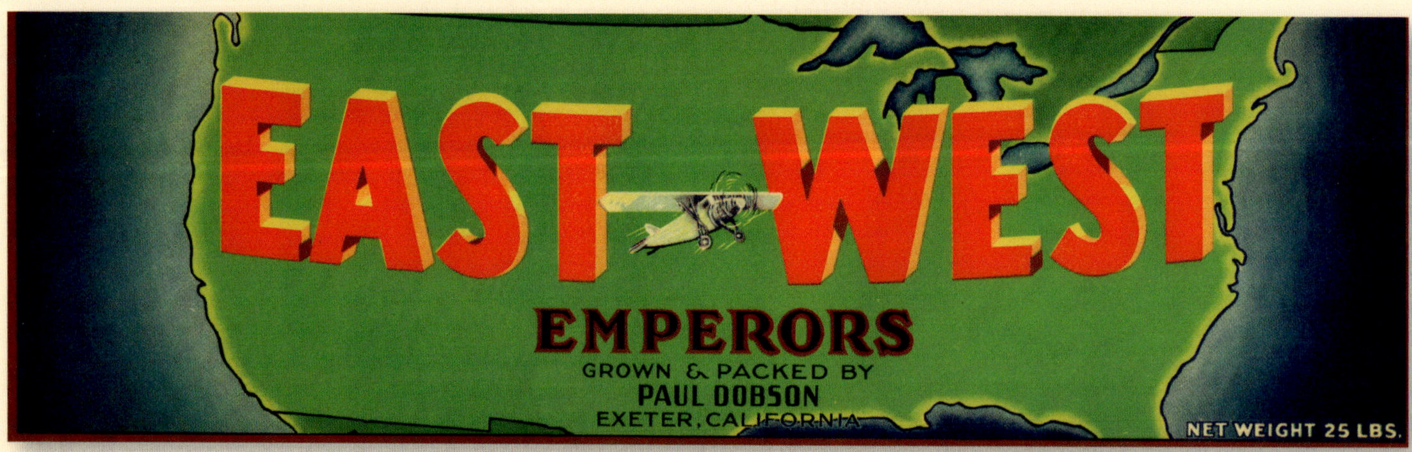

126

PACKED AND
SHIPPED BY
T. O. TOMASELLO CO.
MAIN OFFICE
WATSONVILLE
CALIF.
DOMINATOR
BRAND
PRODUCE OF U.S.A.

127

TEX-ACE
BRAND
PACKED & SHIPPED BY
ENGELMAN PRODUCTS COMPANY
ELSA ★ TEXAS
PRODUCE OF U.S.A.

128

FLYER
BRAND
ORANGE BELT PACKING CO.
EUSTIS · FLORIDA
PACKERS AND SHIPPERS OF CITRUS FRUITS

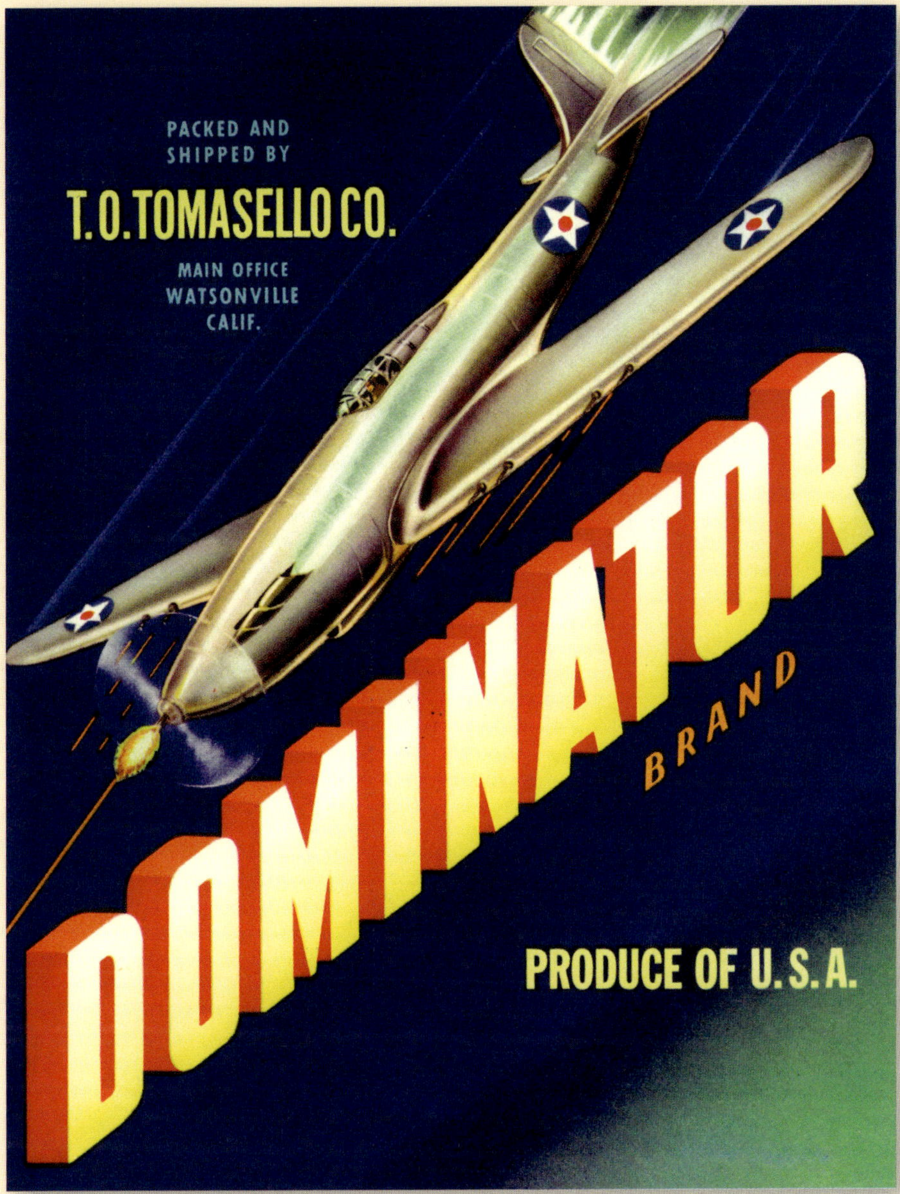

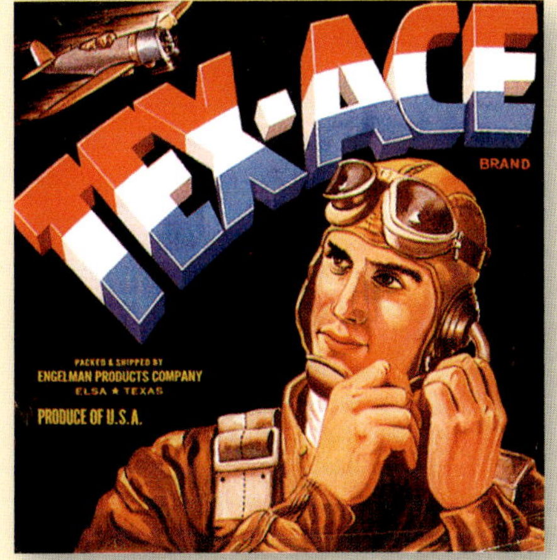

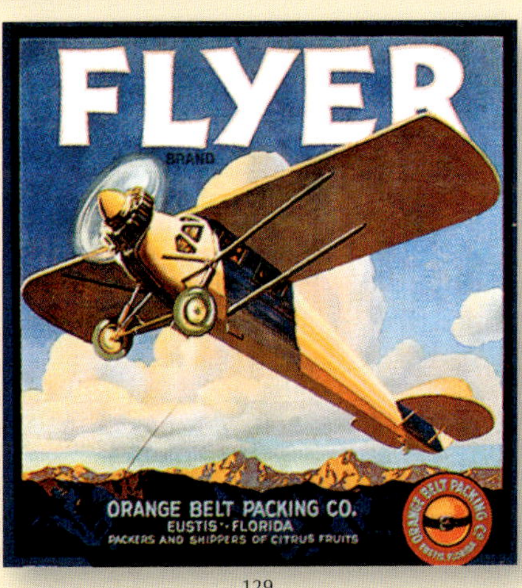

129

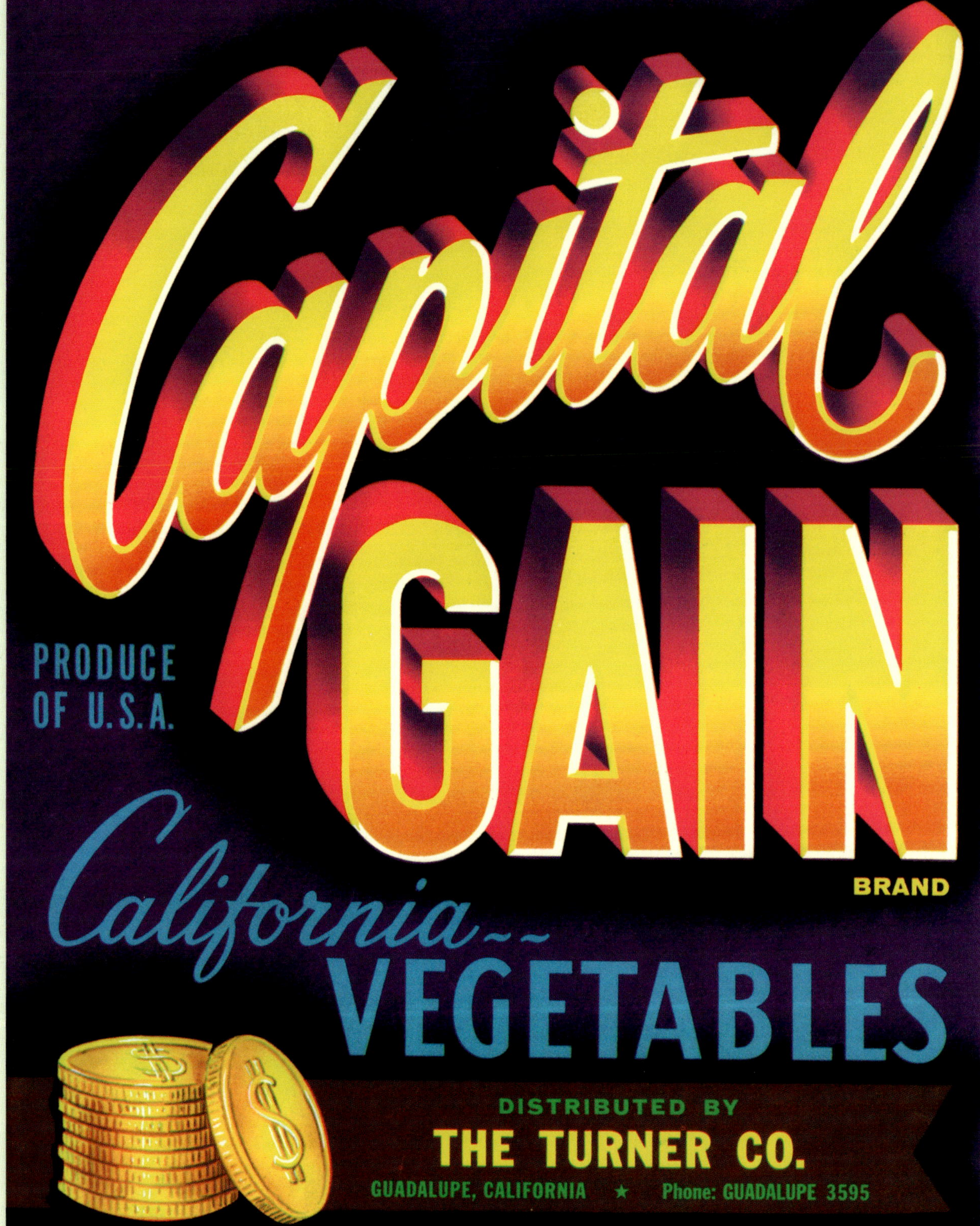

Capital
GAIN
BRAND
PRODUCE OF U.S.A.
California--
VEGETABLES
DISTRIBUTED BY
THE TURNER CO.
GUADALUPE, CALIFORNIA   ★   Phone: GUADALUPE 3595

Herlong's
TREASURE
BRAND
A.S. Herlong & Co. (not Inc.)
Leesburg, Florida

131

NET WEIGHT 28 LBS.
Million Dollar
BRAND
EMPERORS
GROWN & PACKED BY
PAUL DOBSON
EXETER, CALIF.

132

FOR YOUR
PROTECTION
FEDERAL-
STATE
INSPECTED
SAFE
BRAND
Selected Quality
CALIFORNIA GRAPES
PRODUCE
OF U.S.A.
PACKED BY
UNITED PACKING CO.
FRESNO   CALIF.

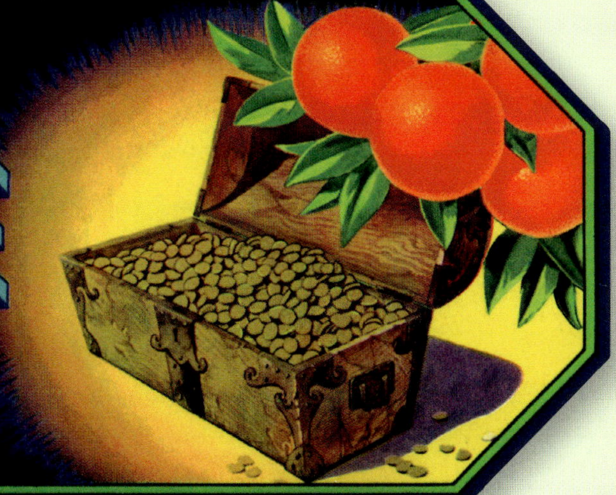

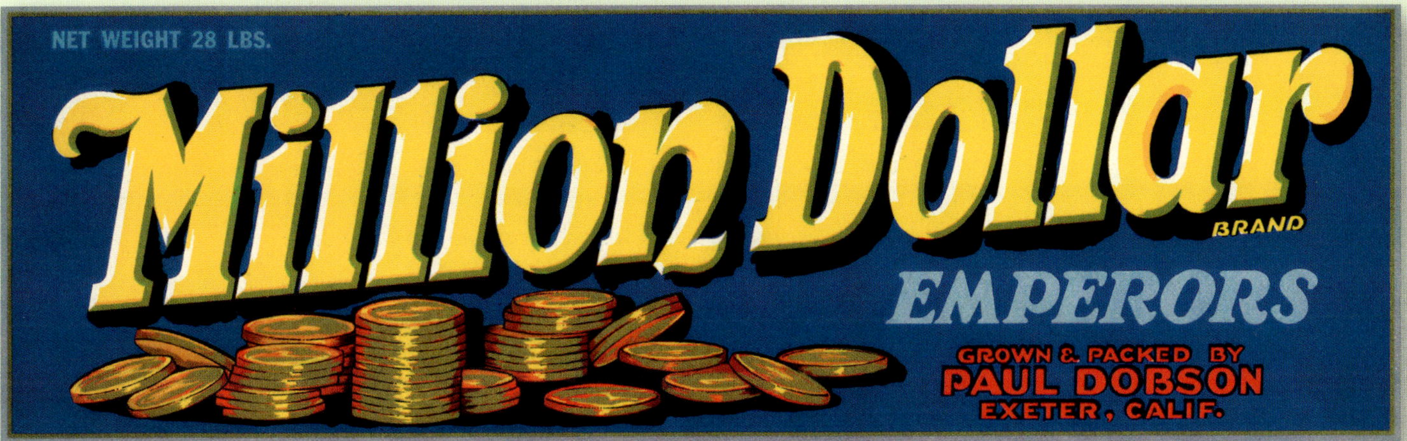

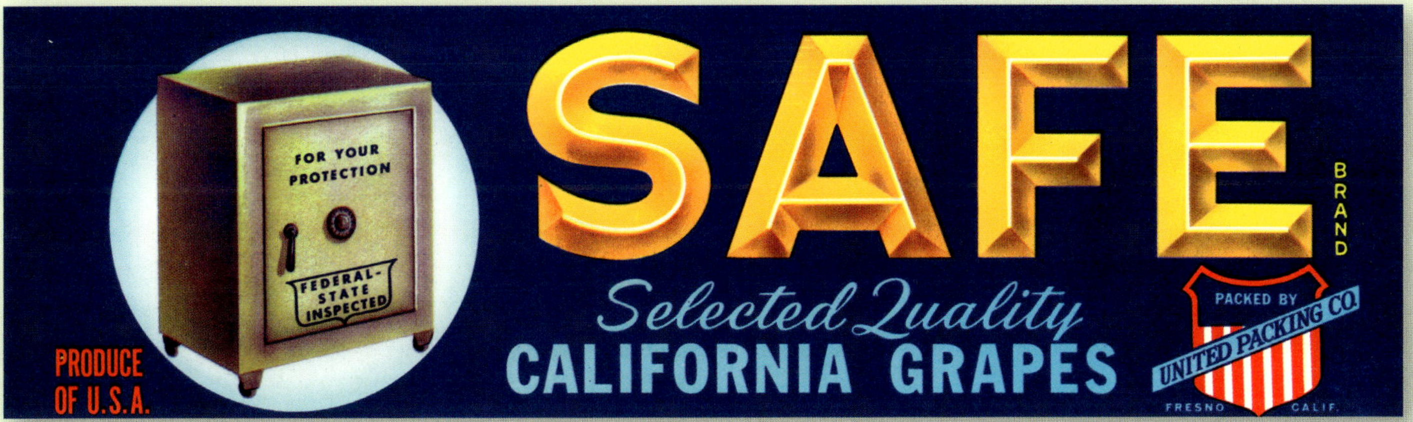

133

FULL
Produce of U. S. A.
WAVERLY GROWERS COOPERATIVE
WAVERLY, FLORIDA

134

Full o' Juice
GROWN IN U.S.A.
REDLANDS ORANGEDALE ASSOCIATION
REDLANDS, CALIFORNIA

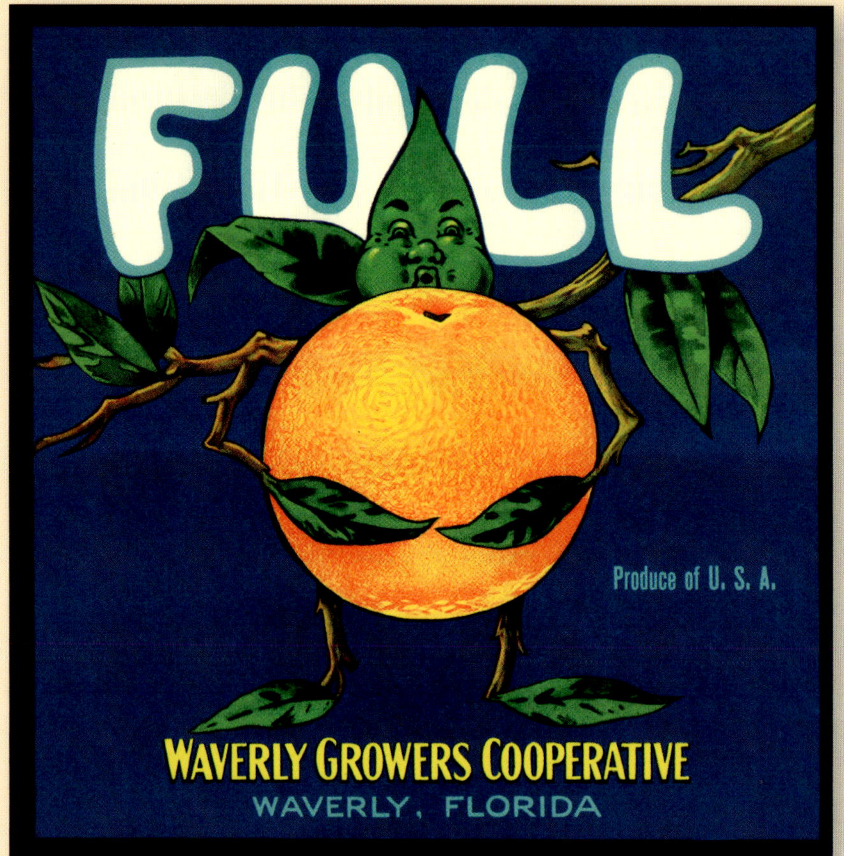

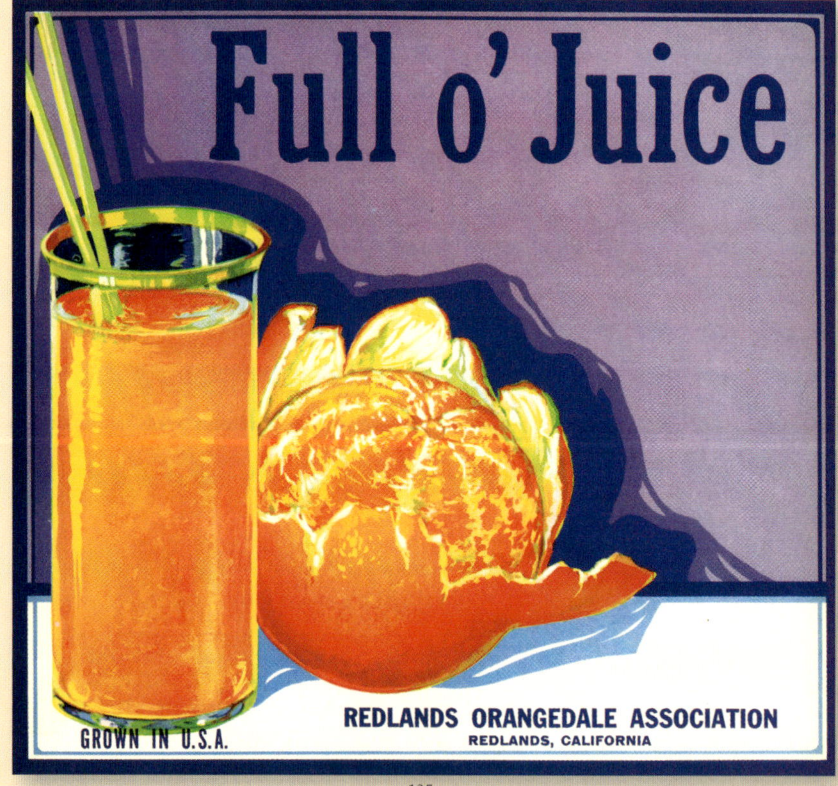

135

BELT
BRAND
GROWN IN U.S.A.
GROWN & PACKED BY
GOLD BUCKLE ASSOCIATION
EAST HIGHLANDS, SAN BERNARDINO CO. CALIFORNIA

136

FANCY
NET CONTENTS
ONE VOLUME BUSHEL.
MORJON
BRAND
洋
行
NET WEIGHT
WHEN PACKED
18.144 KILOGRAMS
CONNELL
BROS. CO. LTD.
公
利
PRODUCE OF U.S.A.
SAN FRANCISCO. U.S.A.
APPLES

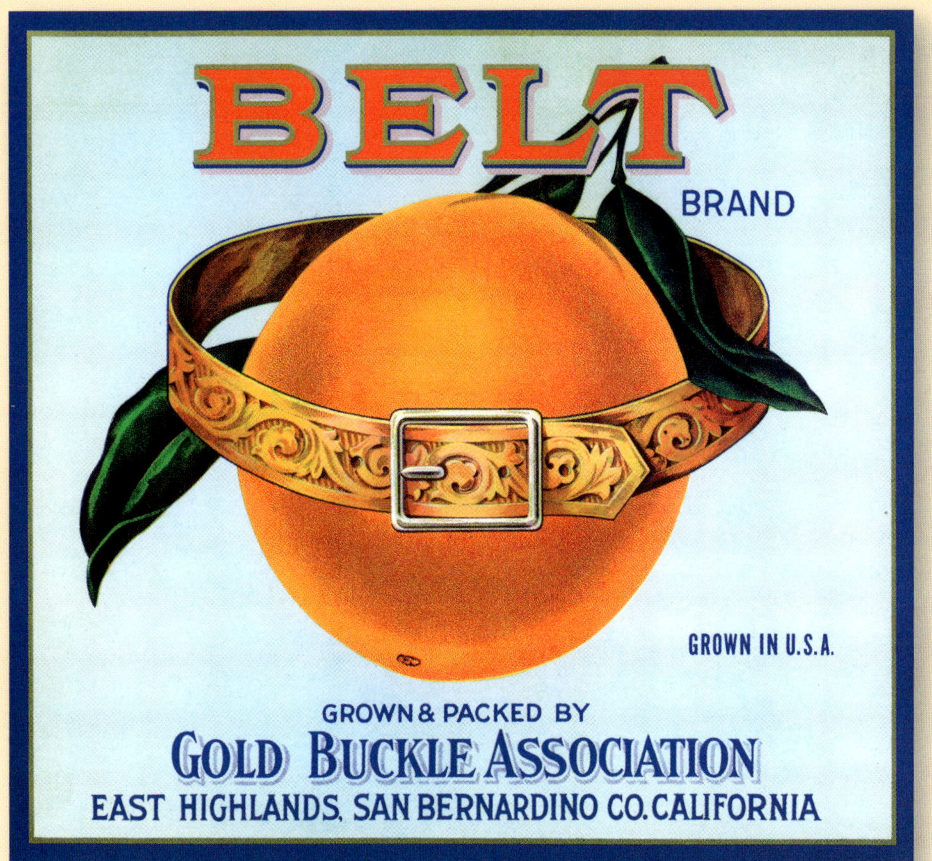

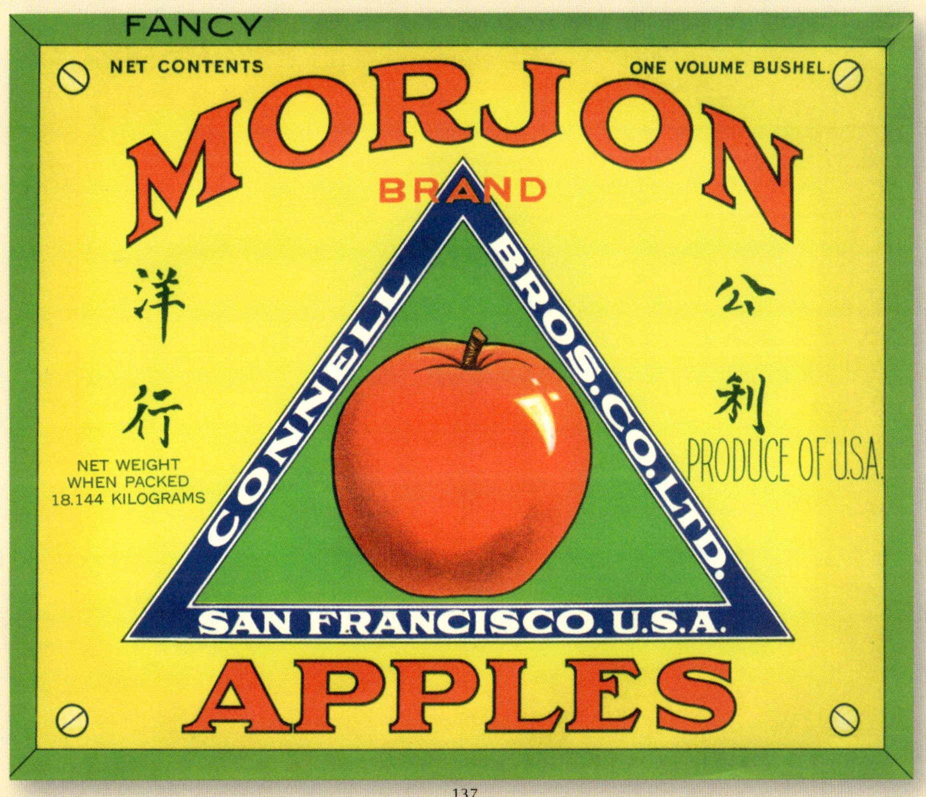

137

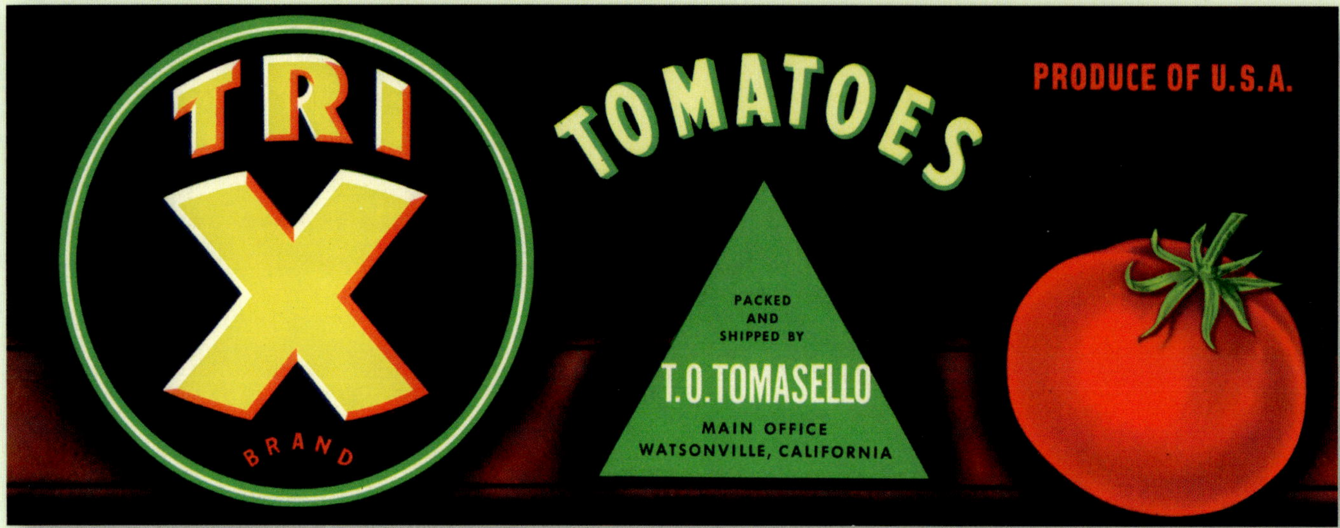

TRI X BRAND
TOMATOES
PRODUCE OF U.S.A.
PACKED AND SHIPPED BY
T. O. TOMASELLO
MAIN OFFICE
WATSONVILLE, CALIFORNIA

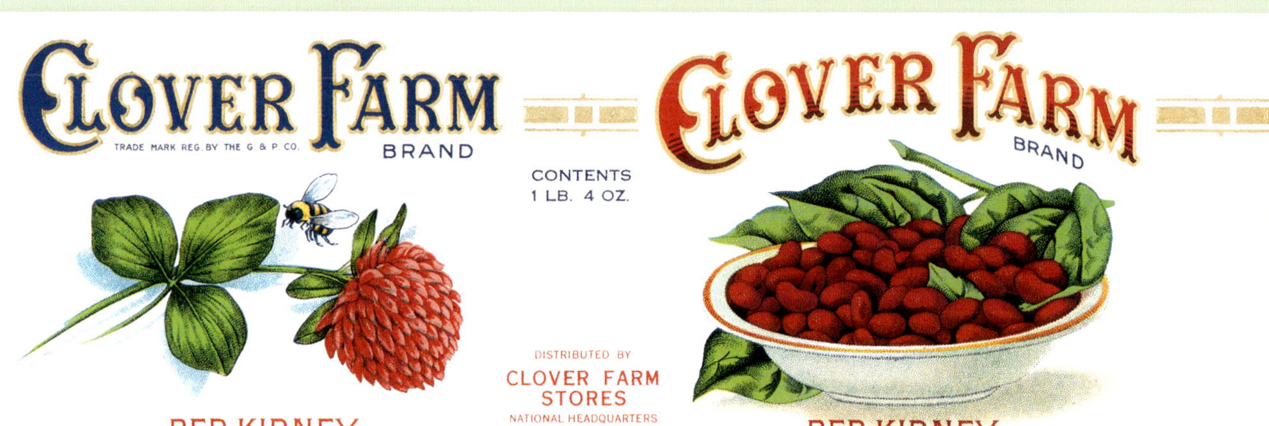

CLOVER FARM BRAND
TRADE MARK REG. BY THE G. & P. CO.
CLOVER FARM BRAND
CONTENTS 1 LB. 4 OZ.
RED KIDNEY BEANS
DISTRIBUTED BY
CLOVER FARM STORES
NATIONAL HEADQUARTERS
CLEVELAND, OHIO
RED KIDNEY BEANS
STECHER LITH CO ROCH N Y

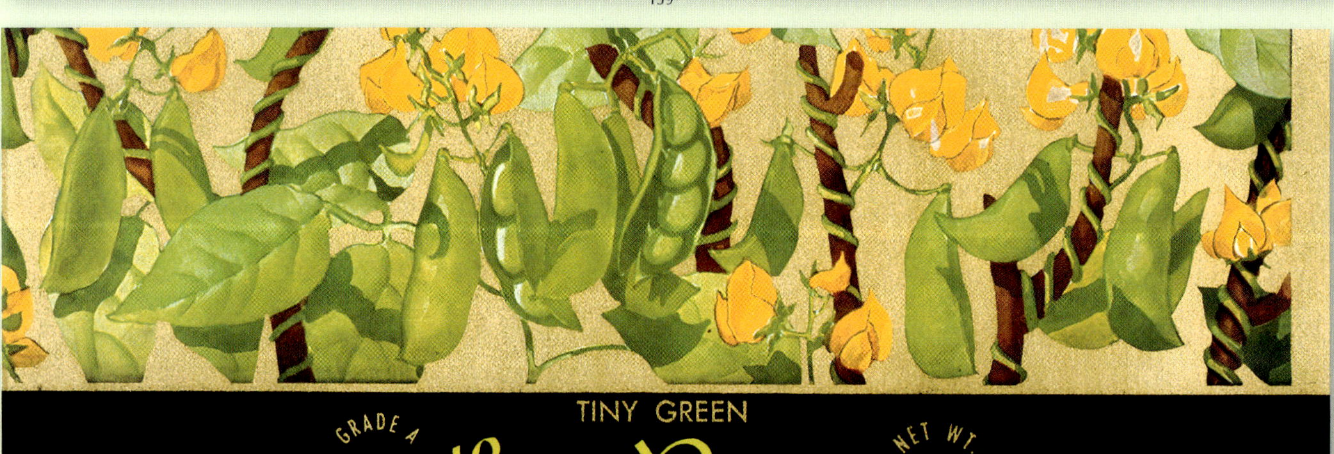

TINY GREEN
GRADE A
Lima Beans
NET WT.

King's Cadets
BRAND
CALIFORNIA GREEN
ASPARAGUS
F.S. AND F.E. CLARKSBURG CALIF.
KING

141

ASPERGES
EN BRANCHES
ALIBEL
MARQUE DÉPOSÉE
ASPERGES EXTRA GROSSES

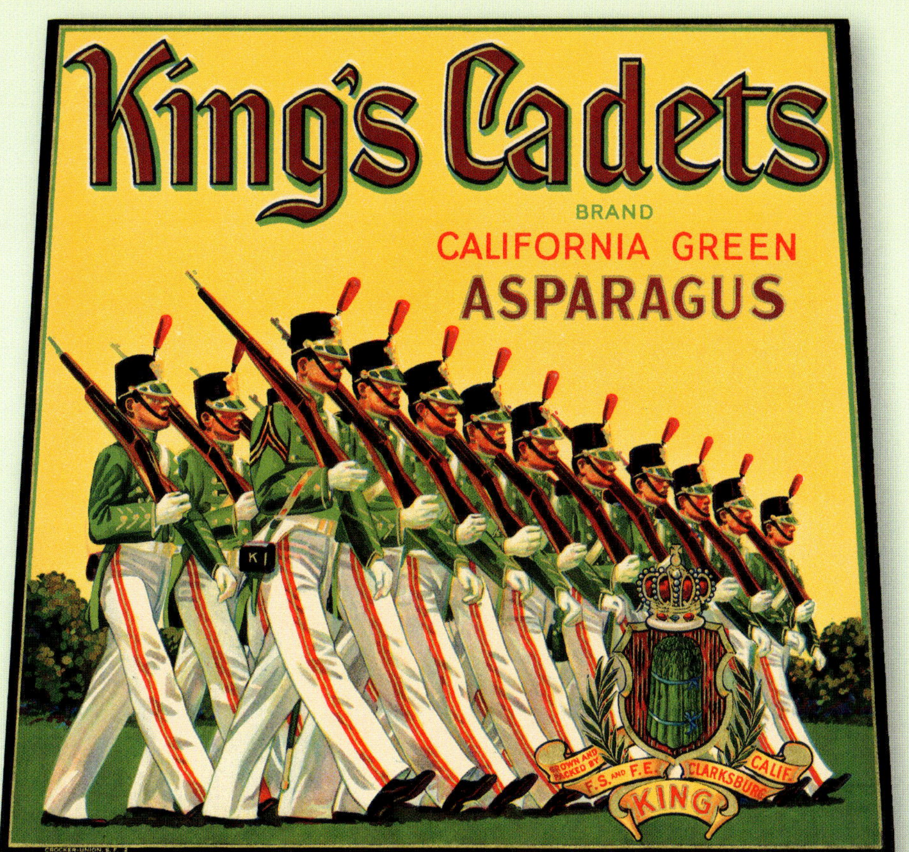

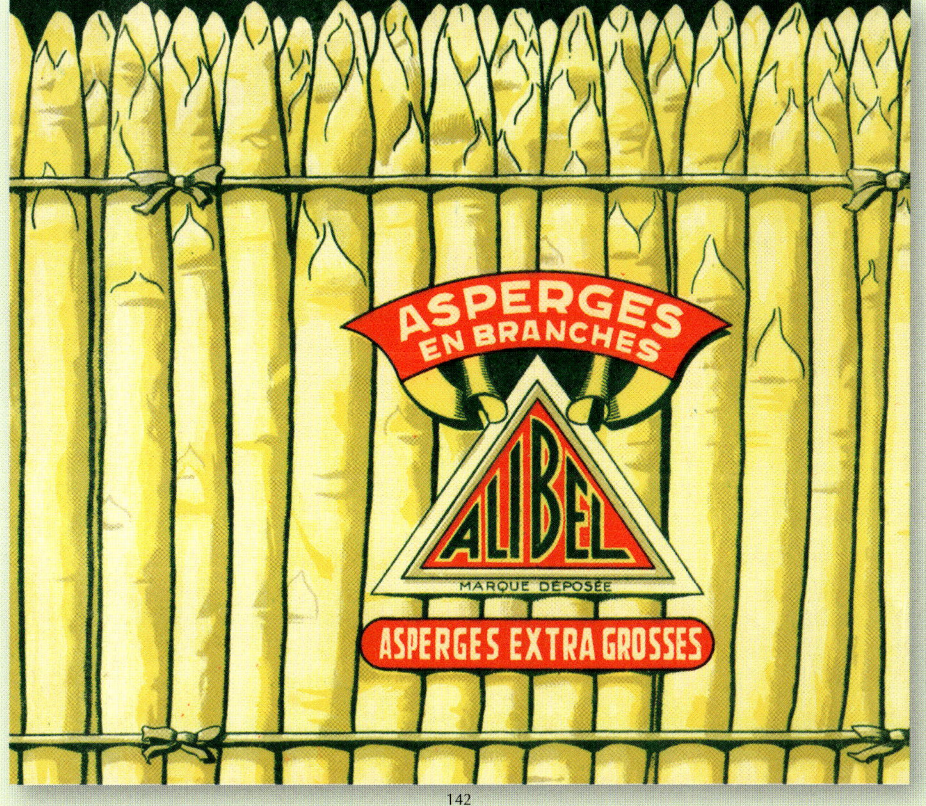

142

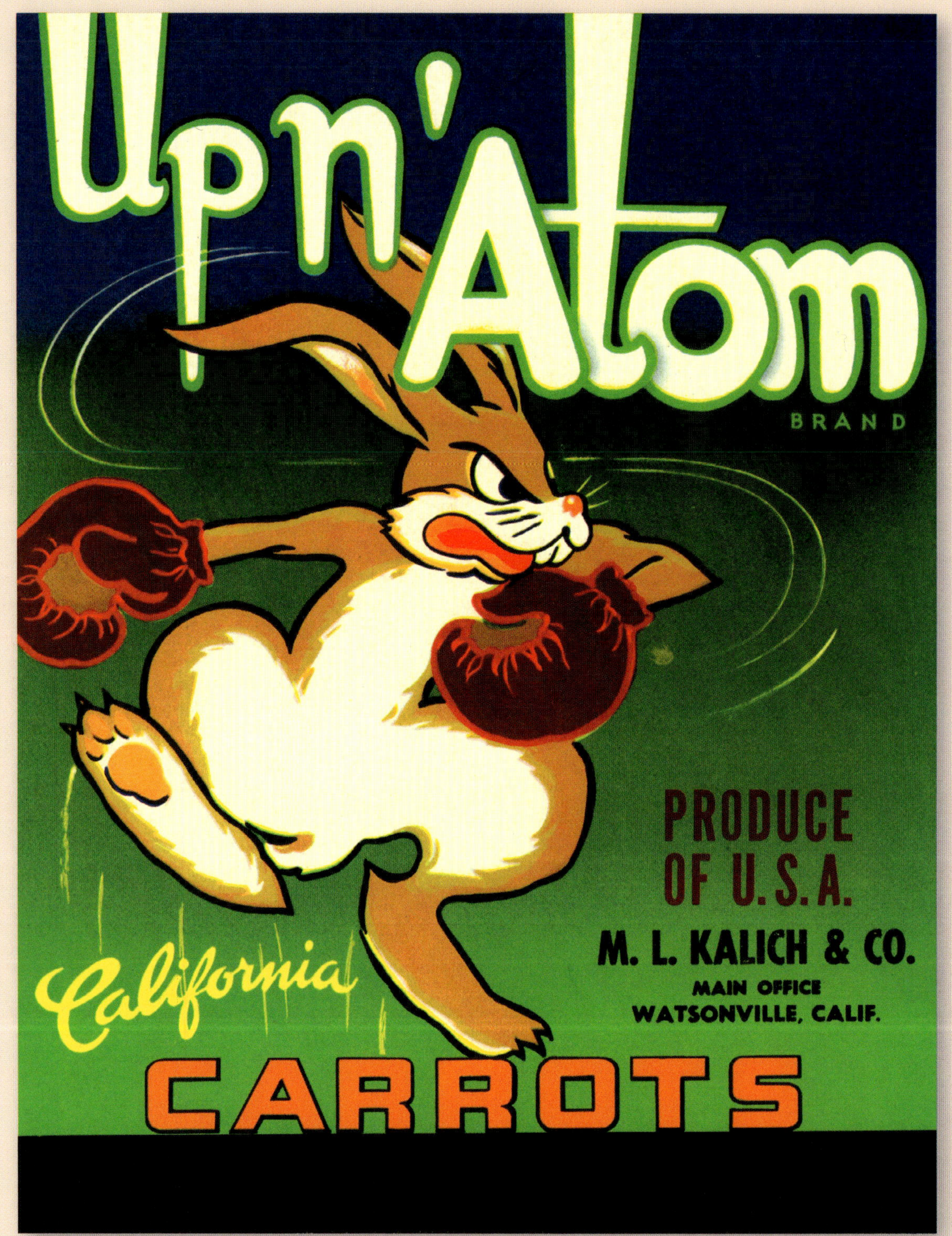
Up n' Atom
BRAND
California
PRODUCE
OF U.S.A.
M. L. KALICH & CO.
MAIN OFFICE
WATSONVILLE, CALIF.
CARROTS

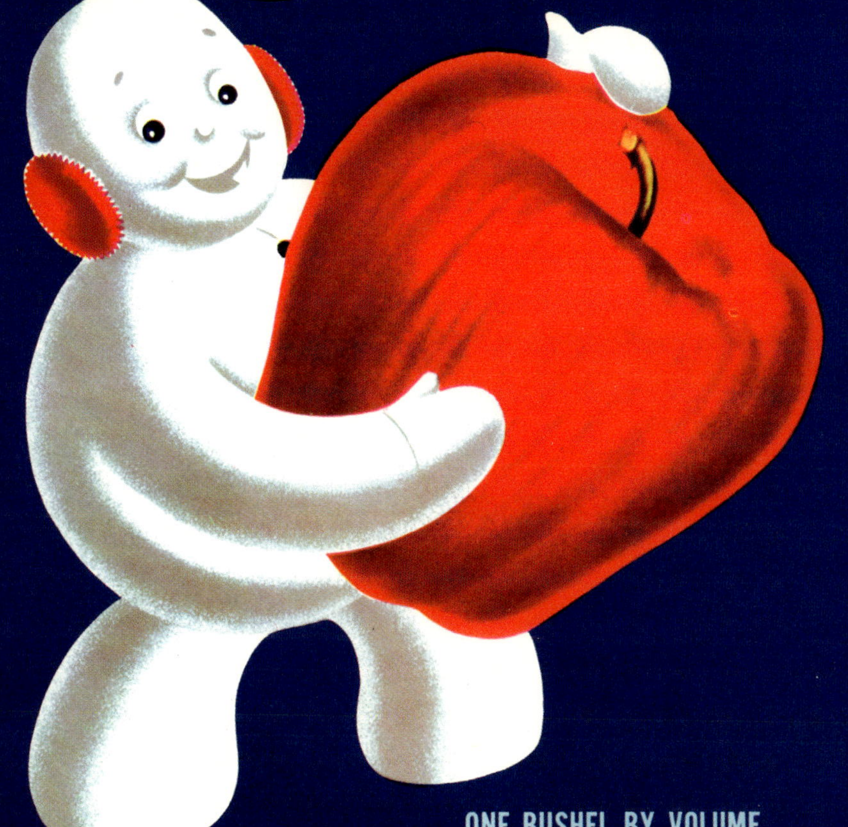

SNOBOY
ONE BUSHEL BY VOLUME
SNOBOY, INC., YAKIMA, WASH., U. S. A.
144

COPYRIGHT 1939 BY R. BROS.
GEORGIA MAID
BRAND
REG. U.S.
PAT. OFF.
SWEET PICKLES
CONTAINS CUCUMBERS, SUGAR, VINEGAR,
SALT, SPICES, ALUM AND TURMERIC.
1 PINT
PACKED BY
RODDENBERY BROS.
CAIRO, GA.

145

Pickle Patch
1 QUART
THE PICK OF THE PATCH
KOSHER STYLE
DILL PICKLES
CONTAINS CUCUMBERS, VINEGAR, SALT,
GARLIC, SPICES, ALUM & TURMERIC.
© 1939 BY
REG. U.S. PAT. OFF.
PACKED BY
W. B. Roddenbery Co.
CAIRO, GA.

146

MOTHER HUBBARD
BRAND
CONTENTS
16½ FL. OZ.
SWEET RELISH
PACKED BY
ADAM BROTHERS CO.
NEW ORLEANS, LA. & HOUSTON, TEXAS.
CONTAINS 1/10 OF 1% BENZOATE OF SODA

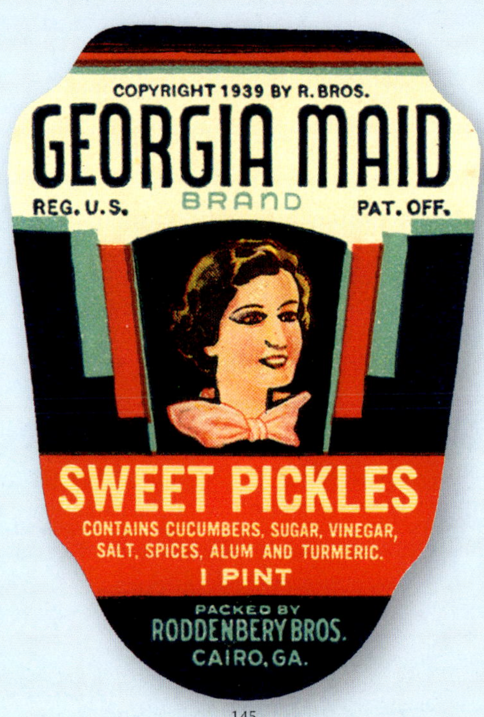

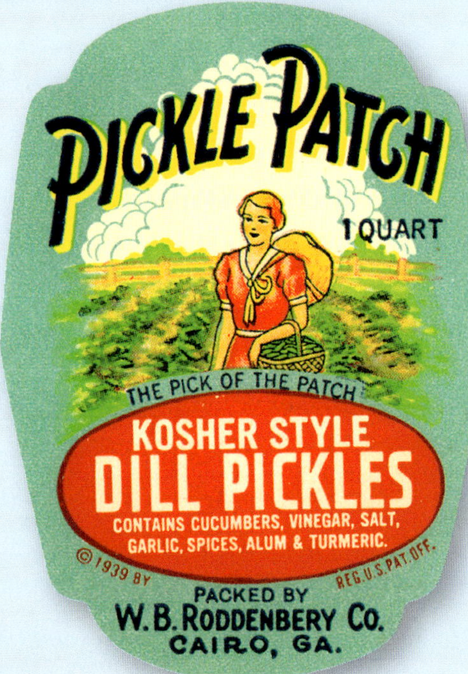

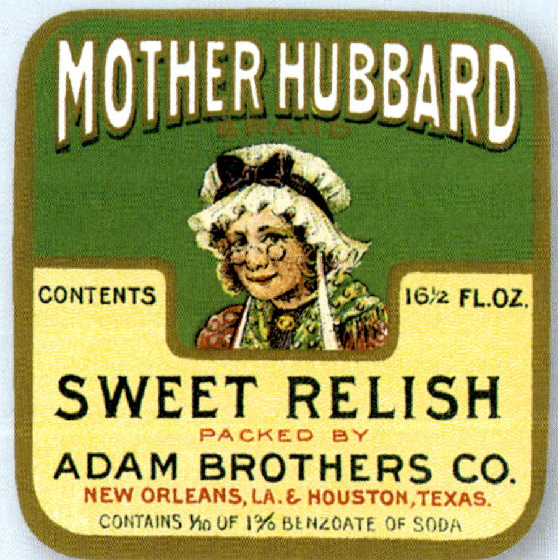

147

HAPPY KIDS
REG. U.S. PAT. OFF.
©1934 BY W.B.R. CO.
IT BRINGS A HAPPY SMILE
NET WT.
BITS O' NUT
1 POUND
PEANUT BUTTER
MADE FROM ROASTED PEANUTS AND SALT
Packed by W. B. RODDENBERY CO., Cairo, Ga.

148

NET WT.
1 LB. 7 OZ.
OH! BOY
BRAND
HOMOGENIZED
PEANUT BUTTER
CAREFULLY SELECTED RADIANT RAY
ROASTED PEANUTS, HYDROGENATED
PEANUT OIL AND SALT
PACKED BY
RODDENBERY BROS.
CAIRO, GA.

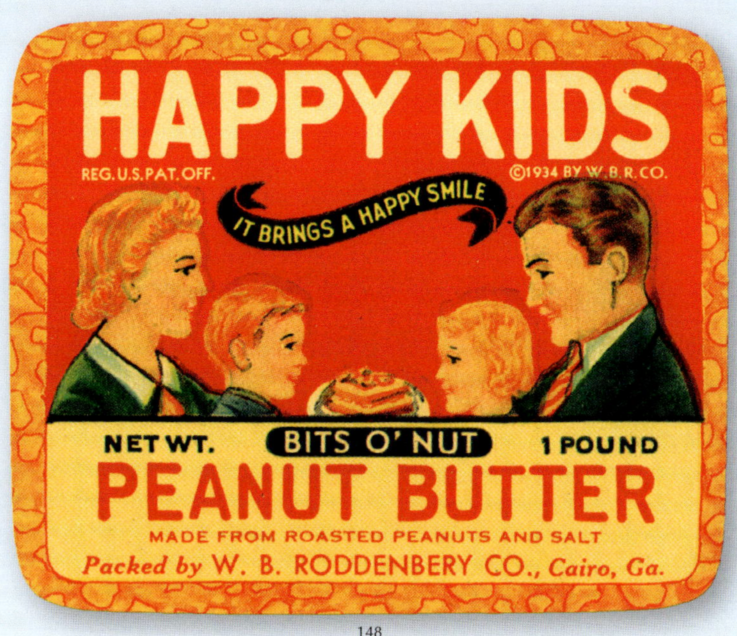

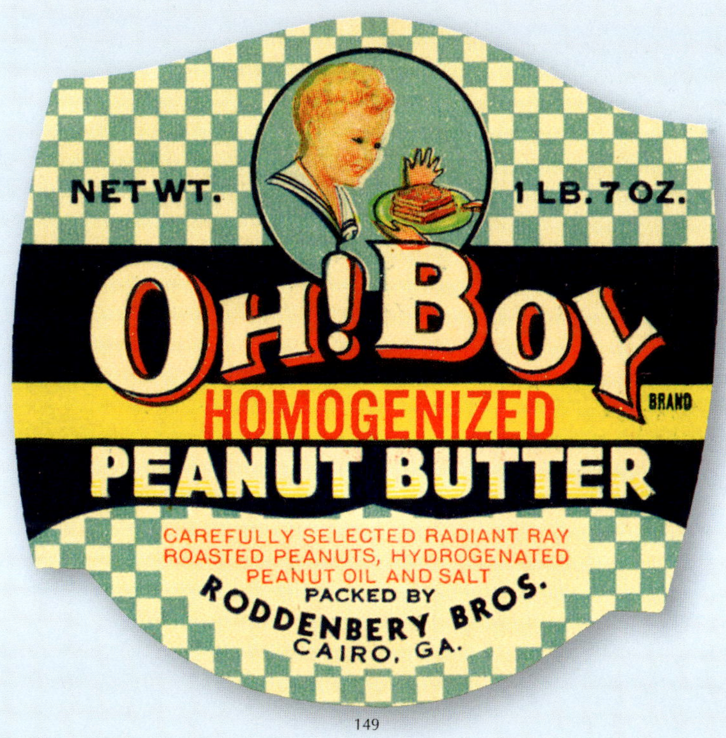

149

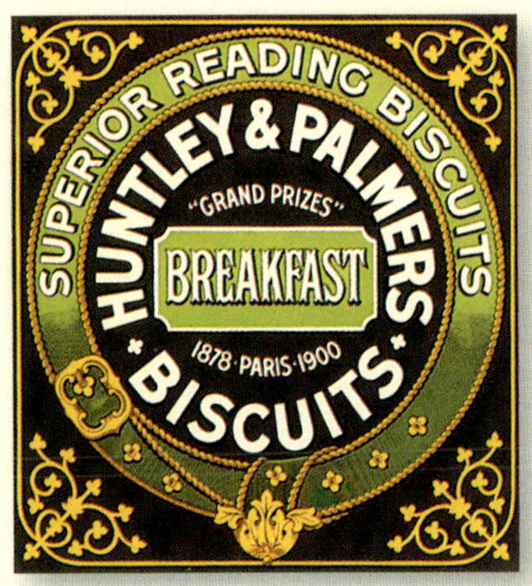

150

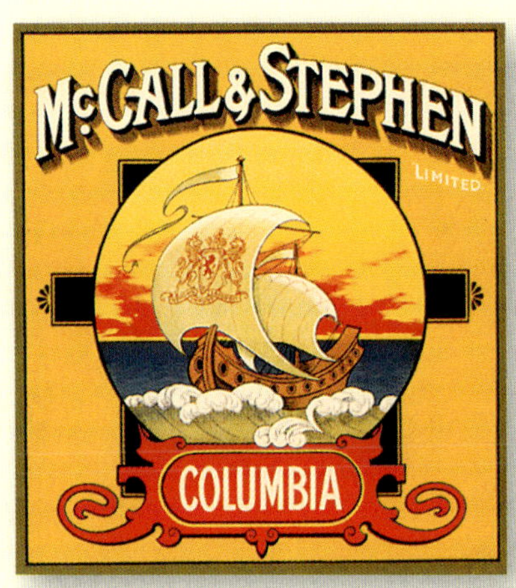

151

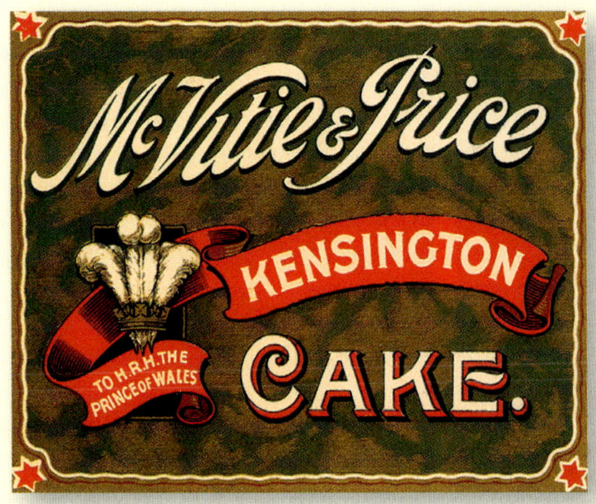

152

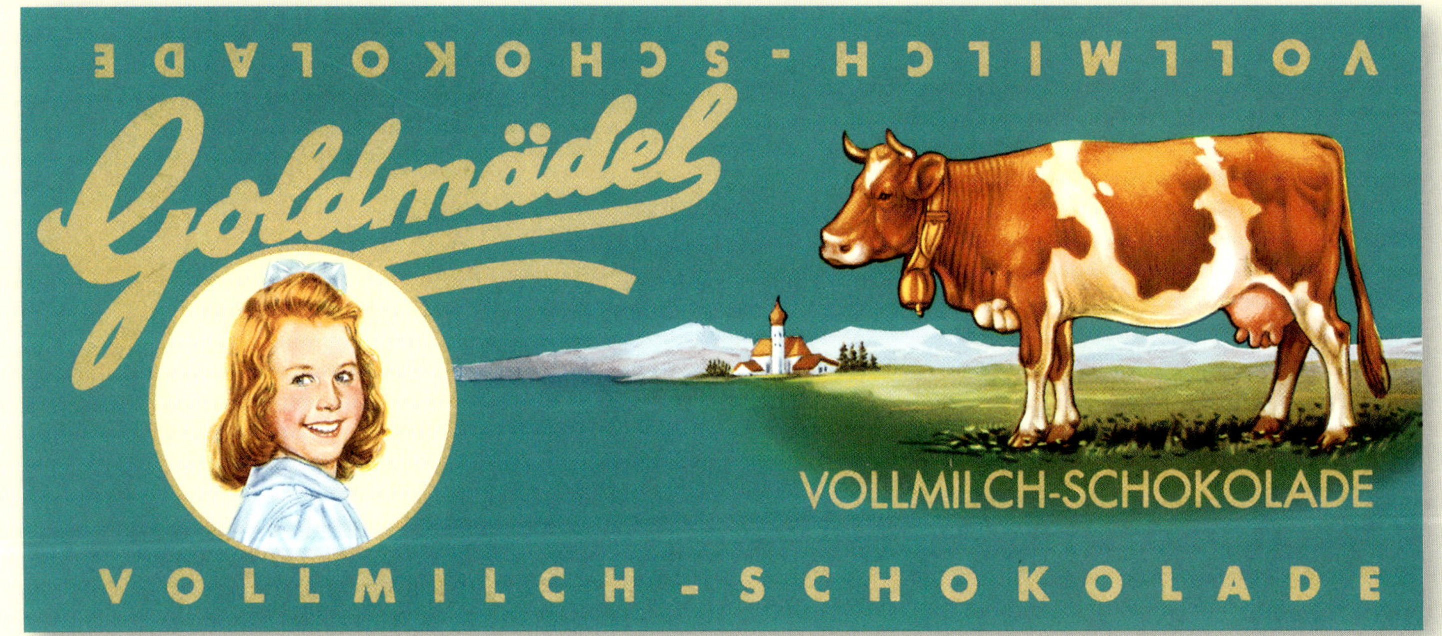

153

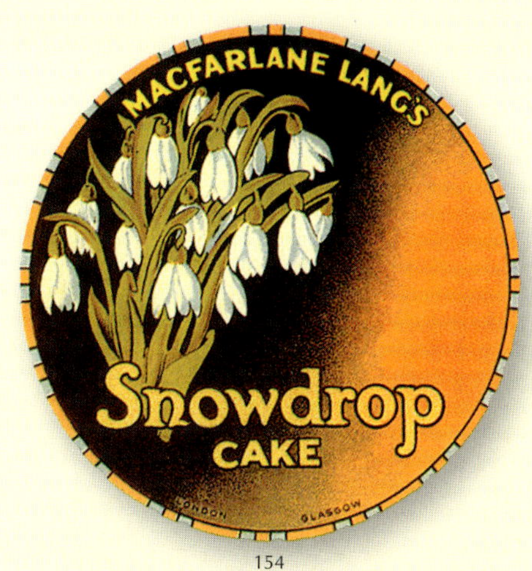

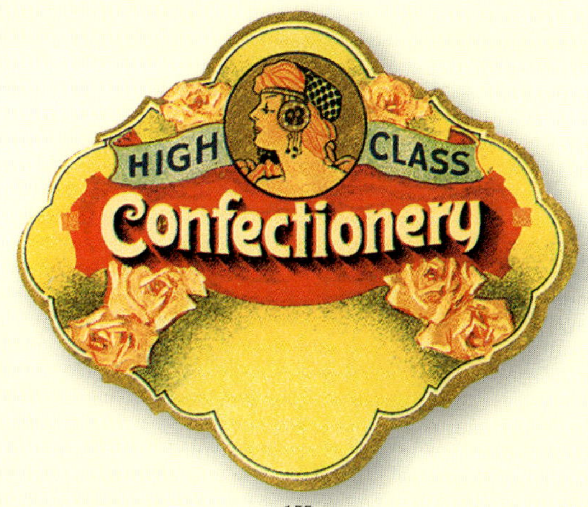

154

155

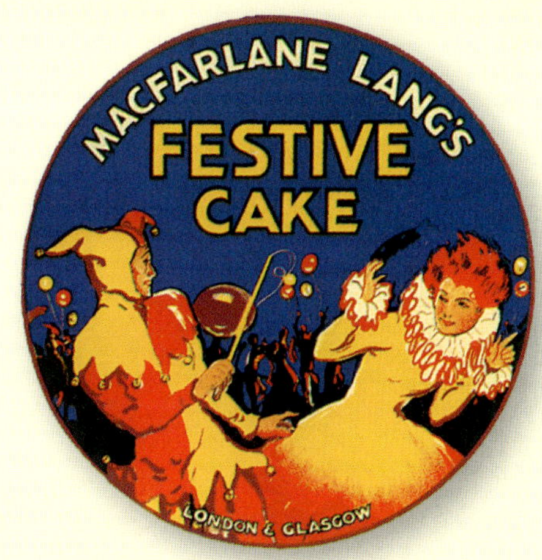

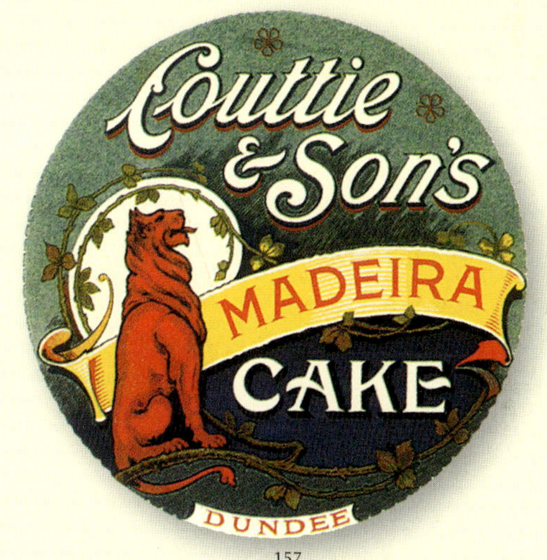

156

157

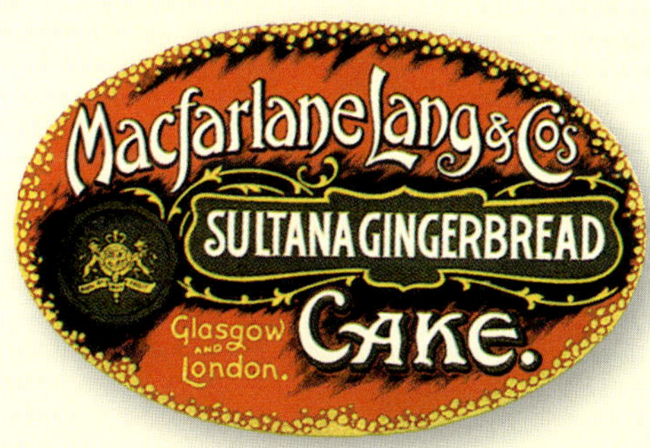

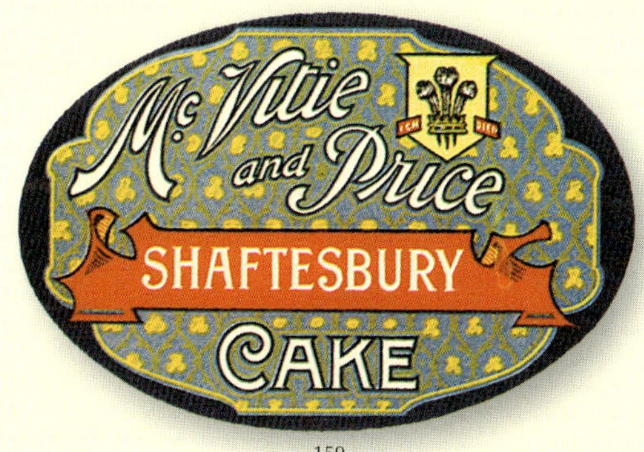

158

159

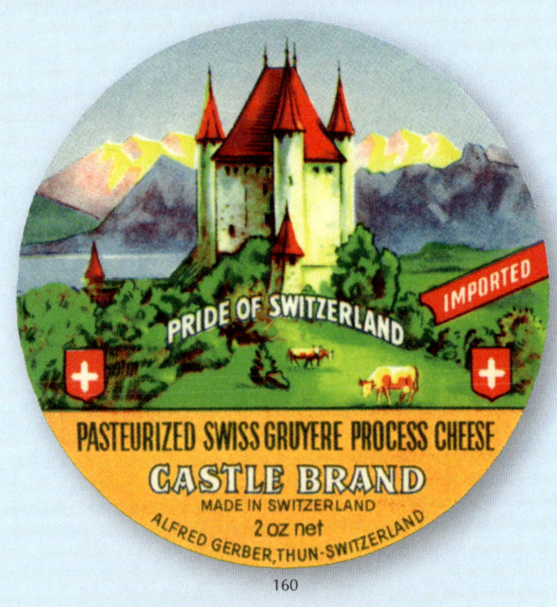

160

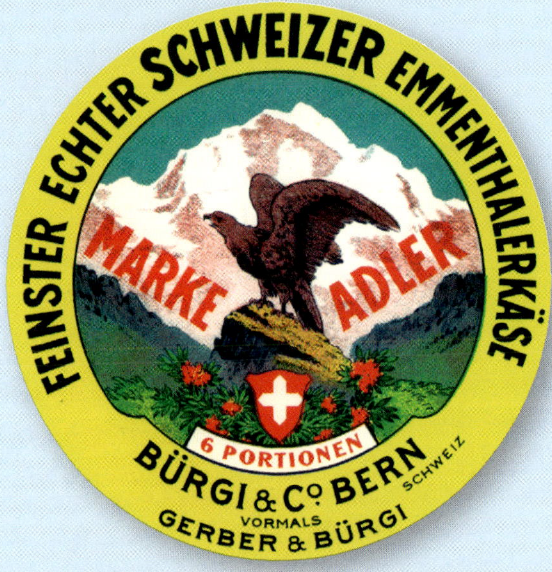

161

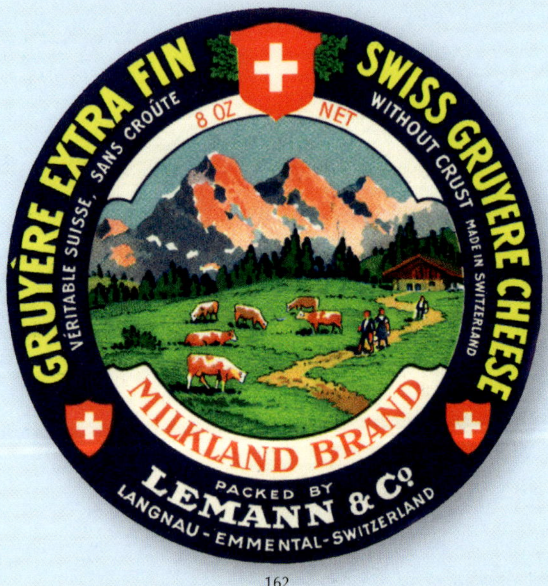

162

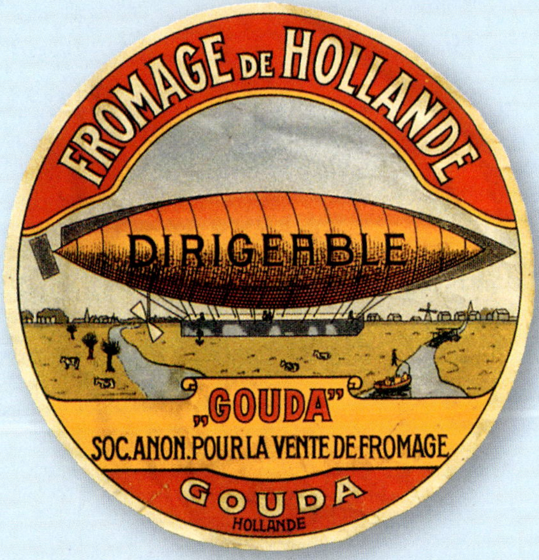

163

Libby's
MADE IN ENGLAND
WELSH RAREBIT

164

Swift's
MADE IN ENGLAND
Welsh Rarebit
SEASONED READY FOR USE

165

Brookfield
WELSH RAREBIT
SEASONED READY FOR USE   MADE IN ENGLAND

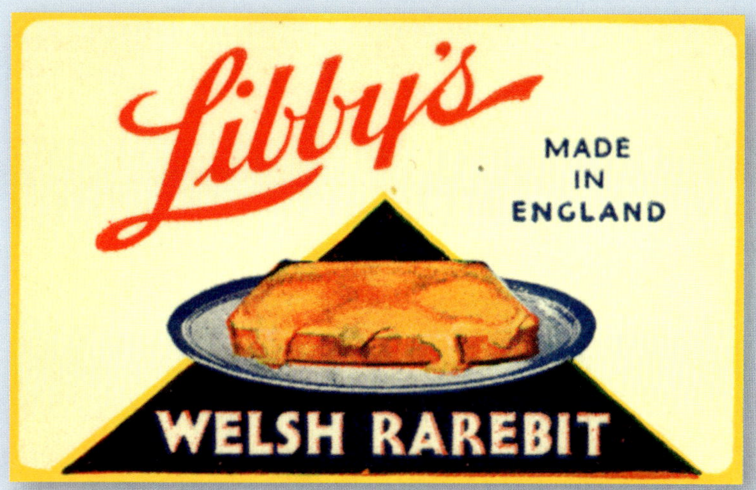

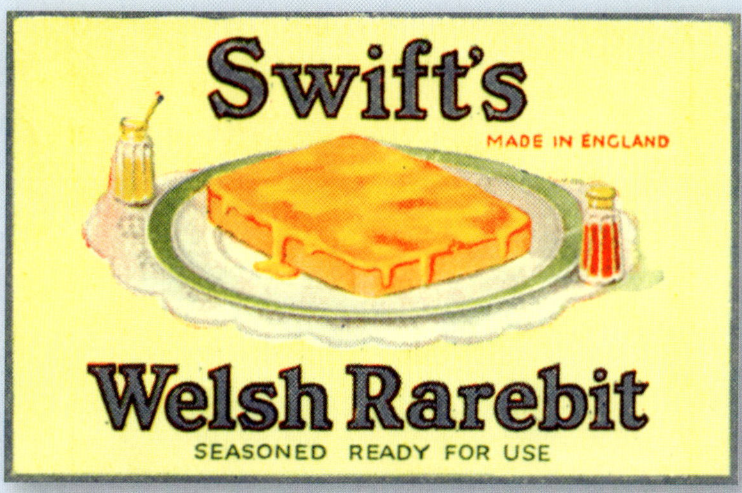

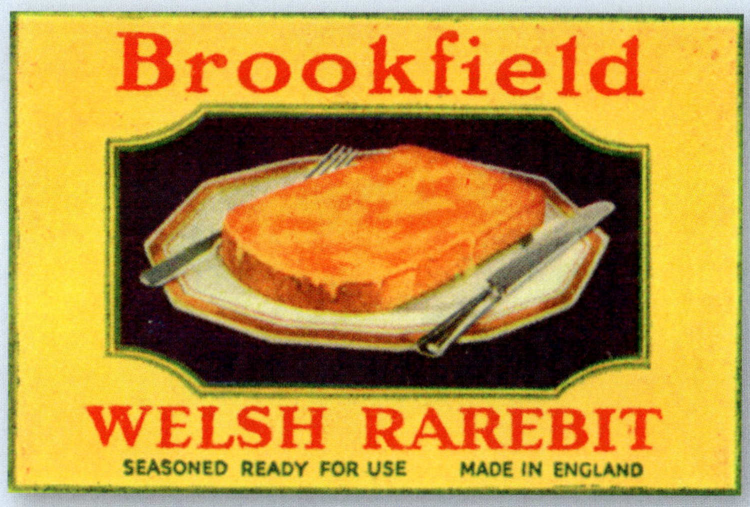

166

ONE POUND NET
CAPITOL
BRAND
BAKING POWDER
PACKED FOR
H. G. HILL COMPANY
NASHVILLE, TENNESSEE

167

COLONIAL
BAKING POWDER
ONE POUND NET

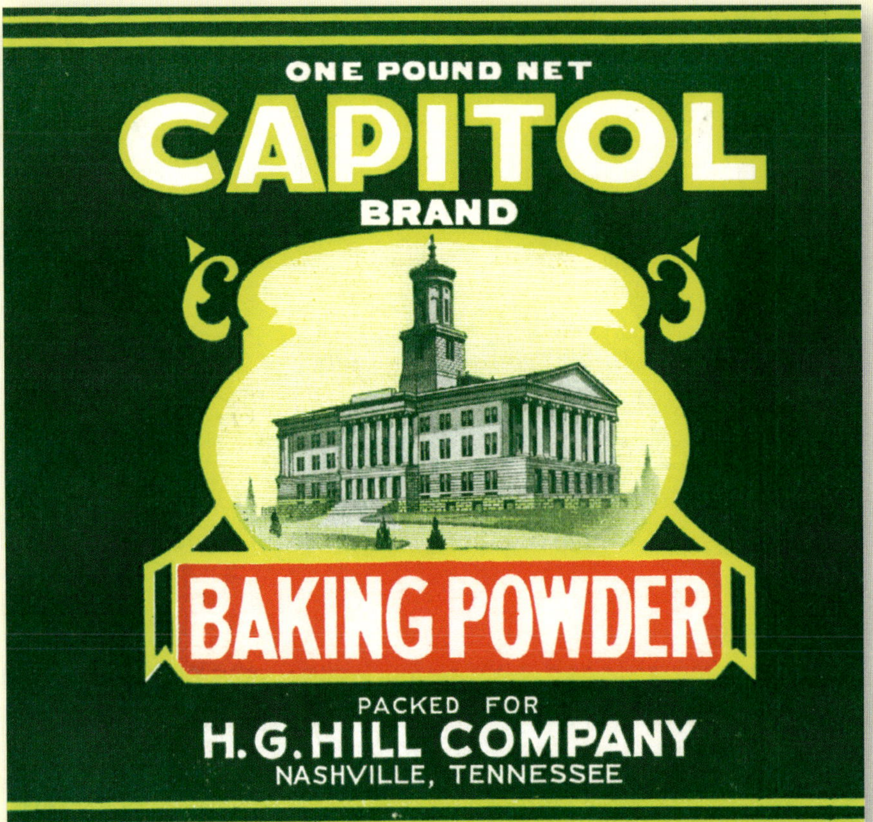

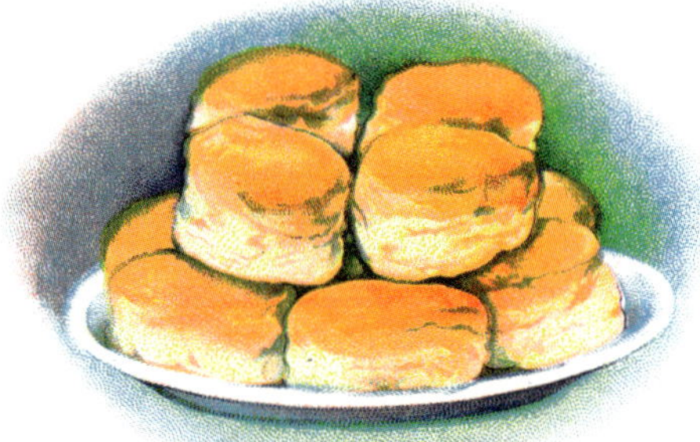

168

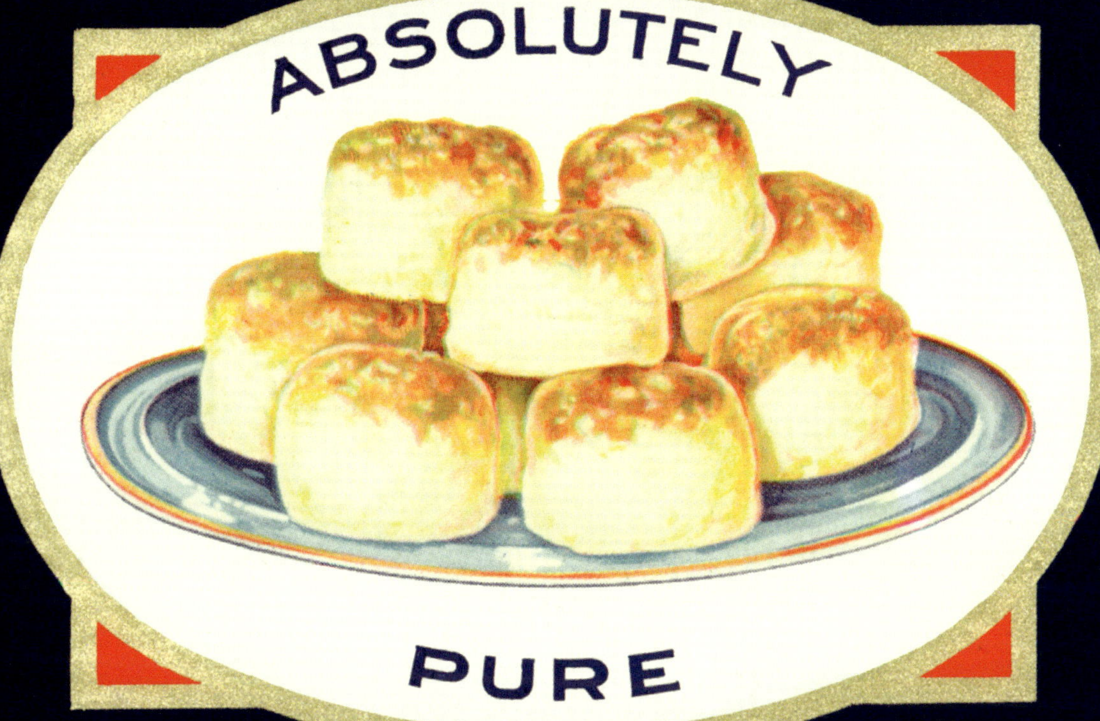

AUTOCRAT
BRAND
REG. U.S. PAT. OFF.
ABSOLUTELY
PURE
BAKING POWDER
ONE POUND NET

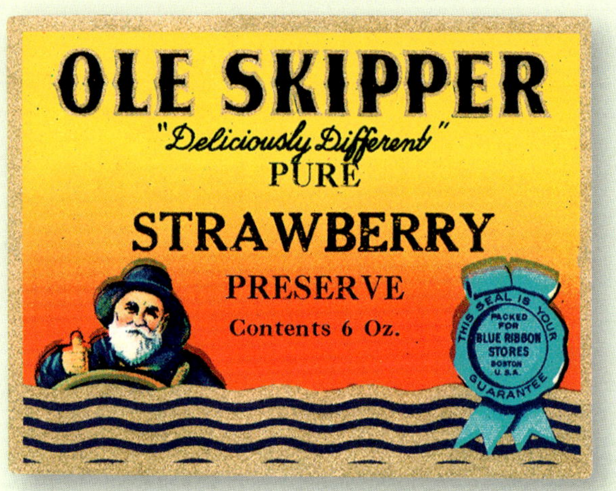

170

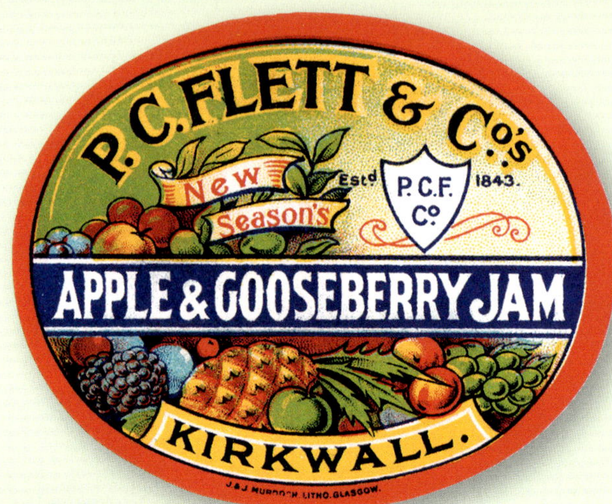

171

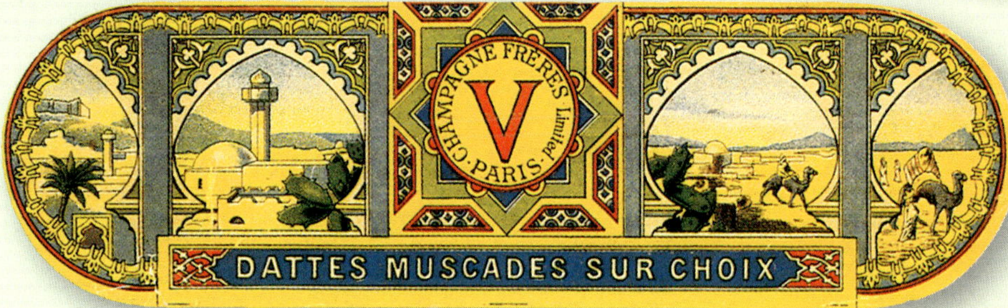

172

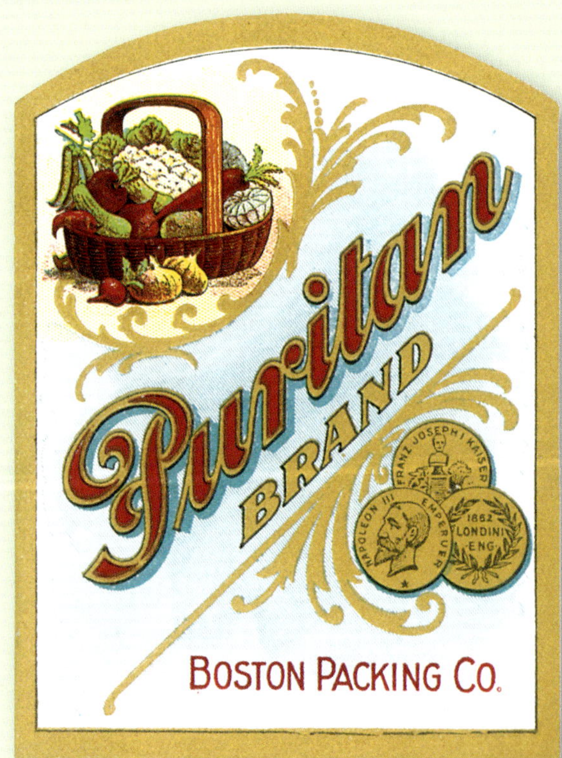

173

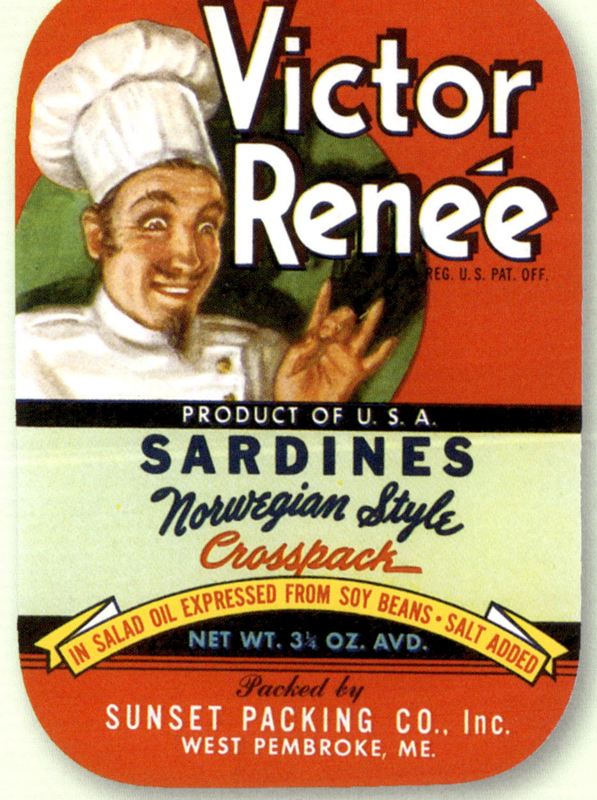

174

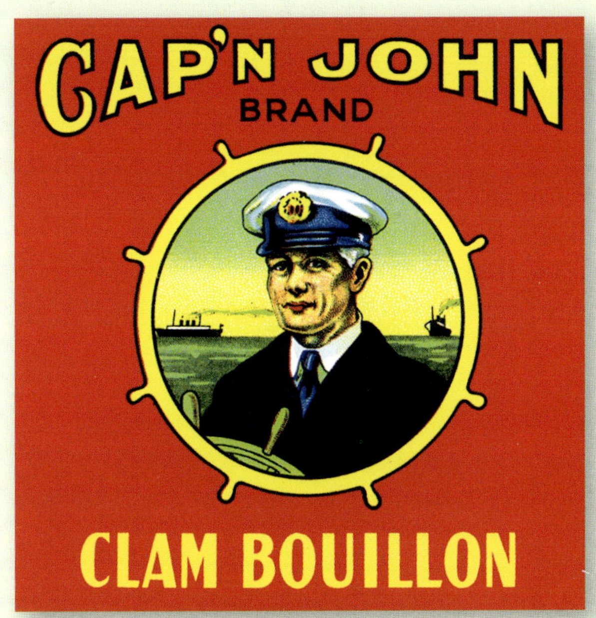

175

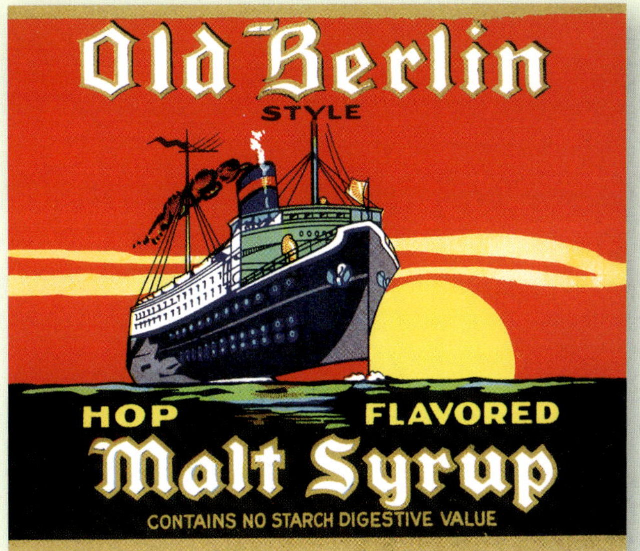

176

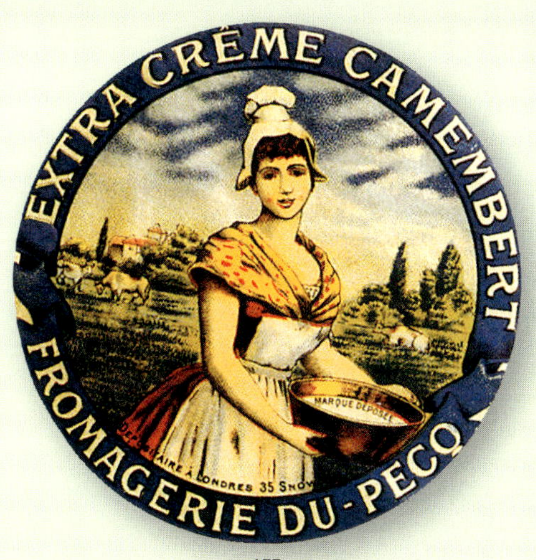

177

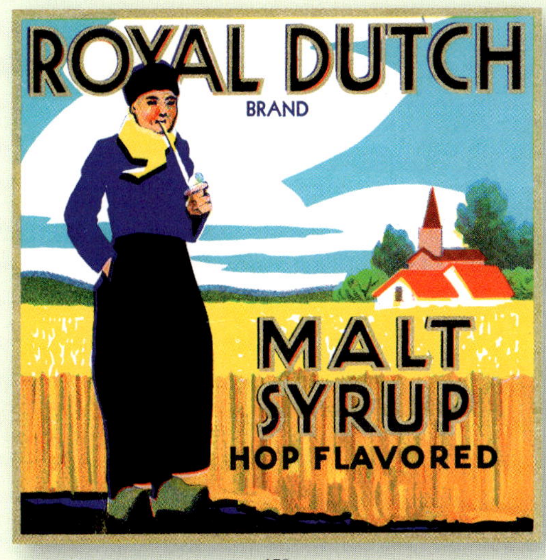

178

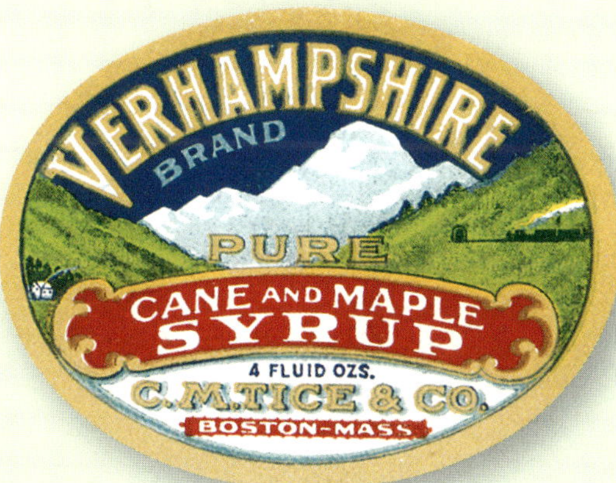

179

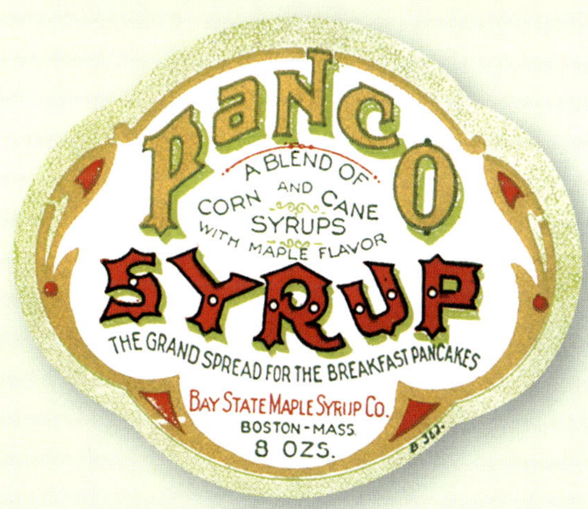

180

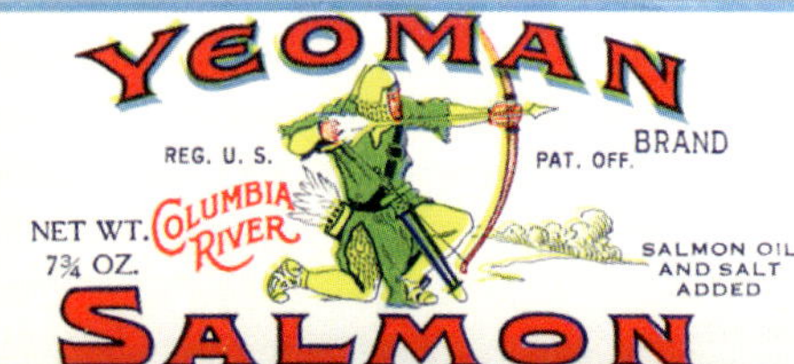

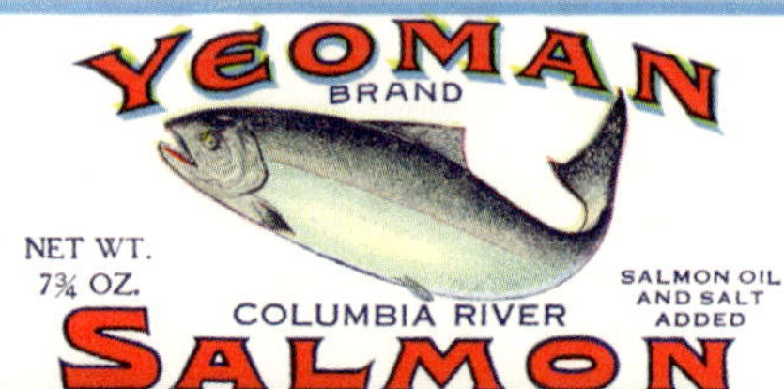

181

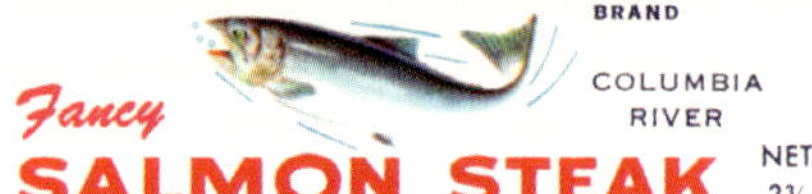

182

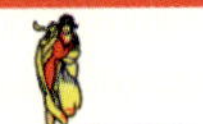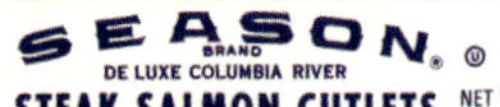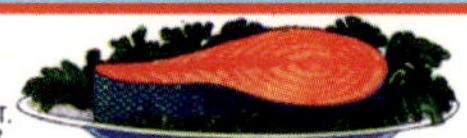

183

184

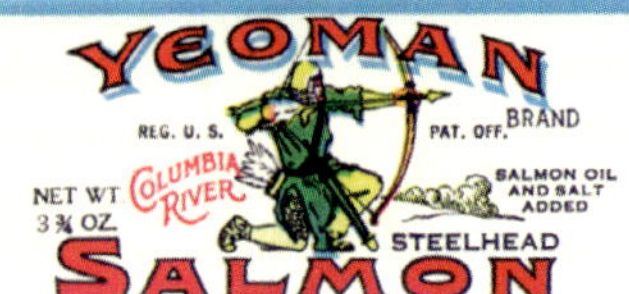

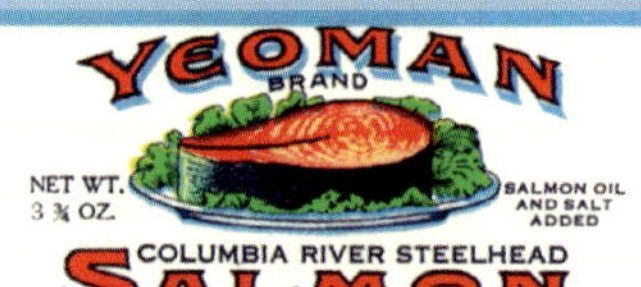

185

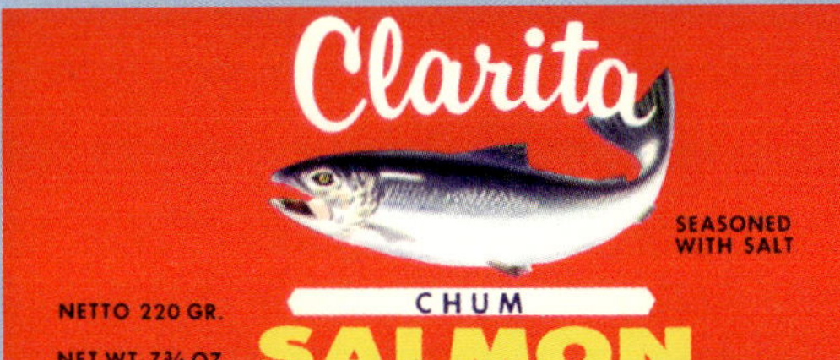

CONFEZIONATO SECONDO LE LEGGI VIGENTI
ZALM NETTO 220 GR.
POIDS NET 220 GR.
PRODUIT DES ETATS UNIS
PACKED FOR
ALLIED CANNERS AND PACKERS, INC.
SAN FRANCISCO, CALIFORNIA 94111
PRODUCT OF U.S.A.
PRINTED IN U.S.A.

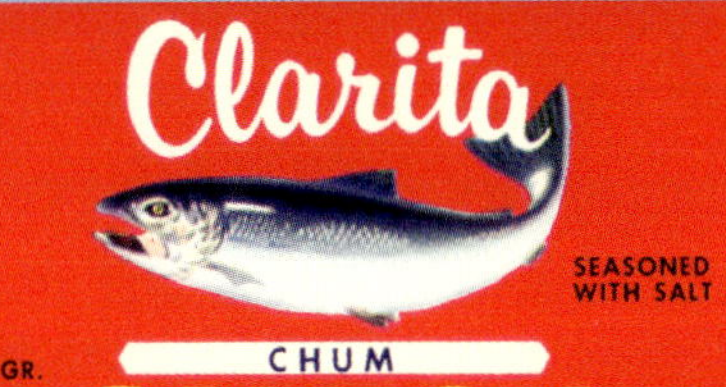

186

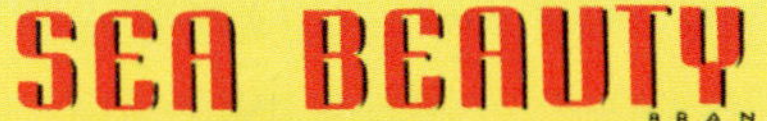

INGREDIENTS:
SALMON & SALT
PRODUCT OF U.S.A.

DISTRIBUTED BY
WASHINGTON FISH
& OYSTER CO.
SEATTLE, WASH. 98104
U.S.A.

187

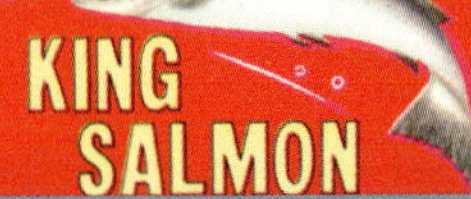

KASHRUT & QUALITY
SALMON OIL AND SALT ADDED
I. EPSTEIN & SONS, INC.
DISTRIBUTORS
IRVINGTON, NEW JERSEY

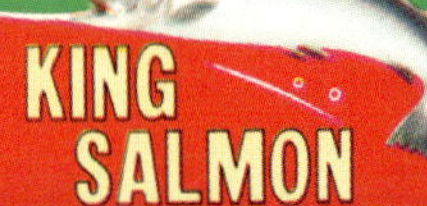

TRADE MARK
REG. U.S. PAT. OFF.

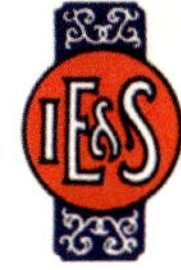

188

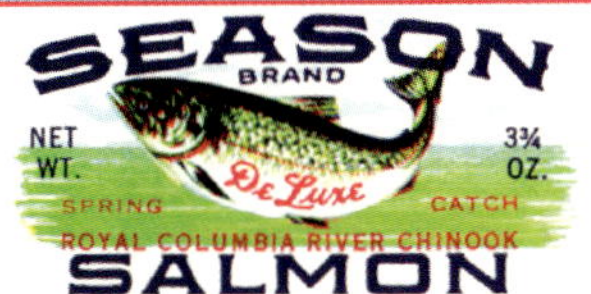

NET WGT. 3¾ OZS.
SALT ADDED
PACKED FOR
M & R
IMPORTING CO.
NEW YORK, N. Y.
U.S.A.

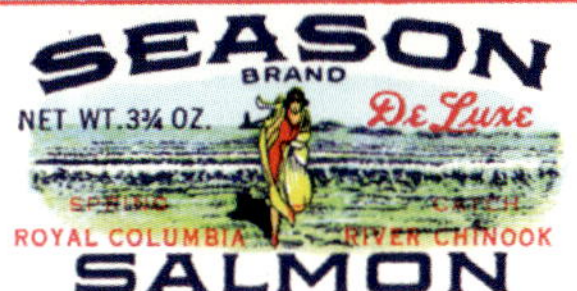

189

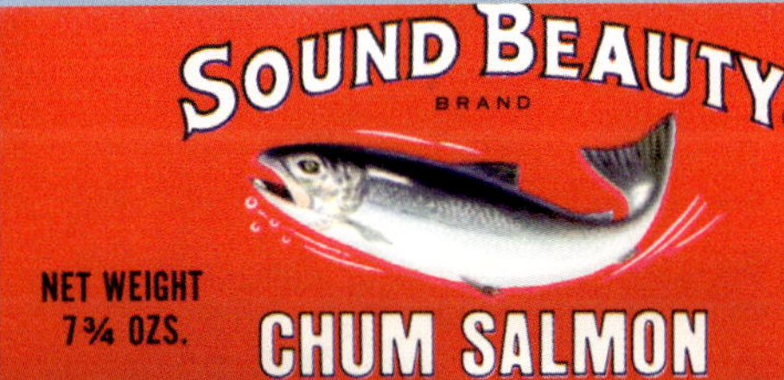

INGREDIENTS:
SALMON
SALT

DISTRIBUTED BY
WASHINGTON FISH
& OYSTER CO.
SEATTLE, WASH. 98104
U.S.A.

PRODUCT OF U.S.A.

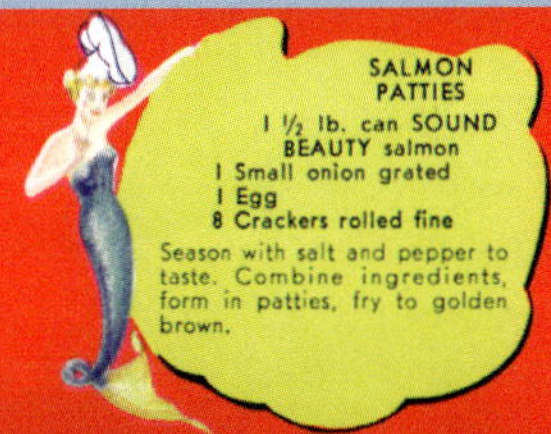

190

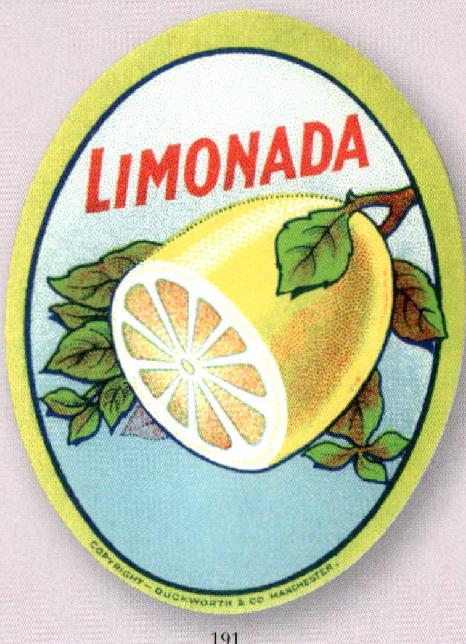

191

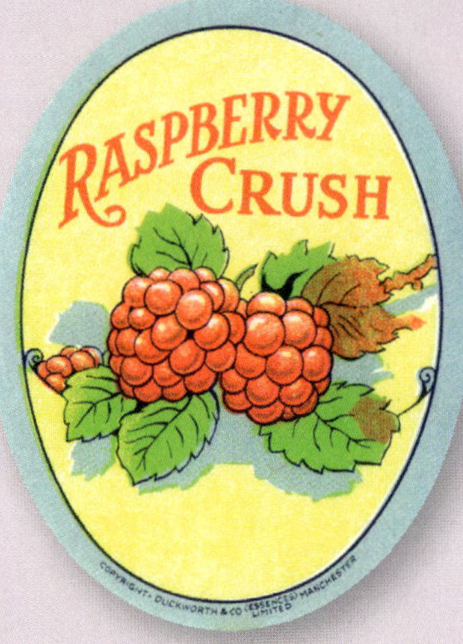

192

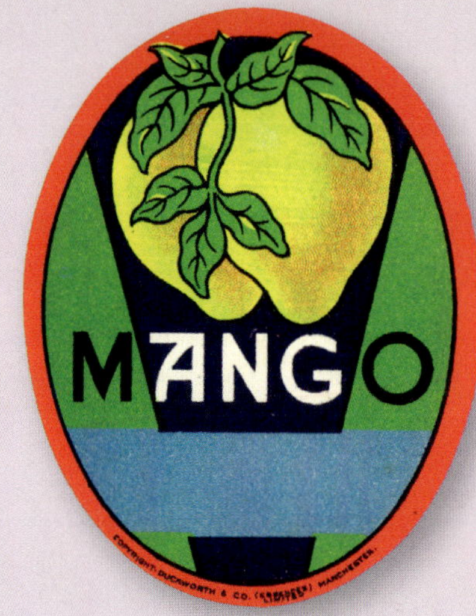

193

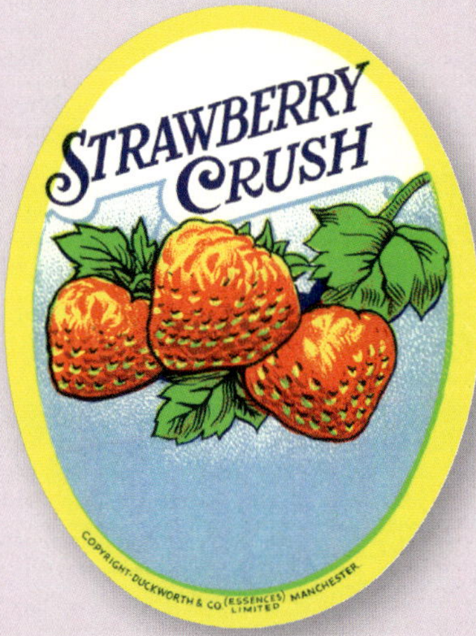

194

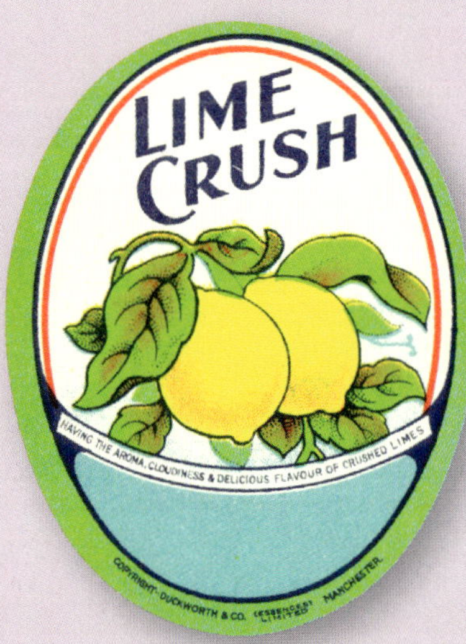

195

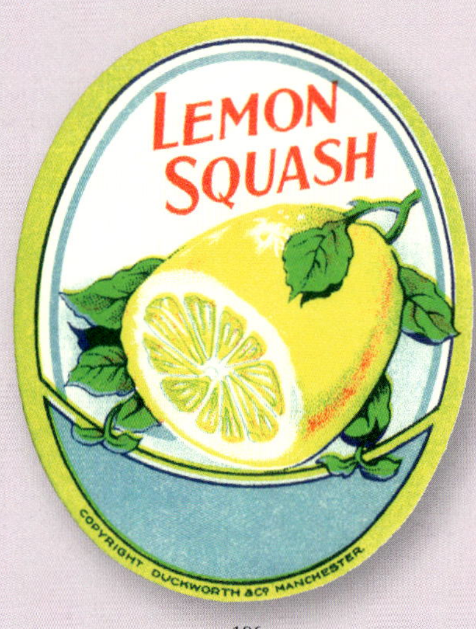

196

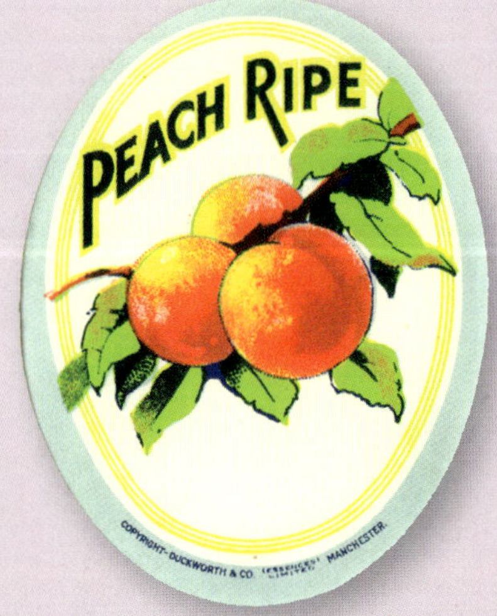

197

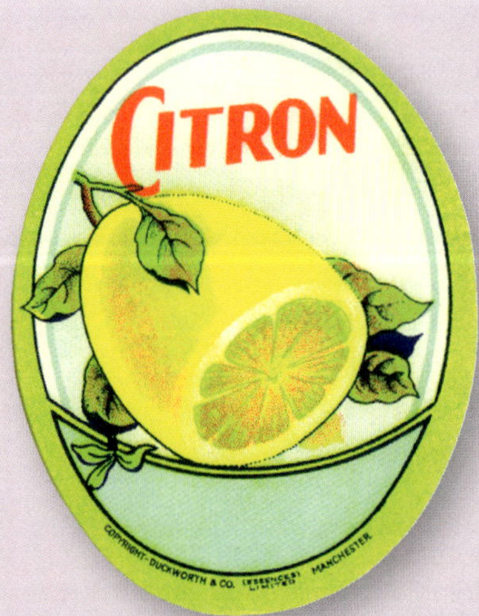

198

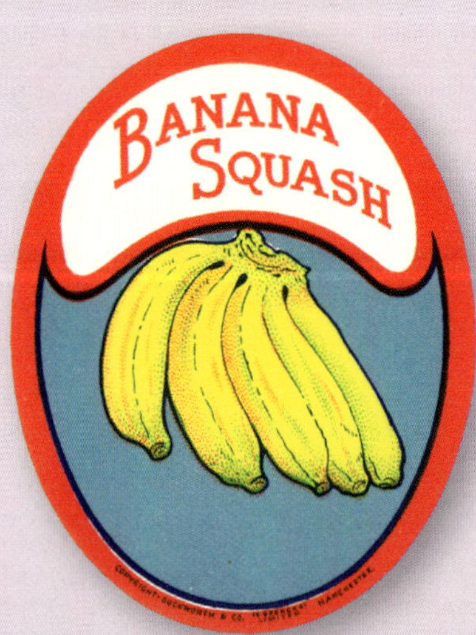

199

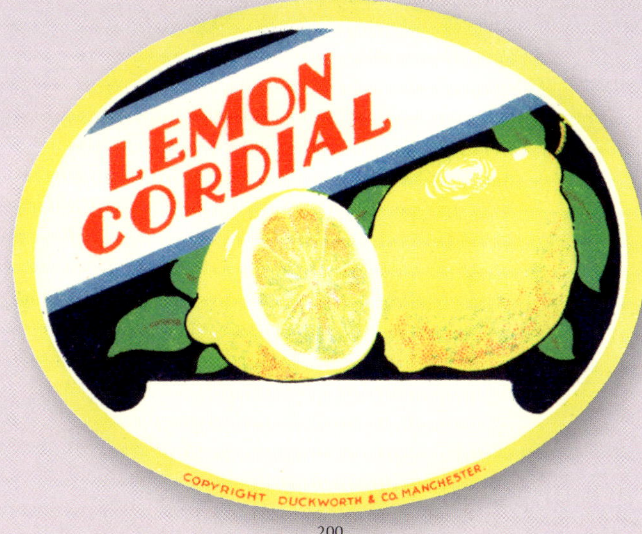

200

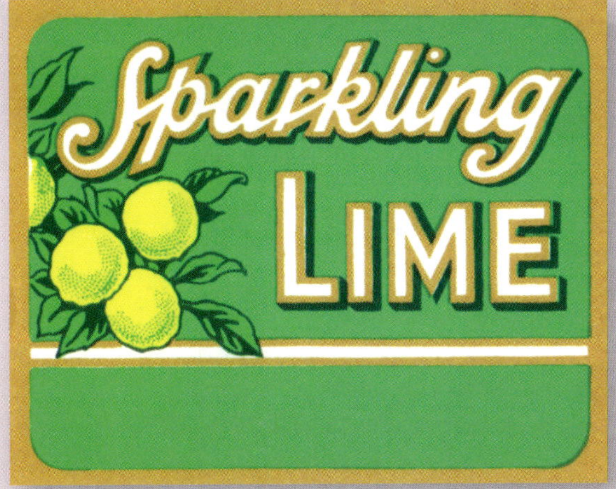

201

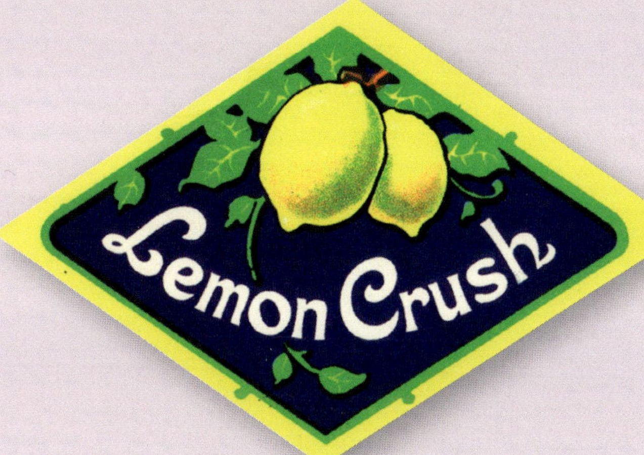

202

203

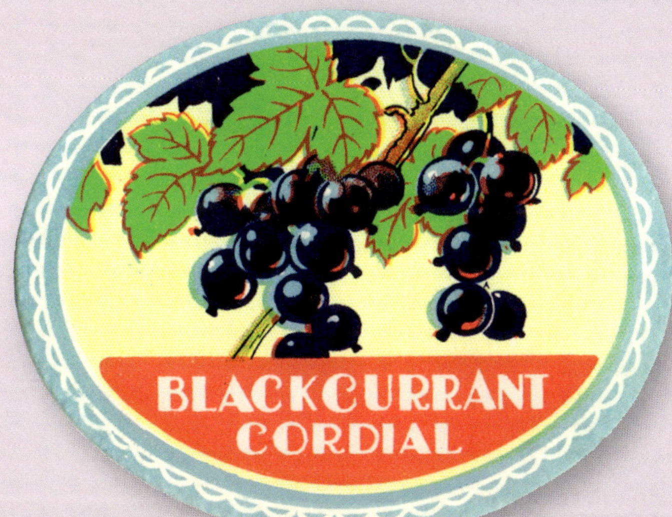

204

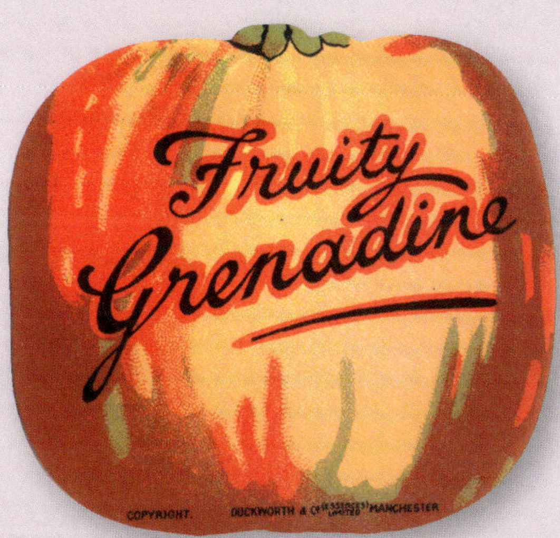

205

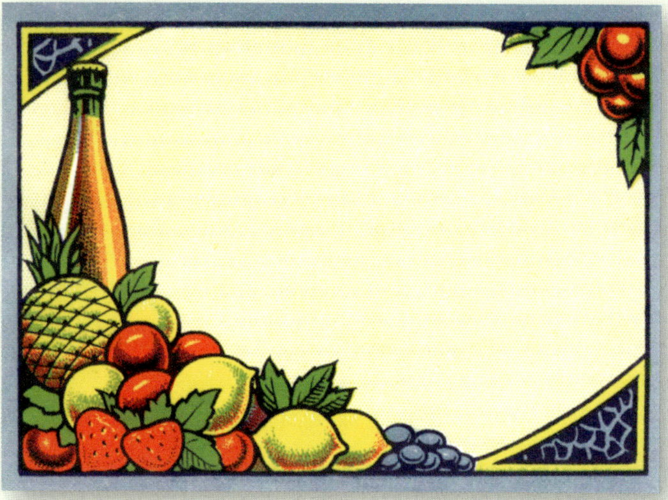

206

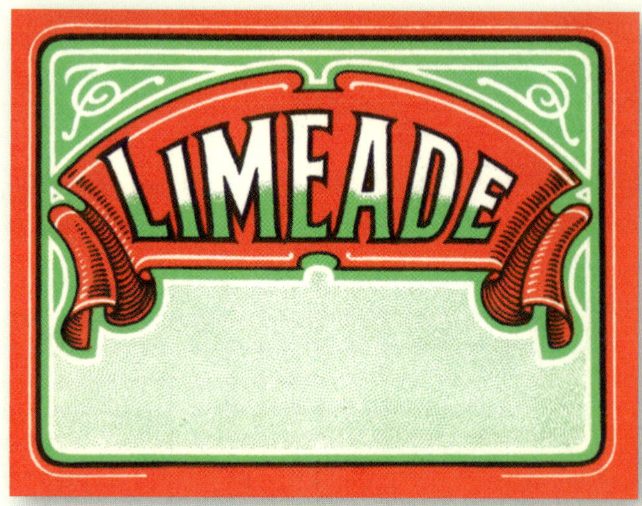

207

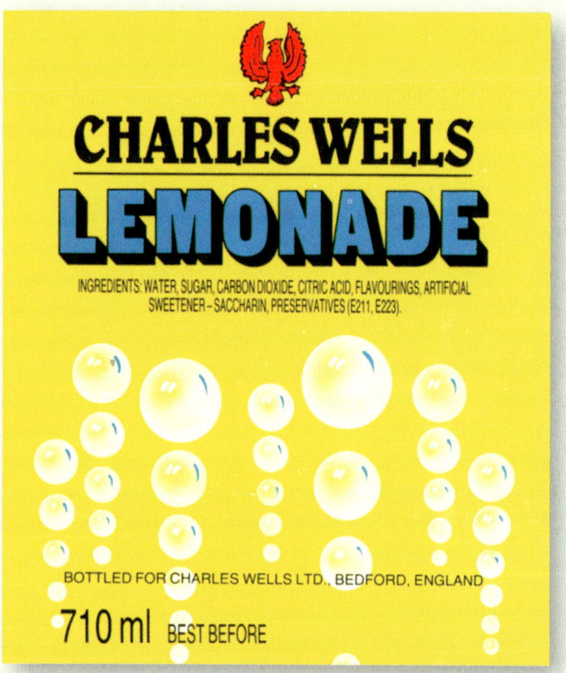

208

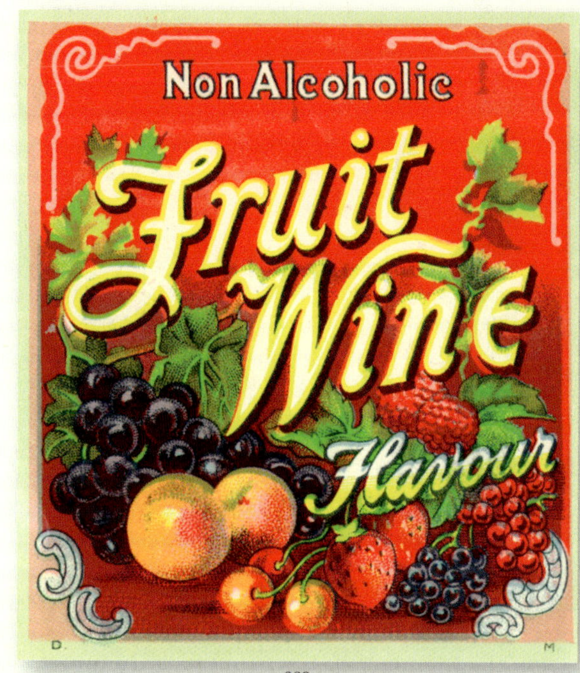

209

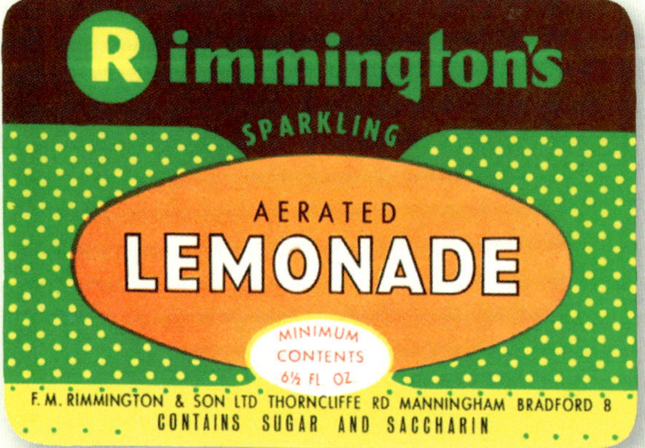

210

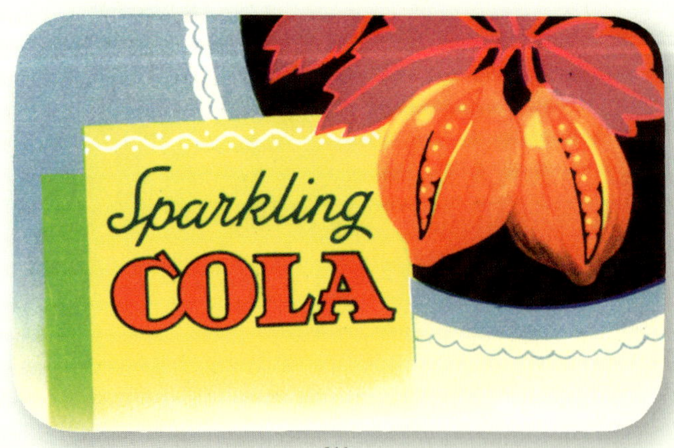

211

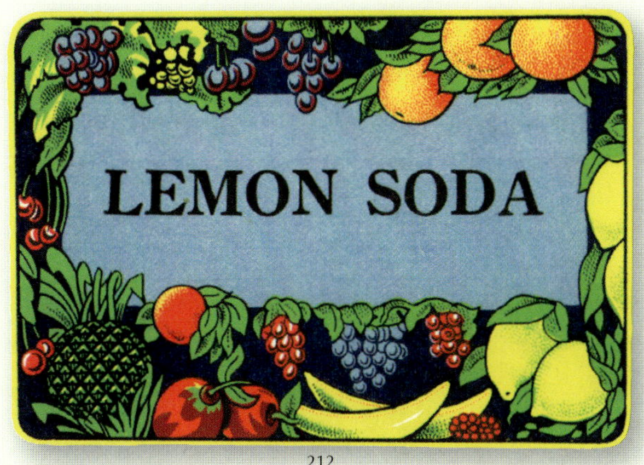

212

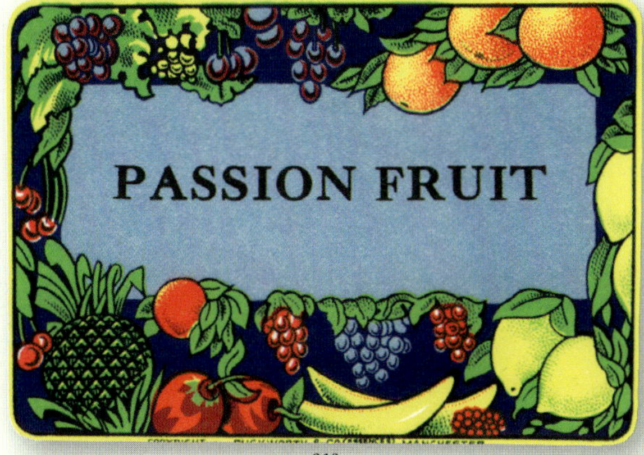

213

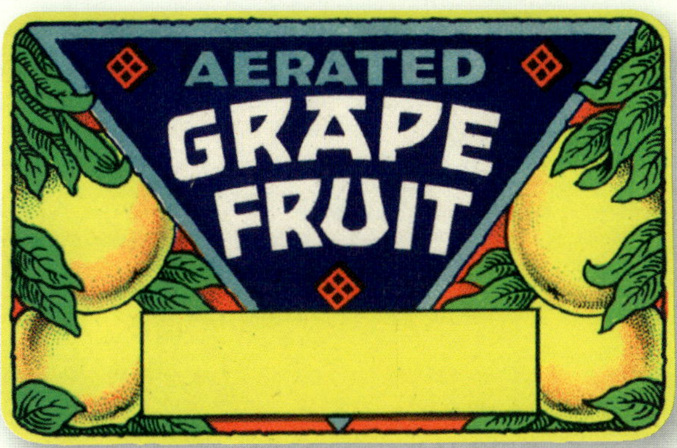

214

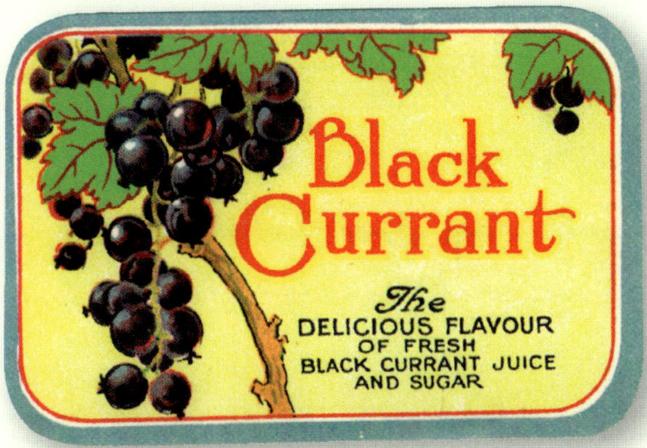

215

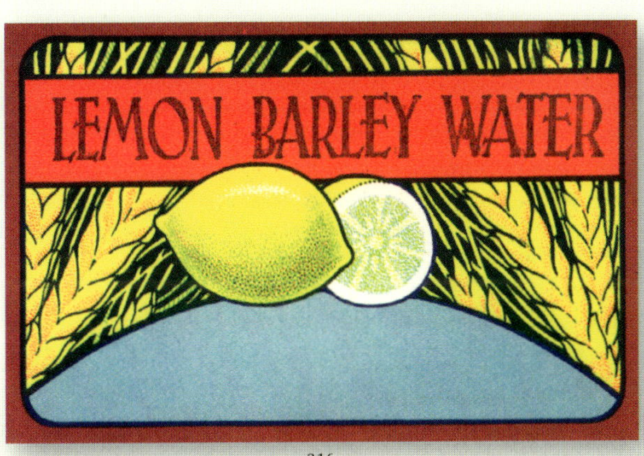

216

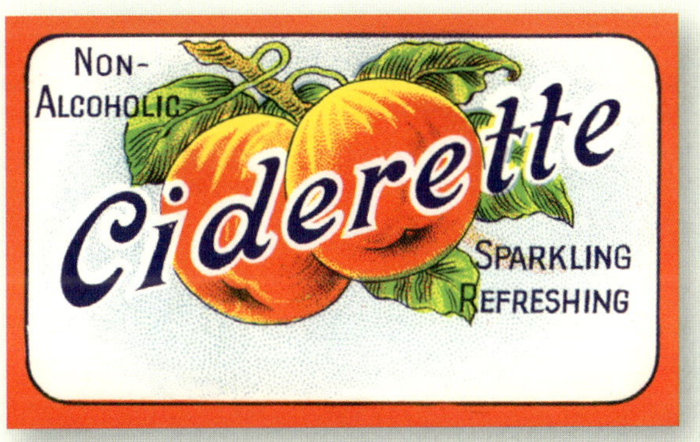

217

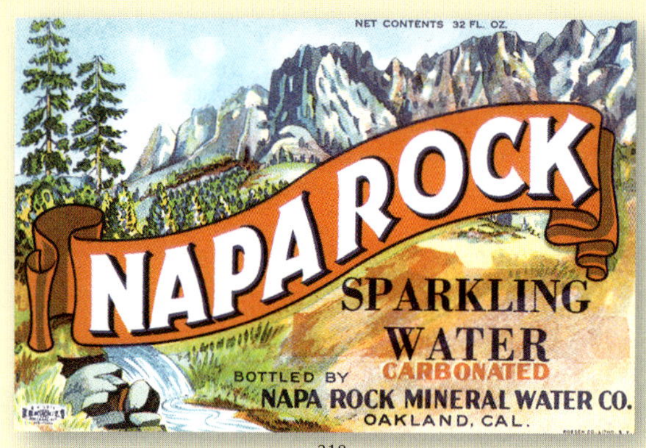

218

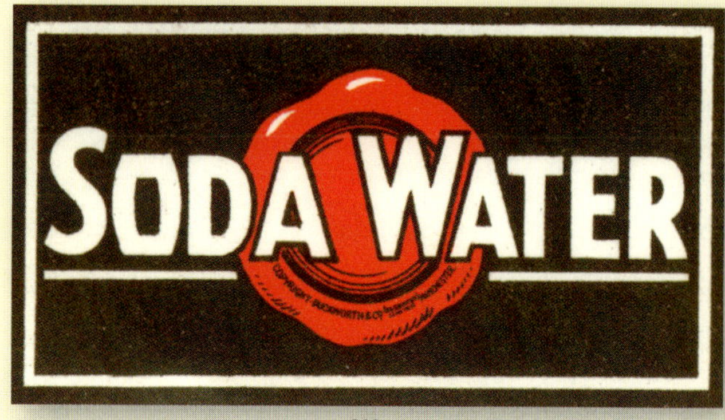

219

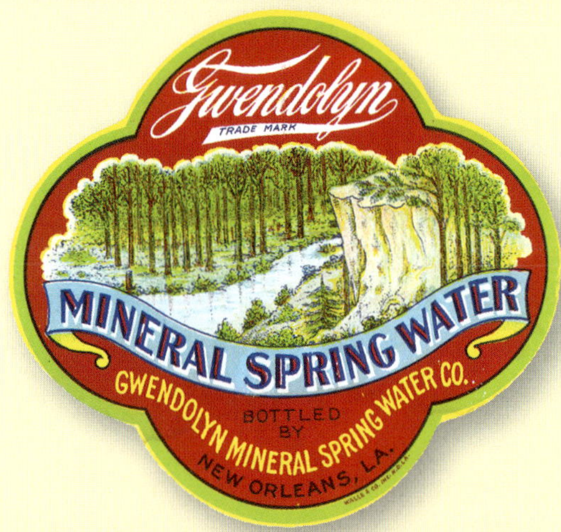

220

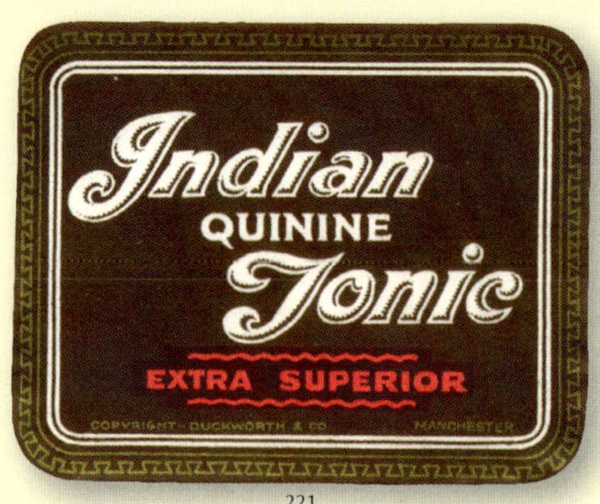

221

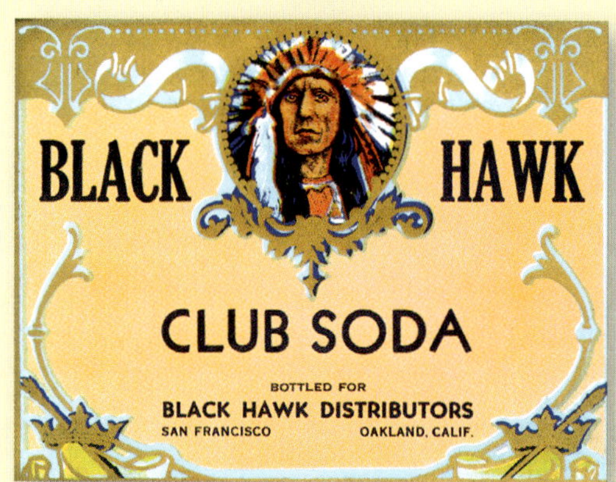

222

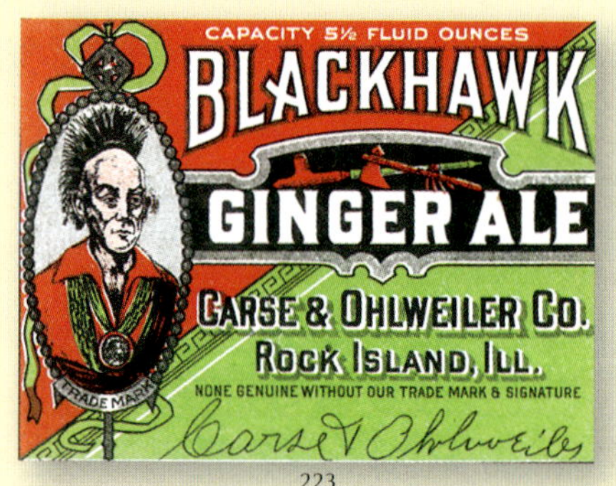

223

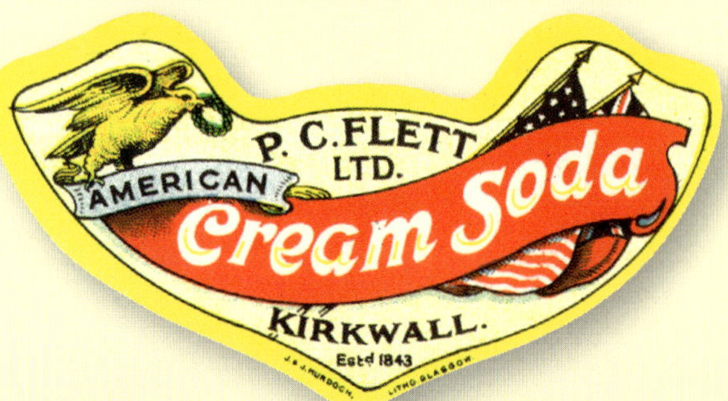

224

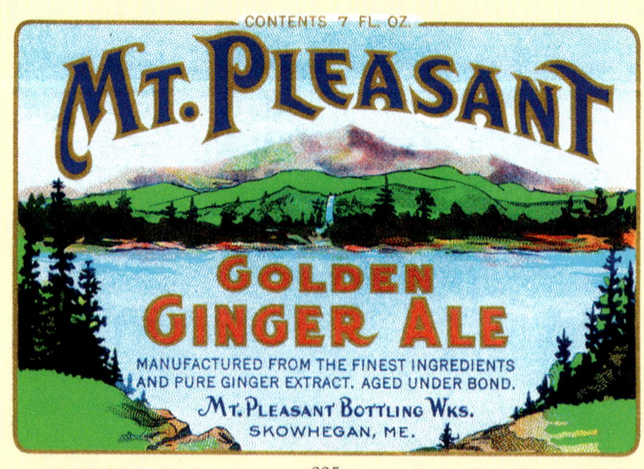

225

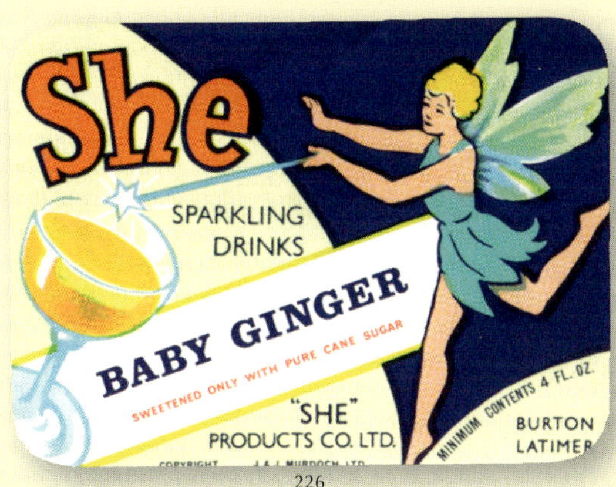

226

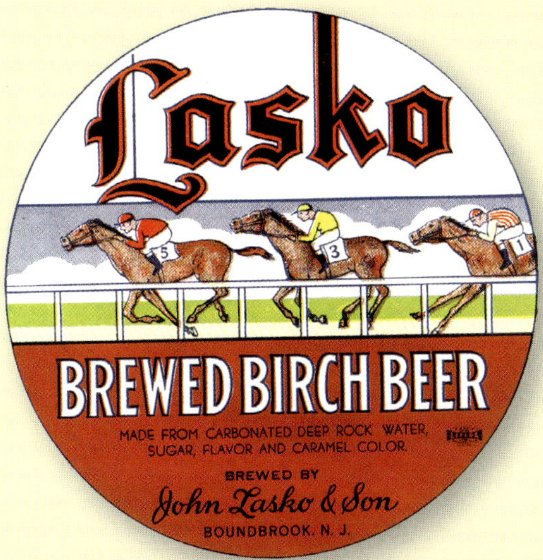

228

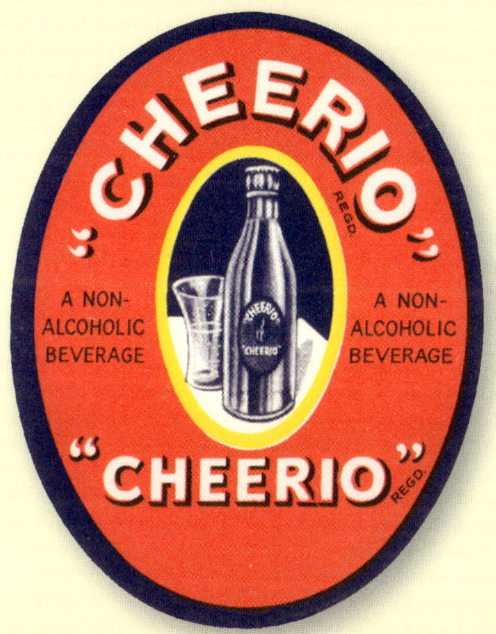

230

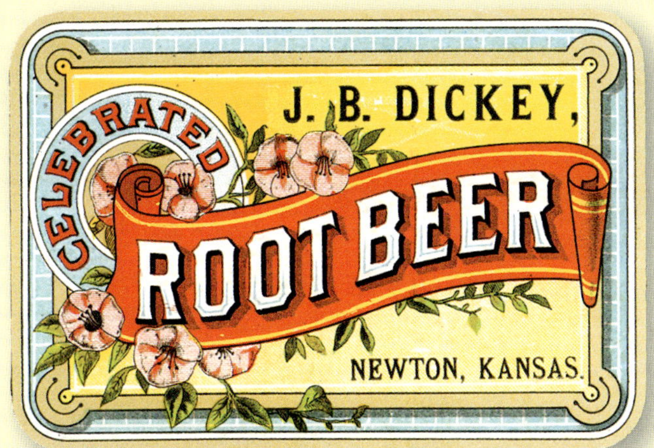

227

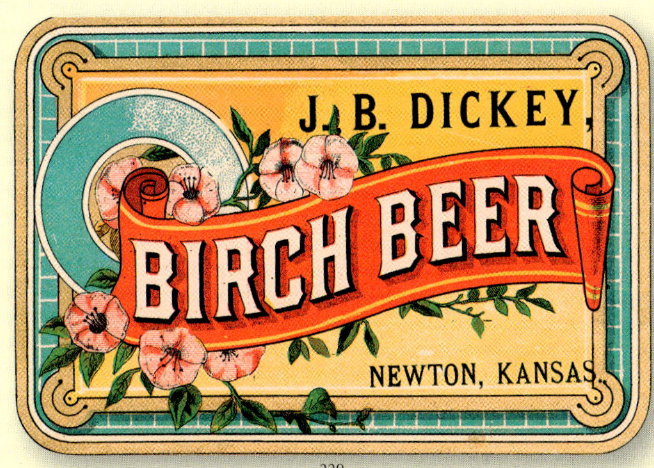

229

231

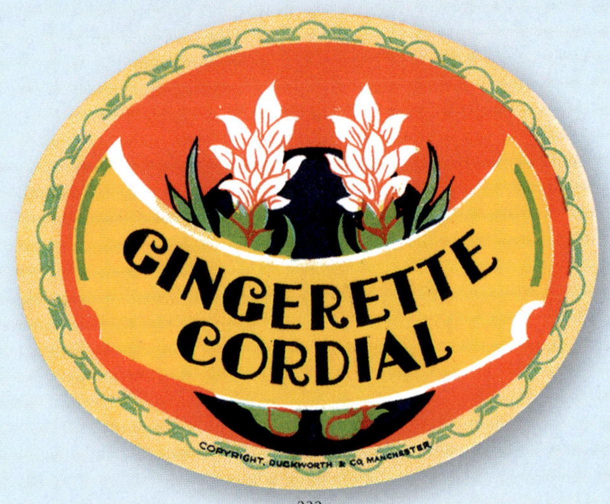

232

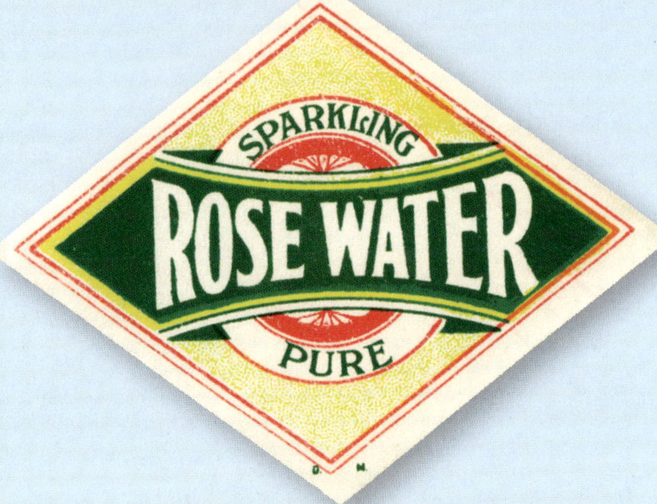

233

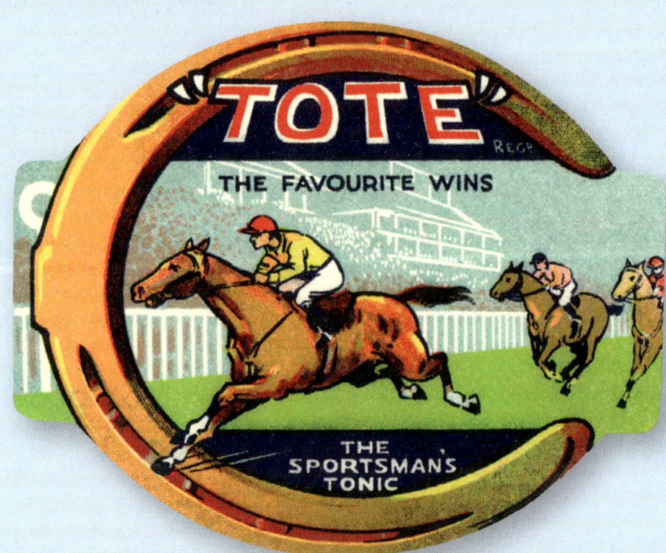

234

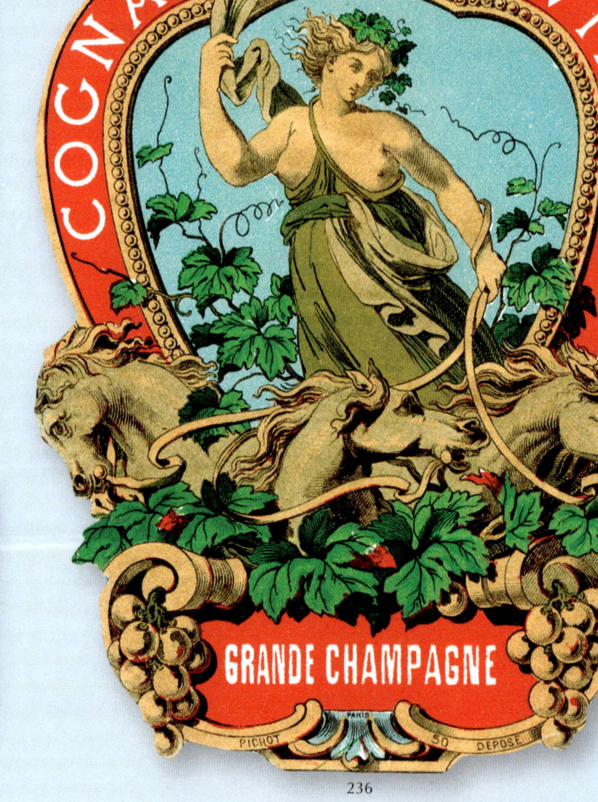

235

236

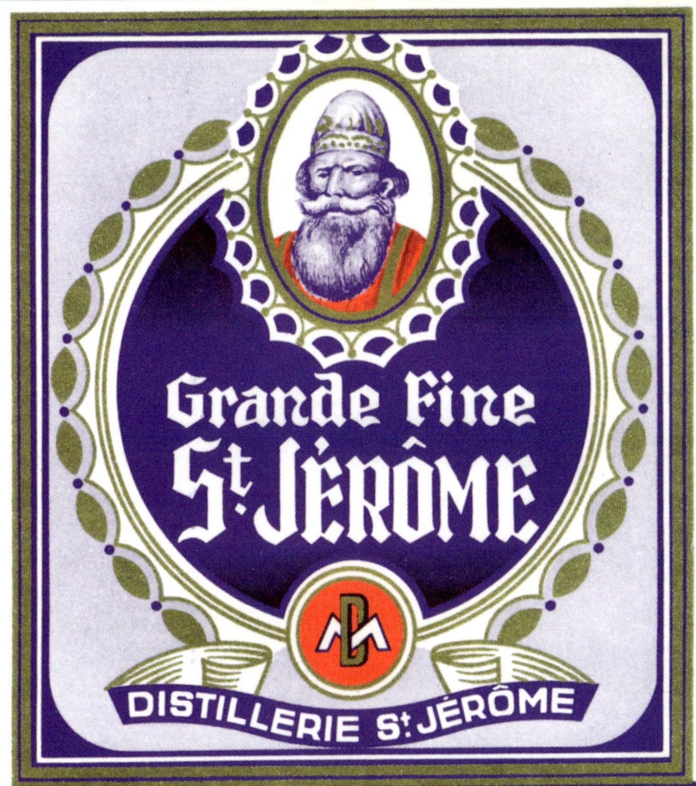

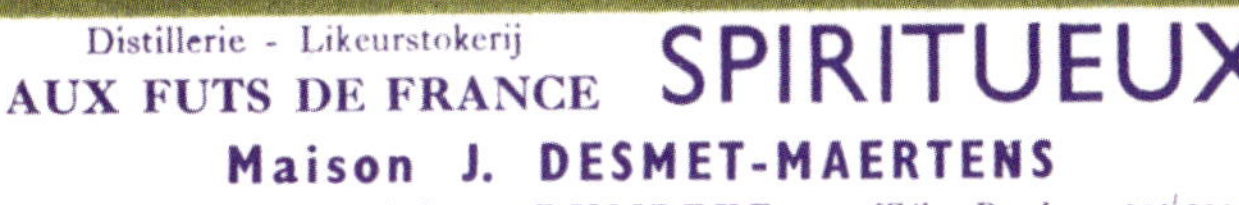

237

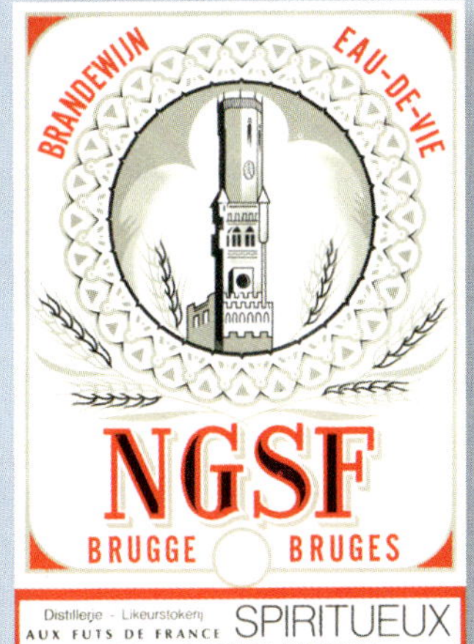

239

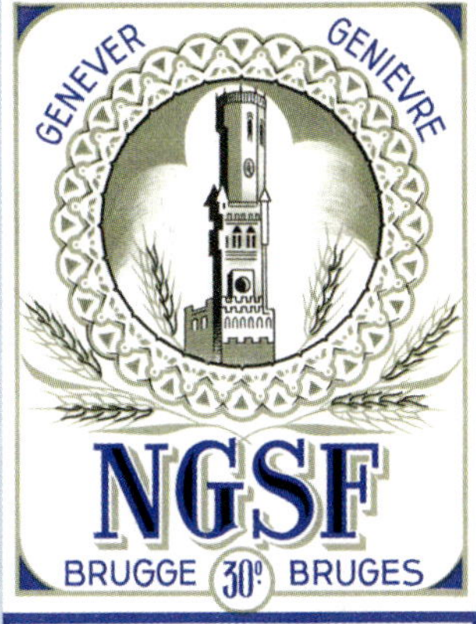

240

Kermis Vreugde label:

238

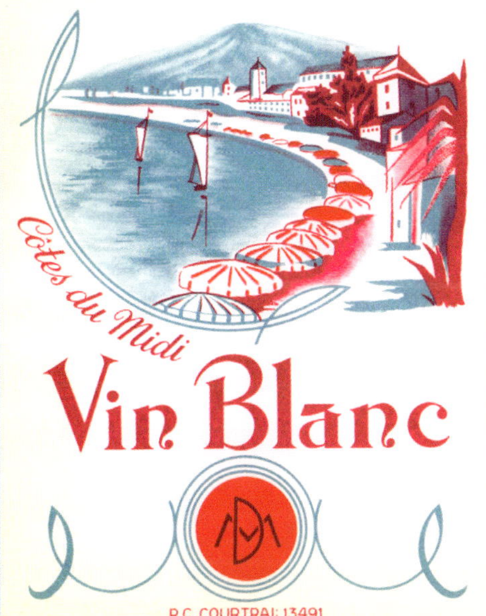

241

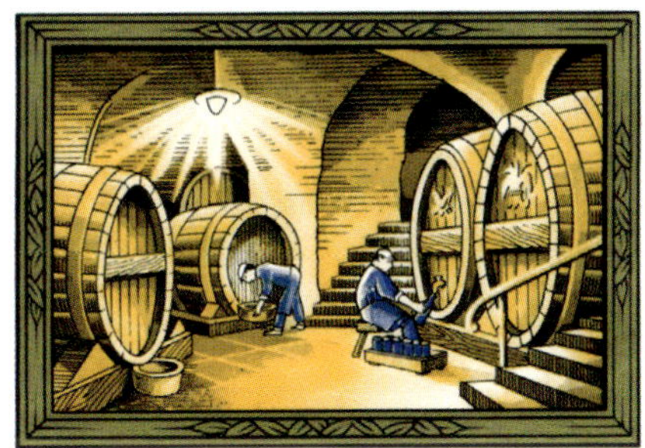

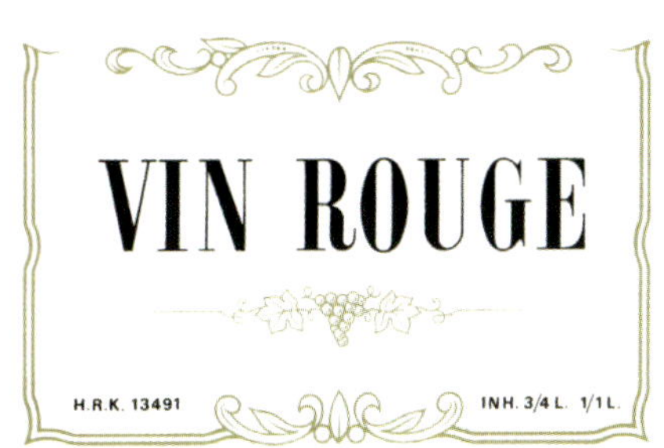

242

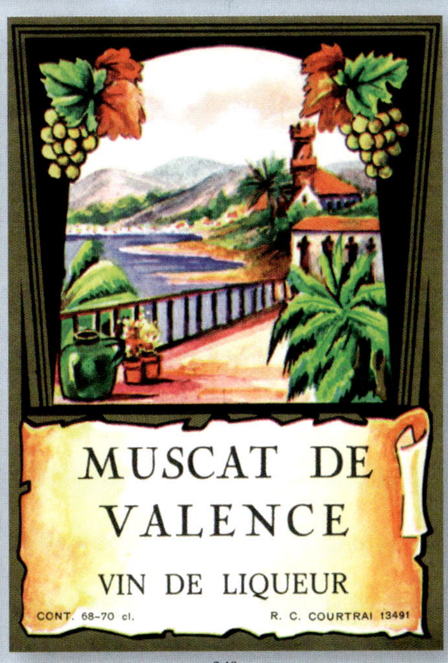

243

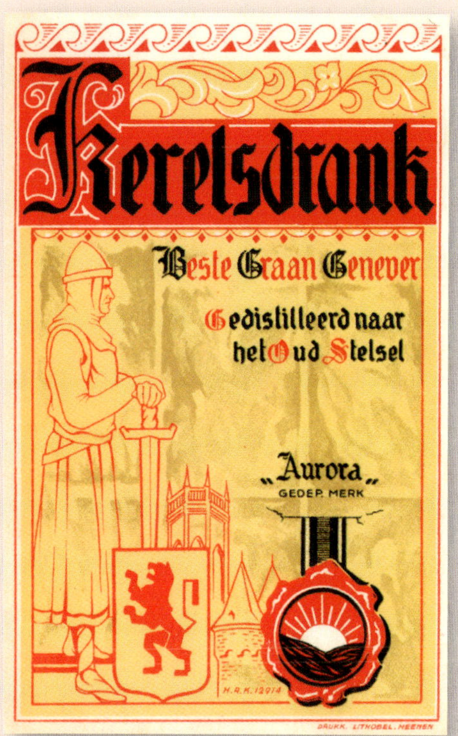

244

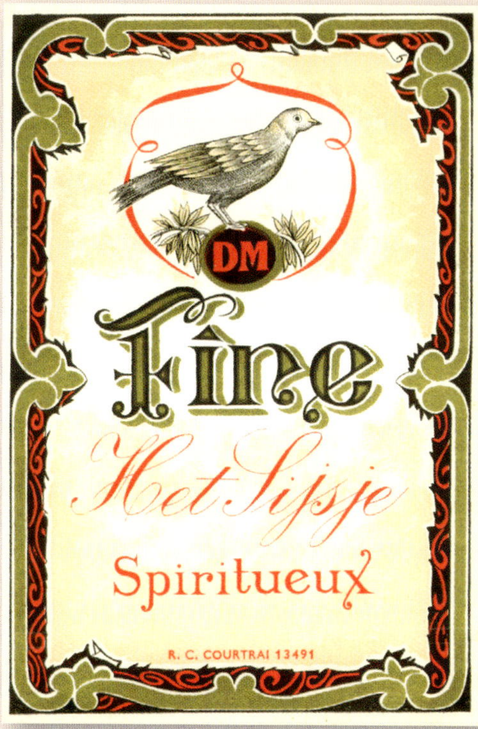

245

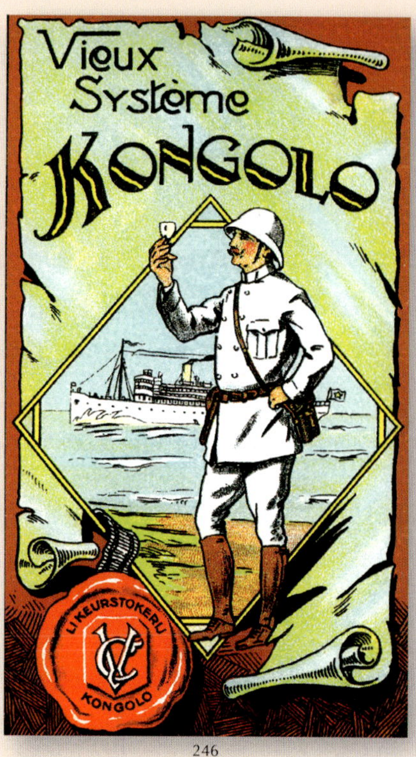

246

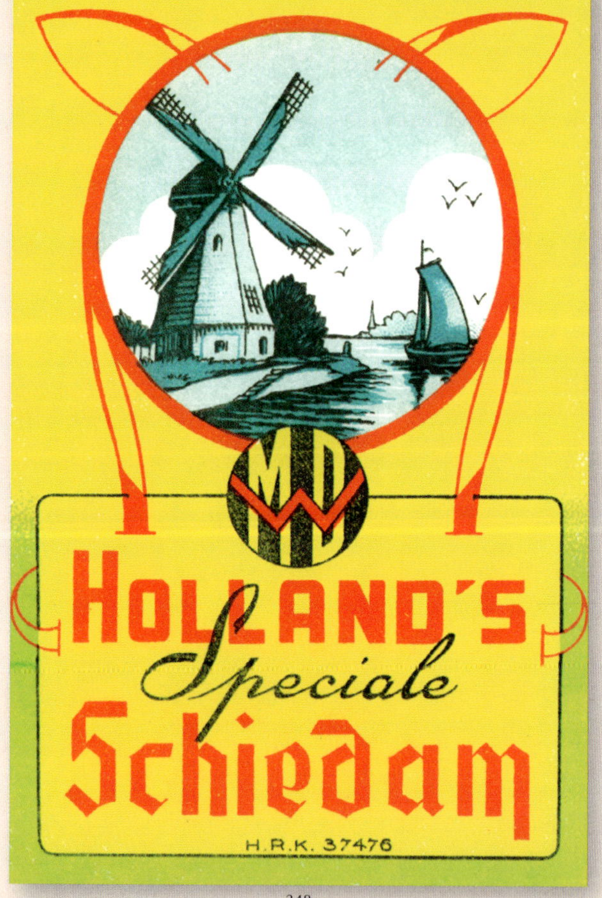

247

248

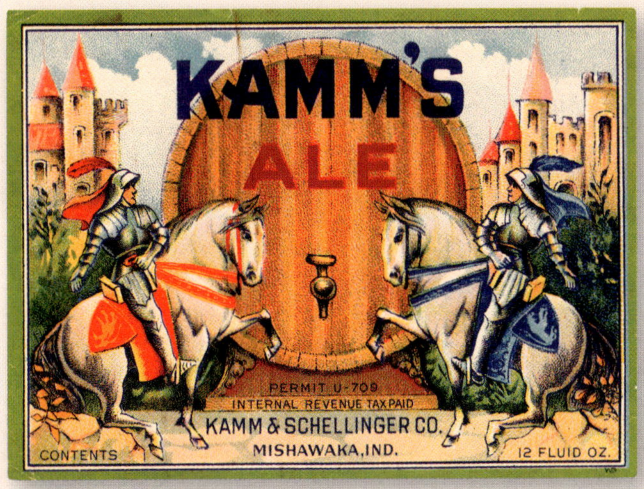

249

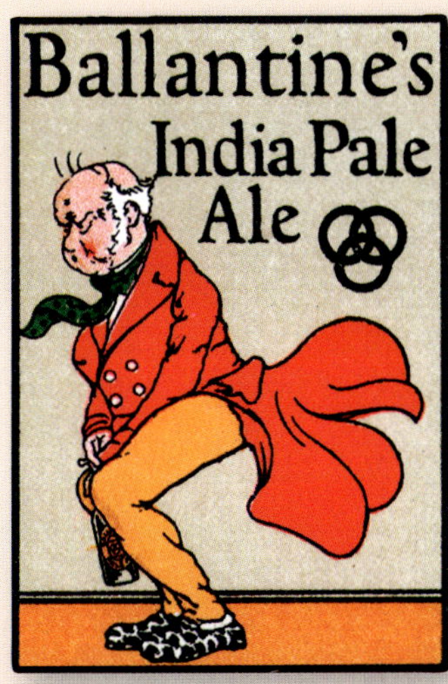

250

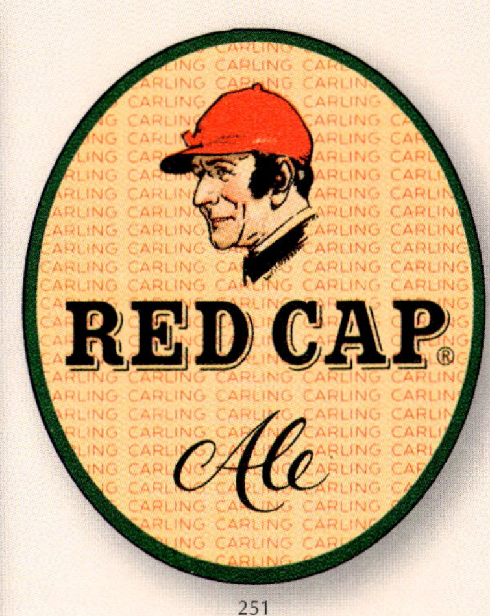

251

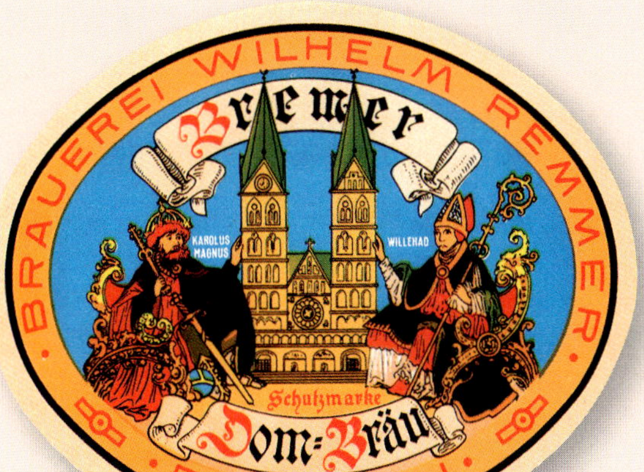

252

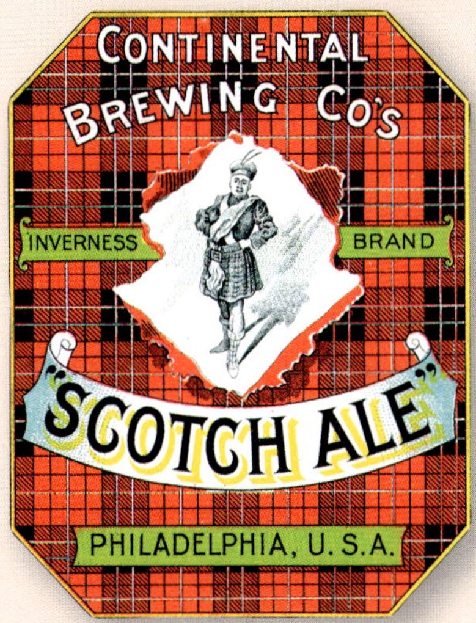

253

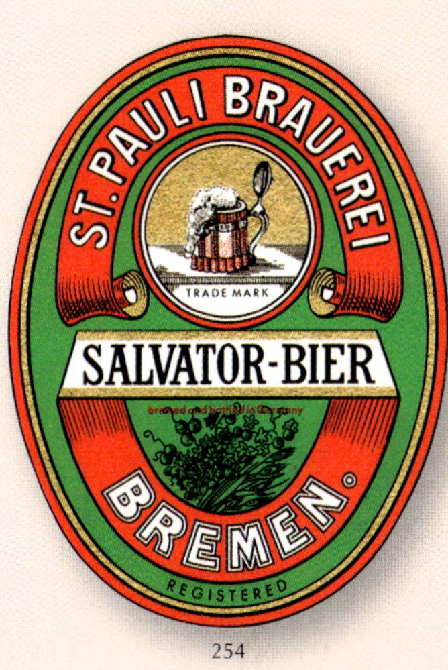

254

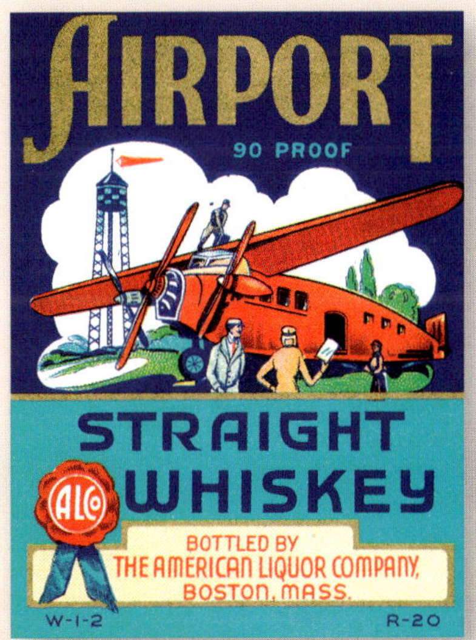

255

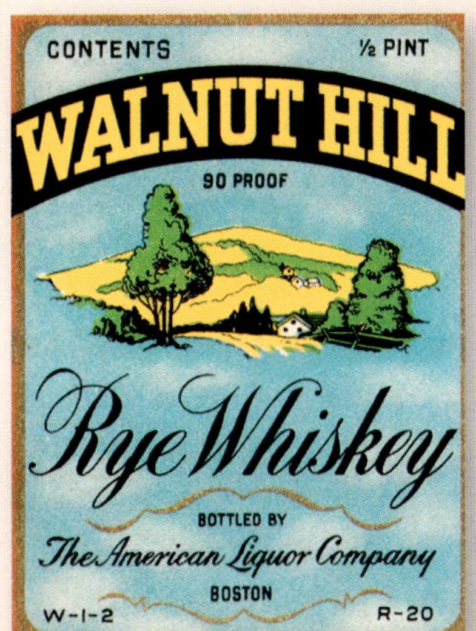

256

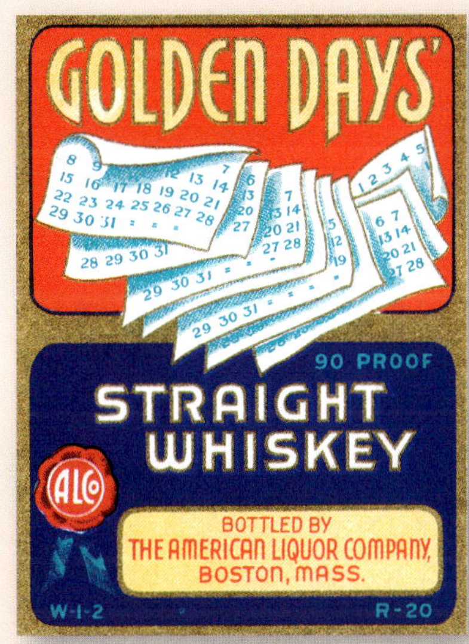

257

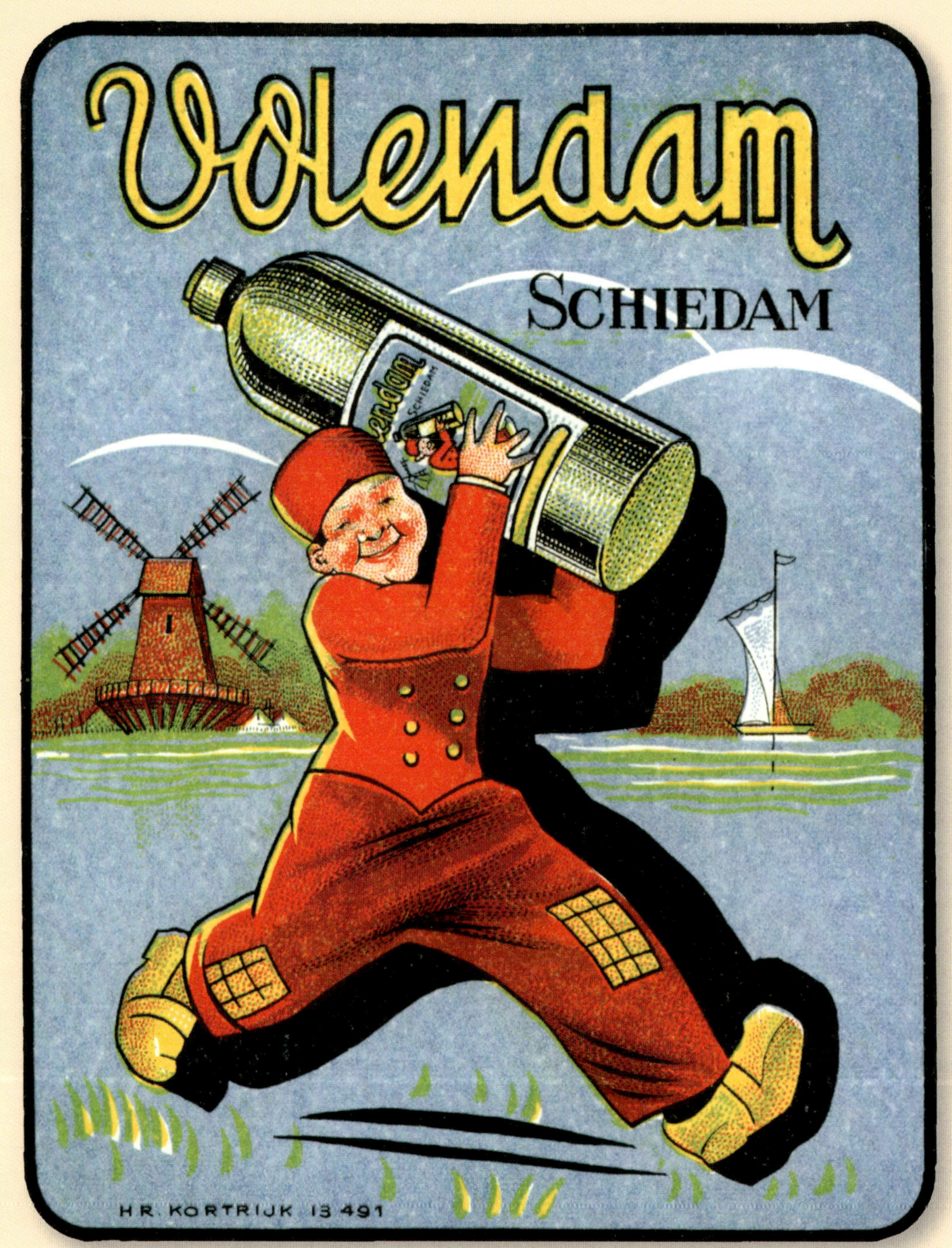
Volendam
SCHIEDAM
H.R. KORTRIJK 13 491

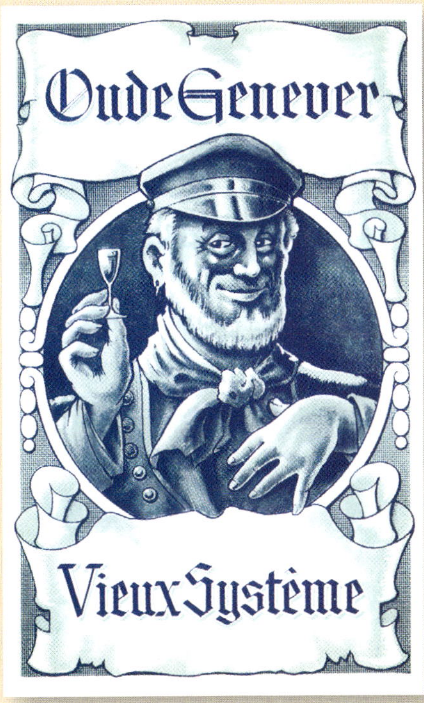

259

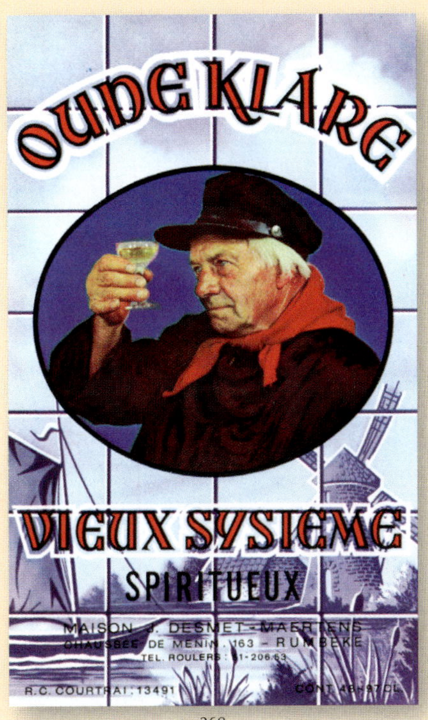

260

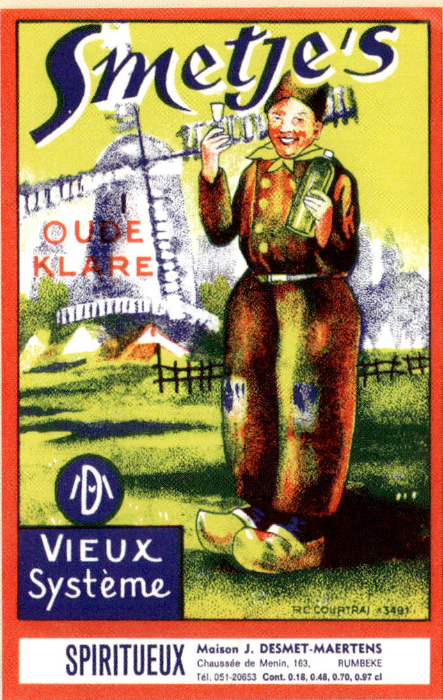

261

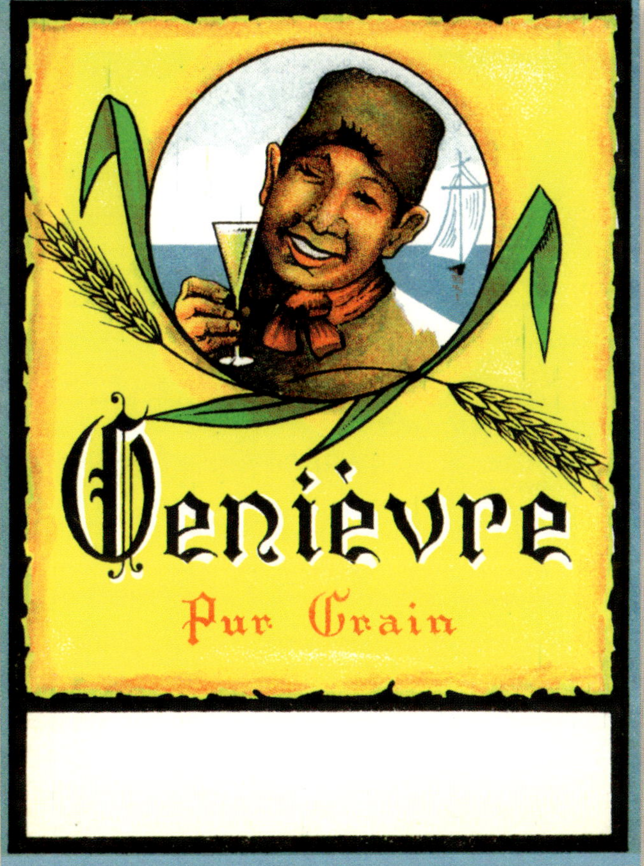

262

263

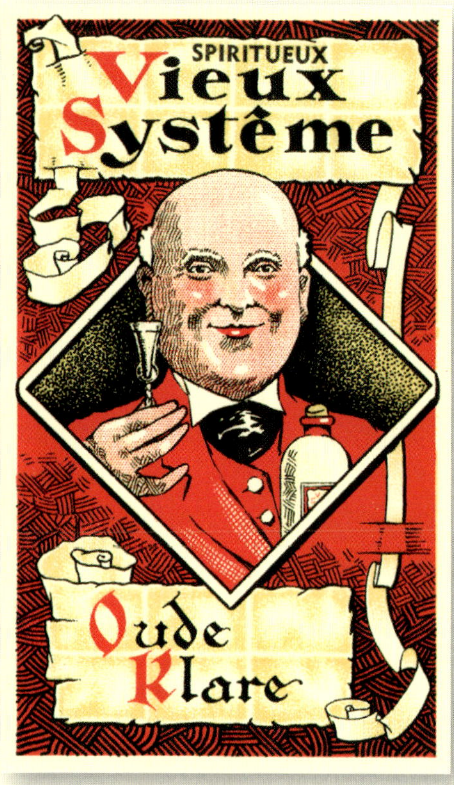

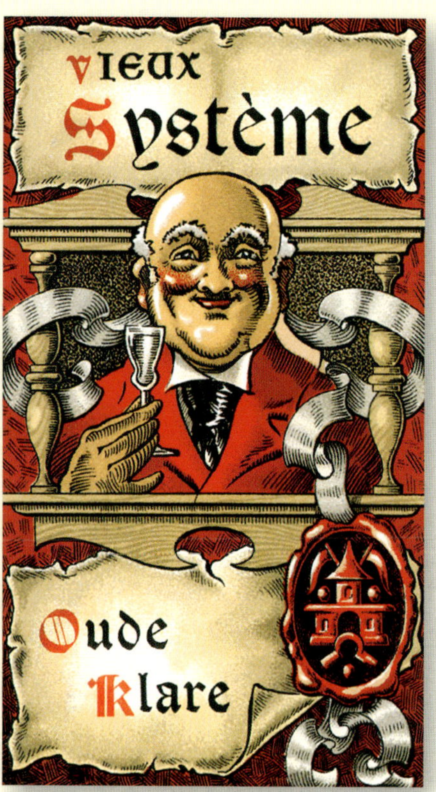

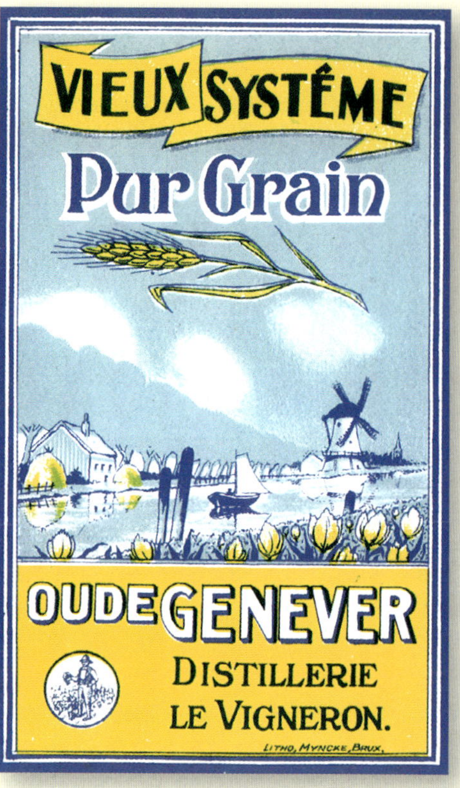

264   265   266

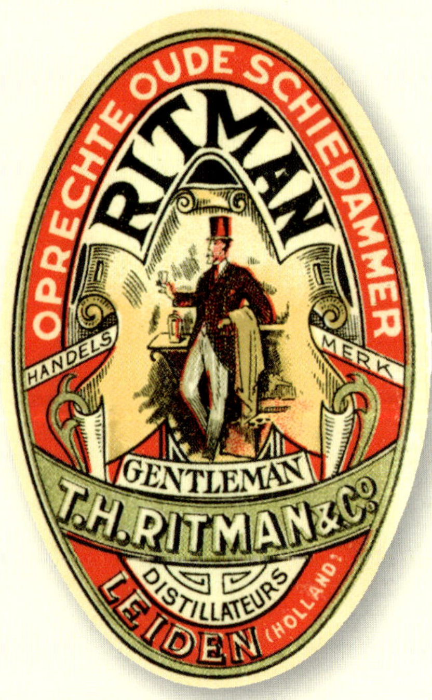

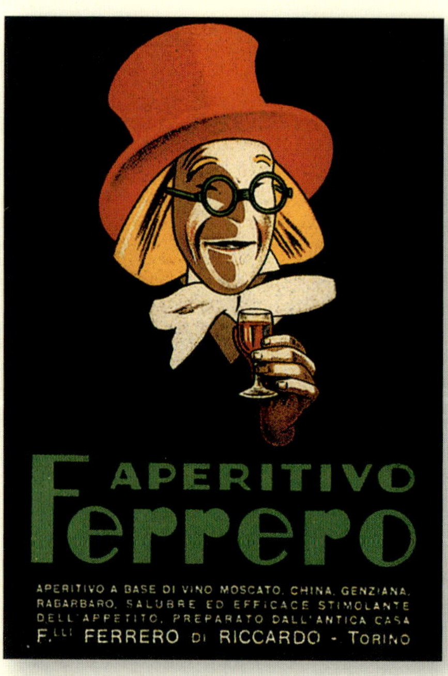

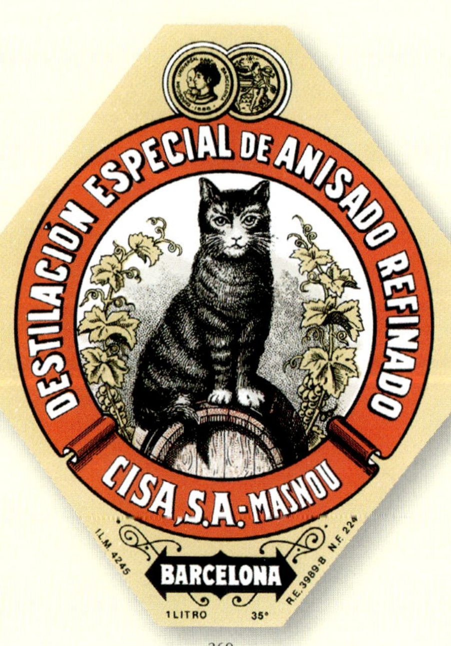

267   268   269

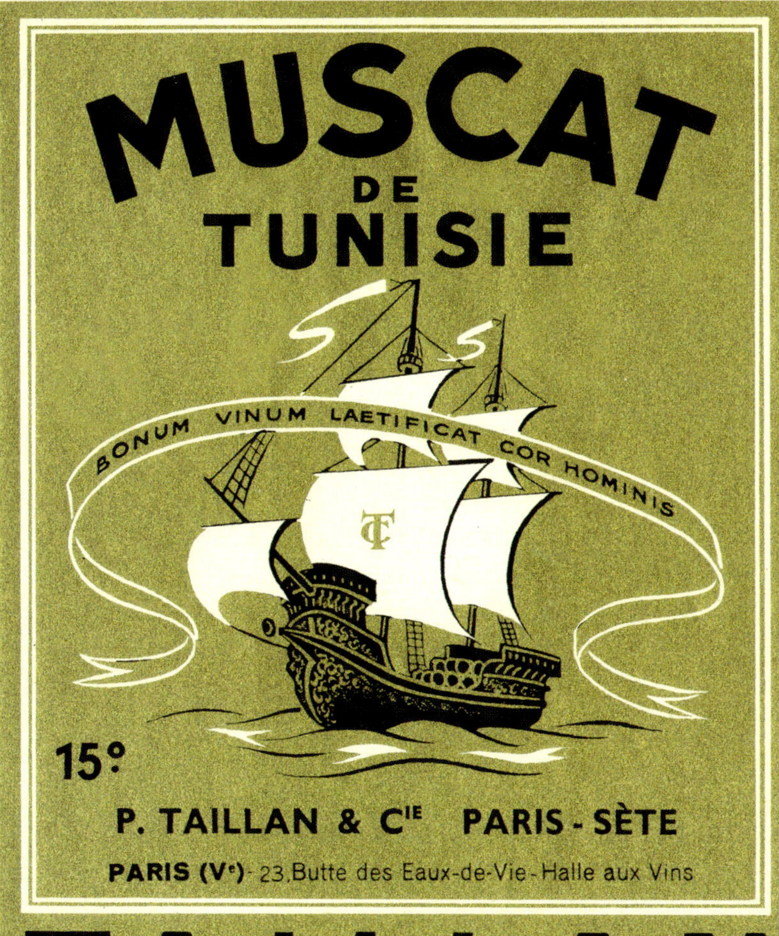

270

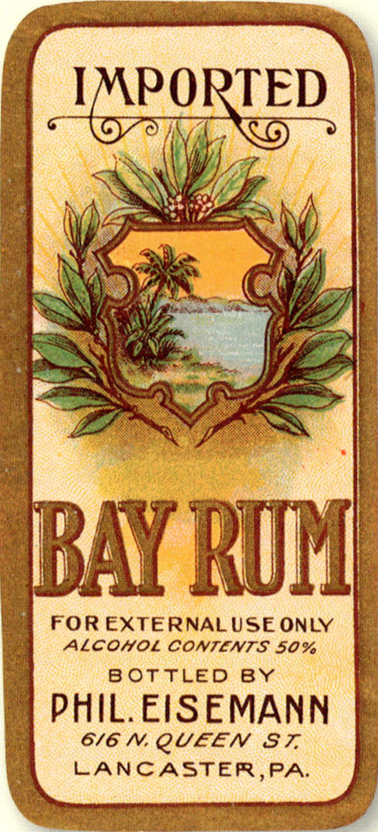

271

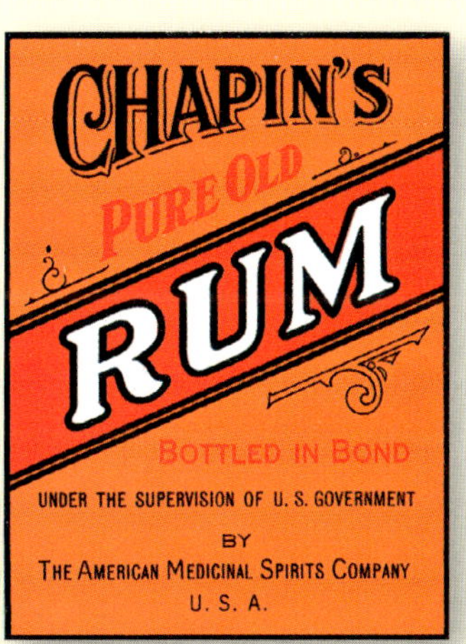

272

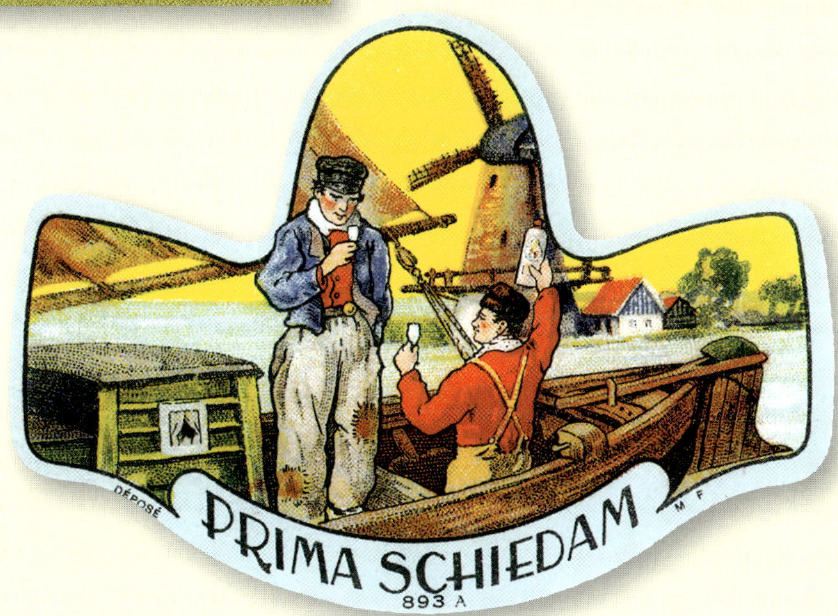

273

VIN SIERE I WIJN
BORDEAUX
Appellation Bordeaux Contrôlée
1979
Entrepôts et Caves A. V. F.
CONT. 70 CL.
R.C. Courtrai 78466

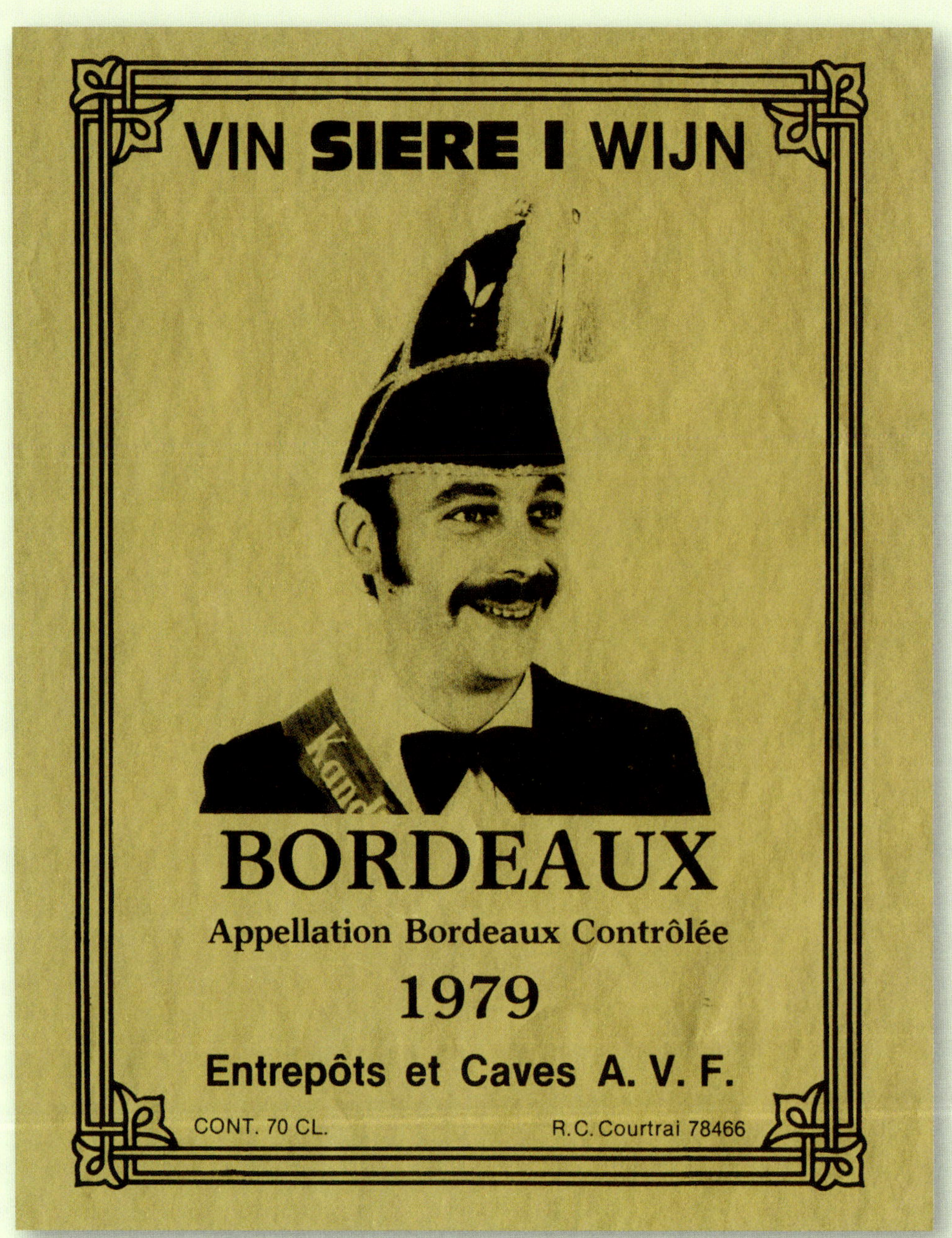

271

RHUM
KWANGO
SPIRITUEUX
MAISON
J. DESMET-MAERTENS
MENENSTEENWEG 163
RUMBEKE
TEL 051 20653
RC COURTRAI 13 491
CONT 018-048-
070-097L

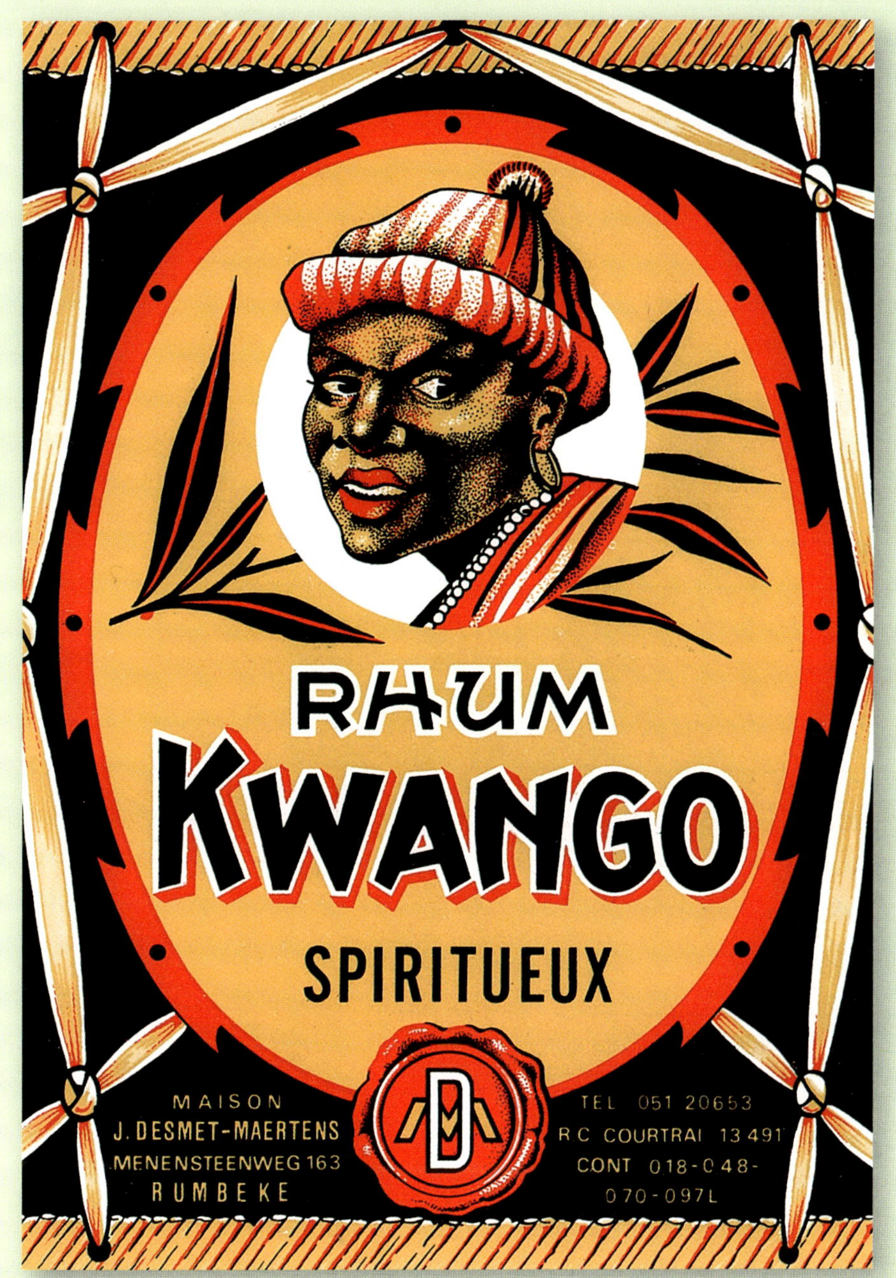

275

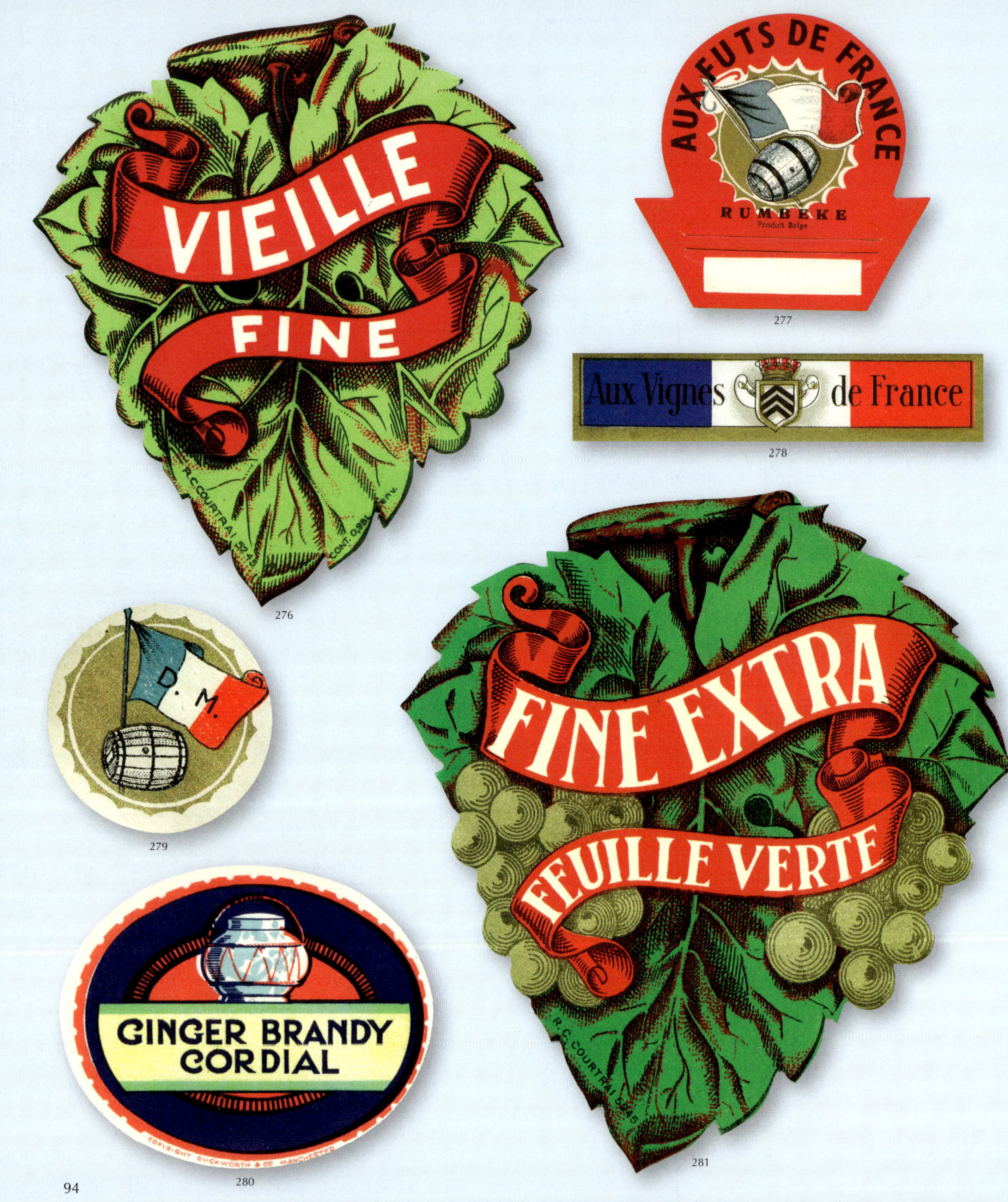
VIEILLE FINE
R.C. COURTRAI 5245 CONT. 0.98L
276
AUX FUTS DE FRANCE
RUMBEKE
Produit Belge
277
Aux Vignes de France
278
D.M.
279
GINGER BRANDY CORDIAL
COPYRIGHT DUCKWORTH & CO. MANCHESTER
280
FINE EXTRA
FEUILLE VERTE
R.C. COURTRAI 5245
281

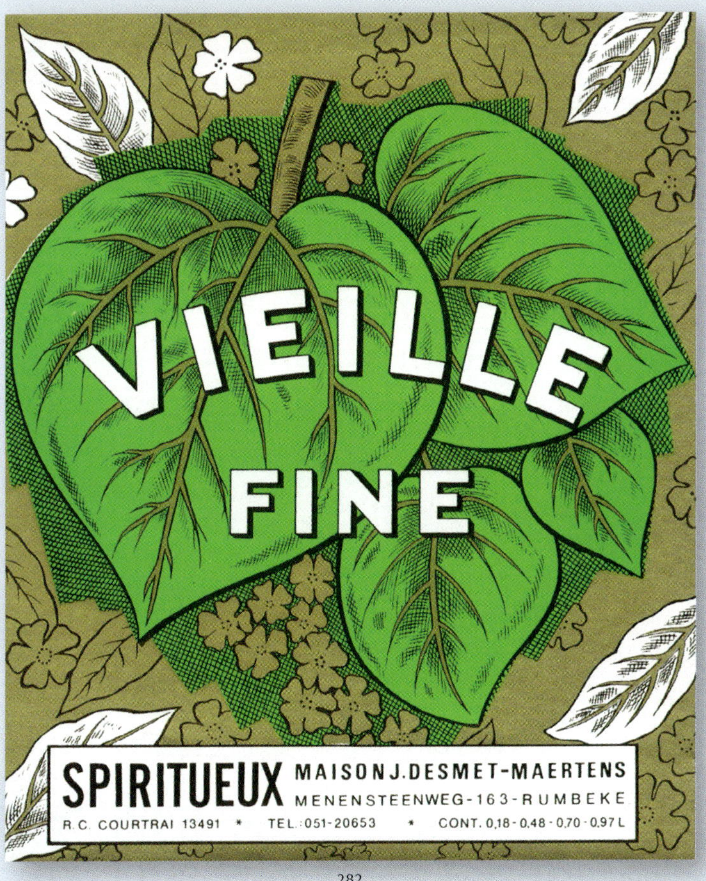

282

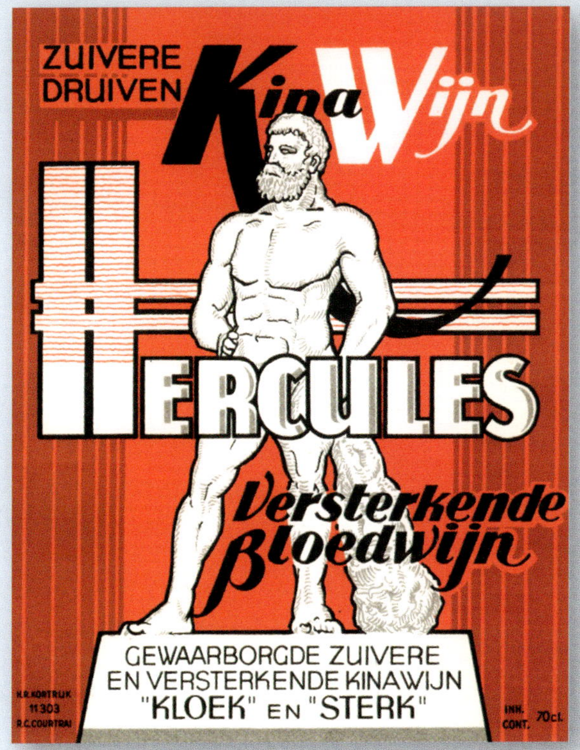

283

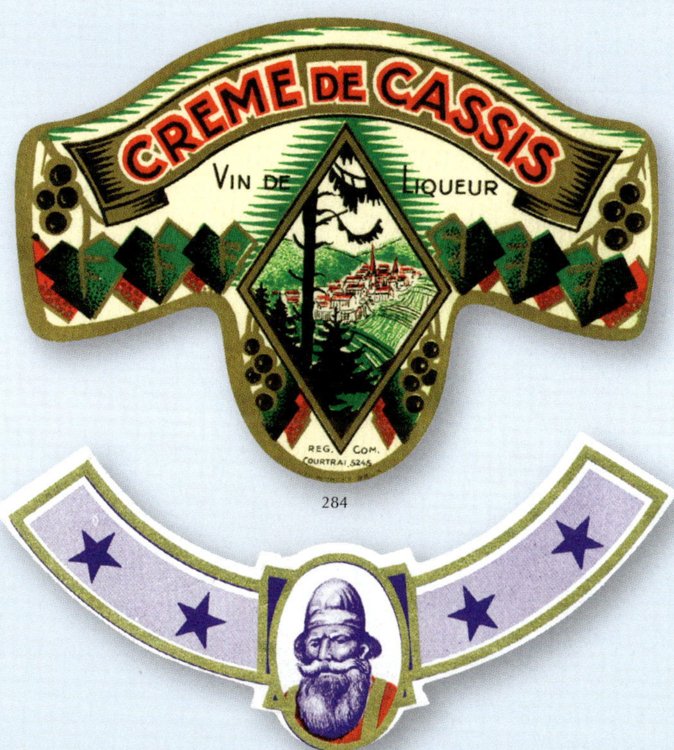

284

285

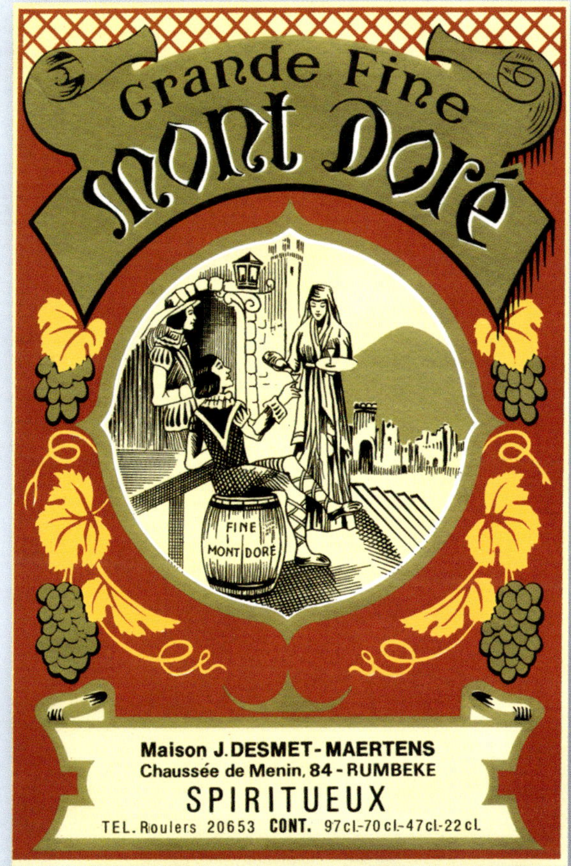

286

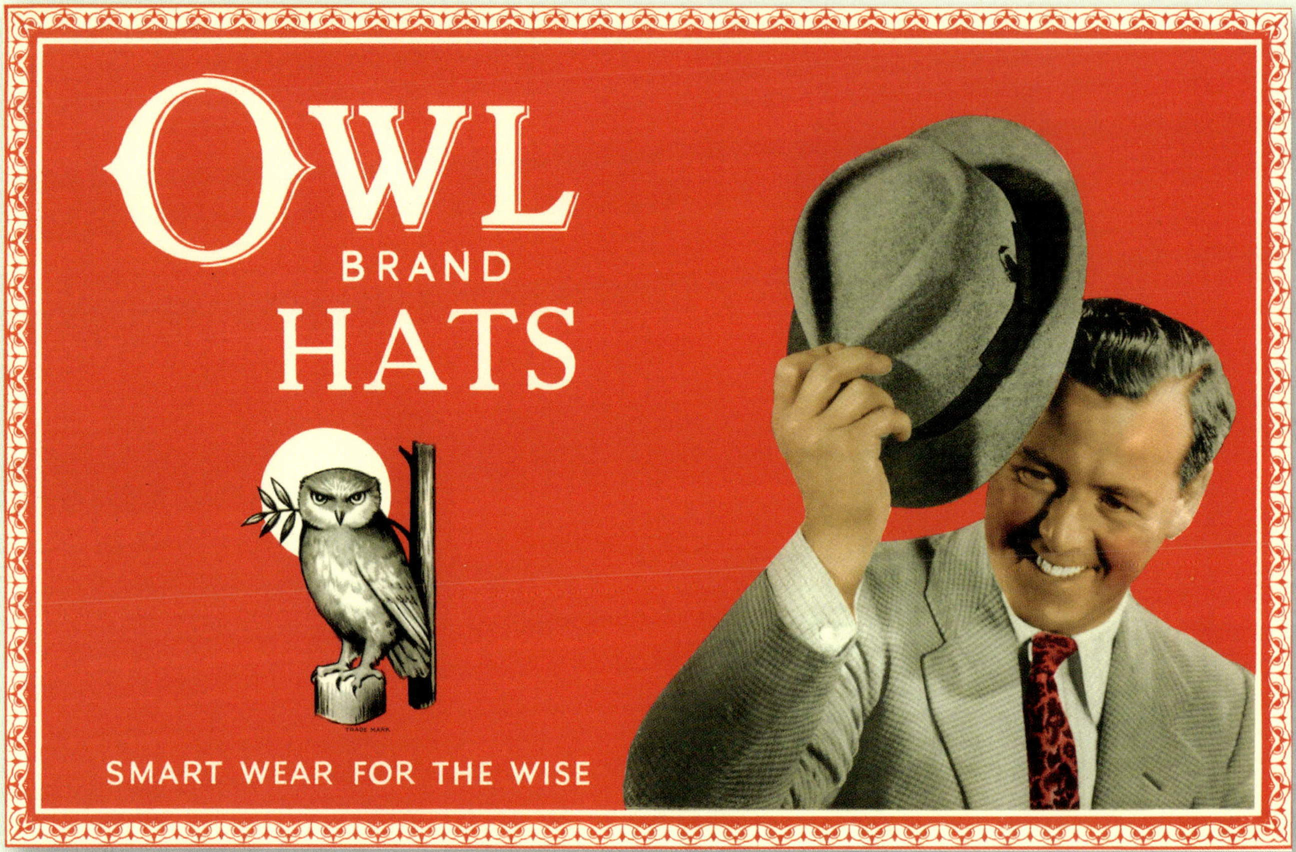

OWL
BRAND
HATS
SMART WEAR FOR THE WISE

287

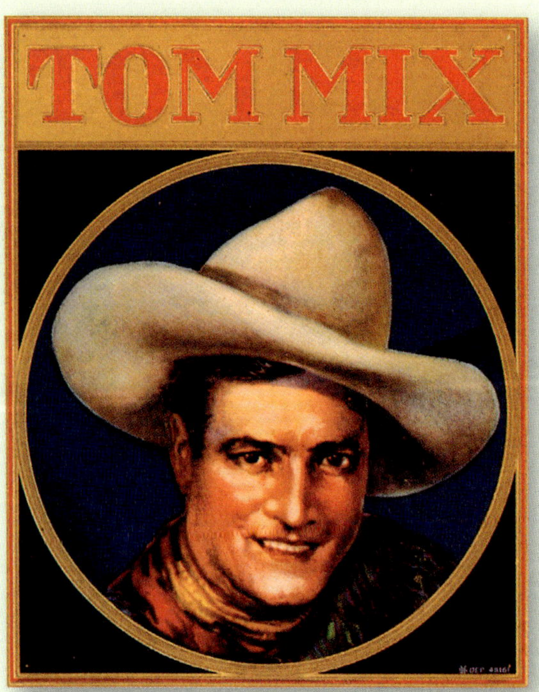

288

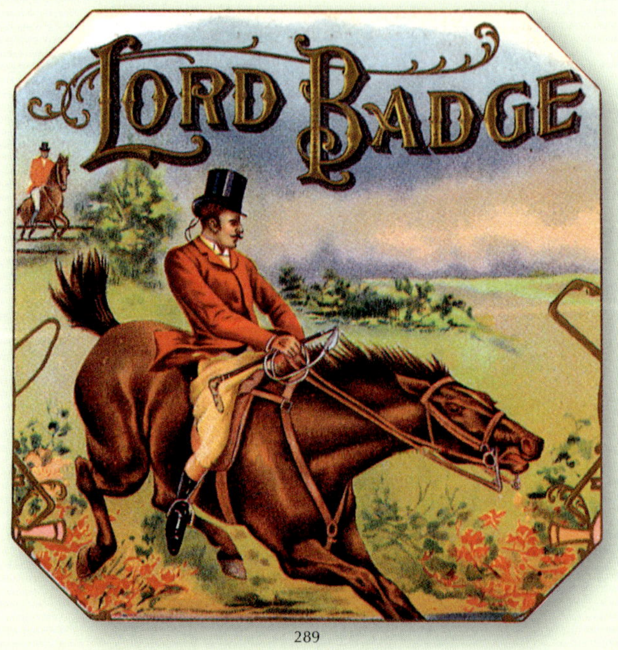

289

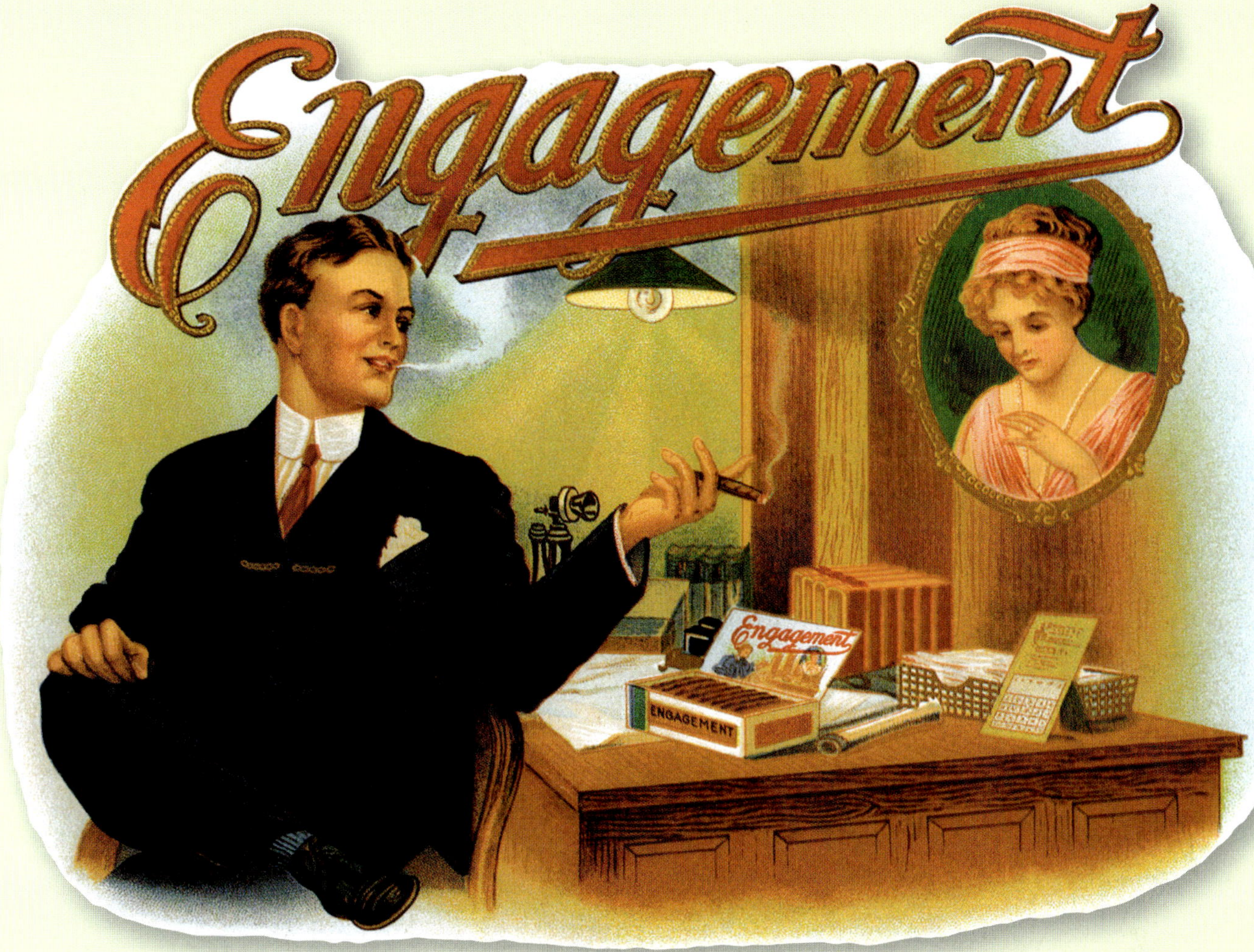

Engagement

290

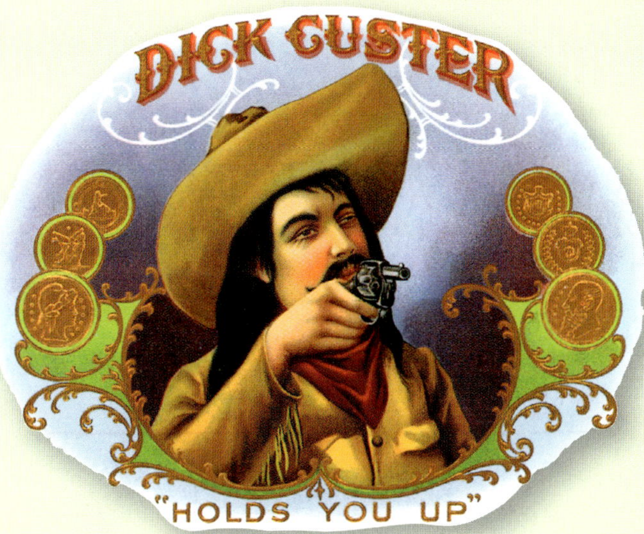

291

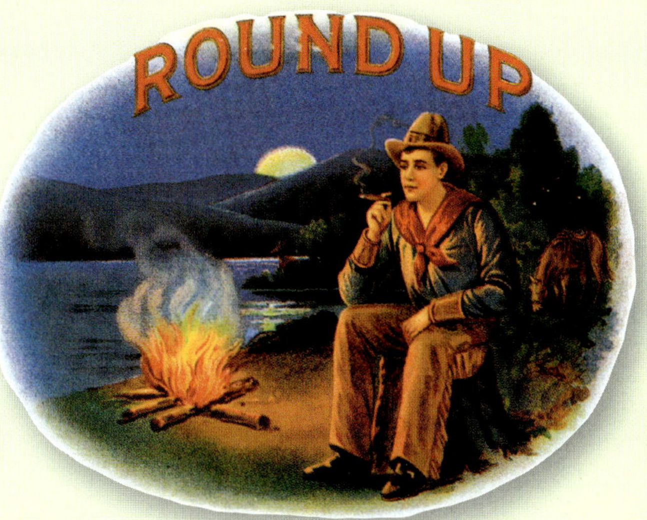

292

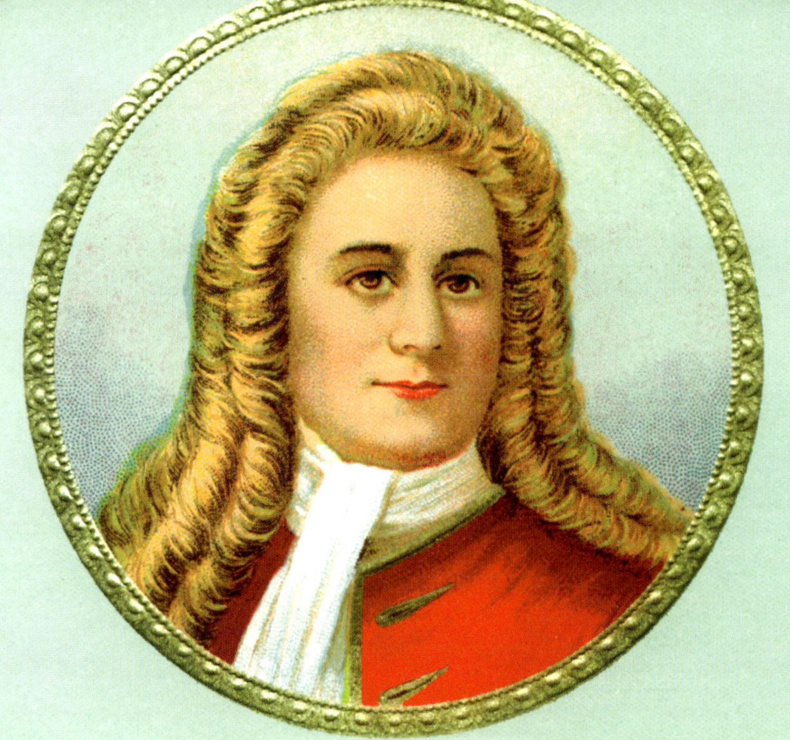

PETER SCHUYLER
G.W. VAN SLYKE & HORTON
ODD MOMENTS
ODD MOMENTS
ODD MOMENTS

CLINT FORD

294

RED TIPS
RED TIPS
RED TIPS
RED TIPS
RED TIPS
RED TIPS
RED TIPS
RED TIPS
RED TIPS

295

BIG JOHN
PLUG CUT
TOBACCO
MADE BY
JOHN WEISERT
TOBACCO CO.
ST. LOUIS
U.S.A.
BIG JOHN
The World's Greatest
SMOKE or CHEW
BIG JOHN
PLUG CUT
TOBACCO
MADE BY
JOHN WEISERT
TOBACCO CO.
ST. LOUIS
U.S.A.
BIG JOHN
The World's Greatest
SMOKE or CHEW
FACTORY
No. TP-81
OF MISSOURI

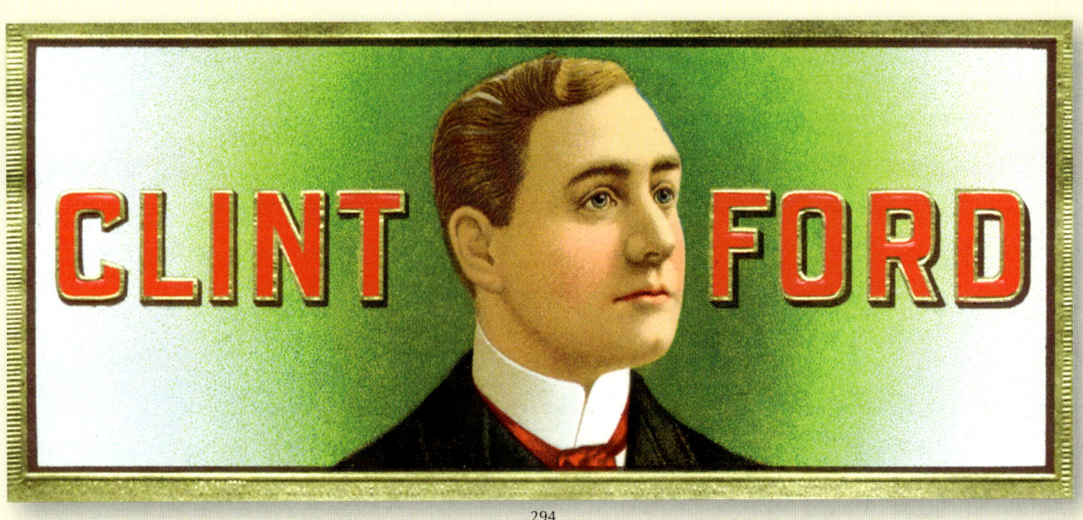

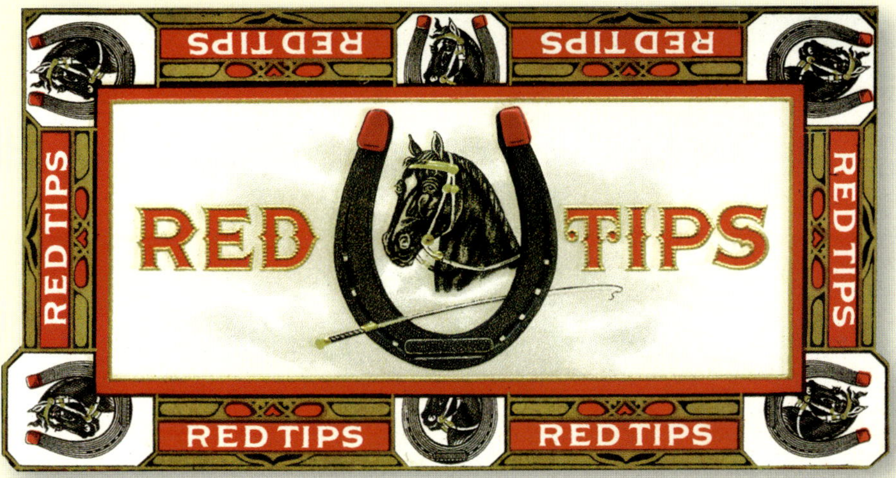

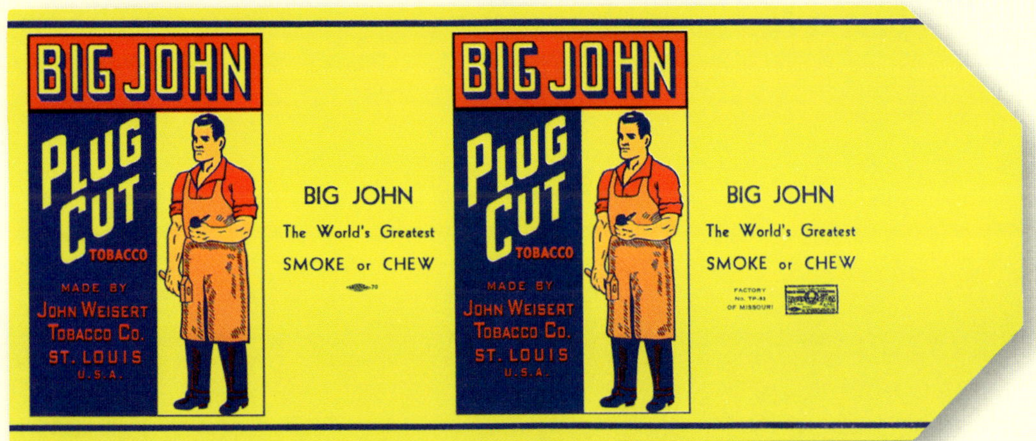

296

CHECKERS
MILD & MELLOW

297

SONNY BOY

298

SHERLOCK HOLMES
SHERLOCK HOLMES

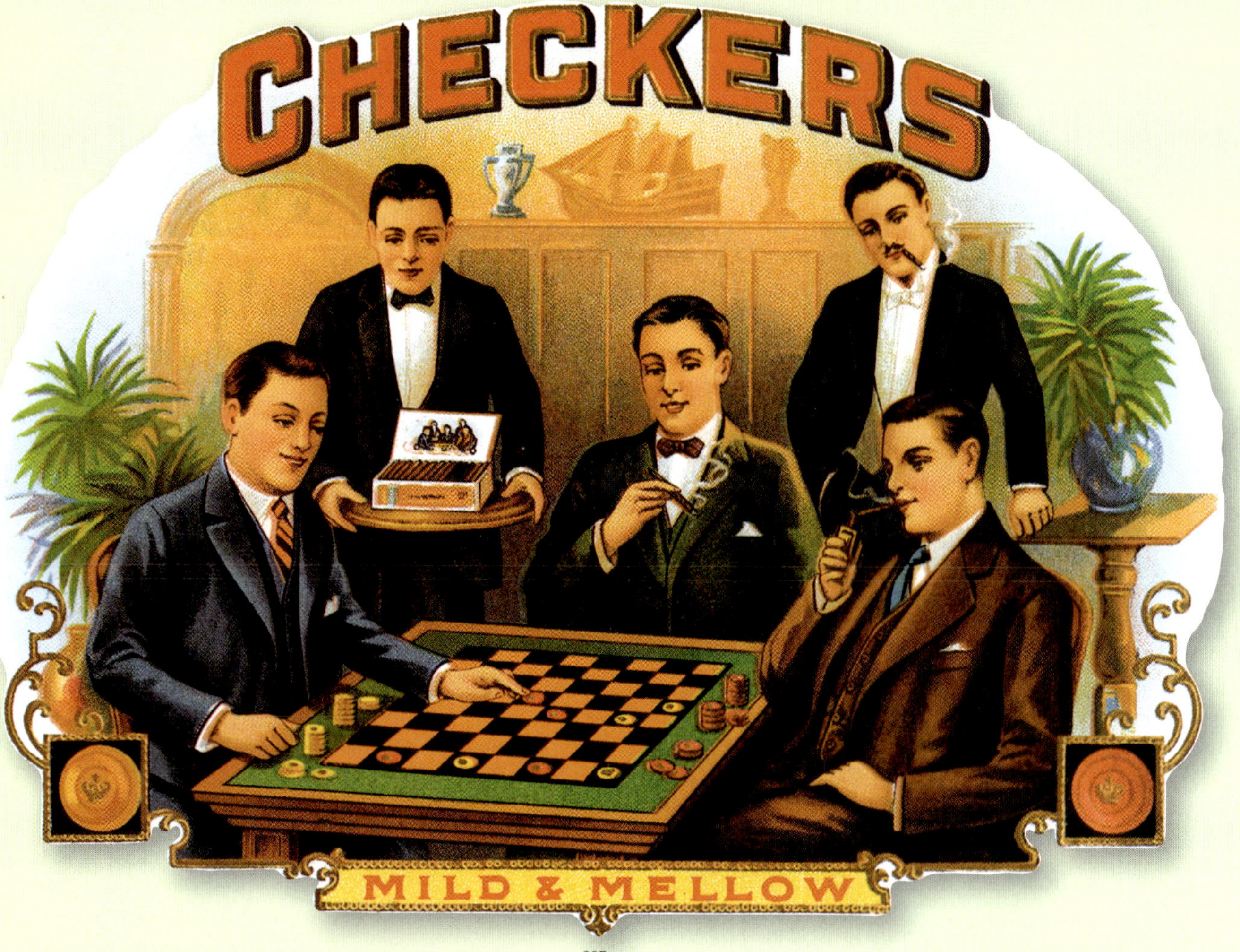

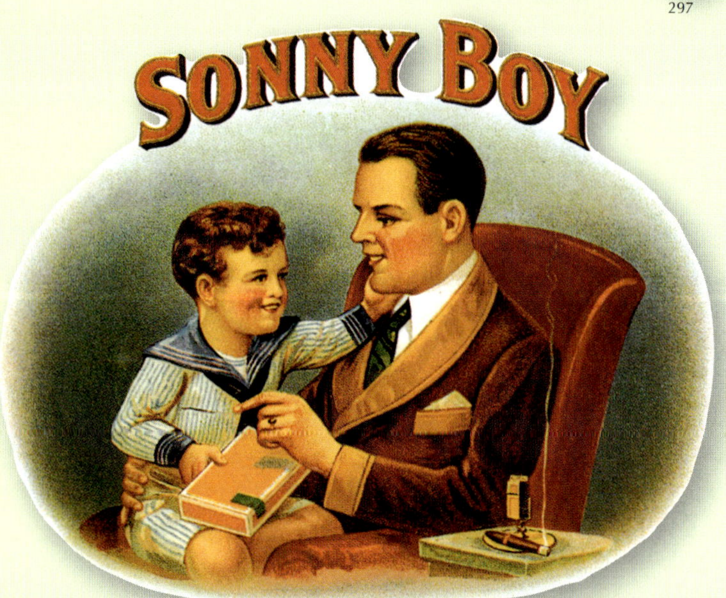

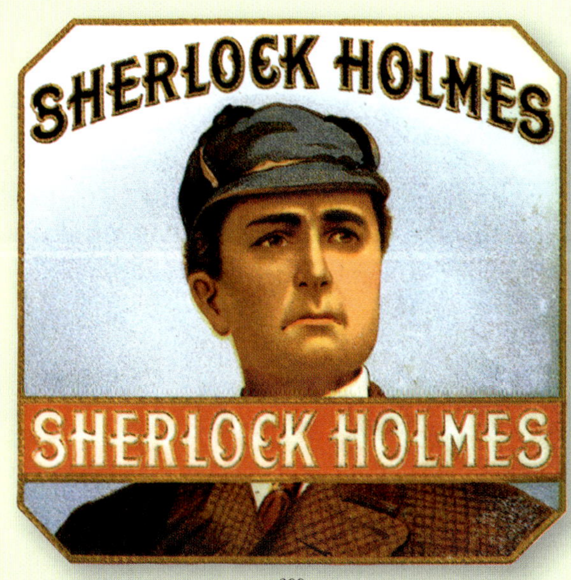

299

JOLLY BAND

300

RIGOLETTO
RIGOLETTO
RIGOLETTO

301

CAPTAIN CORKER

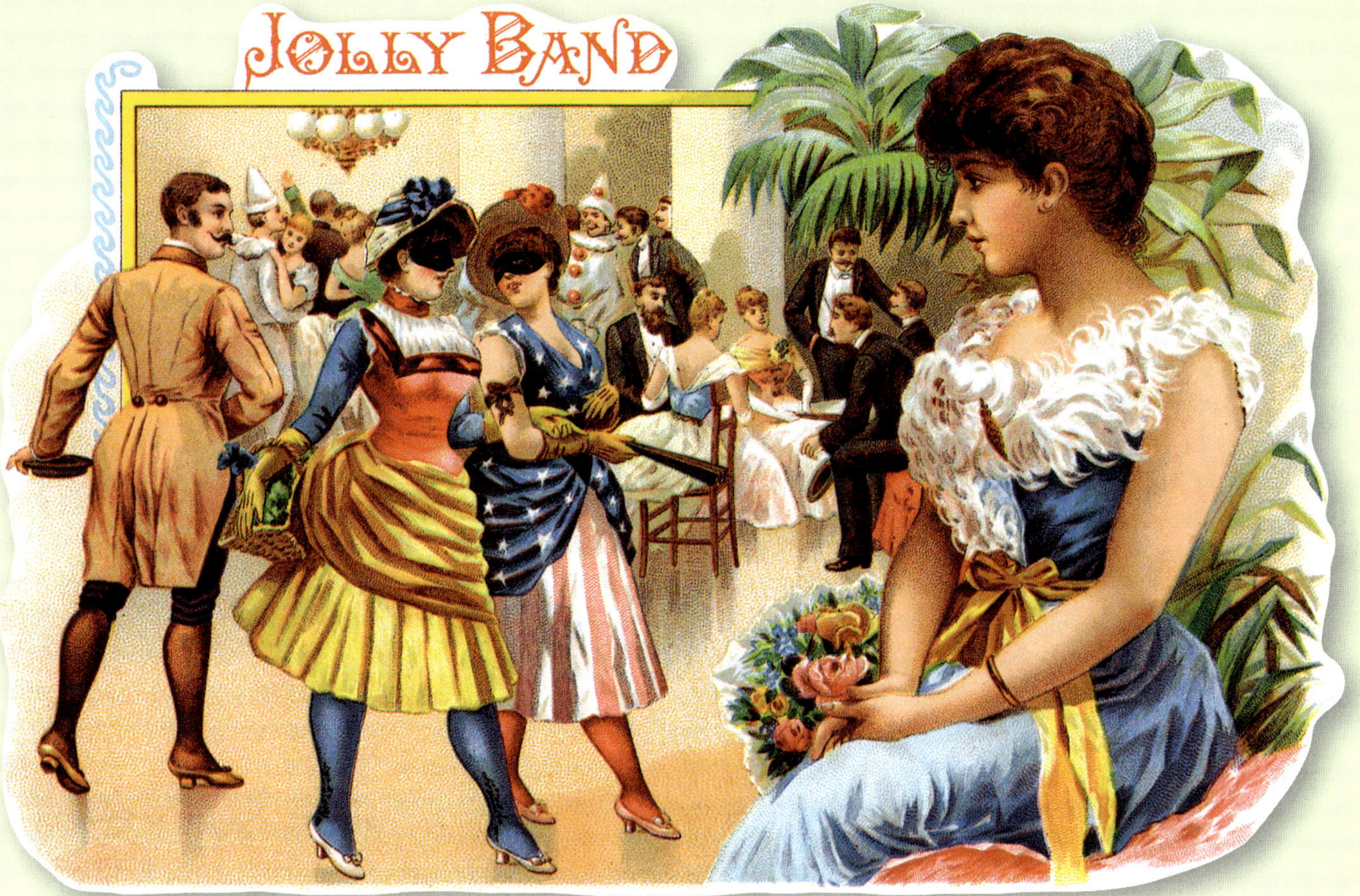

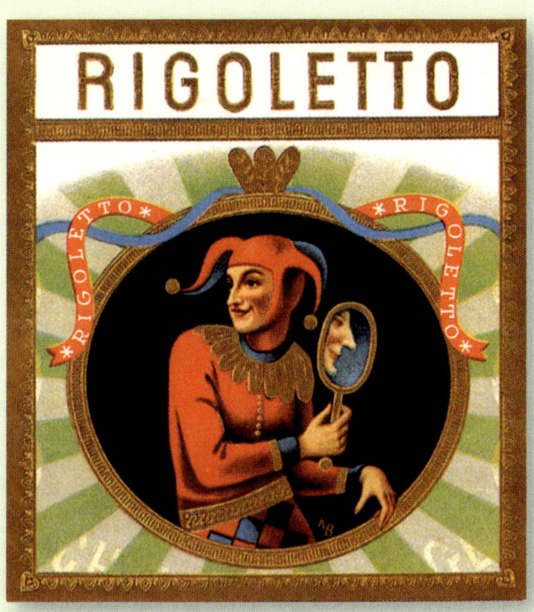

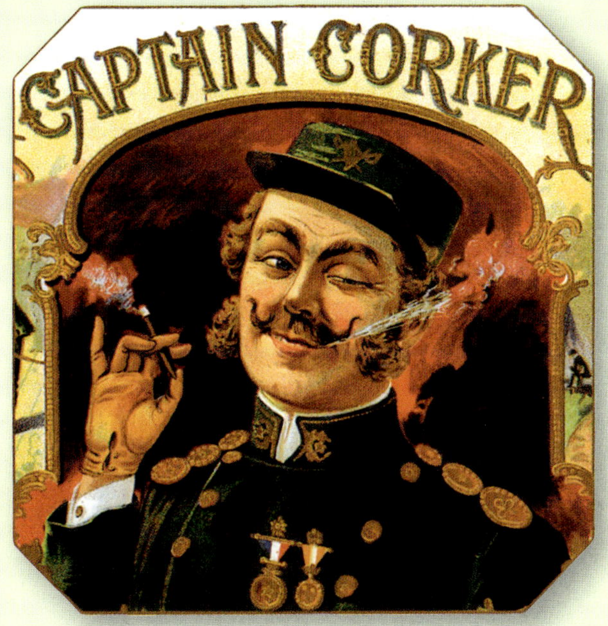

302

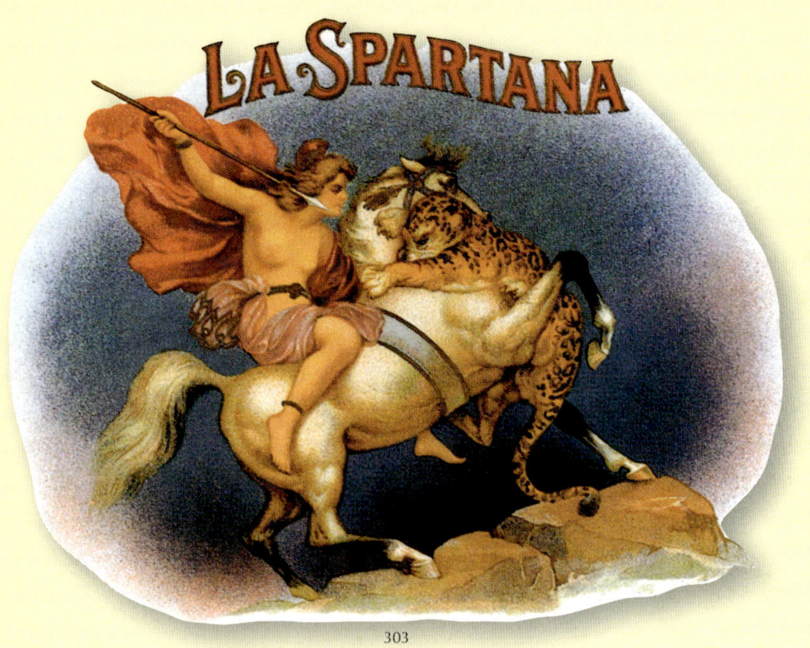

303

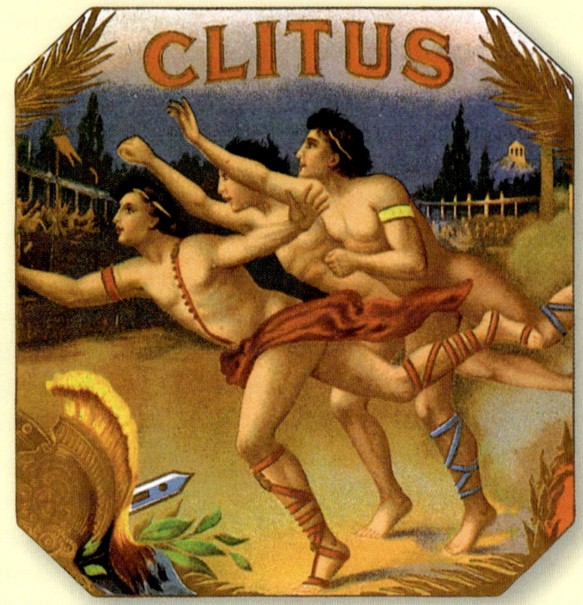

304

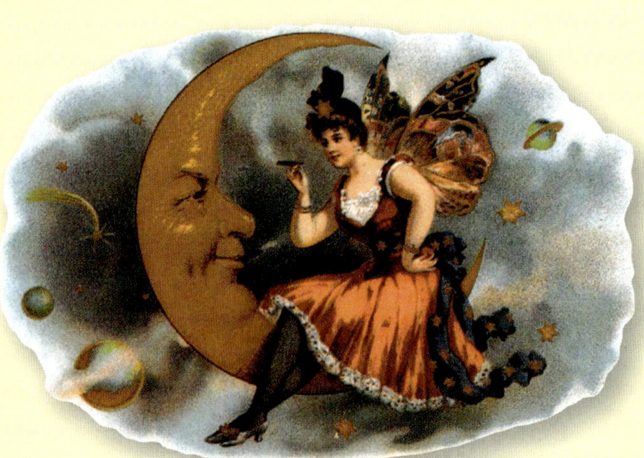

305

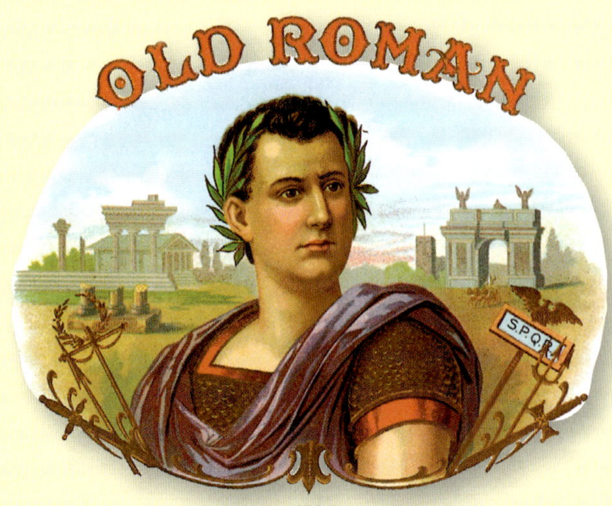

306

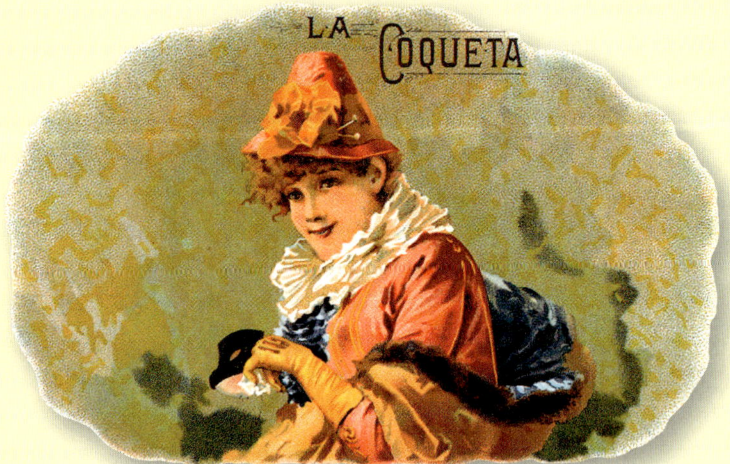

307

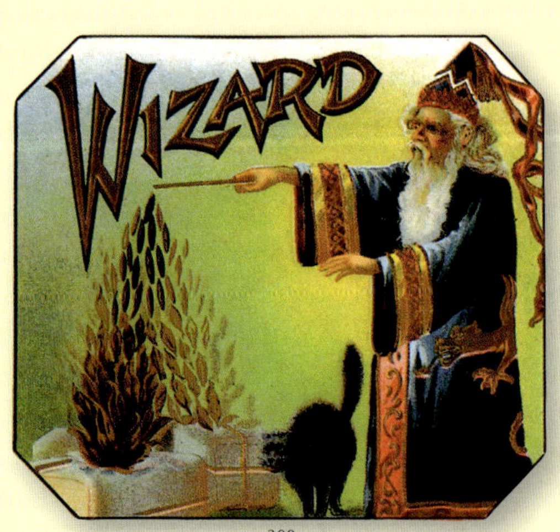

308

IRISH SINGER

309

LA FESTA

310

FORGET ME-NOT

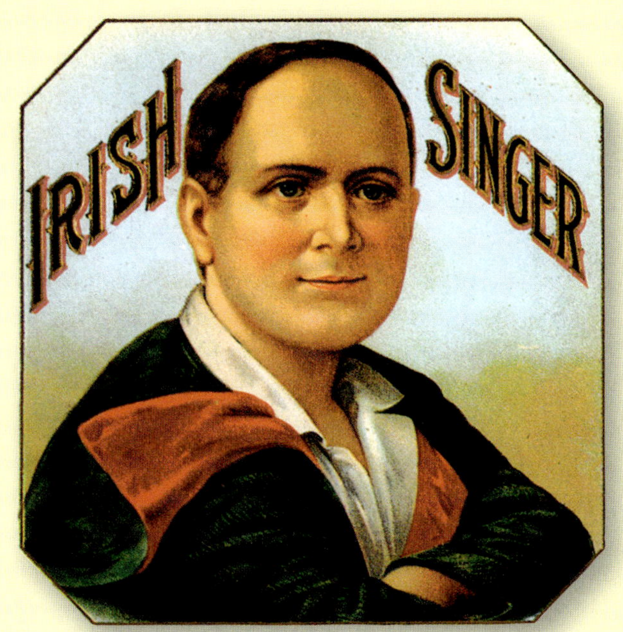

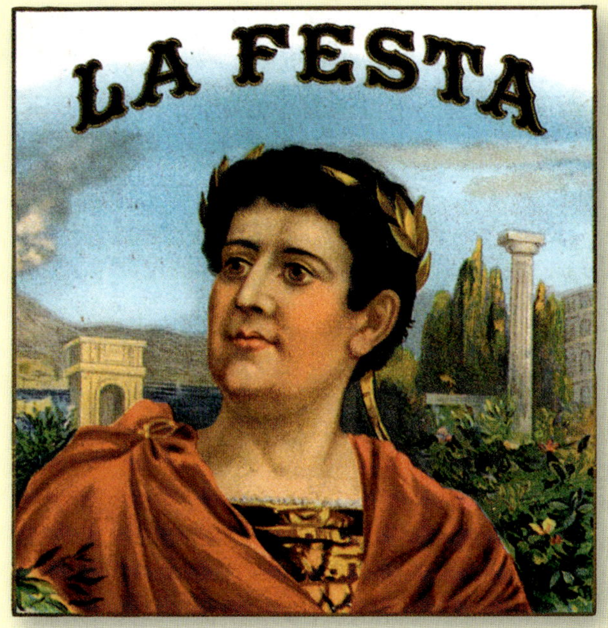

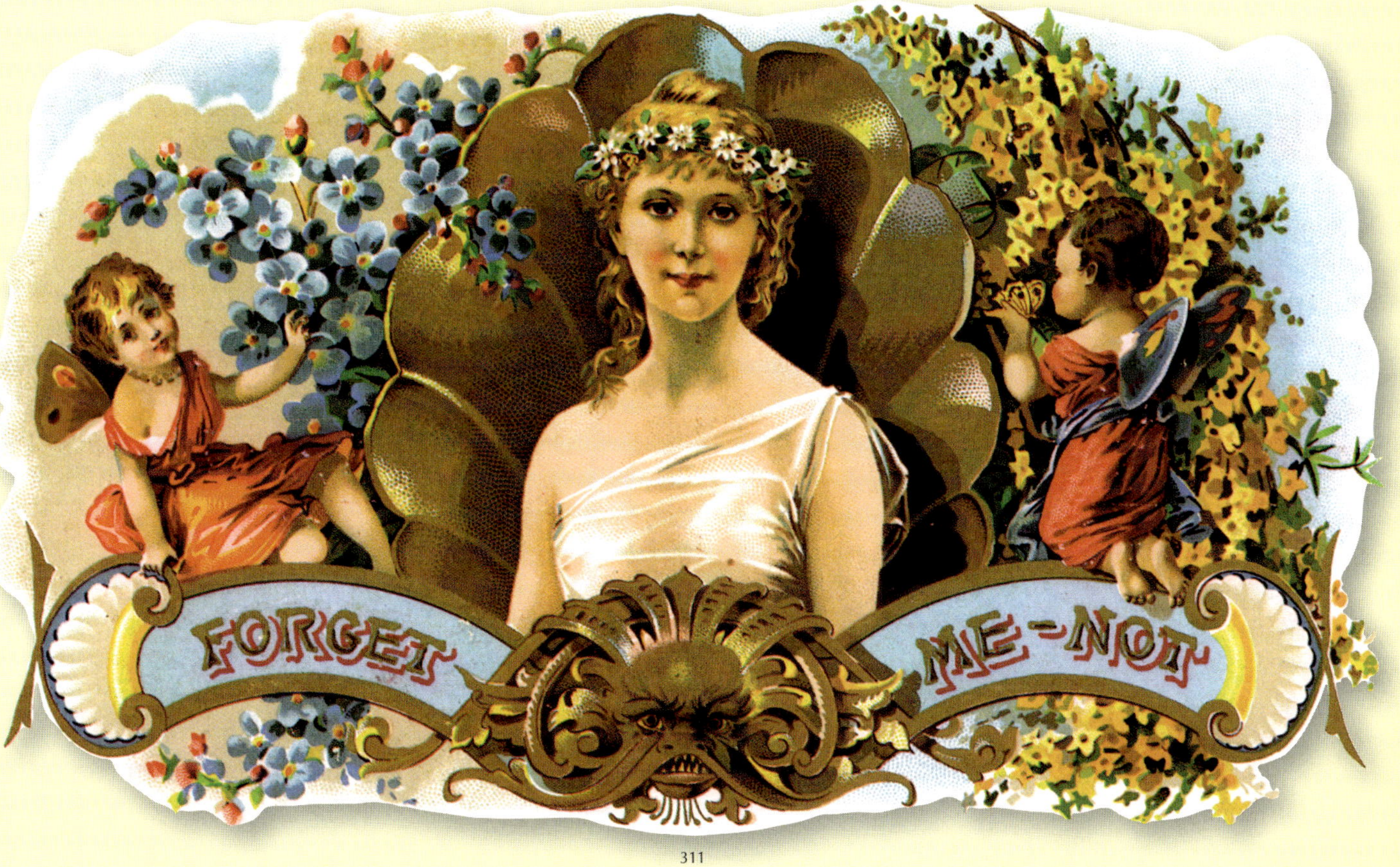

311

OLDEN TYMES.

312

IDLE HOUR

313

BLUE BELLE

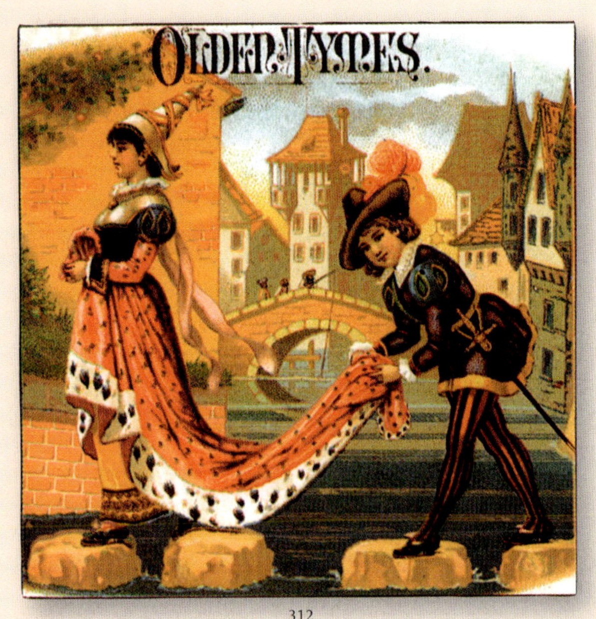

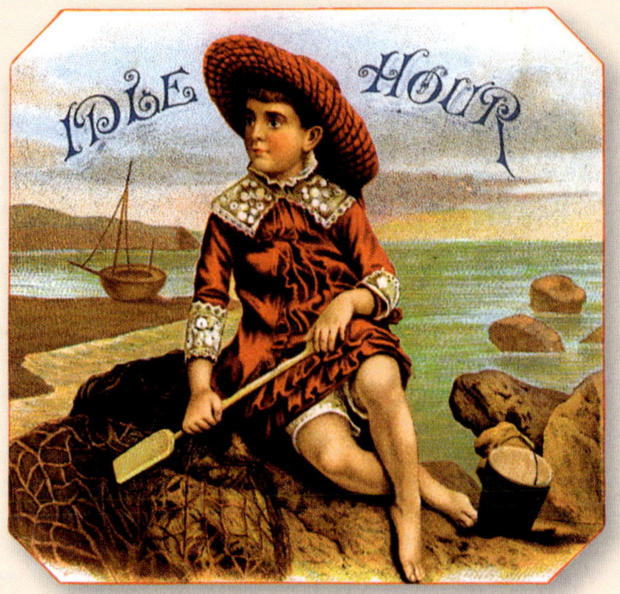

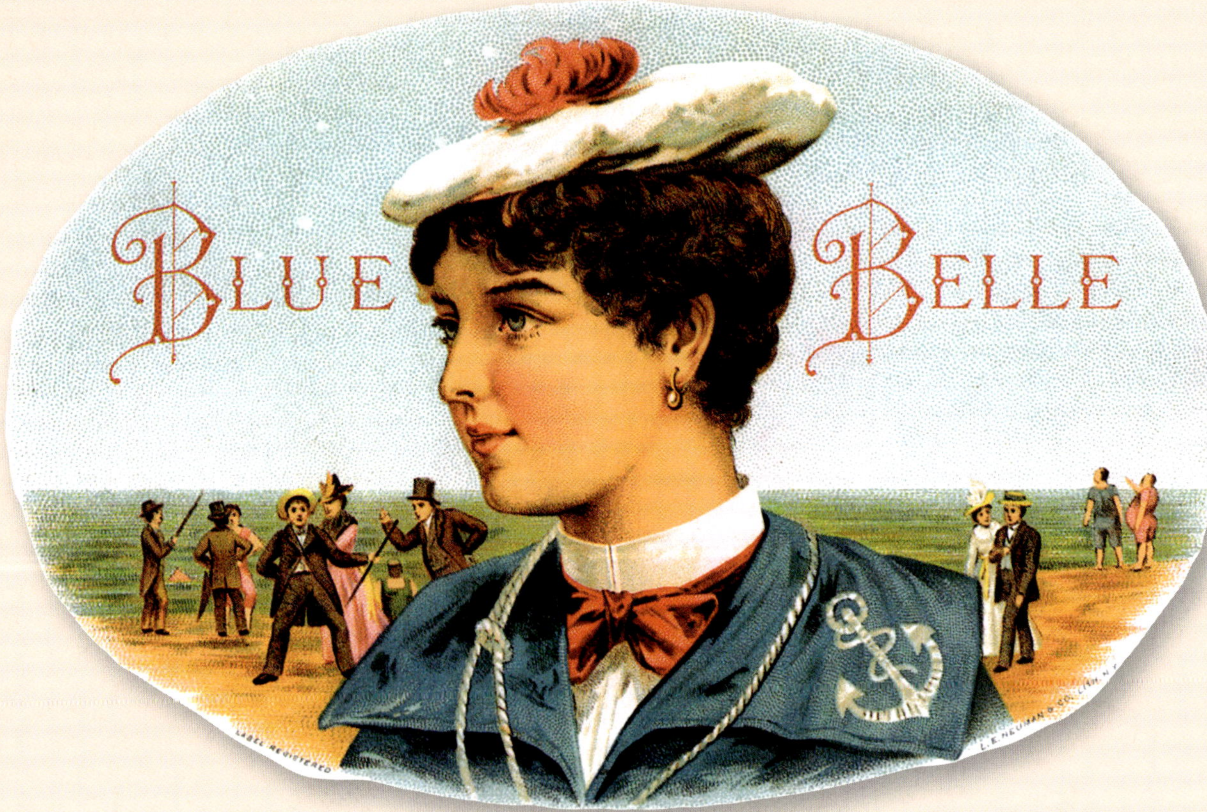

314

Wedding Veil
HAVANA
CIGARS
TRADE MARK REGISTERED

315

Cigarros Finos

316

LA SABILLA
TRADE MARK REGISTERED

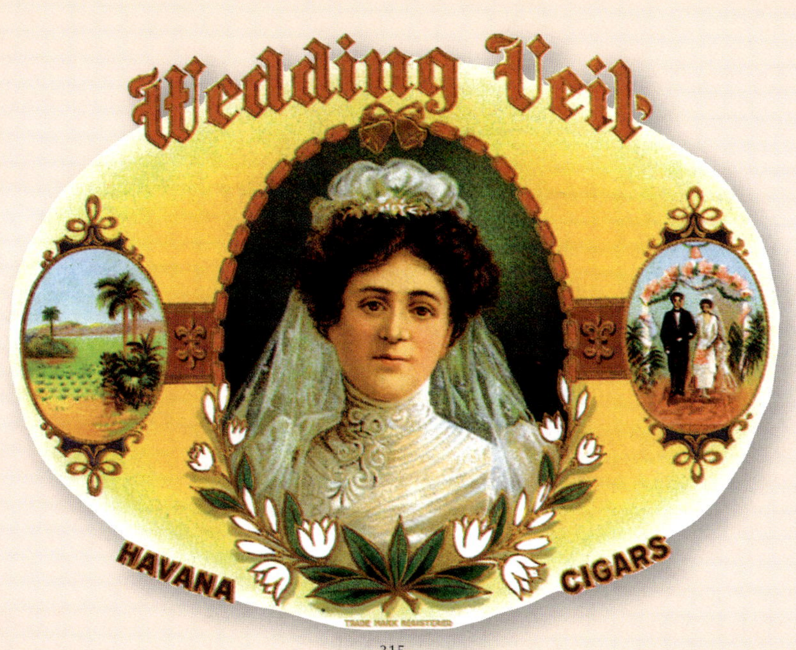

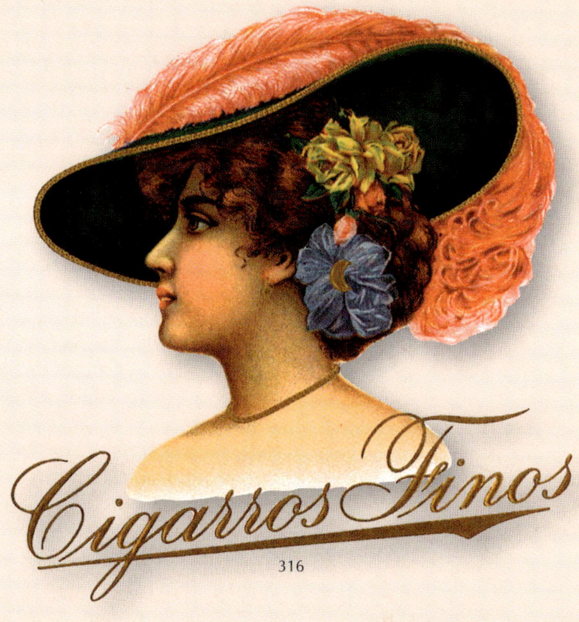

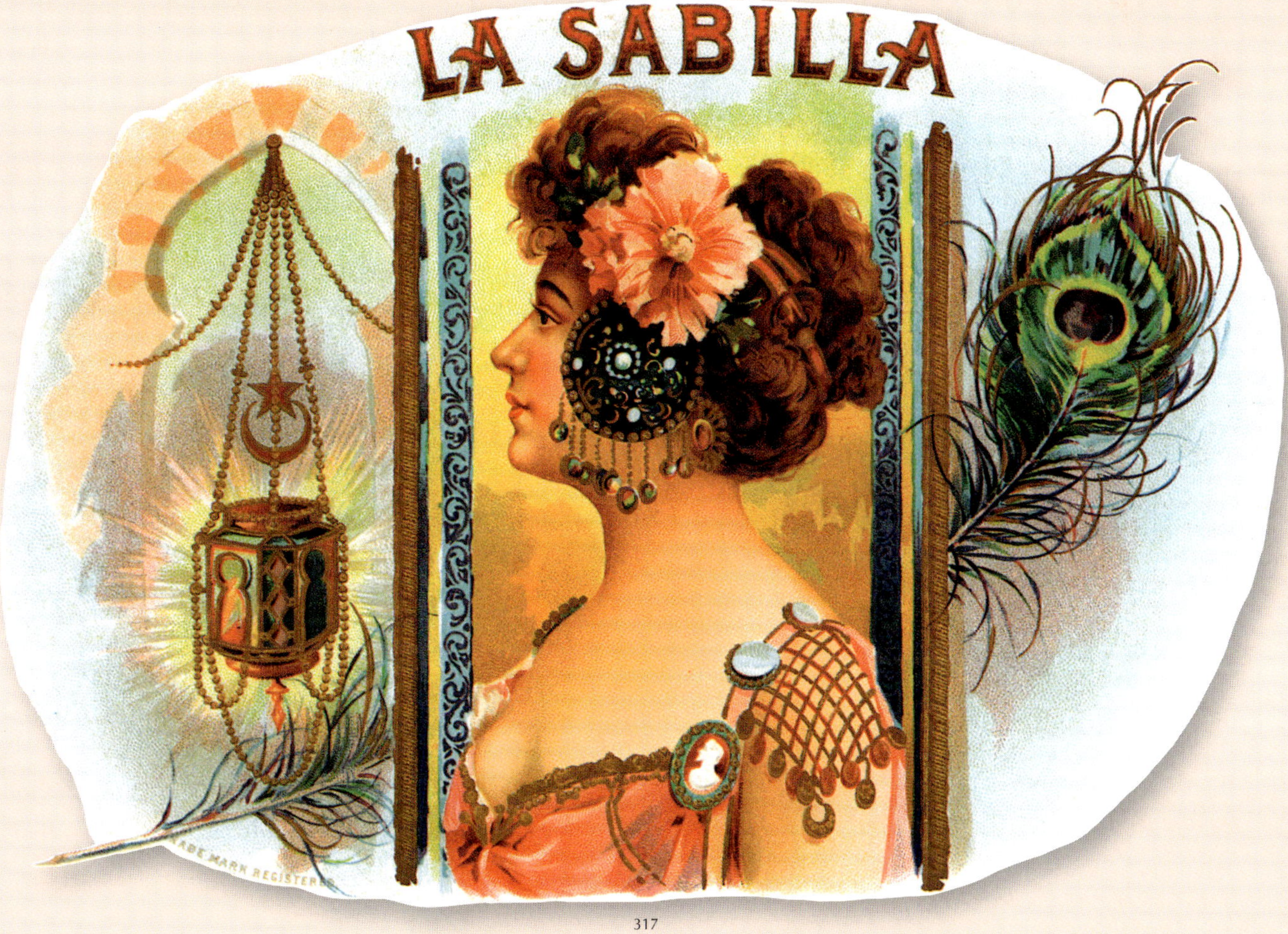

317

SEA ROBIN
W.B.L.

318

EL GAURDO
EL GAURDO

319

White-Cat
White
CAT.
STANDARD QUALITY

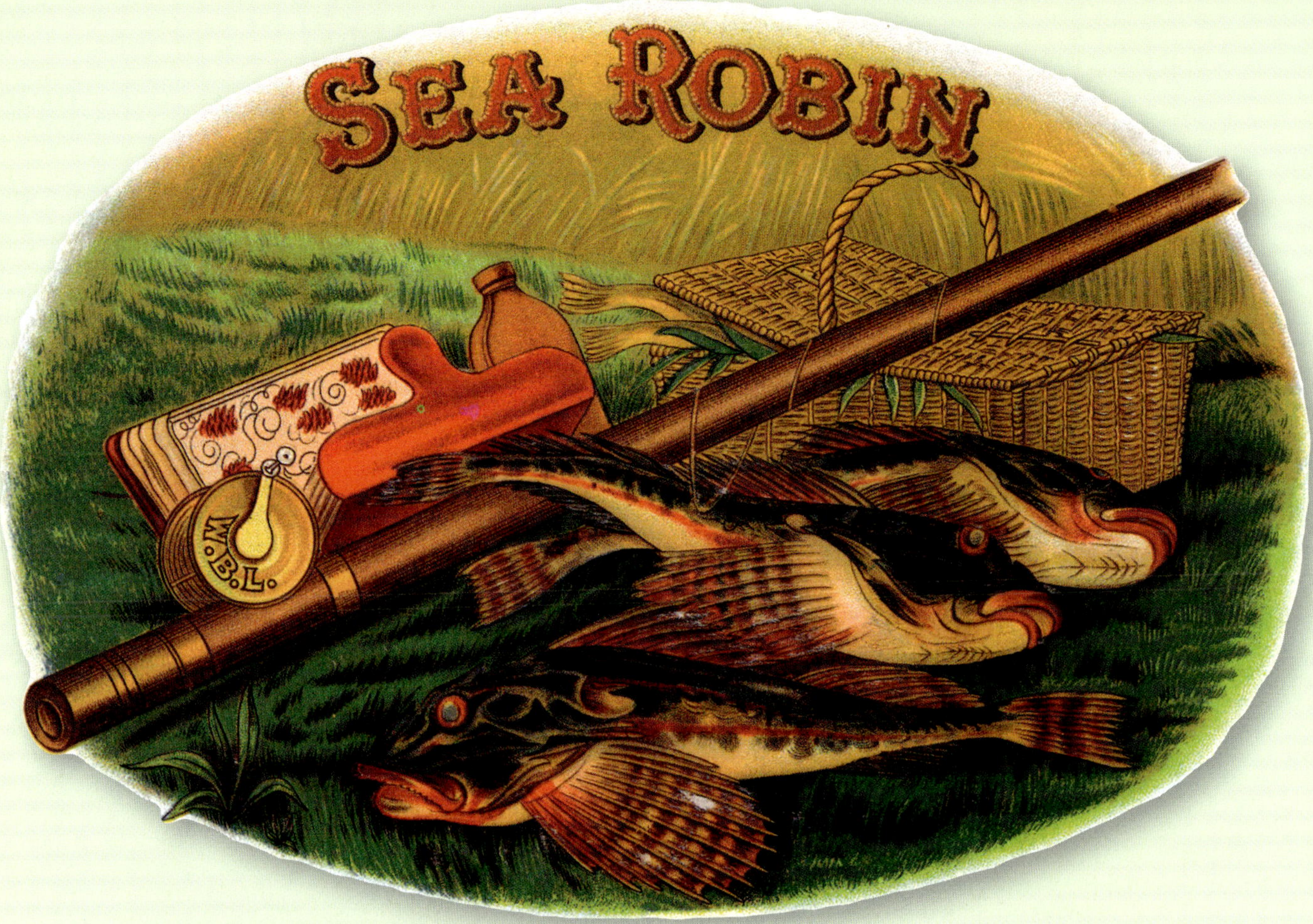

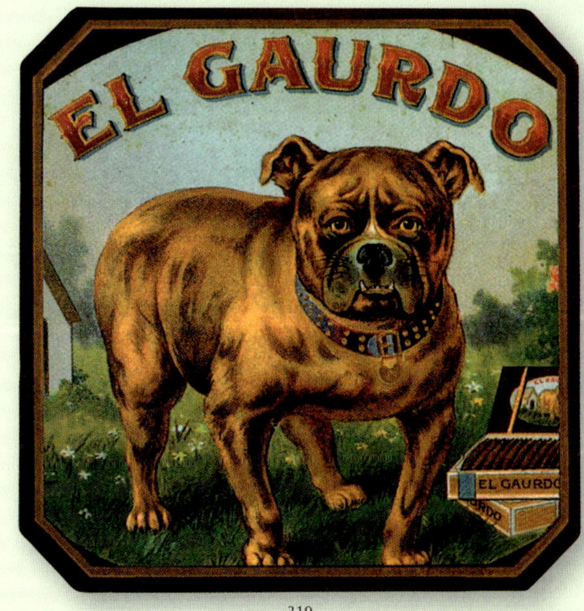

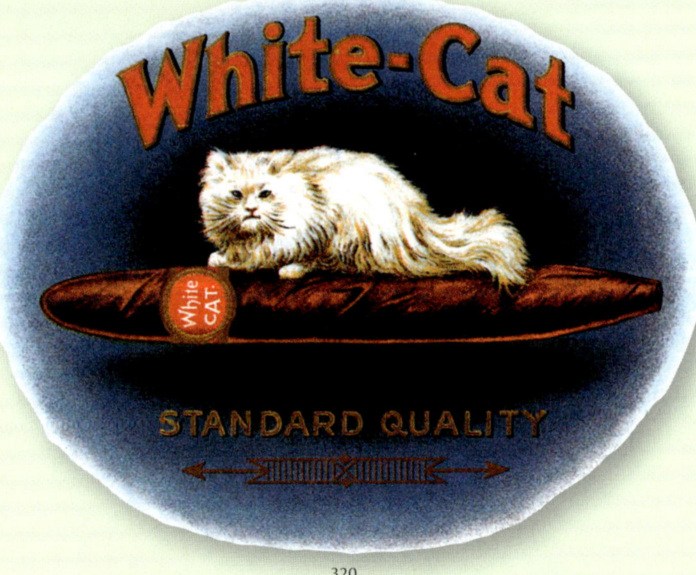

320

OMAR

321

CUBAN

322

MADAME BUTTERFLY

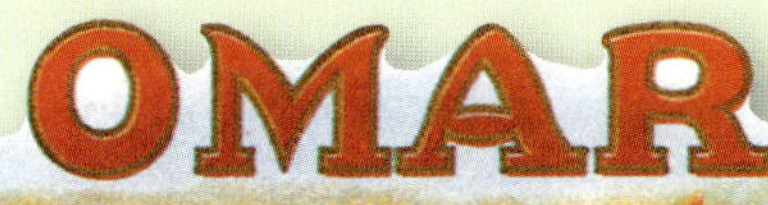

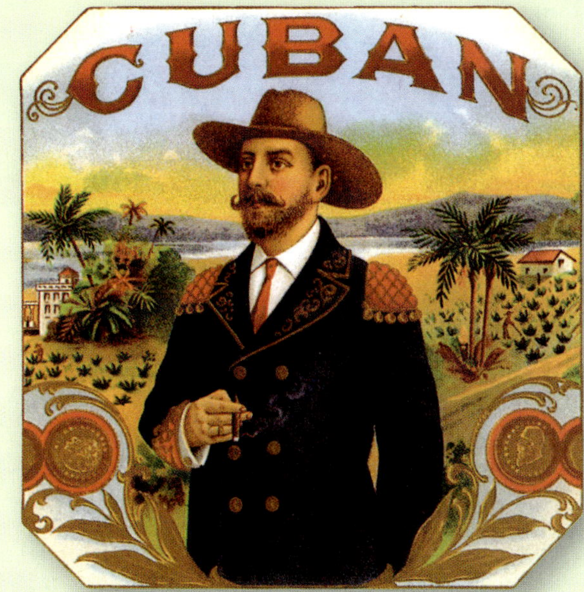

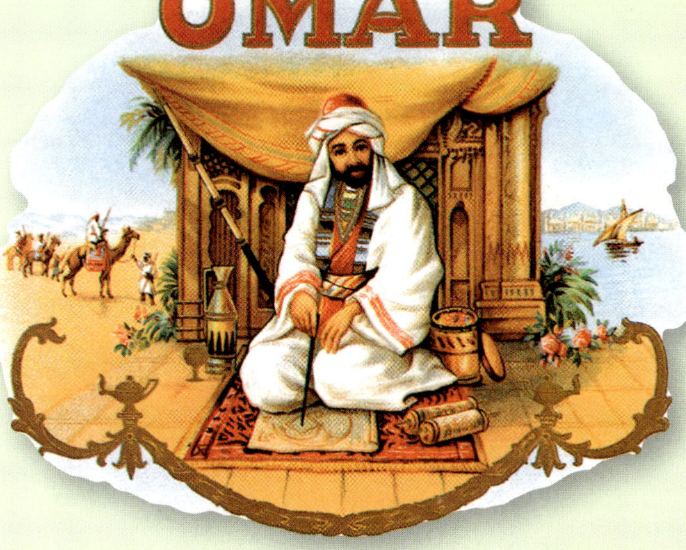

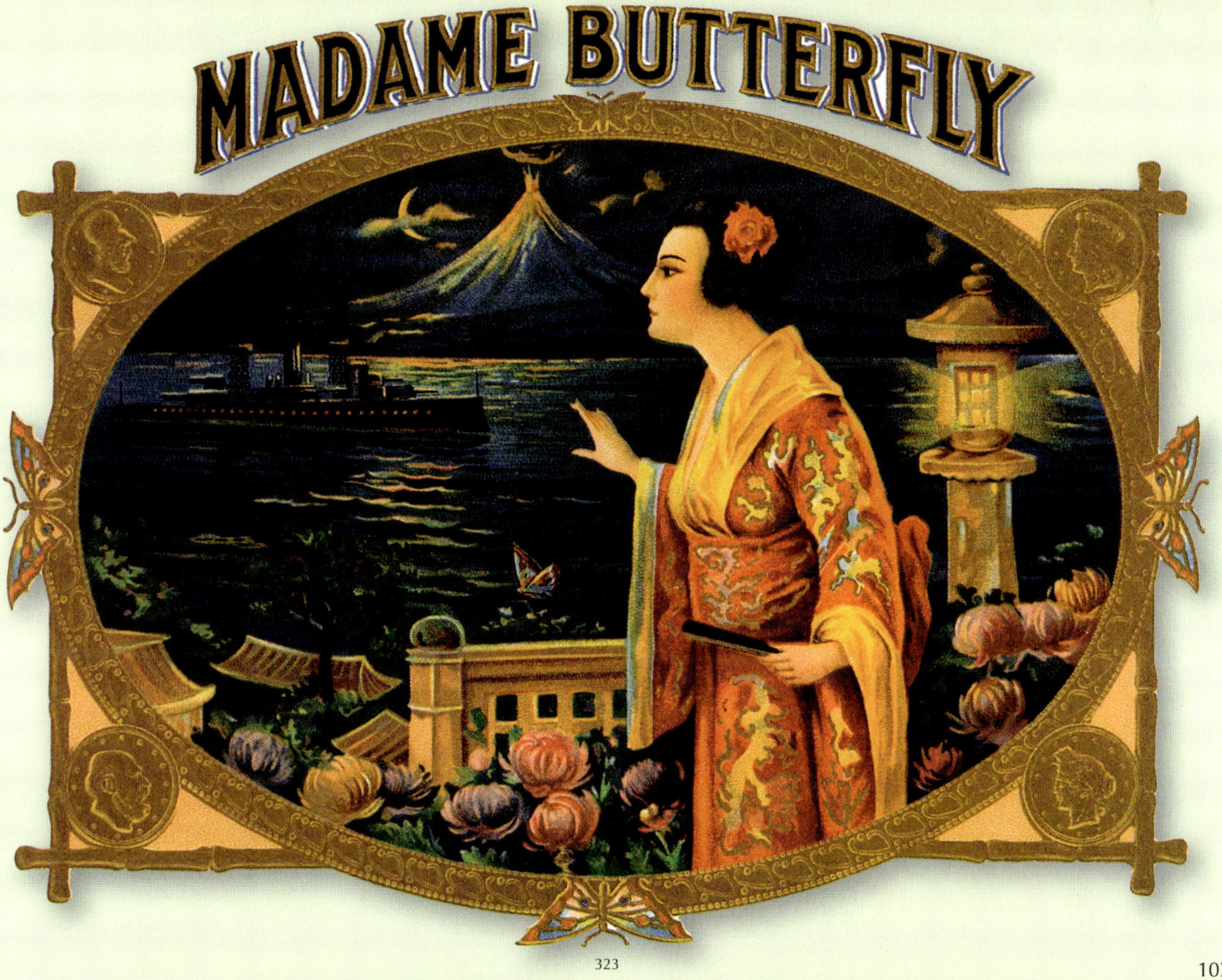

323

RIP VAN WINKLE
MAY YOU LIVE LONG & PROSPER

325

WALT. WHITMAN

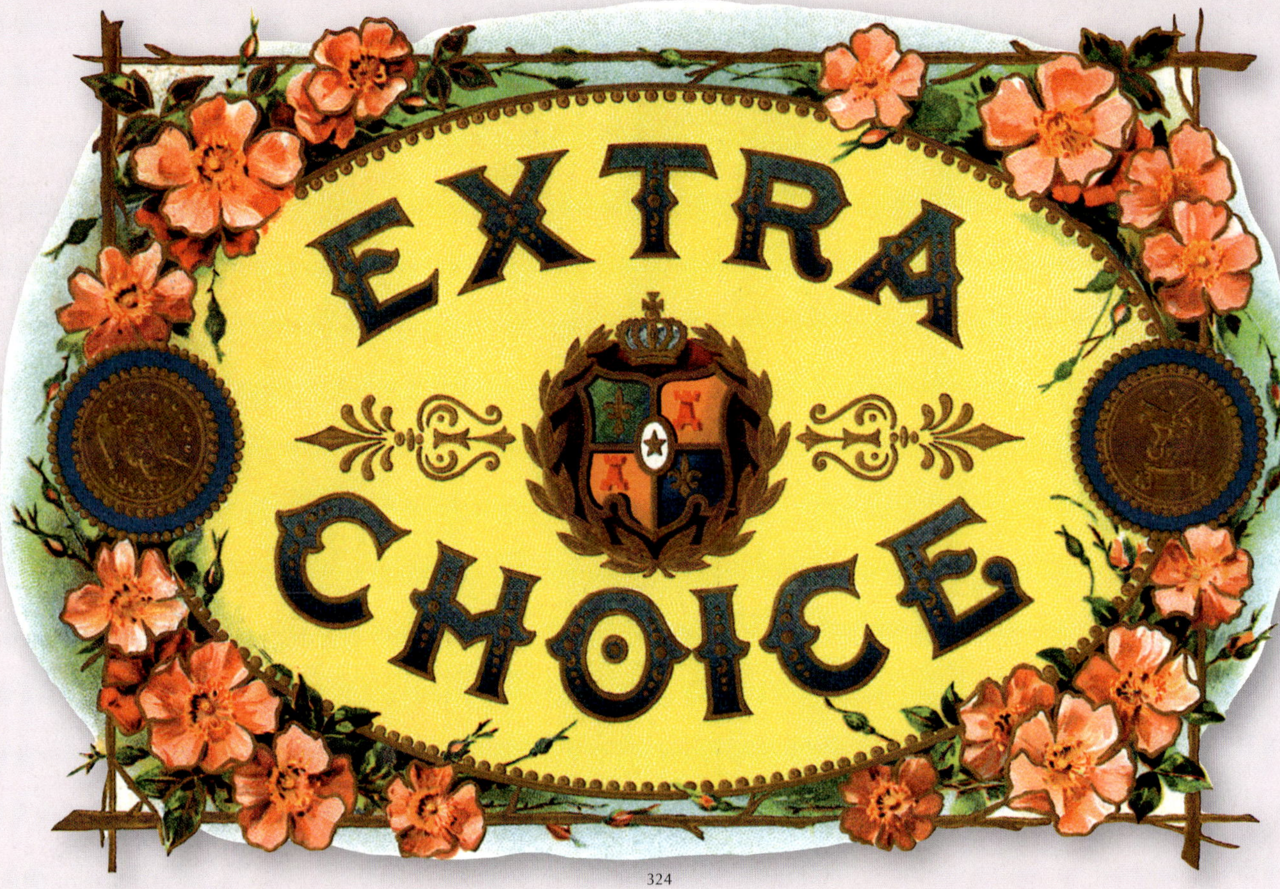

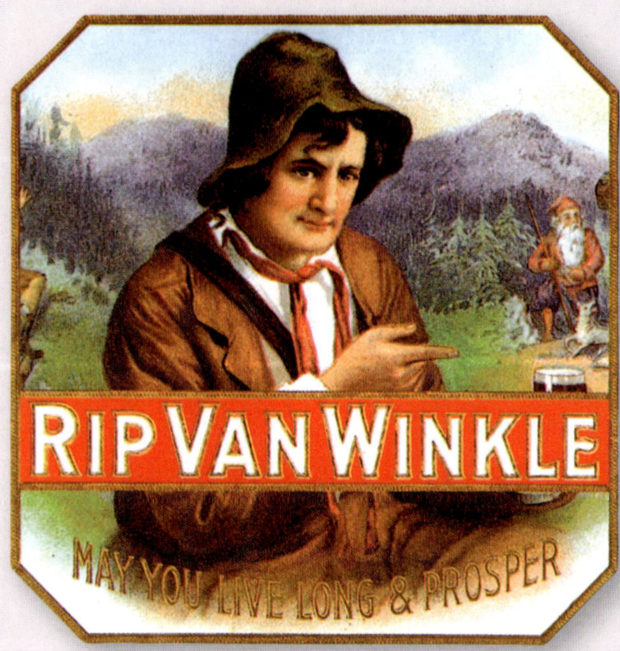

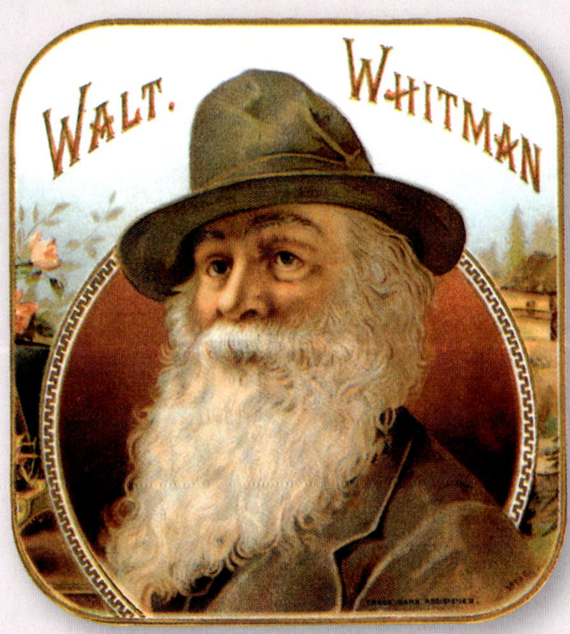

326

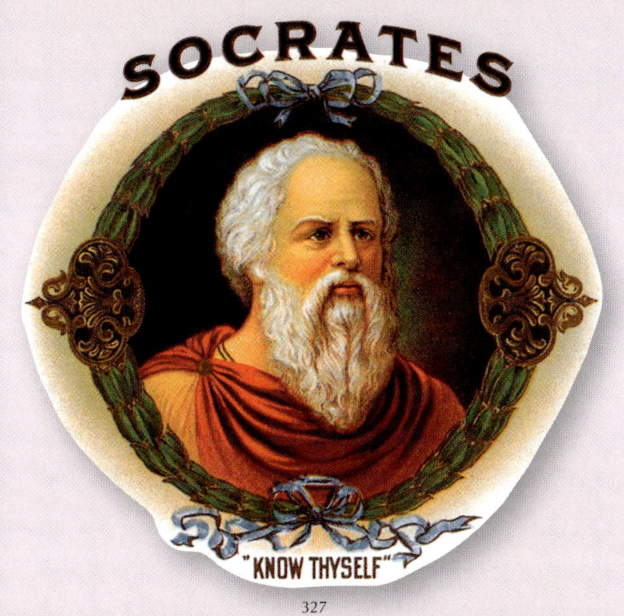

327

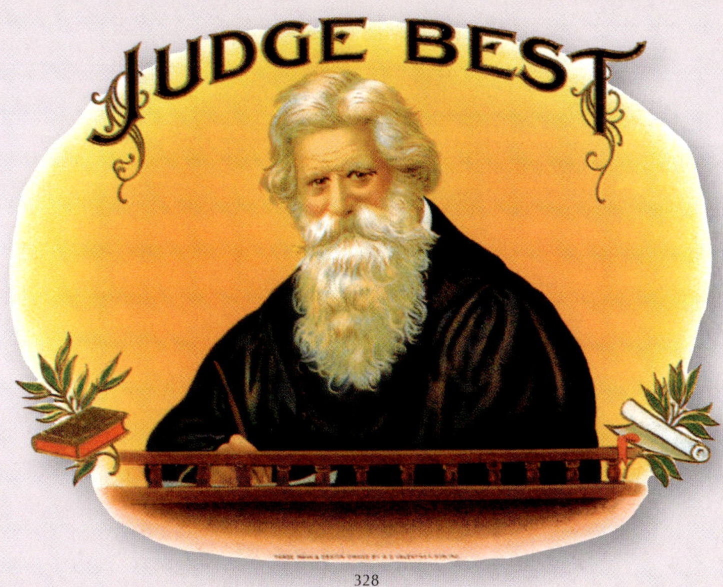

328

POLITANO

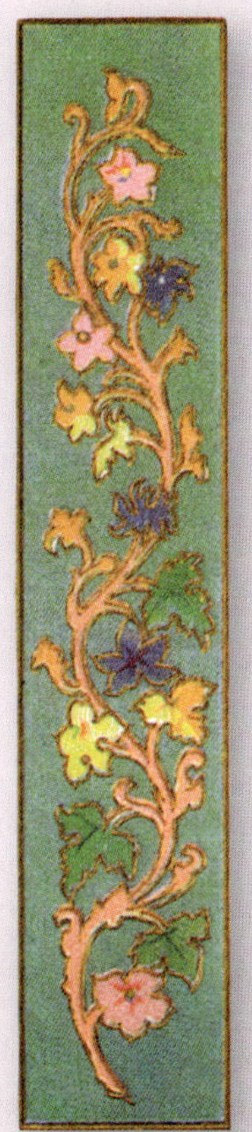

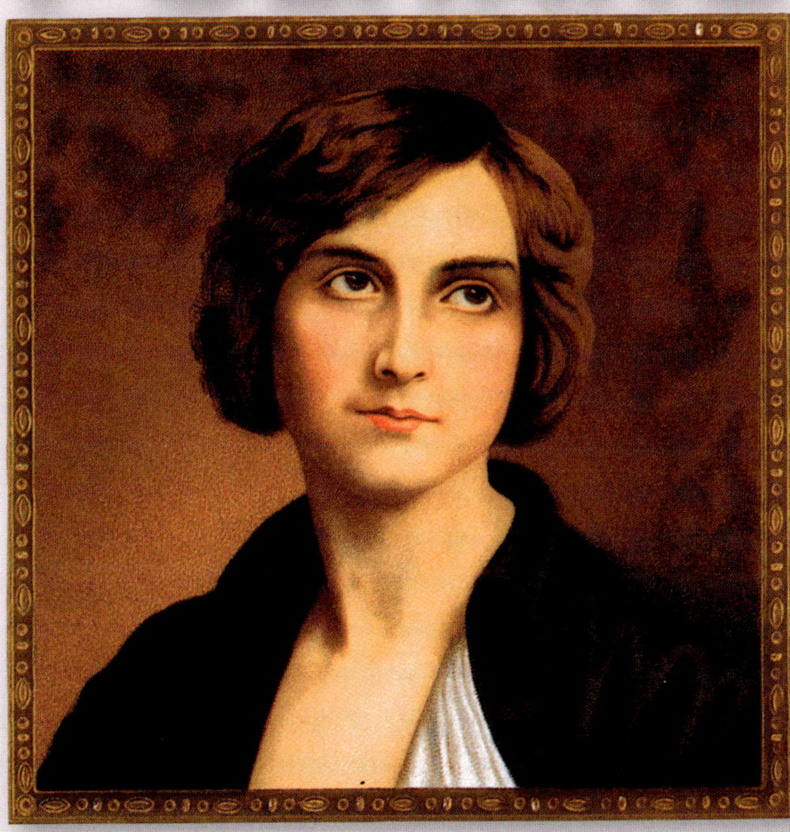

329

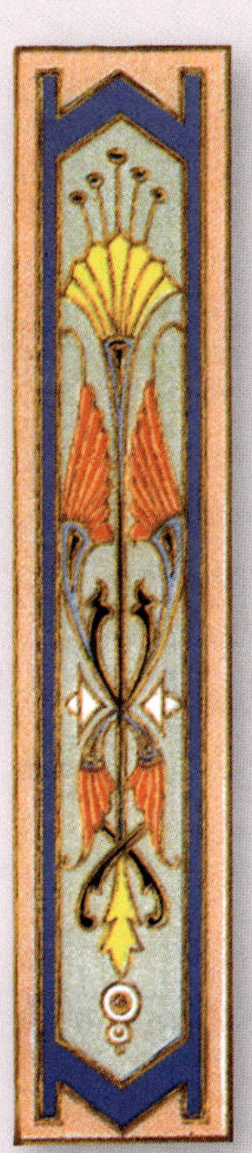

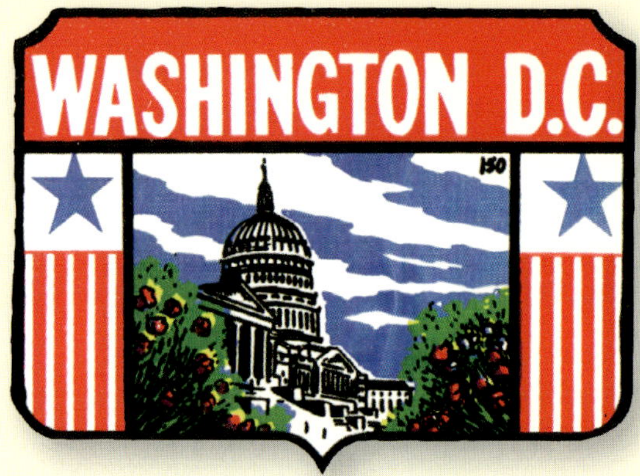

330

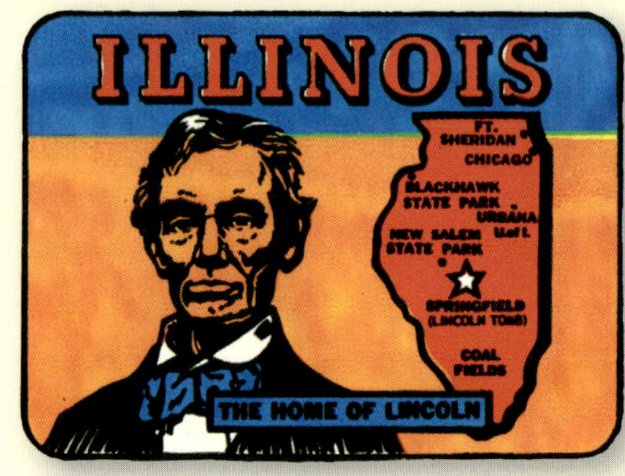

331

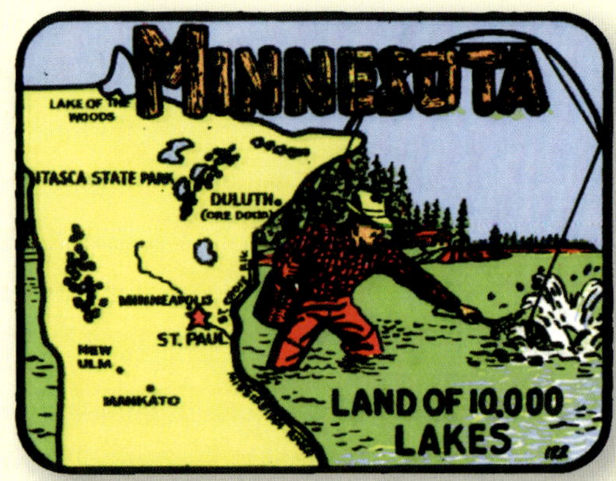

332

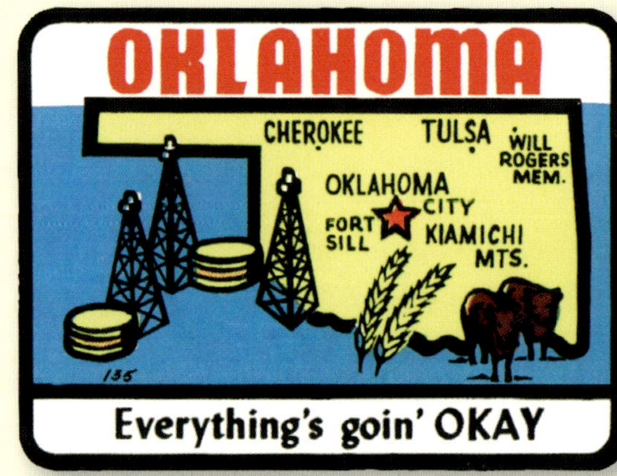

333

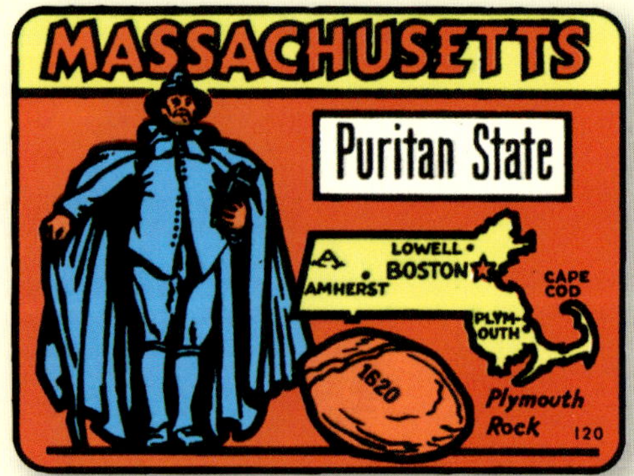

334

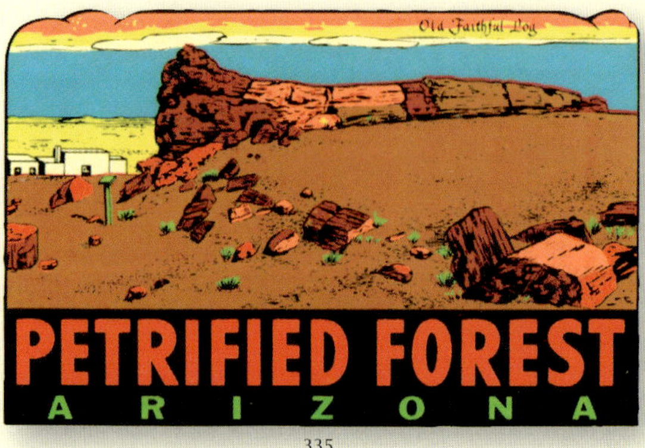

335

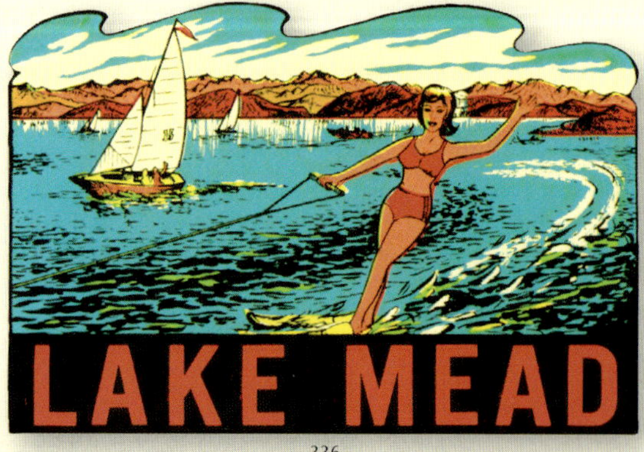

336

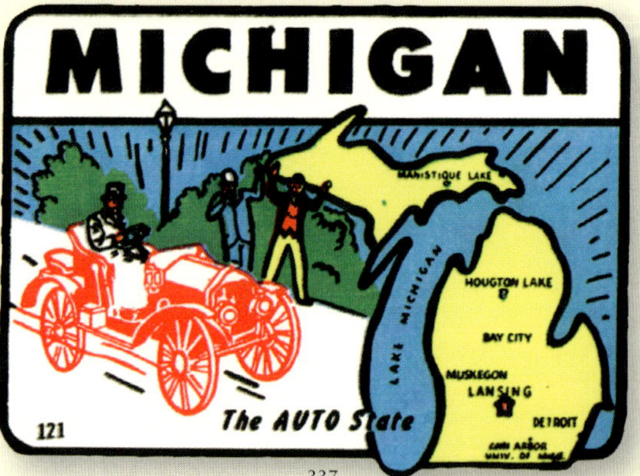

337

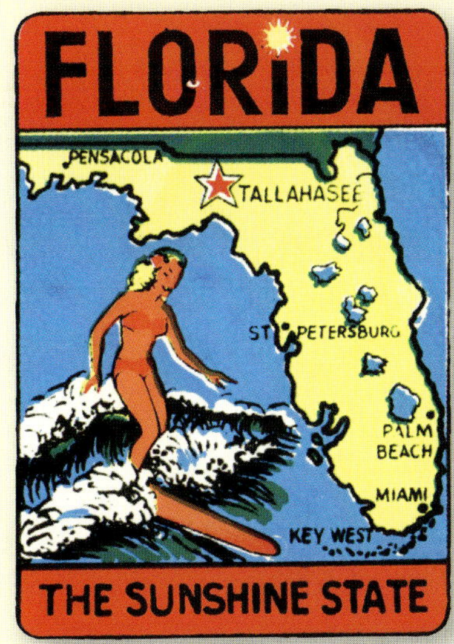

338

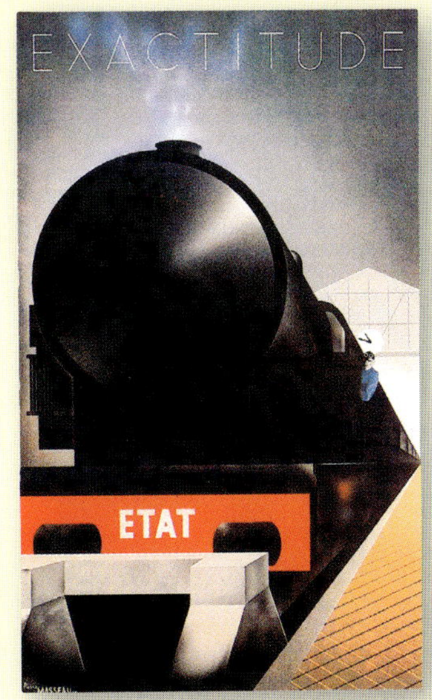

339

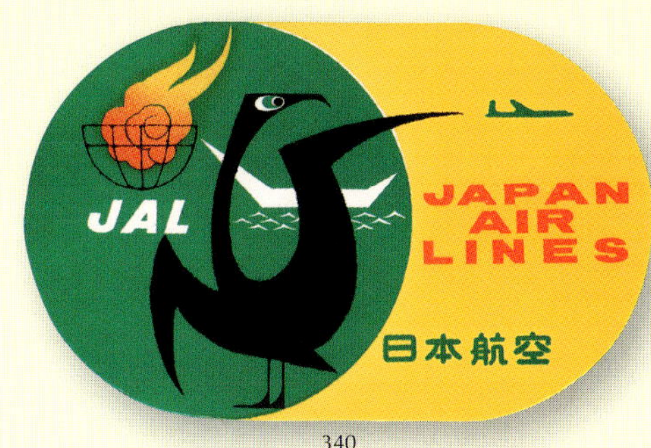

340

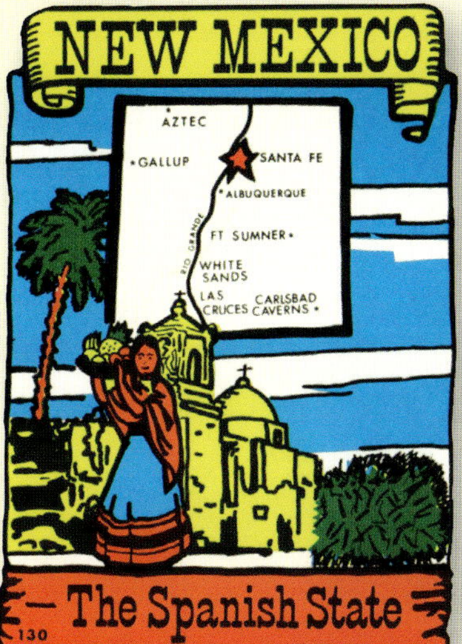

341

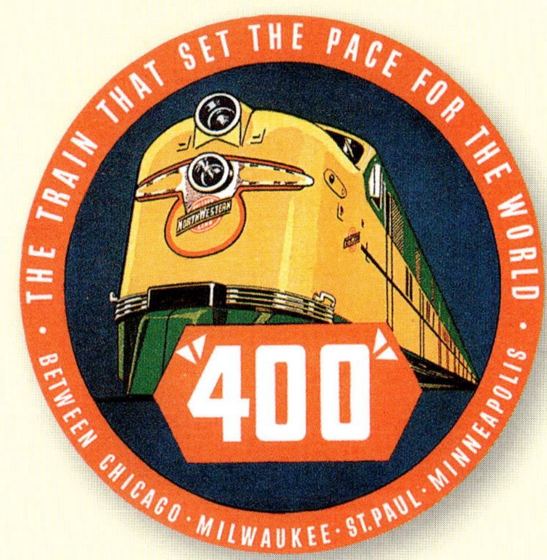

342

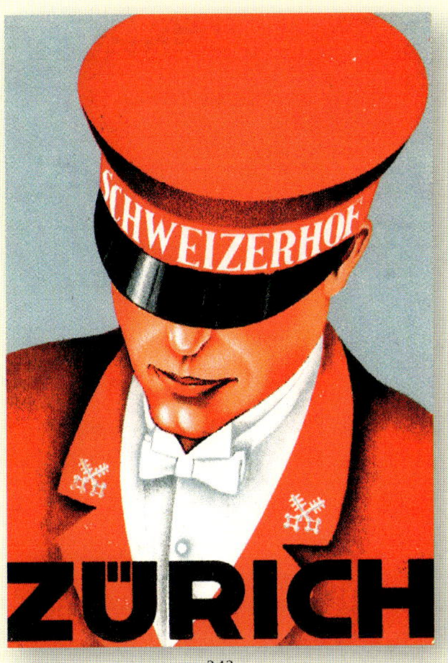

343

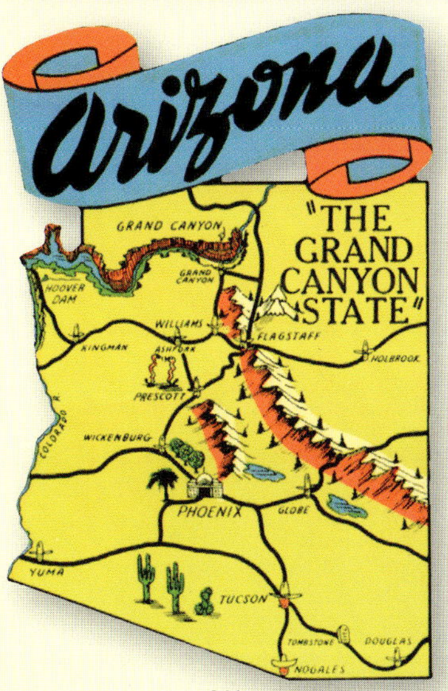

344

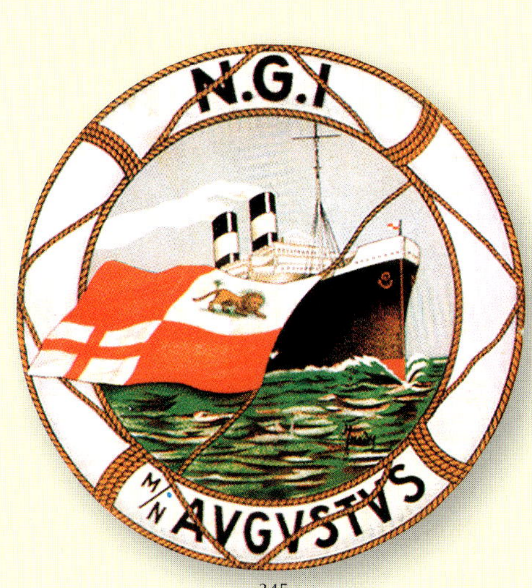

345

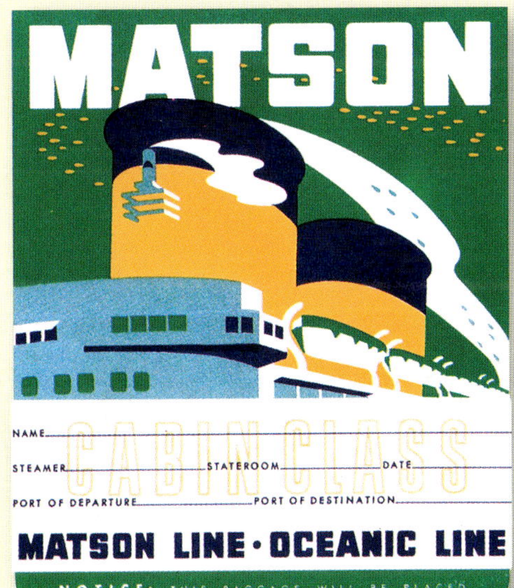

346

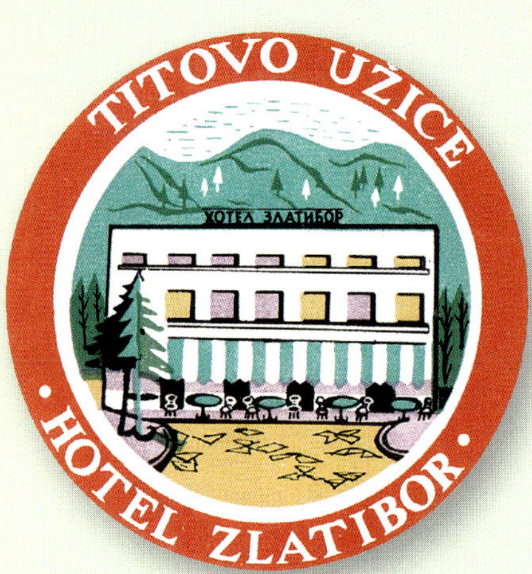

347

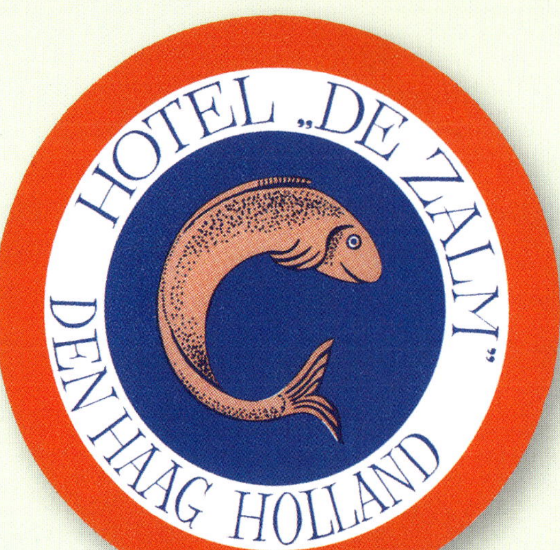

348

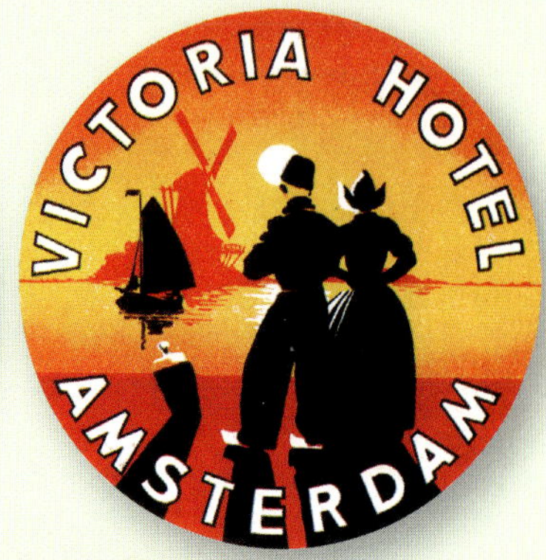

349

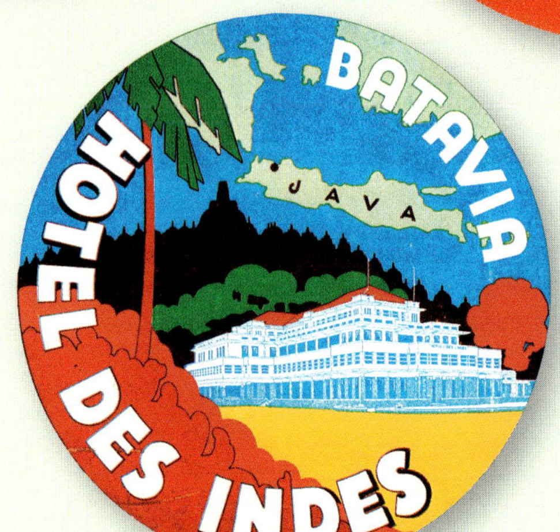

350

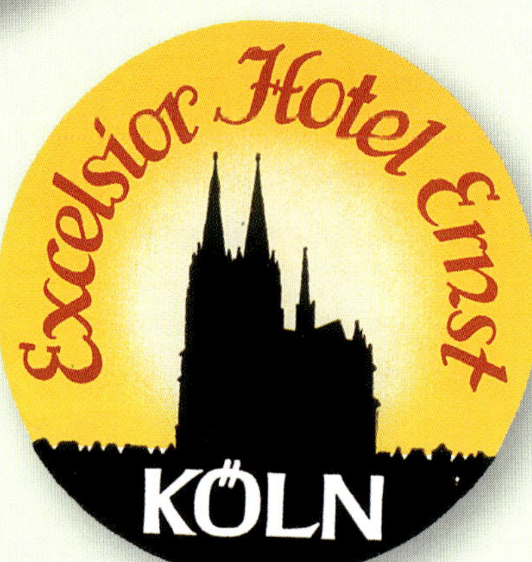

351

353

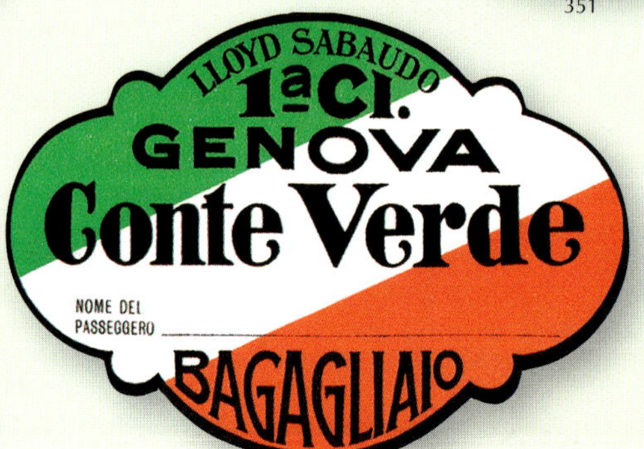

352

354

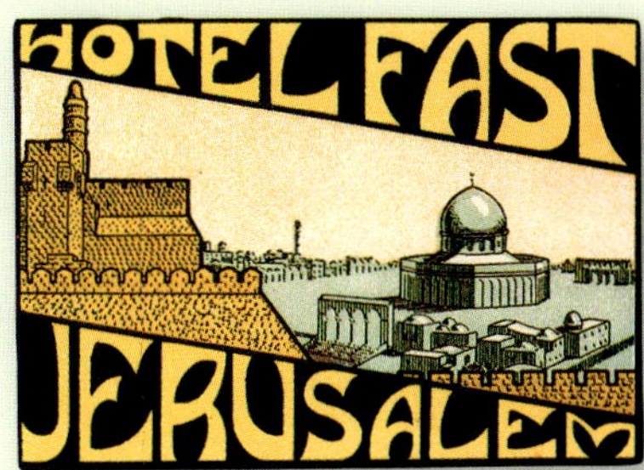

355

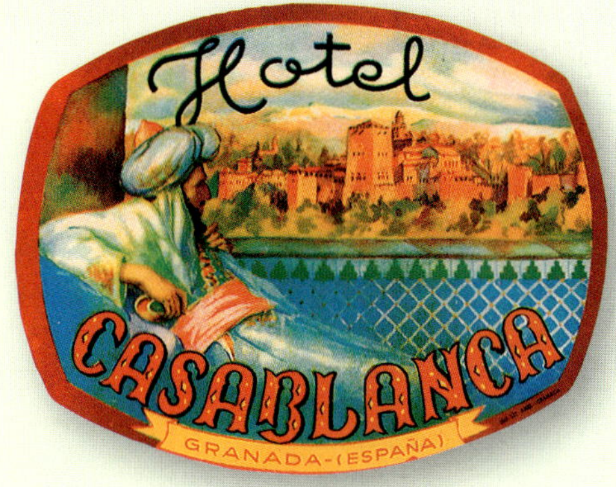

356

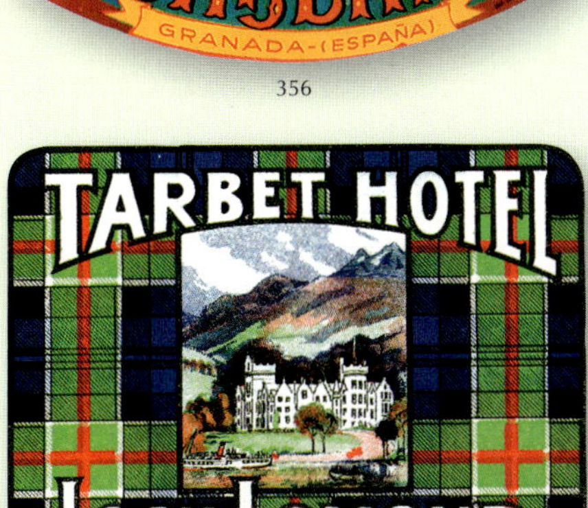

358

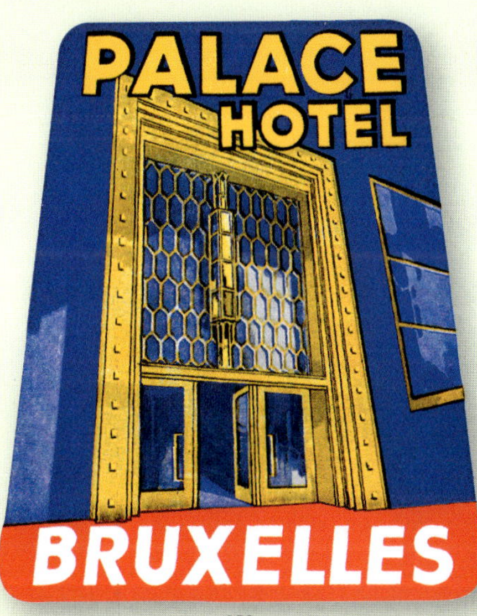

359

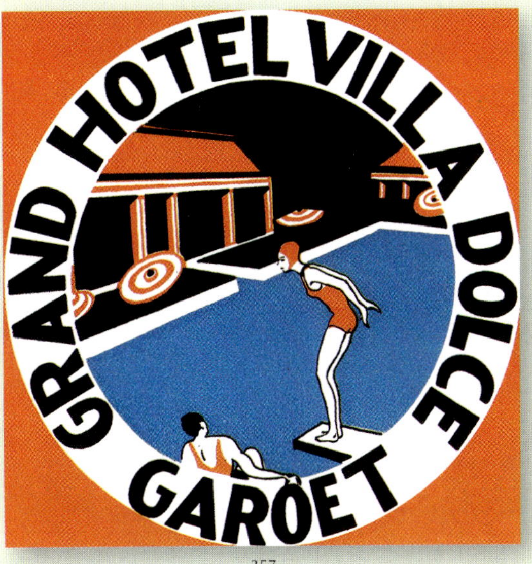

357

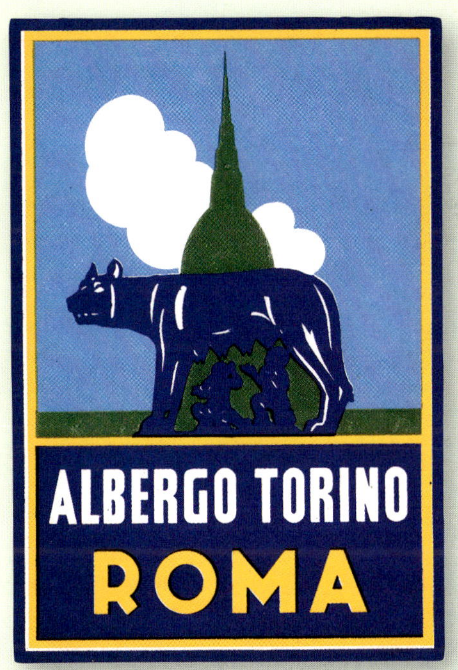

360

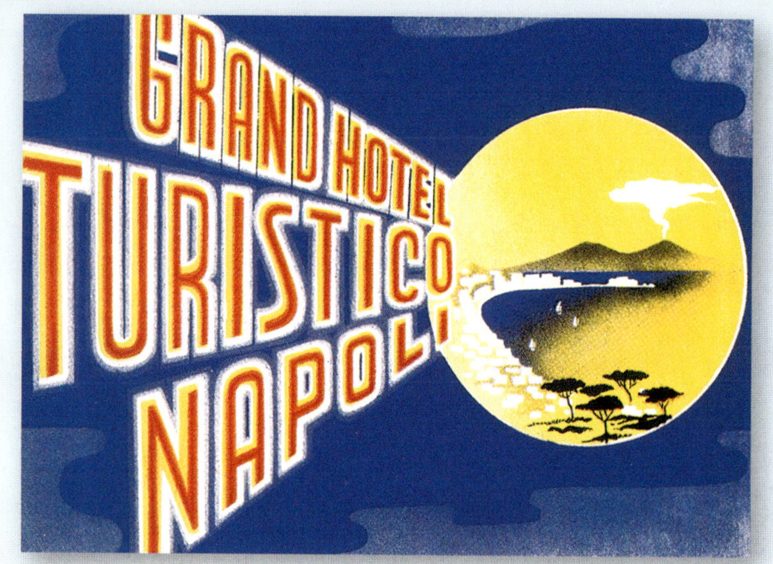

361

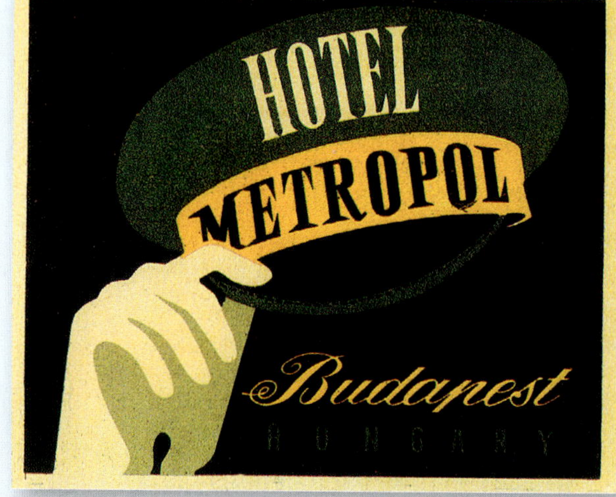

362

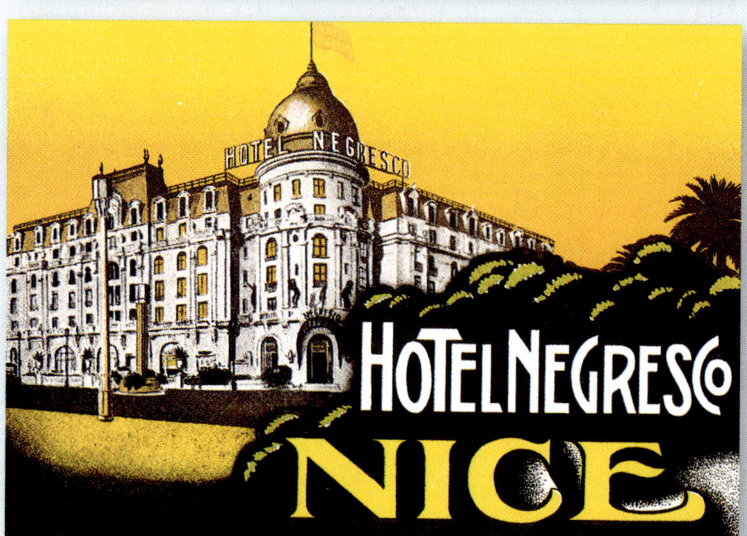

363

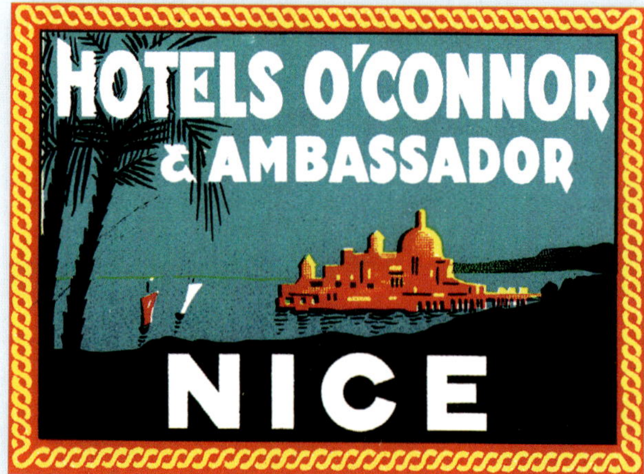

364

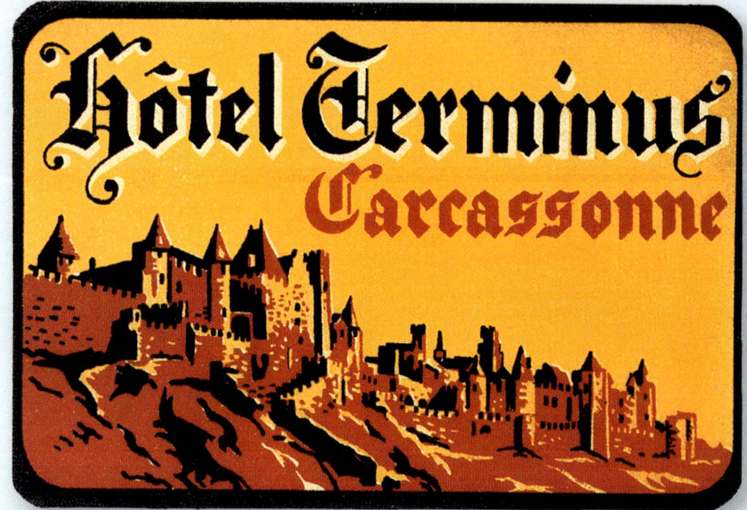

365

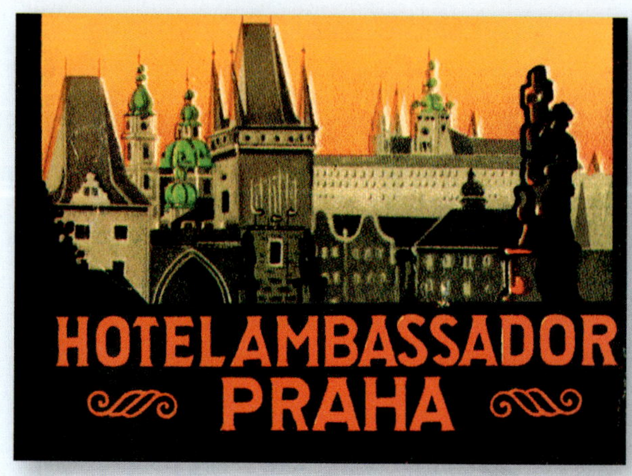

366

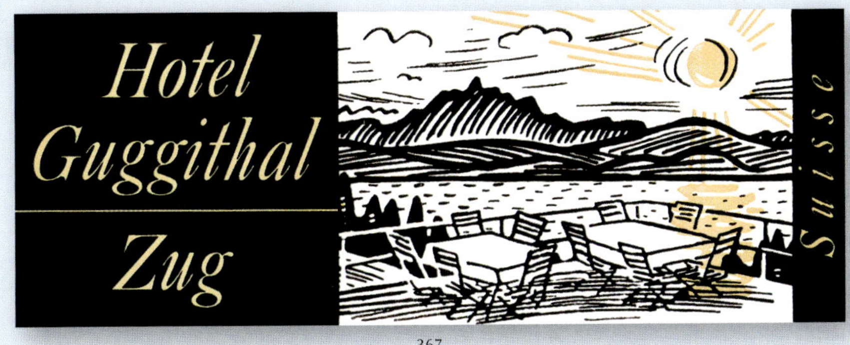

367

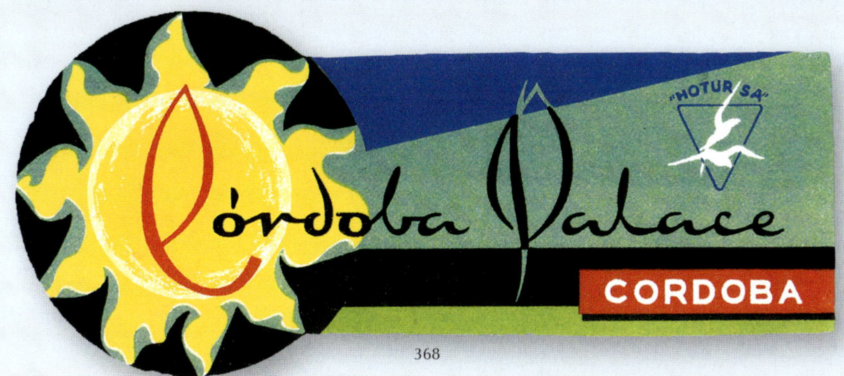

368

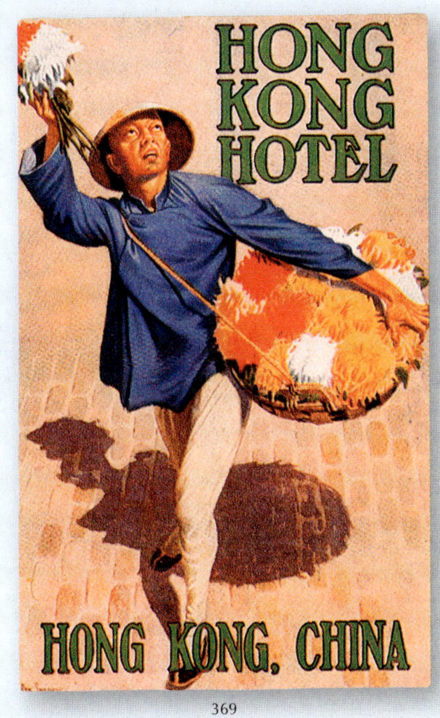

369

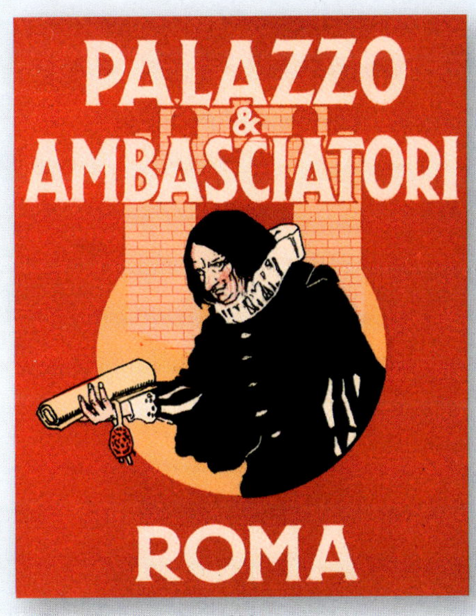

370

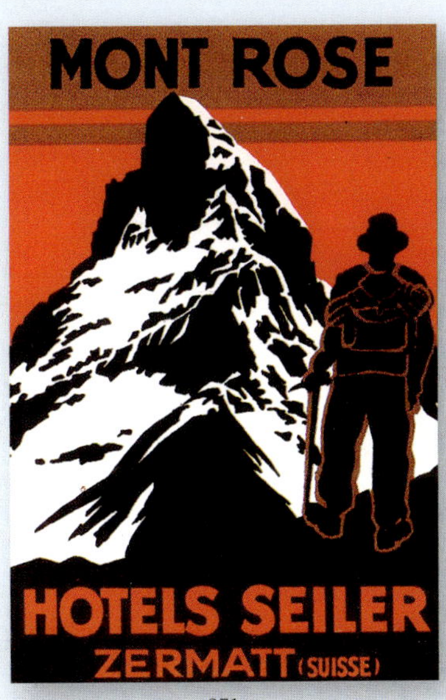

371

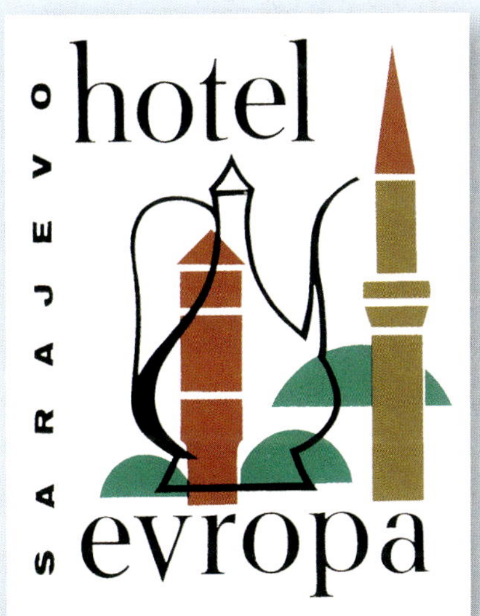

372

BOU-SAADA
ALGERIE
HOTEL
TRANSATLANTIQUE

373

ANFA-HOTEL
CASABLANCA

374

HORRIS HOTEL
CAIRO
فندق حوريس
القاهرة

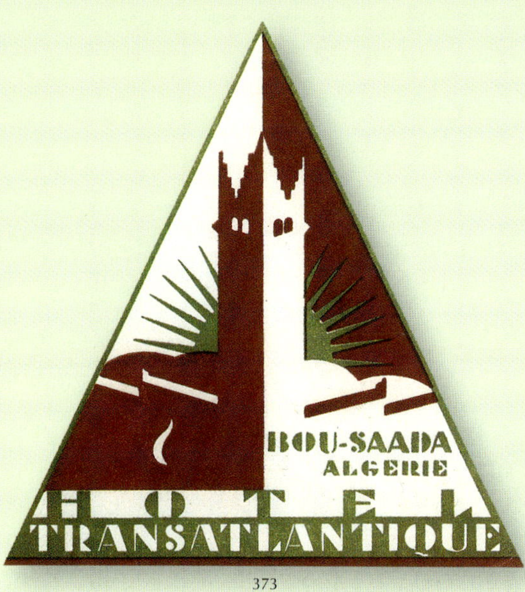

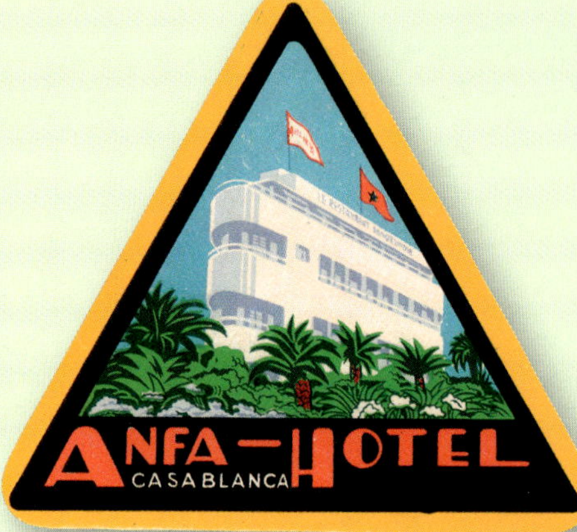

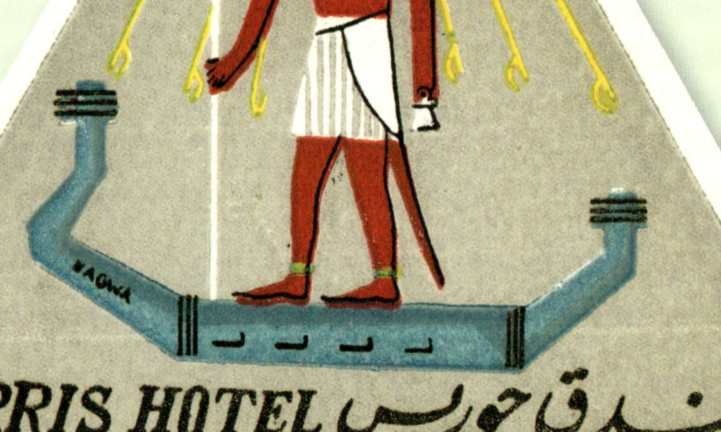

375

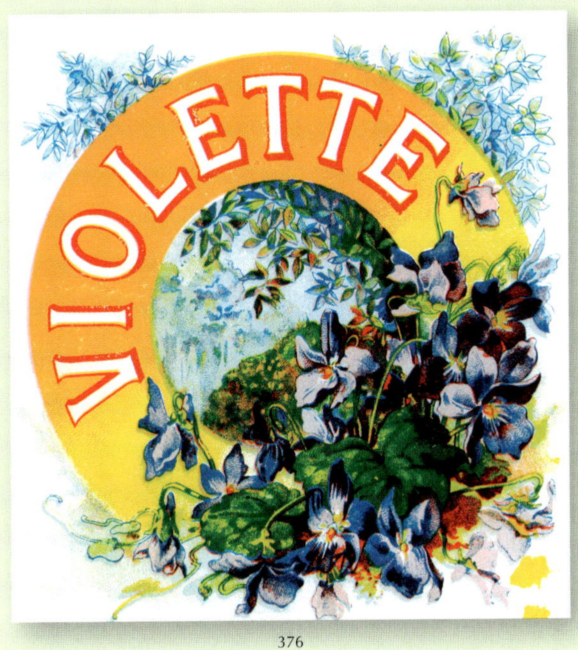

376

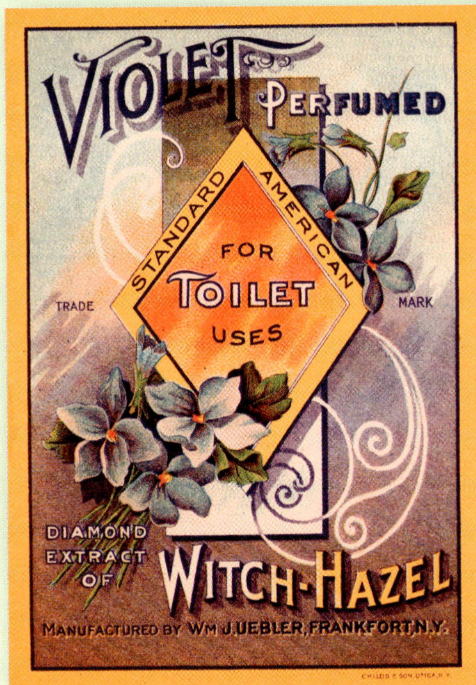

377

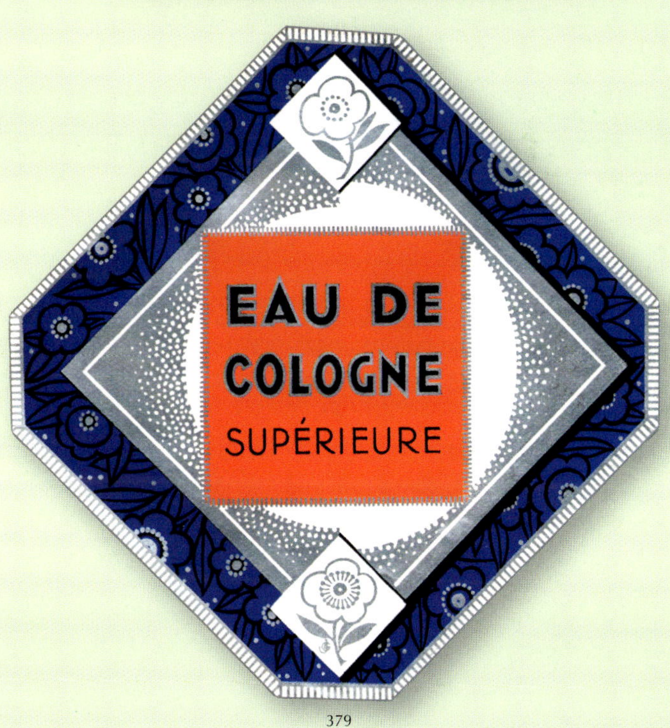

379

Rock Lily
TOILET WATER
NOT OVER 50% GRAIN ALCOHOL.
THE
BUERGER BROS. SUPPLY CO.
DENVER, COLO.

378

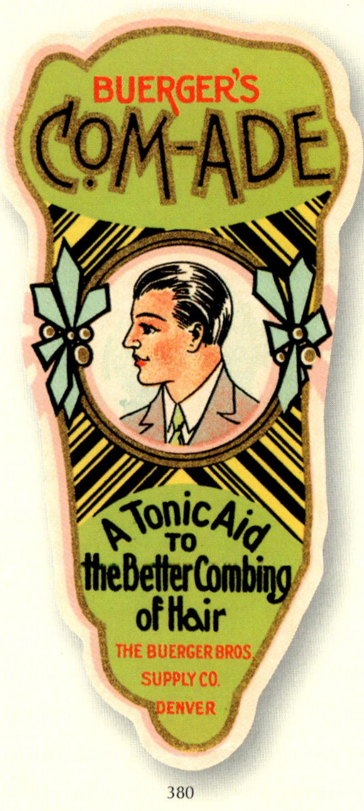

380

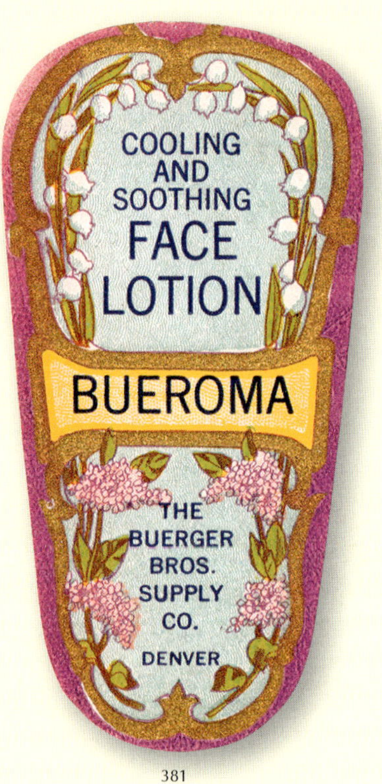

381

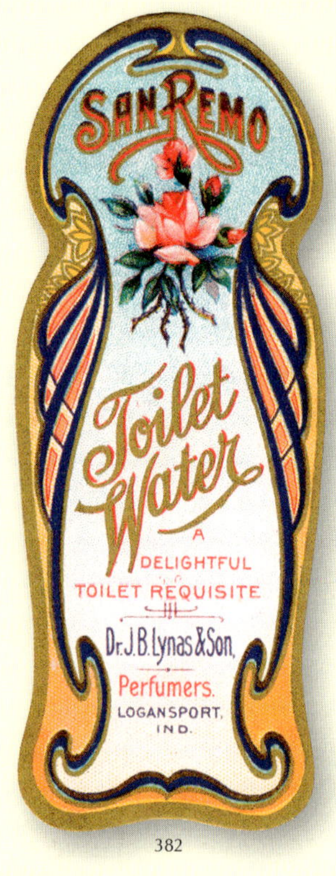

382

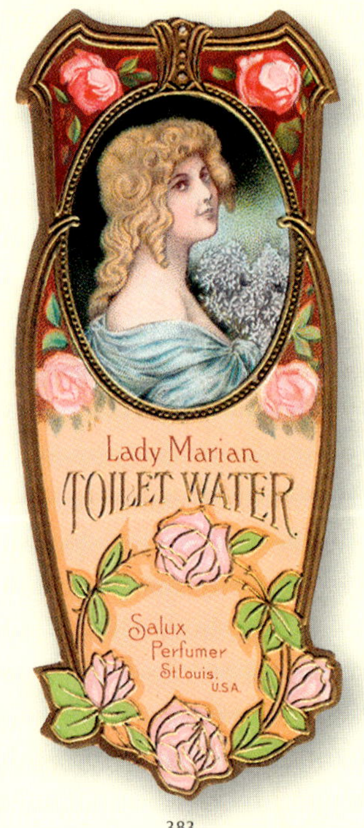

383

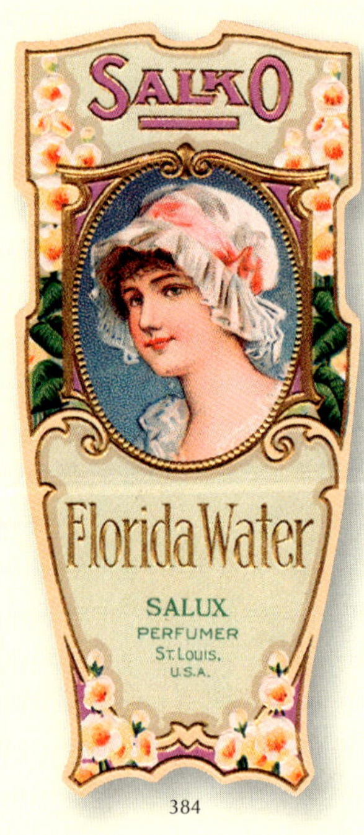

384

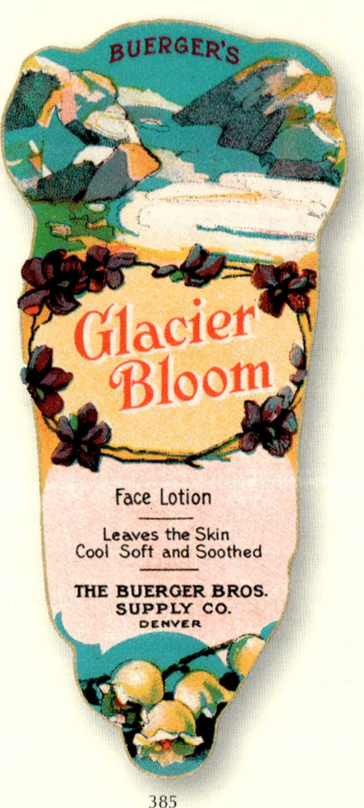

385

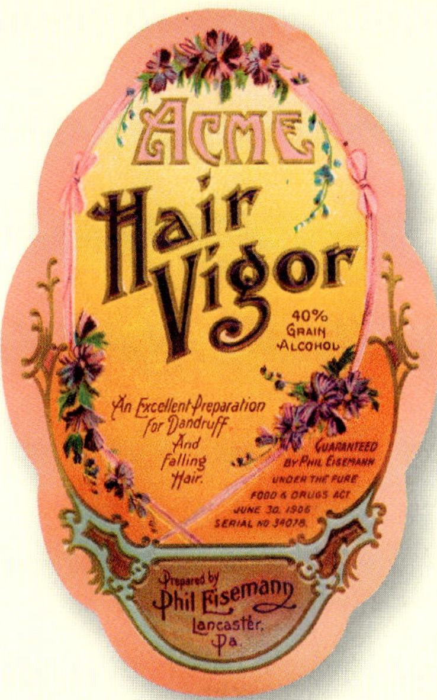

386

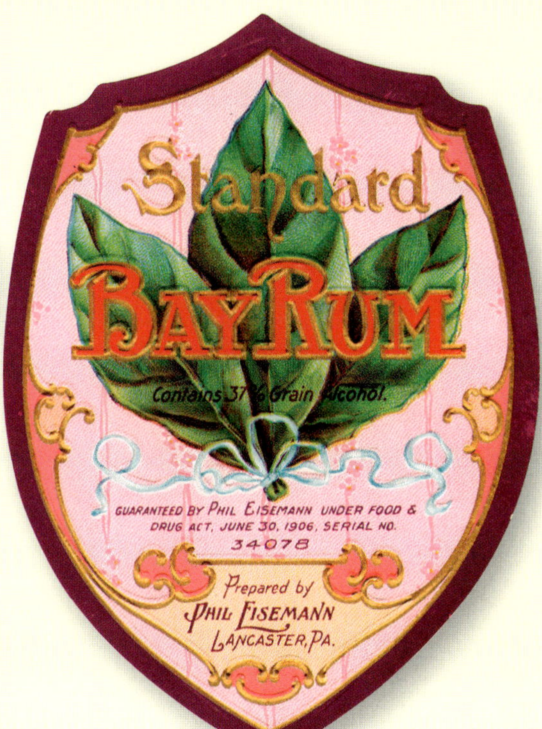

387

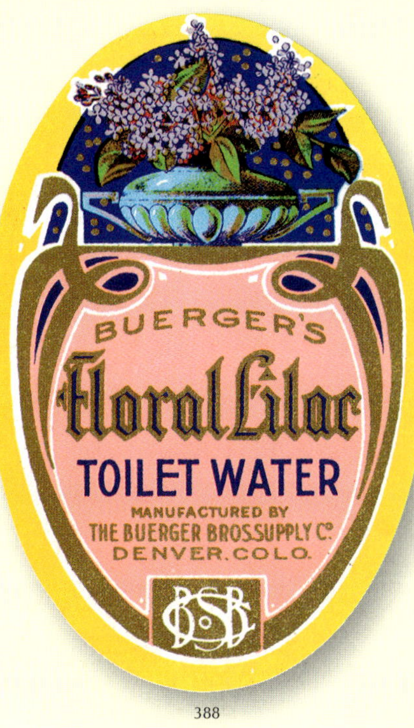

388

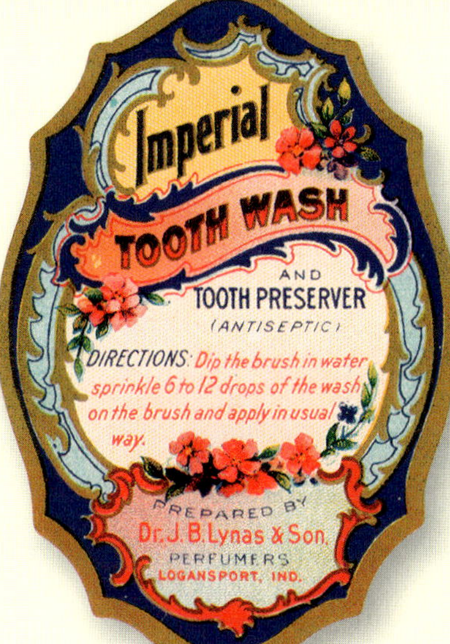

389

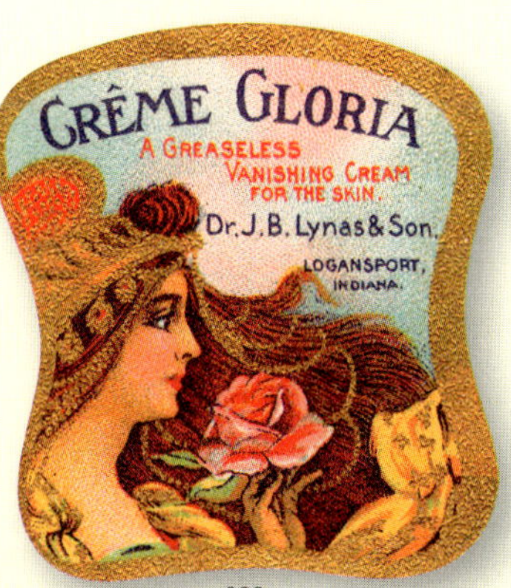

390

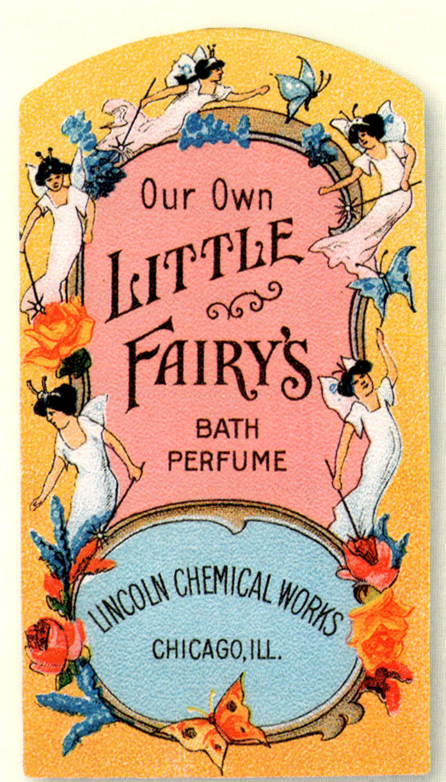

391

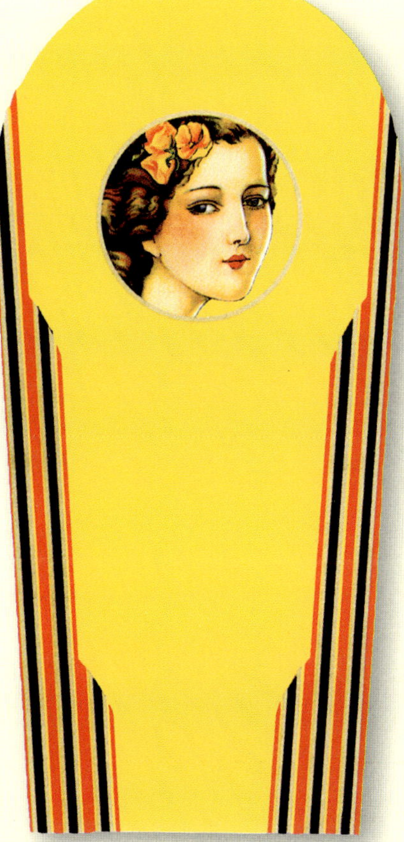

392

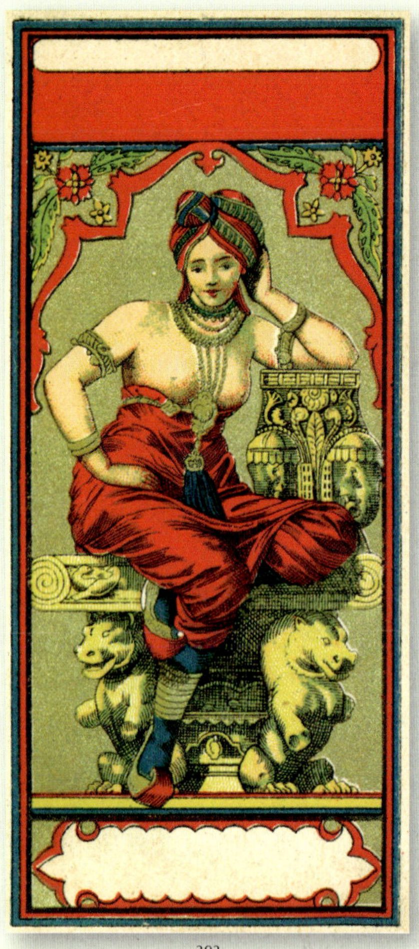

393

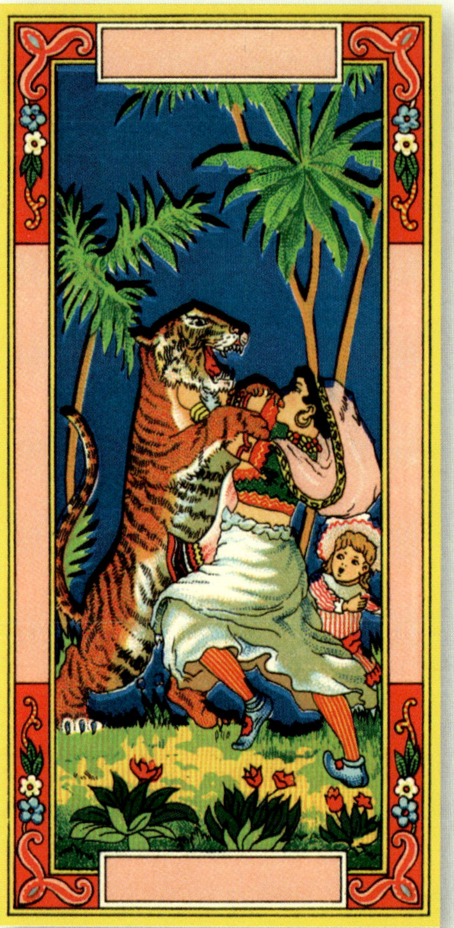

394

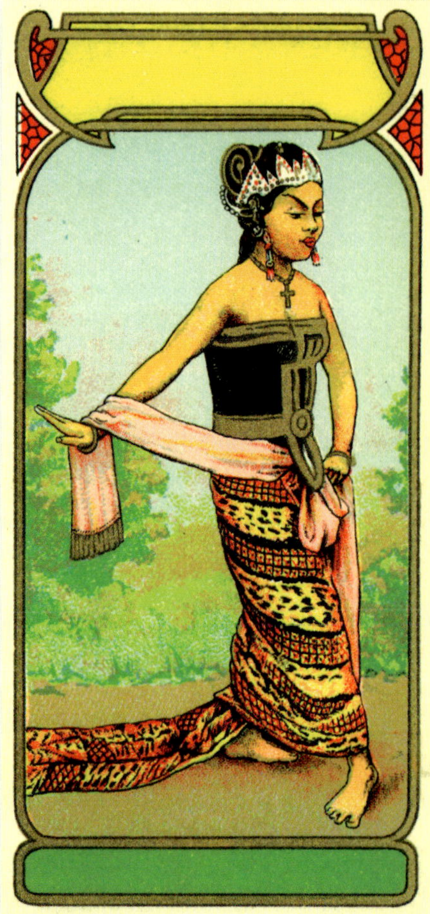

395

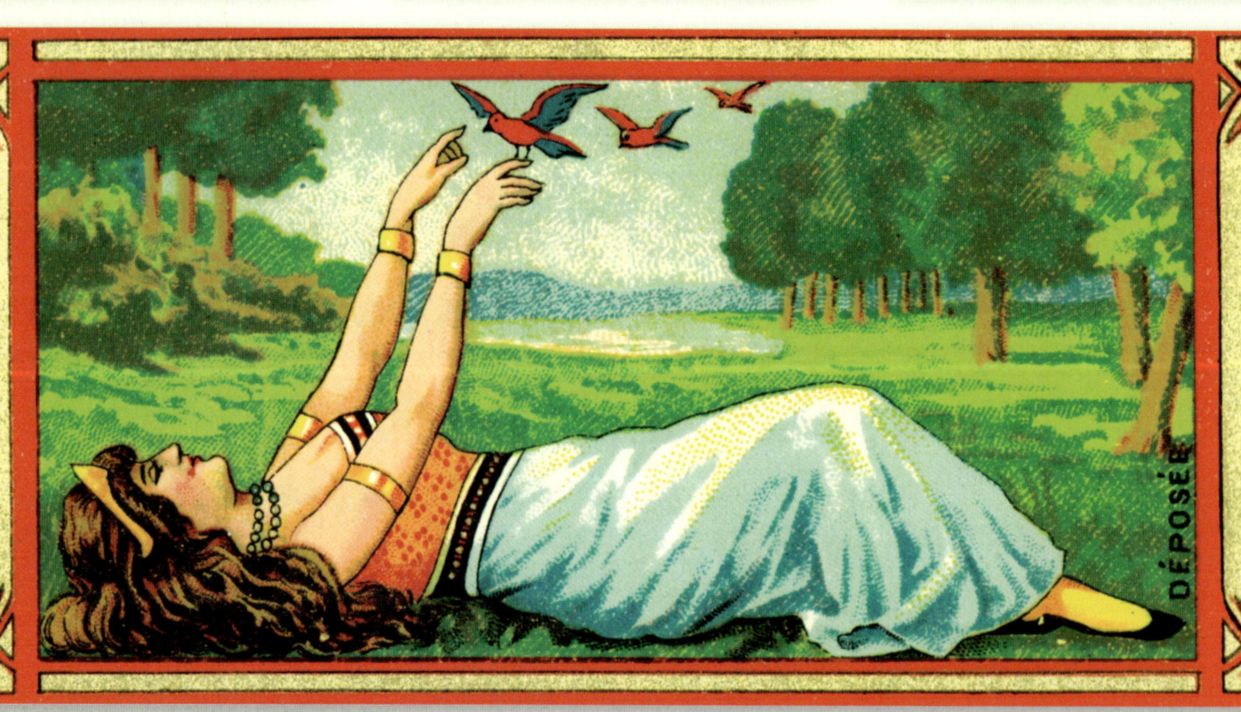

396

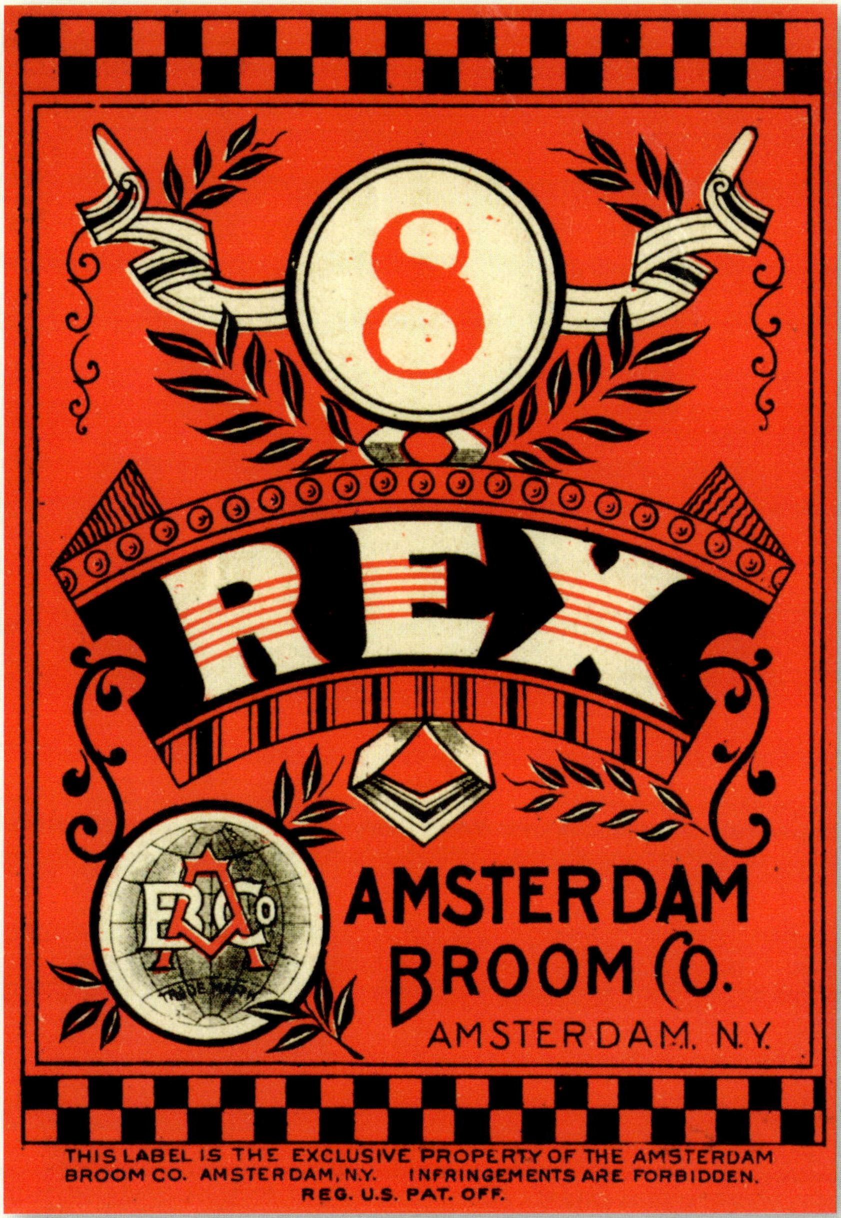

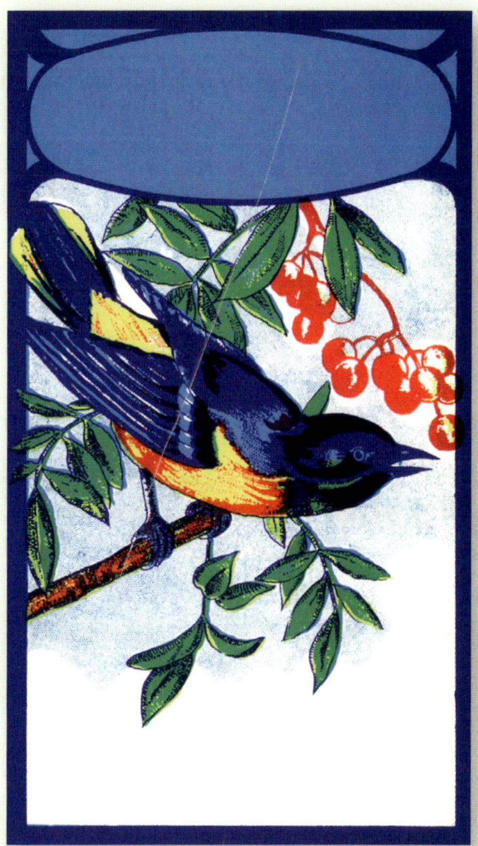

398

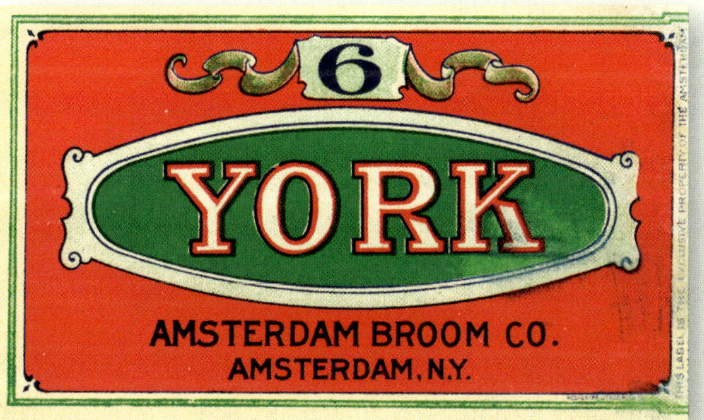

8
REX
AMSTERDAM
BROOM CO.
AMSTERDAM, N.Y.
THIS LABEL IS THE EXCLUSIVE PROPERTY OF THE AMSTERDAM
BROOM CO. AMSTERDAM, N.Y. INFRINGEMENTS ARE FORBIDDEN.
REG. U.S. PAT. OFF.
397

6
YORK
AMSTERDAM BROOM CO.
AMSTERDAM, N.Y.
399

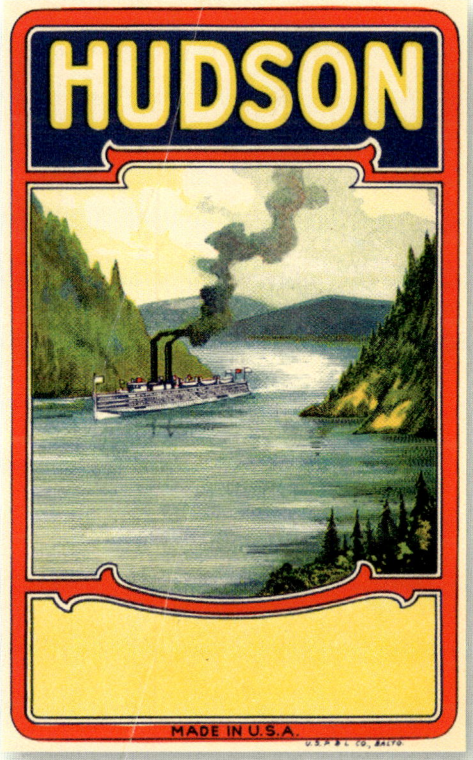

HUDSON
MADE IN U.S.A.
400

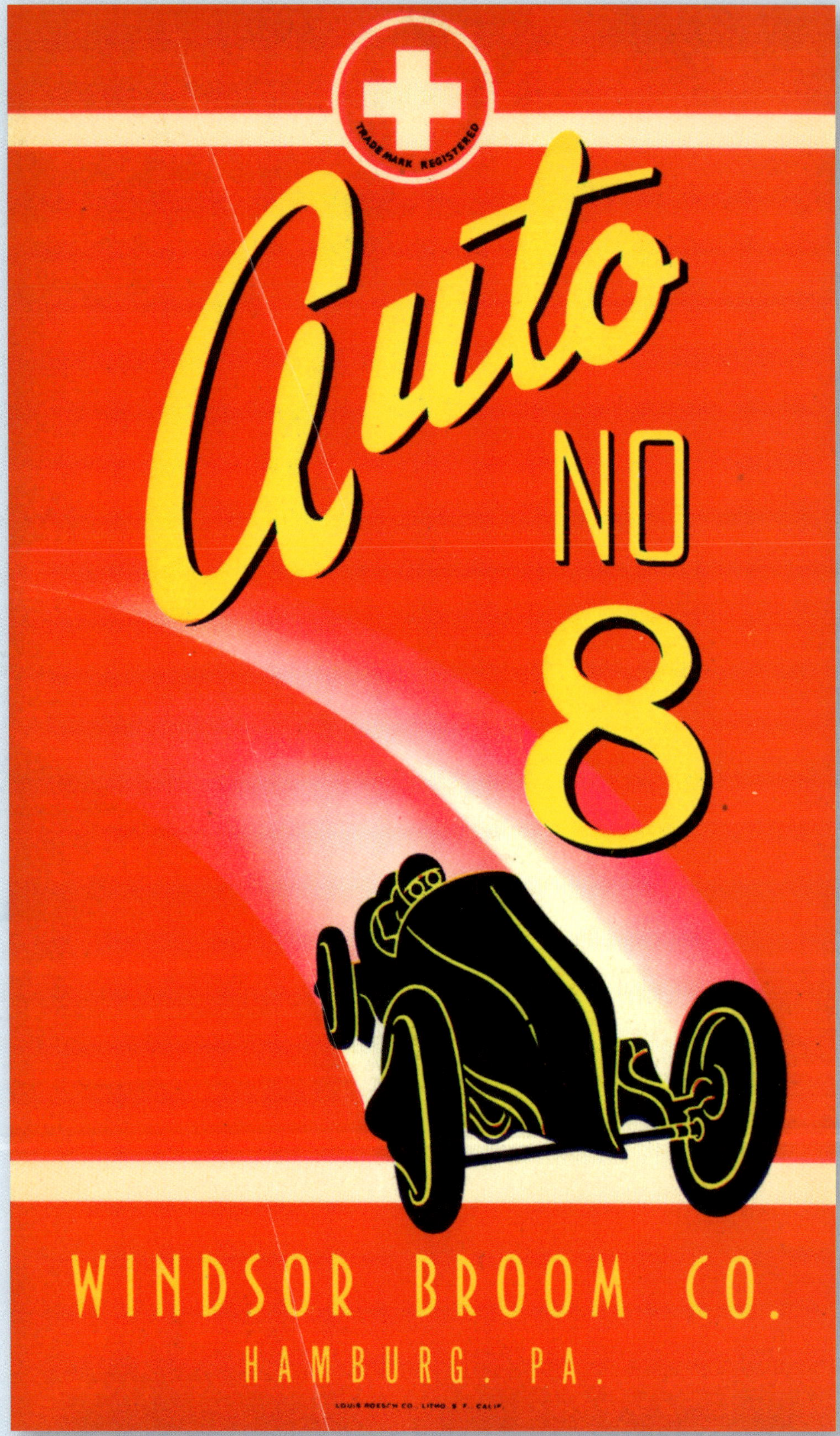

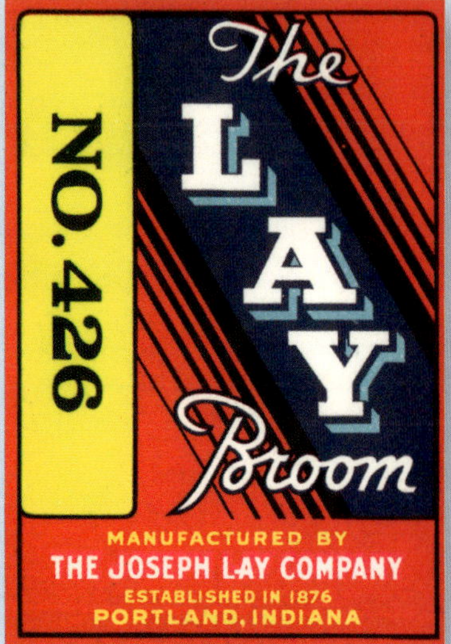

402

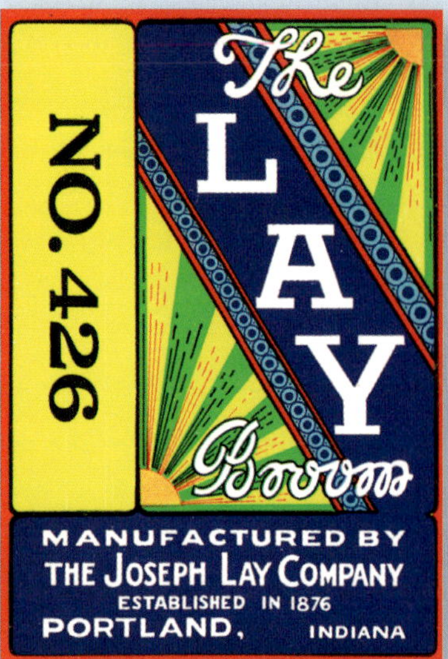

403

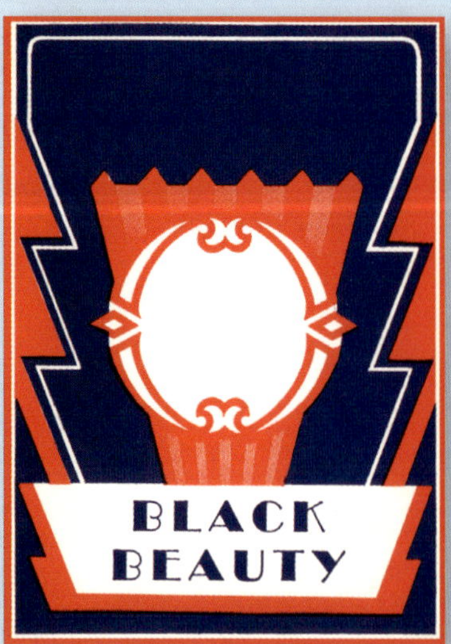

404

401

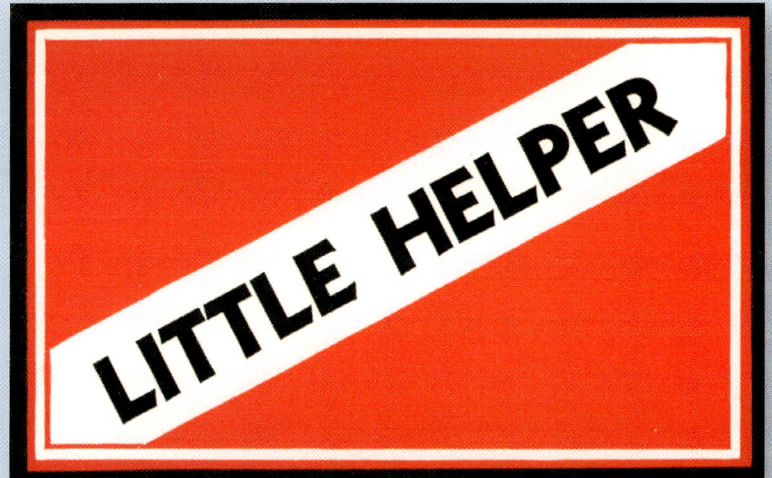

405

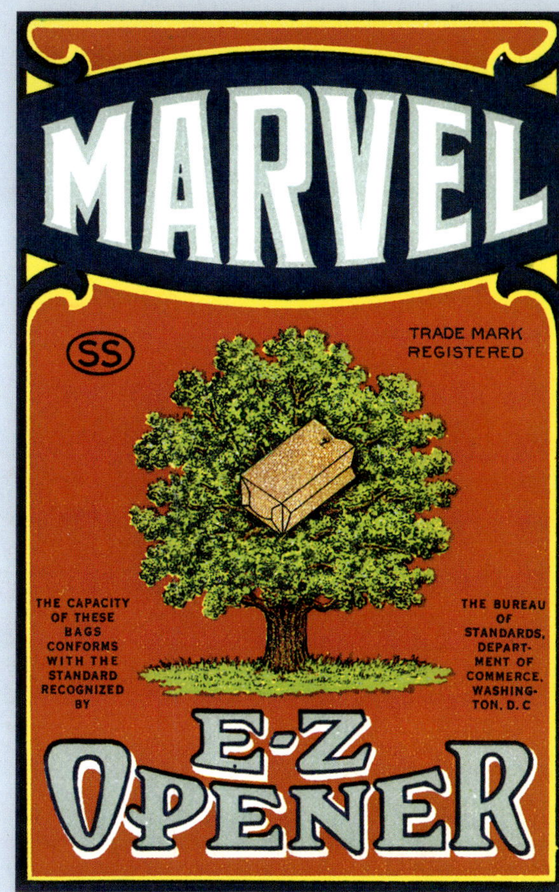

406

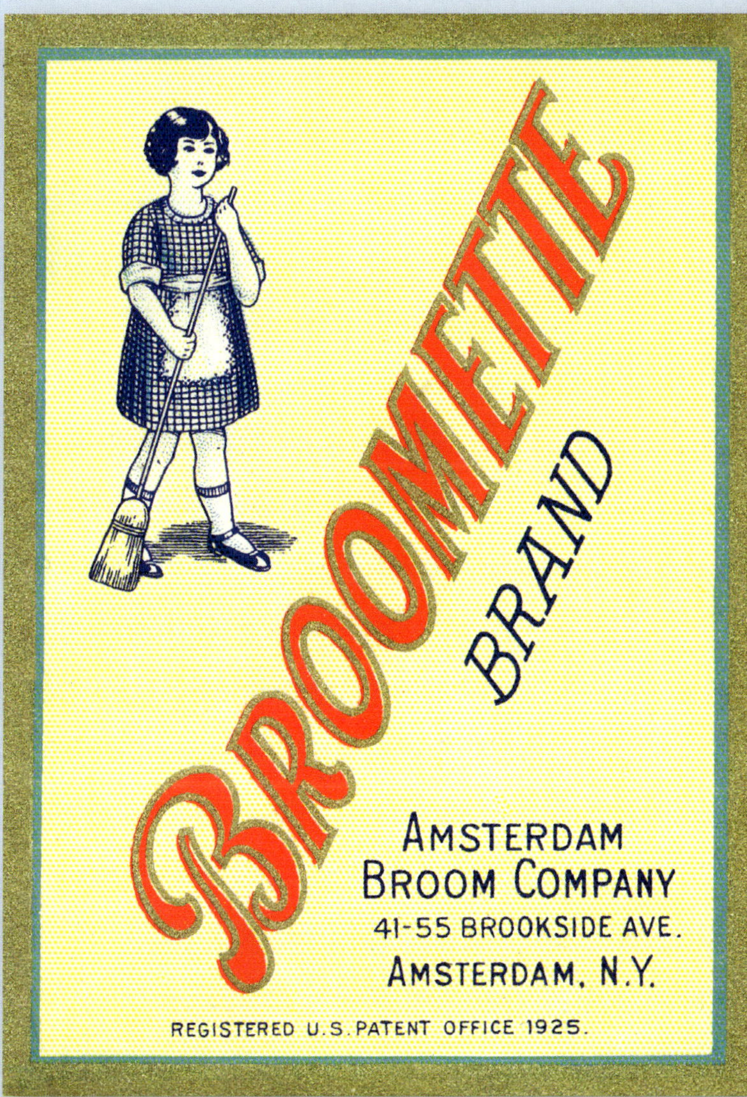

407

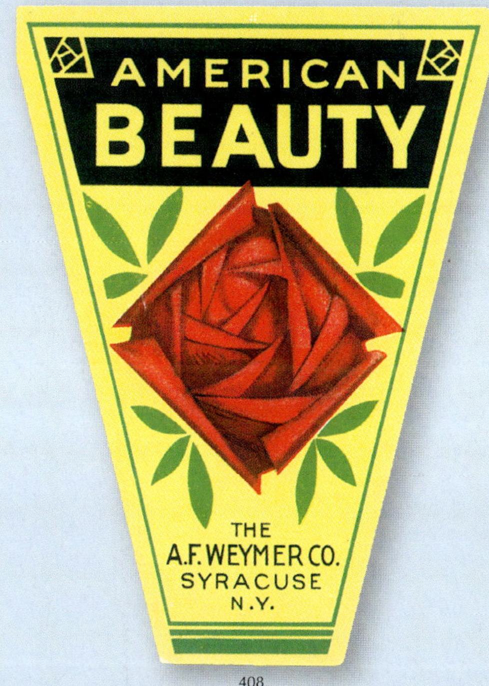

408

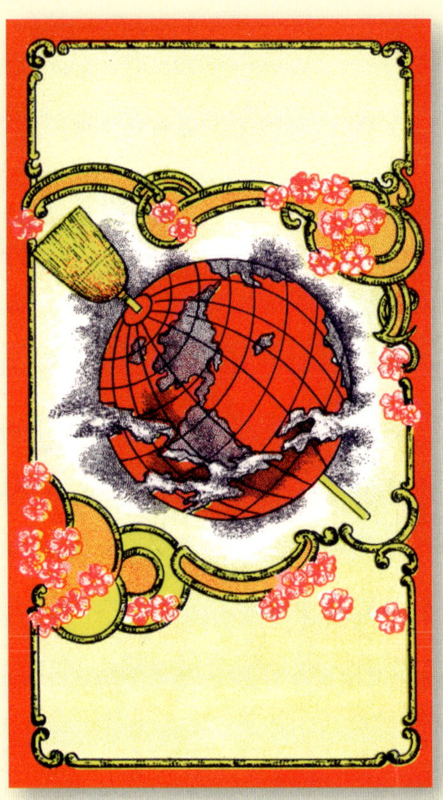

409

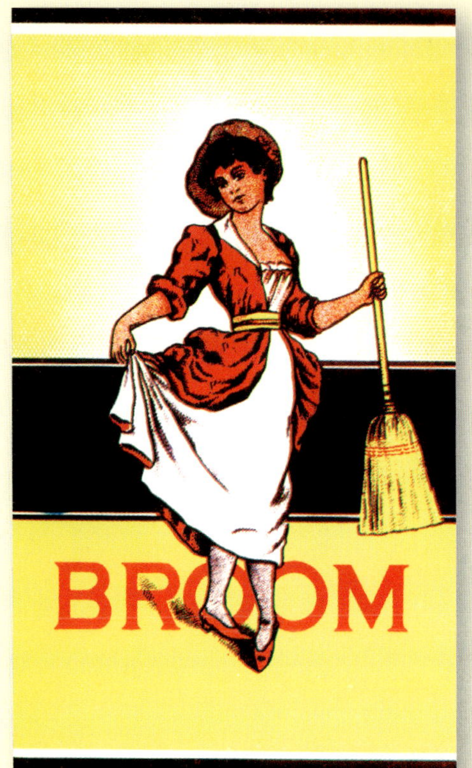

410

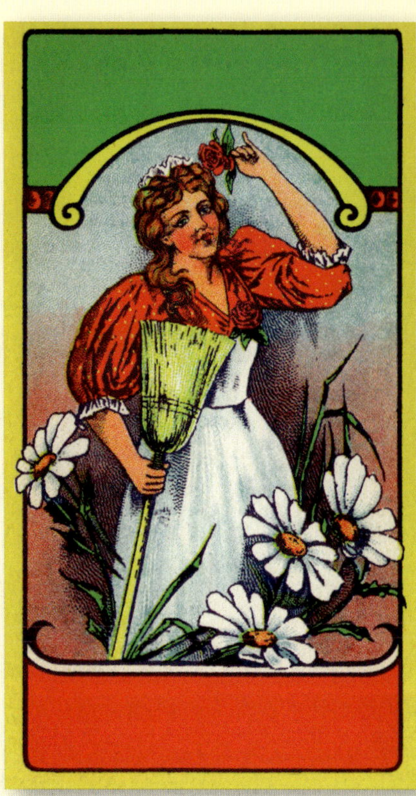

411

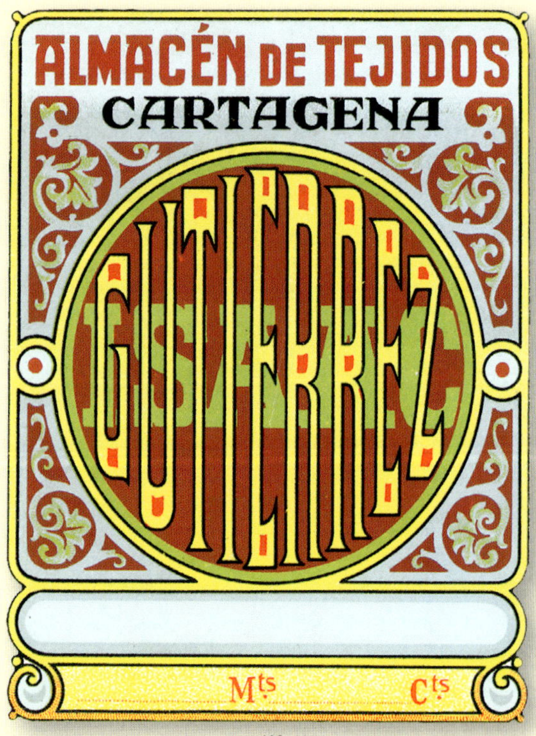

412

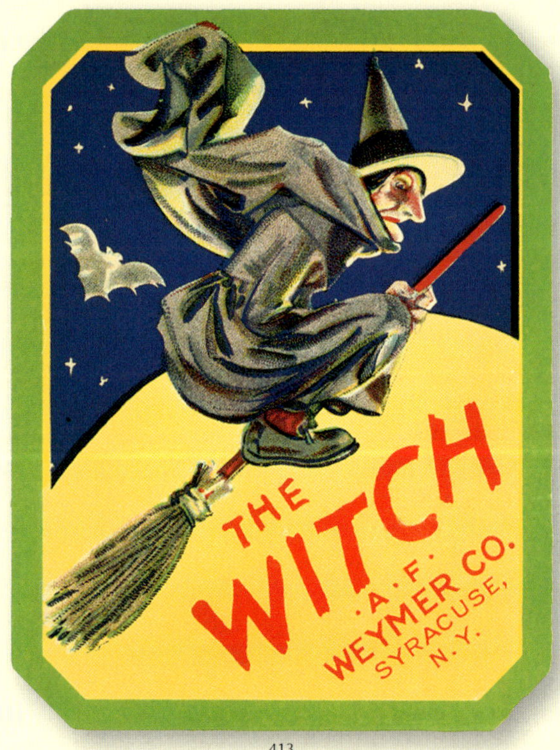

413

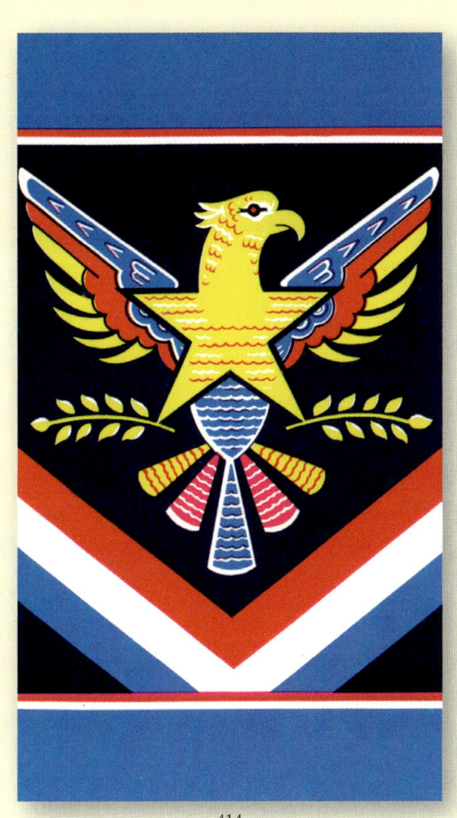

414

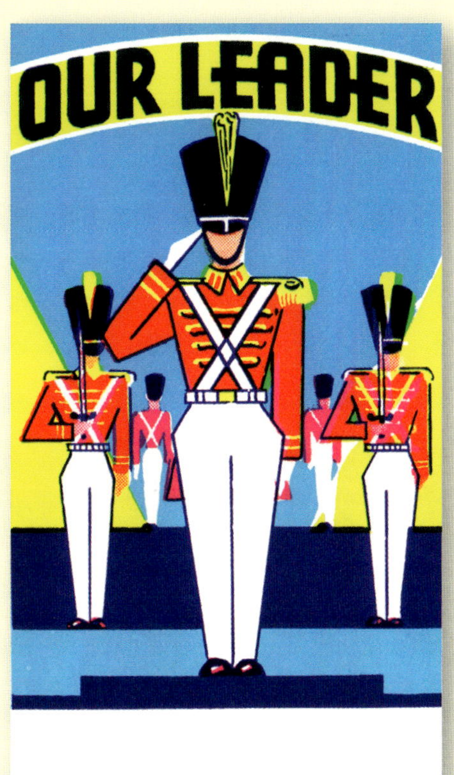

415

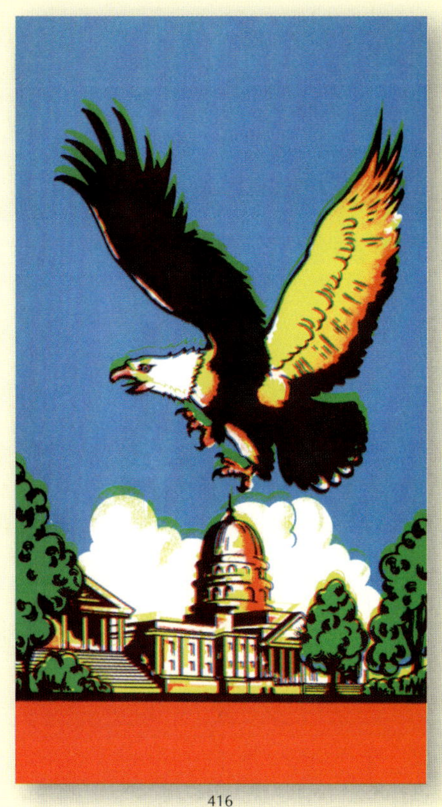

416

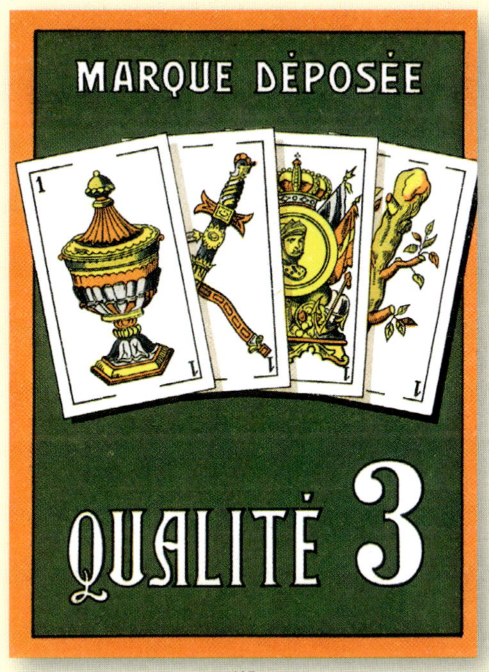

417

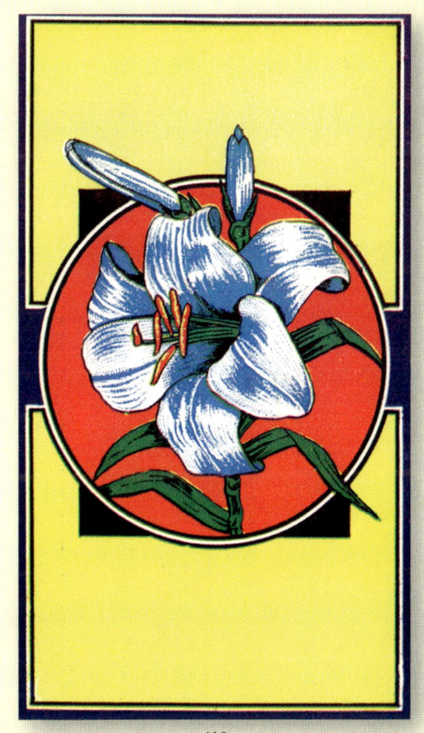

418

419

420

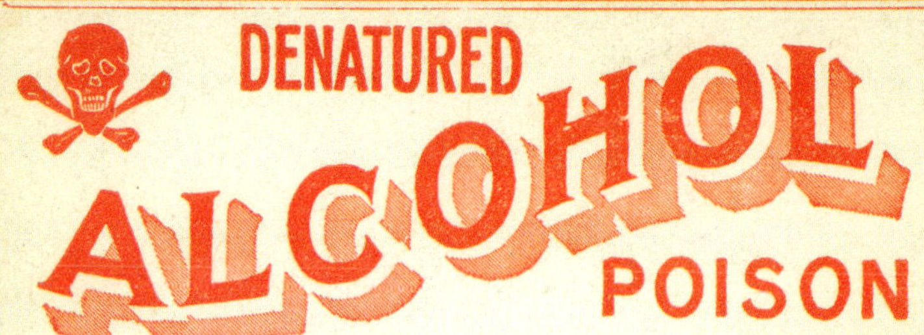

421

422

423

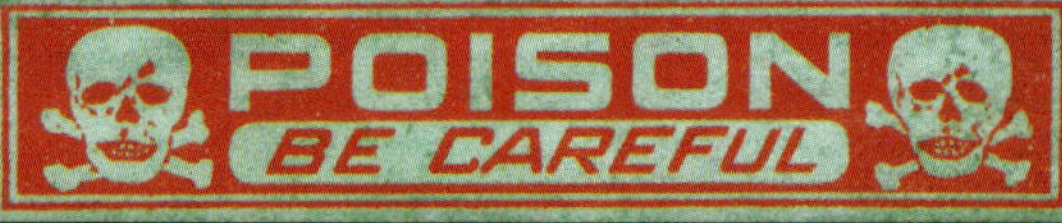

424

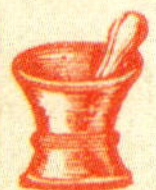

425

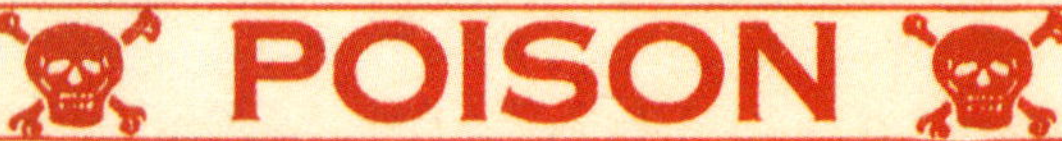

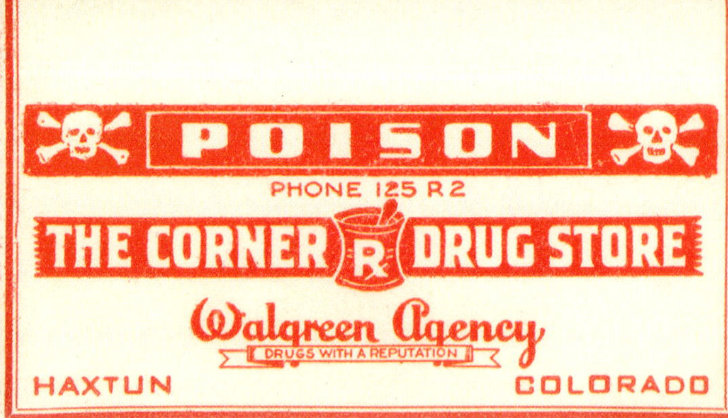

426

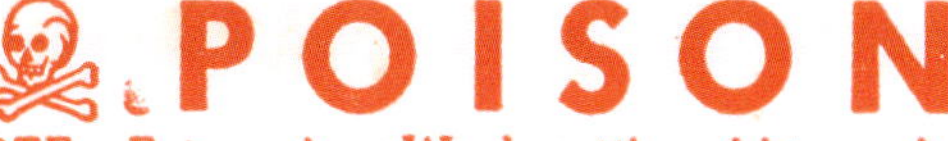
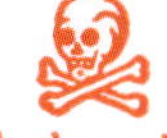

SHEEP DIP

Active Ingredients: not less than,
Carbolic Acid......%, Coal Tar Oils......%

POISON

ANTIDOTE—External—Wash with rubbing alcohol and follow with soap and water. Internal—Give a tablespoonful of salt in a glass of warm water and repeat until vomit fluid is clear. Give milk or white of eggs beaten with water. Have patient lie down and keep warm. Call a physician.

DISTRIBUTED BY   NET CONTENTS............FL. OZS.

HENNEY & COOPER

PRESCRIPTION DRUGGISTS

136 WEST CENTER ST.   MARION, OHIO

427

Carbolic Acid

POISON !

Antidote: Give draughts of strong Brandy, Whisky or diluted Alcohol; then an emetic of wine of Ipecac or salt water, and finally Epsom Salts.

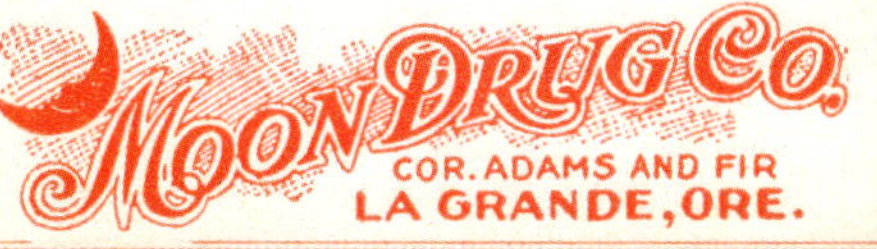

428

POISON

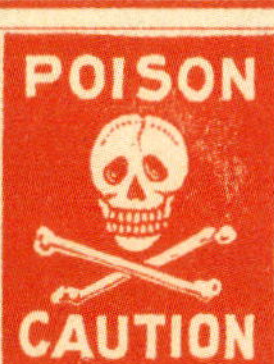

CAUTION

NITRIC ACID

ANTIDOTE—Carbonate of soda, potash, lime, magnesia, chalk, calcined magnesia, followed by demulcent drinks, white of egg or milk. Apply heat to extremities; stimulants as needed.

THE A. WELLER DRUG CO., DeGraff, Ohio

429

MURIATIC ACID

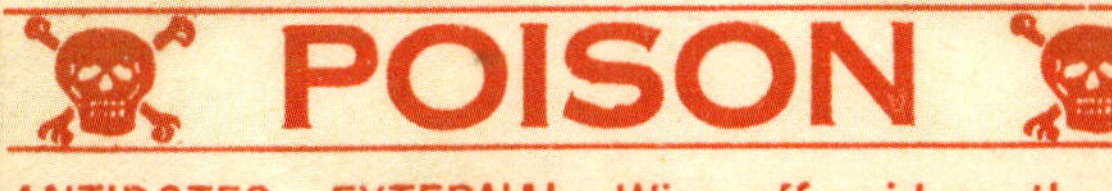

POISON

ANTIDOTES----EXTERNAL: Wipe off acid gently, immediately flood the surface with water, using soap freely, then cover with moist magnesia or soda.
INTERNAL: Drink a teaspoonful or more of magnesia, chalk, whiting or wall plaster or small pieces of soap softened with water, in milk, mucilage or raw egg white. Call a Physician.
CAUTION: To be used only by or on the prescription of a physician, if for medicinal use.

CONTENTS   FL. OZS.   PACKED BY

430

TINCT. ACONITE U.S.P.

CONTAINS ALCOHOL 66.5 PER CENT.

DOSE: 5 to 15 drops As required.

ANTIDOTE: Mustard mixed in water, then strong Coffee, without milk or sugar.

POISON!

THE *Rexall* STORE.

LEMMON'S DRUG STORE

ROY LEMMON, Mgr.,   GUTHRIE CENTER, IOWA

431

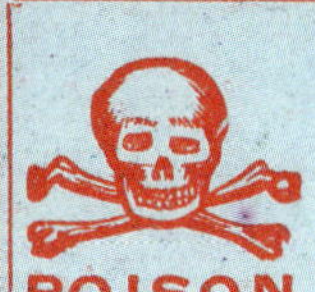

SUGAR OF LEAD

ANTIDOTE—Give Milk or White o. Eggs in large quantities.

POISON

THE *Rexall* STORE.

LEMMON'S DRUG STORE

ROY LEMMON, Mgr.,   GUTHRIE CENTER, IOWA

433

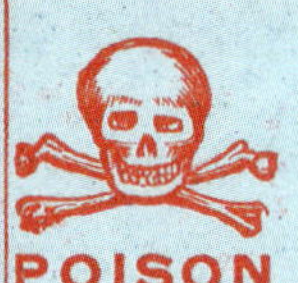

STRYCHNINE

ANTIDOTE—Emetic of Mustard or Sulphate of Zinc, aided by warm water.

POISON

THE *Rexall* STORE.

LEMMON'S DRUG STORE

ROY LEMMON, Mgr.,   GUTHRIE CENTER, IOWA

432

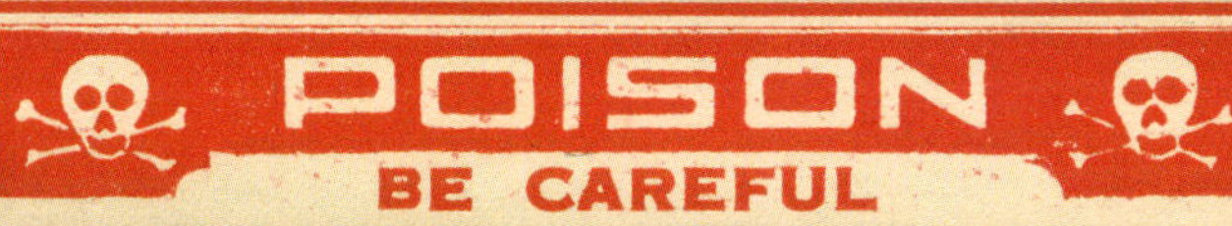

434